BEYOND

THE

COLD

An American reflects on a year spent in Norway as a child, on subsequent trips and experiences as an adult during a 35-year period and discovers a deep affection – and warmth – for a country, people and culture not his own.

By Michael Kleiner

Copyright © 2006 by Michael Kleiner

ISBN 0-7414-2854-7

Cover photo of Geirangerfjord, the most dramatic and
narrowest fjord in Norway, by Michael Kleiner.

Published by:

INFI∞ITY
PUBLISHING.COM

1094 New DeHaven Street, Suite 100
West Conshohocken, PA 19428-2713
Info@buybooksontheweb.com
www.buybooksontheweb.com
Toll-free (877) BUY BOOK
Local Phone (610) 941-9999
Fax (610) 941-9959

Printed in the United States of America

Printed on Recycled Paper

Published March 2006

DEDICATION

TO MY PARENTS, PARTICULARLY MY FATHER,
WHO FIRST TOOK ME TO NORWAY,

AND TO ALL OUR NORWEGIAN FRIENDS,
WHO HAVE MADE ALL THE TRIPS WORTHWHILE

Table of Contents

Foreword

In the summer of 1969, as my family was preparing to go to Norway for a year, a young man of 10, already a committed sports enthusiast, asked me to tell him something about this country we were going to. I told him about my previous experiences in Norway as a soldier at the end of World War II. I also told him that Norway, this country of only four million people, had won the most medals at the 1968 Winter Olympics than any other country in the world.

"Wow, that must be a nice place!" he said.

That was the end of the discussion, but it was enough to stimulate his interest in the coming trip.

Little did I know at the time that my son, Michael, would write a book about Norway more than 25 years later. Of course, after that first year, I also had no idea of the depth of the meaning this experience had for him, or what it would lead to in the intervening years. During those years, the family saw his affection for the country mature and his appreciation of its culture, its social system, language and people grow as well. The family witnessed his reading, traveling, writing and talking about Norway, as well as his commitment to studying the language.

I think the visit of our close friends, the Dalgard family, to the United States in 1972-73 cemented his intellectual and emotional ties to this country, which were to develop even further and blossom so fully when he returned to Norway for the first time, as an adult, in January of 1986, and then on subsequent visits.

As the plans and discussions for the book began to crystallize, I became increasingly aware and impressed with how much people miss in the experiences and emotional reactions of those close to them even though they may be together physically. When we share those same experiences, we may laugh together; we may cry together, or do the opposite at the same time. We don't always know what stimulates such reactions in others, although we often think we do.

When Michael initially asked me to write an introduction to the book (which at the time was to end after Chapter 7), I told him that I would have to read the manuscript first. After all, I wanted to know why I should encourage others to read it. At the outset, I have to disagree with him on one or two details. In his Introduction, he says that I'm the only other person who could have written this book, but that he is a better writer. I must say, unconditionally, that he is the only person who could have written this book, and the reader will soon find out "why." He and I can debate who is the better writer.

My first reactions to the book are that it is charming and most engaging. It is written with warmth and sensitivity, with humor and caring, with appreciation and insight.

My second set of reactions is somewhat more complicated and is also influenced by questions raised by friends and colleagues. They ask: "Is it a travel book? Is it autobiographical? Is it psychological?" It is not any of these specifically. It is all of these and more. It is about a relationship between an individual and a country he came to know over a 35-year period. It is about how an individual, from childhood to adulthood, was repeatedly influenced by accumulating past experiences and by new ones in that relationship. As the book unfolds, he shows with great skill how Norway's natural environment, history, culture and the characteristics of its people permeated and molded this relationship and how it influenced the author himself. He also juxtaposes this process with the influences of selective aspects of American history, culture and the characteristics of many Americans during this same period of time and himself as well.

However, the reader may not be looking for all of these complexities, and may only be interested in having a warm intimate experience with Norway. This book will provide just such an experience. It is in the tradition of the romantic poets and writers. Read and enjoy!

Dr. Robert Kleiner
originally written in July 1994/revised 2005

Introduction

"I have not much interest in anyone's personal history after the tenth year, not even my own. Whatever one was going to be was all prepared before that."

-Katherine Ann Porter

I will have to beg to differ with Katherine Ann Porter, and I hope my readers will too. This book is about my life after 10, how important that life at 11 was, and how it influenced me and my development as a person. My father took our family to Norway for a year in 1969-70, fulfilling a 21-year promise to himself. I was a 10-year-old, turning 11 while I was there. Even though it was only one year, Norway was a major part of my childhood. Though Norway remained special throughout my teens and early adulthood, it didn't take on the great significance in my life until my recent return trips. The why of these special feelings also developed to a greater degree during and after those trips. I did not return to Norway until 1986, even though my father returns two or three times a year. It was 16 years later when I was a 27-year-old adult. That particular trip was a very emotional, nostalgic experience, and as I write in the chapter about that journey, "It is not many people who can return to a place 16 years after being there, having crossed a childhood-adult timeline...Perhaps, this trip was a type of rite of passage, a final crossing between childhood and adulthood."

One of the major experiences of that 1986 trip was the warmth of our Norwegian friends, which made me want to make subsequent trips. I have not been disappointed with the later journeys in June and

December of 1990 and in the summers of 1992, 1996 and 1997.

That in part answers the question, why a book on Norway? My motivation for writing this book derives from many reasons and factors. There are many friends – Norwegian and American – and relatives who might say there may be no better American than I to write this type of book about Norway. Unless, of course, it was my father, but I'm the better writer.

There is also a comment that Berit, one of my father's student research assistants in 1969-70, said during my June 1990 trip that made me curious. She said to my cousin, "You will find no bigger fan of Norway than Michael Kleiner." If it was said in 1992, I could understand. I only recall her coming to Philadelphia once after we returned home in 1970. Then, she saw me during the 1986 trip. She really only knew me as a young child, but how did she recognize that feeling? I wasn't even sure about my own feelings.

As my Norway allegiances grew, I would go into bookstores and browse in the travel sections. One might find travelers' language-phrase books in Swedish or Danish, but not always in Norwegian. There might even be travel books about Sweden or Denmark, but Norway would usually be included in the Scandinavian books. Rarely would there be a book just on Norway. Sometimes, the "hopping" capitals of Stockholm or Copenhagen were compared more favorably to the more laid-back Oslo, as if every traveler is looking for a bubbling metropolis. Even the friends who accompanied me on the trips, with no offense intended, would intimate about making side trips to Copenhagen or Stockholm, as if Oslo and Norway had nothing much to offer, when it was Norway we were visiting. In June 1990, we did manage to squeeze in an exciting two-day adventure, a trip to Denmark and Sweden, to say we were there, but not to Copenhagen or Stockholm. Of course, there is a Norwegian bias or "chauvinism" here. You also need a good amount of time to see all the Scandinavian countries. It can't be squeezed into a week. Years later, my cousin would comment that though that spontaneous excursion was exciting, he regretted not having enough time in Oslo. He has never had a chance to return to Norway.

I felt there was a need for a book on Norway, but I didn't want it to be a regular travel book of "this is what to see." I could add more: a special touch, feelings and emotions. While describing what to see, I also wanted to express an appreciation of Norway, the people and their culture. Having friends in the country gives me an advantage over other travelers and travel writers. Through these "pictures," it might encourage people to travel to Norway. Then again, would people be interested – or care about – my experiences and the people I knew?

I was inspired when I read two books in the spring and summer of 1992 before and during a trip to Norway. They were *Three In Norway by Two of Them* and *Wall to Wall: From Beijing to Berlin By Rail* by Mary Morris. The former book is a humorous account of the experiences of three British men traveling through Norway in the 1800s written in diary form. *Wall to Wall* details Morris' search for her grandmother's birthplace near Kiev by traveling on the Trans-Siberian Railroad from China (Beijing and the Great Wall of China) to Moscow in 1986. She isn't able to travel to her grandmother's village, so she detours and travels to Berlin – and the Berlin Wall. She writes beautifully about the situations she encounters, the people she meets and the sites she sees. Morris does her homework by including the background and history of things she sees. *Wall to Wall* is the only book by Morris I have read, but she has also written similar books about her travels in Mexico. These books showed me that travel books could be written that weren't simply, "This is what I saw; and this is how much it cost."

The friendliness, warmth, genuineness and generosity of the Norwegian people were the most important aspects I wanted to convey. Still, this presented the problem I just mentioned. The people I am writing about are our friends and not the readers'. The average traveler will not know anyone in Norway who can help them enjoy the country, and certainly will not be able to call on our friends. That was resolved by remembering other experiences I had with Norwegians outside this established circle of friends.

There is a "stereotype" that Norwegians are reserved, somewhat cold and hard to get to know. I want to dispel that myth. I would prefer to say Norwegians are more relaxed, less tense and less fast-paced than we Americans. The people we know who come closest to that "reserved" type are friends in Bergen. Yet, beneath that reserved quality is graciousness. Our family had not seen this family in 20 years when we visited in December 1990. The mother of the children, now grown women, opened her home to my friend and me then, and again in the summer of 1992, even though she wasn't there. She gave us gifts on that first trip and sent me a holiday card in December 1992 with a picture of the house in winter. Her graciousness and thoughtfulness were also shown in 1997.

When I returned from the December 1990 trip, I searched for a Norwegian instructor. I finally found a Norwegian student at the University of Pennsylvania, who was more interested in teaching his country's language to someone than making a lot of money. When he graduated, I contacted the goalie on the Drexel University soccer team, who was similarly interested. I had met him previously when Philadelphia College of Textiles and Science, where I worked as sports information director, played Drexel. He was personable from the first time I met him.

On my 1992 trip, my friend and I had a four-hour layover at London's Heathrow Airport. Suddenly, a woman turned to us and offered us the rest of her sandwich. She was from Oslo and was waiting for the same plane. Soon, we were playing Scrabble and by the end of the flight, she was inviting us to dinner. Our schedule kept us from following up on the invitation. When we visited Frognerseteren, an old part of Oslo in the mountains, we stopped a couple to ask them questions about some old buildings. The next thing we knew, the man was driving us around Frognerseteren showing us different views and then dropping us off at the train stop.

The purpose of the summer 1992 trip was to attend the International Summer School. The hospitality of the Norwegian staff, from receptionists (who helped students with their Norwegian), houseparents, office workers to tour guides, was extremely friendly. Afterwards, my friend and I traveled to the Lofoten Islands in the Northern part of the country. Our initial plans were to stay with my family's friends, but a problem arose and we couldn't stay with them. Our friends arranged for us to stay with their friends. The hospitality of these strangers to two foreign strangers was most touching. On the first night, the hostess took us on a drive around the island. They offered us the use of their car and bicycles, and they served us traditional Norwegian meals. And, there are probably other examples. I feel these incidents dispel the "stereotype" and show that the average traveler can also experience the kindness of Norwegians. Thus, in part, is the notion behind the title of the book.

I also had to write this book for myself. The Norway experience of 1969-70 and the Norway experiences of the subsequent trips have been important parts of my growth and maturity. Writing this book pulls a lot of things together for me, both in my feelings for and reaction to Norway.

Looking back, the years 1968-72 were important in my development in different areas: educationally, socially and politically. The year 1969-70 was in the middle of that time. I attended four different schools from 1968-72. The fifth grade in 1968-69 was my greatest year of elementary school. I had my best teacher.

I announced to my fifth-grade class that I was going to Norway by presenting a report on Norway. Then I found myself in a Norwegian school, where I had mixed experiences. There were good times, but many hard times. There were four Americans in the school – my brother and a brother and sister. We were a minority in a strange land. Further, Norwegian students start school a year later than we do. So I was in sixth grade at age 11 with boys 12 and 13. There was school on Saturday as well. There were times of intense loneliness. I realize now that the activities my brother and I did together were (unknowingly) survival techniques. I should mention that the people I have seen on the return trips have not been classmates.

In addition, the years 1968-72 were also a politically turbulent time. My parents are politically aware people, but even without politically aware parents, it was hard not to know what was going on.

The year away was a good lesson because we could observe the events from a distance and a different perspective. We read in the *Herald Tribune* about the peace marches on Washington in 1969, the bombing of Cambodia in April 1970 and the killing of students at Kent State a few days later. My father and other Americans got together and wrote a letter to protest the bombing and Kent State killings. We would read and listen to Nixon and Henry Kissinger talk about "peace with honor...to maintain our respect around the world." Then we would listen to Norwegians who didn't respect American actions, and some of this came from students at school!

It was hard for this not to impress itself on a young boy. Reading the *Herald Tribune* introduced me to political satirist Art Buchwald. Soon, to keep myself busy, I was not only writing my sports stories, but political satire as well.

At the same time, the year in Norway and Europe was important as far as my Jewishness was concerned. There were 825 Jews in Oslo. We sought out the Jewish communities in Oslo, Stockholm and Helsinki, and our hotel in Amsterdam happened to be in the old Jewish community. We came away with stories from survivors of the Holocaust and people who had been rescued. We visited the Resistance Museums in Oslo and Copenhagen, which showed how these countries, with small Jewish populations, resisted the Nazis and helped the Jews. We visited the Anne Frank House in Amsterdam and saw bullet holes in buildings in Dunkirk, France. Our way of communicating was through my mother's Yiddish. Meeting these people and seeing these sites made me feel a close connection to my people's past.

Because my trips to Norway have been so personally developmental is one of the primary reasons for the style in which I have written. I chose to write in journal style with day-by-day entries. In some cases, I am writing about the same sites, but from a different perspective and feeling than at another time. For instance, in 1969-70, we lived around the corner from Frogner Park, which has the great statues by Gustav Vigeland. For me, the park in 1969-70 represented where I skated, skied and played soccer more than the statues. Returning to the Park so many years later, as an adult, evokes those memories, but I also appreciate the Park for the magnificence of the statues. It is better to write about the background of the Park on the trips after 1969-70.

I am also visiting those sites with different people – four friends, a wife and a cousin – and they are adding their viewpoints. By the same token, I am visiting people who are known to me, but with a person who doesn't know them and vice versa. What are these American friends' reactions to the Norwegians? What are the Norwegians' reactions to them? It was pretty consistent. The Norwegians accepted them, and for the most part, the American friends were taken with that acceptance.

I also kept a journal on the June 1990, 1992, 1996, and 1997 trips, which made describing those trips easier. The challenge and the fun of this project were writing about the other trips without a journal. It forced me to dig deep inside myself to remember what happened each day and to remember feelings and emotions. To be writing in 1992 and 1993 about 1986 and 1990 and balancing the 1992-93 retrospective on those years with the feelings at the earlier times were among the greatest challenges. I had to be careful in writing about 1969-70; I had to remember it from a young boy's perspective. I amazed myself. I had photo albums from January 1986 with each picture captioned and December 1990 without captions. I recreated the day-by-day accounts by looking at each picture. I proved to myself that a picture is worth 1,000 words. It was amazing how much came back just by looking at photos. As for 1969-70, I have not seen the films in a long time, but have seen them a number of times over the years; the images are ingrained in my head. So, much of the 1969-70 story came from my head – from my recollections and memories. The book project was so much a part of me that at many different hours of the day, I would suddenly remember something that happened more than 20 years ago.

By writing in this style, I have taken the experience of the year abroad, which included negatives at school, to the completely different positive and fond view of the country that I hold now.

I also accomplished the early parts of this project during a time of unemployment. I began writing in September 1992 after I returned from Norway and completed a first draft describing the trips, in June 1993. It kept me active, involved and gave me something to focus on. (But I did not have a closing chapter until 1994.)

This book was to end after the chapter on 1994, with the 1996 and 1997 trips to Norway to be part of a sequel. The time it has taken to get the first *Beyond the Cold* to press made me decide to put all these trips together. To wait for two books to be published might make the stories ancient history, stale and dated. The chapters on 1996 and 1997 may be the best written and include enough unique information, perspectives and experiences that it won't bore the reader with repetition. And the 1997 trip, being my honeymoon, sheds a new light on my Norway experience and probably offers a segue into a second book, if there is one.

This has also been important as far as my writing ability is concerned. I have been able to pull the Norway experiences together. I have a deep affection for the country and its people. Norway makes me believe in the potential of human kindness and friendship. I can only think of one friend in the United States who I still know after 30+ years. In Norway, I have several, and they're friends for life. Norway and this book have made me whole. I felt it was time for me to share my experiences with others. It is my hope that people will not just think of cold weather and stereotypes when they think of Norway, that they will think 'Beyond the Cold.' It's time for you to see for yourself. Turn the page, drift back into time, travel 4,000 miles with me to the special country of Norway.

Glede seg! Enjoy.
Vennlig hilsen/Friendliest greetings,

Michael Kleiner
originally written in 1993/revised 2004

Acknowledgments and
The Story Within the Story

There is always a story within the story, the pieces behind the scenes that had to come together to complete the project. There are the thanks and the acknowledgments.

I, of course, thank Norway and the people I know and have met for providing me with the material for the book; and my parents for their interest, support and editorial comments and suggestions.

I thank Jan Booker, a writer and friend, who took a glance at the manuscript, as it was, in the summer of 1994, encouraged me to continue, and gave advice on how to get it published.

Drs. Len Blumberg, Holger Stub and Robert West, for their interest and encouragement at the weekly Temple lunches with my father and me. It was Blumberg who, in offering advice about selecting a title, asked me what I thought of when I thought of Norway. I, then, turned the question around and contemplated what *other people* thought of when they thought of Norway. The results were cold weather and to a "degree" "cold" people, and I was countering that by writing of a country that I knew was a lot more than cold weather. Therefore, *Beyond the Cold.*

In the summer of 1994, I undertook what would become one of the most interesting parts of the book process. I decided to contact as many people I mention in the book as possible for permission to use their real names. I devised a release form and sent out letters covering close to 100 people. These were sent to nine countries – United States (Minnesota, Washington State, Florida, Texas, Pennsylvania, Utah, Massachusetts and New Jersey), Norway, England, Germany,

Israel, Canada, Russia, Slovakia and Bulgaria. The list included people I had not seen or talked to in 25 years.

Only one letter was returned for a wrong address. Only three people requested to see the excerpts. The *response* rate was 89 percent, and the yes vote was 94.3 percent. The condition was a lack of a response meant approval. I heard from some of the people I hadn't seen since 1970. What was even more touching and gratifying was the notes people wrote to me, particularly students from the International Summer School (Chapter 5), congratulating me, wishing me luck, looking forward to reading the book, and wondering how they managed to be included in this "opus."

It turned out to be a great way to stay in touch – and enlarged my visiting list for the next trips to Norway. I wasn't sure if the mail would get to Russia, Slovakia or Bulgaria, and I heard from each person I wrote to in those countries; two sent the letters back by special delivery. Unfortunately, we also learned of one death of a friend in Norway (but we might not have heard without this process).

And I came within an answered telephone of being reunited with a childhood friend. My cousin e-mailed a letter she saw on the Internet from a Jewish man in Norway. He turned out to be a good friend of my parents – who I didn't know – and they had said he might be able to tell me how to contact this childhood friend. After two weeks of e-mails, he sent me a telephone number in Paris. Two calls weren't answered, but if the phone had been answered....

I repeated the process in 2005, contacting people my wife and I met on our honeymoon, which included people from England and Australia. I also wrote recent Norwegian friends. Despite the lack of contact, the responses were heartwarming.

High school classmate, novelist Howard Coale, read the first 50 pages in 1996 and said with a few changes the book had a lot of potential. He also challenged me to think and remember about my feelings in certain situations.

I would like to thank Mary Chris Brownell, middle school English teacher at Abington Friends School when I worked there, for reading the manuscript and offering positive feedback; as well as author/client Lois Young-Tulin, Ph.D. for being a reader; and Cathy Kessler for her copy editing.

Thank you to Infinity Publishing for making it all happen: to John Harnish for his encouragement, advice through a couple of difficult situations and his "enjoy oftens;" to Michelle Shane for guiding me through the process and always willing to answer my questions promptly; to cover designer Chris Master for presenting ideas objectively while being open to my suggestions and getting my fjord picture on the cover! It was not the cover I initially envisioned, but I love it. Now, after four years of attending Infinity conferences talking about my book, I will now attend the conference with my book on the table.

I thank my wife, Lisa, for selecting Norway as a honeymoon destination, to "see this country you talk about."

February 2006

Part 1

Chapter 1
1969-70

"Writers, if they are worthy of that designation, do not write for other writers. They write to give reality to experience."

-Archibald MacLeish

17 August 1969

The day had finally arrived. We were leaving for a year in Norway via London and Copenhagen.

Norway had been part of our vocabulary for about a year. There had been a possibility we would go in 1968-69, but it didn't come about. All we really knew about the country was that my father had been there in 1945 with the Allied liberation forces at the end of World War II and again in 1948 as a student. However, he was lovesick and returned to America to marry my mother-to-be in December 1948. He promised himself that one day he would return with his family. We knew that, and the story about goat's milk.

As he tells it, he drank goat's milk while in Norway. When he returned to the States, he tried to convince my mother's uncle and cousin that he drank goat's milk. They refused to believe him, so he said he would go to the store next door and buy some. He bought cow's milk and told them it would taste thicker and sweeter. The uncle and cousin protested the container didn't say goat's milk.

"Regular milk containers don't say it's cow's milk," said my father.

"That's true," they responded.

1

They poured the milk into glasses, and the uncle and cousin said, "You're right. It is thicker and sweeter."

I certainly hoped I wouldn't have to drink goat's milk for a year. These stories were part of family folklore. My father, now a sociology professor, had been approved for a sabbatical leave by Temple University to do research on the aspirations of males ages 18-25 and compare them to similar studies in the United States. He chose Norway to do the research, so his promise would be fulfilled.

As for me, I looked toward this year in another country with excitement and fascination. I brought Norway to school. I was in fifth grade at a public school in Philadelphia. The teacher was the best teacher I had in elementary school. For the December 1968 holiday program, our class performed "Walking in the Winter Wonderland." Each member of the class had to dress up in the costume of a different country. I chose Norway. I wore three sweaters and sweated under the hot lights of the stage. And at the end of the school year, I announced to the class my impending trip by presenting a report on Norway. My final report card was six A's and six B's.

I spent four weeks of the summer at day camp, and the highlight might have been when the Phillies' baseball star Richie Allen, who lived around the corner from the camp, stopped by the camp. I would not see a baseball, football or basketball game – live or on TV – for a year or really listen to one either.

Then came the farewells. There was one in New York at my grandmother's apartment for the New York family. My father had received goat's cheese at a Philadelphia party with friends. He walked up to the same uncle he played the trick on 21 years before and said, "You know a friend gave me Norwegian goat's cheese as a sendoff gift."

"Let's not start that again!" exclaimed the uncle.

Now, the day had arrived. We were at my Uncle Dave and Aunt Beverly's (my mother's sister) house in Cherry Hill, New Jersey. They and the two girls, Beth, four, and Sandy, a year-and-a-half, would be taking care of

Pebbles, our dog. The last meal I'm sure was my aunt's great lasagna. No dog and no lasagna for a year. My Uncle Dave had gone to medical school in Kansas City and done residencies and internships in Detroit, Mt. Clemens and Lansing, Michigan. Now, he finally got a job in Cherry Hill, nearby, and we were heading 4,000 miles away. And within months of our return, Dave would get a job in Houston, and they've been there ever since.

We loaded up their turquoise Chevrolet station wagon and my mother's brother Marvin's car. The caravan drove us to Philadelphia International Airport for the Pan Am flight to London.

I stood along the side at the check-in. The reality of this trip was setting in. Excitement was mixed with anxiety. I felt trepidation. I was leaving friends and family. For a year. That's a long time. I was a 10-year-old. What would it be like? Would I have friends? Would it be lonely? Would people be nice? Would I get sick on this seven-hour plane ride, as I had been prone to do on domestic flights? I don't remember where my sister, Wendy, 13½, and my brother Albie, 8, were at these moments.

Meanwhile, there was a commotion at the desk. The airline had a weight restriction and with our year's worth of luggage, we had exceeded it. Pan Am wouldn't let us on with the luggage, unless we paid for each pound over. We wound up paying, but my father was infuriated when they wanted him to pay for a seat for my mother's guitar.

Finally, we were on the plane for the first leg of this trip, my first time in Europe. In London, we would stay with other names from my father's storybook, a war-time friend, Jack, and his wife, Cissy.

I did get airsick, but was okay by the next morning when we touched down at London's Heathrow Airport.

18-30 August 1969

It was early morning London time. We might be in a strange land, but we were met by people we knew at least by name. My brother and I had never met them while my mother and sister met them on a trip in 1966. For my father, it was the second time in 21 years. Jack, my father's friend, and his son, Ian, greeted us. We piled the luggage into their two cars. Jack had a Rover, one of the popular British cars, and Ian a tiny Austin Mini. I rode in the Rover; my younger brother got the little car.

This was London. They drove on the wrong right side of the road. It was a long ride from Heathrow to the house. We came around a small curve to a small white house. Jack's wife, Cissy, waited for us. There was a short hallway and to the right a staircase. To the left was a living room/dining room. Straight ahead was the kitchen. Upstairs were two bedrooms, a bathroom and a separate room for the toilet. We would soon learn the European term "water closet," or WC, for this room. The three kids would stay with Jack and Cissy, while my parents would stay with Ian, his wife, Carol, and their year-old daughter, Ruth.

Jack and Cissy also had a daughter, Anne, who was about 19 and who we had met the previous summer – 1968 – when she visited the United States. She introduced us to British music, like music by The Association. We introduced her to baseball. We had some fond memories of her stay during that turbulent political summer.

Martin Luther King had been assassinated on April 4, 1968, and Robert Kennedy fell to the same fate on June 6 after winning the California Democratic Presidential primary. The Vietnam War was a hot issue, galvanizing people on both sides. It forced President Lyndon Johnson to decide not to run for reelection and resulted in the campaigns of Kennedy, Eugene McCarthy, who opposed the War, and Vice-President Hubert Humphrey, who was tied to the policies of the incumbent. After Kennedy's death, it became a choice between Minnesotans Humphrey and McCarthy as the Democratic National Convention opened in Chicago in August. Richard Nixon, a staunch supporter of the War, had already won the Republican nomination.

Anne and a friend planned to be in Chicago at the time of the Convention, hoping to see the American political system at work. A couple of days before the convention started, they became nervous when they saw the Chicago police in riot gear and thousands of National Guard units on the streets. They called us and asked if they could come back to Philadelphia. A few days later, we all huddled around the television and watched the horror of the riots unfold.

Now, it was exactly a year later. Nixon was President, and we were in London en route to Norway. There were no conventions or riots in London to worry about.

Over the next 10 days, we would be involved in a whirlwind of activities, in addition to getting to know and love these people. We saw what we could of the changing of the guard at the crowded Buckingham Palace. We visited Trafalgar Square, Windsor Castle, Tower of London, Westminster Abbey, St. Paul's Cathedral. Of course, we ate at Wimpy's, the hamburger "joint" of England, from where Popeye's hamburger-eating friend got his name – or vice versa. My memory of the famous Harrod's department store was not of anything I bought. I cut my elbow on a glass table, creating a need for first aid. My elbow and the shirt were my first casualties in Europe.

Ian was a big football – soccer – fan and had season tickets to the Tottenham "matches" – let's be British, now. He couldn't take us to the "First Division" matches, but took Albie and me to a "Second Division," or minor league match, between Tottenham and Bristol. I still don't understand the English division system. I remember there wasn't a scoreboard or clock and that Tottenham won 2-0. I've been a Tottenham Hotspurs "fan" since.

Anne's boyfriend Michael's passion was cricket; the game that's supposed to resemble baseball. He took us to a field and taught us the finer points of the sport. I tried watching a match on the "telly," but the same match lasted for days.

Albie woke up early one morning to go to work with Jack, who ran a clothing business. Albie helped out, and Jack gave him a day's pay, the first time my brother earned money.

Finally, it was time for us to continue our journey. Again, there would be another stop in Copenhagen, Denmark, for the weekend. My knowledge of Copenhagen was from my dad, who had visited there in 1964 for a conference and filmed the trip. So we had seen the movies. He also bought my mother a sweater, which she wore for years.

On August 29, we departed London. Scandinavian Airlines was great, but again, I got sick. The problem was the bug hung around for the weekend. My thoughts of Copenhagen are limited. The room in the hotel was nice, and the water was some of the best I ever tasted. I had a hard time enjoying the great Tivoli Gardens.

31 August 1969

This was it. Finally, the *real* day had come. We would arrive in Norway. The flight from Copenhagen to Oslo was about 45 minutes. I think I made it through this flight relatively unscathed. Then we touched down at Oslo's Fornebu Airport. It was a late Sunday afternoon. We were actually met at the airport, by a Mr. Magnusen. His parents were renting us their home. He drove us to our new temporary home – Tidemands *Gate* (Street) 20. It was brown – just like our house in Philadelphia – with a porch and small yard in the front. We had to open up an iron gate and walk to the back along a pebbled drive. Even that was a little similar. We opened up a door, and up a few steps was a door with "MAGNUSEN" on it. There were steps that went upstairs to a couple of other apartments. Mr. Magnusen unlocked the door.

There was a long hallway on our left and right. Down the hallway on the left side was a "WC" and the room that

6

would be my sister's. At the end of the hallway, to the left, was the kitchen; to the right, a dining room. Down the hall, to the right of the front door, was the bathroom, my parents' room and at the end of the hallway the room my brother and I would share. That wouldn't change. Straight ahead from the front door was the living room. Off the living room was a window and door leading out to the porch. To the right of the living room was a small room. There was a desk with a telephone on it. Then, there were steps going down. A basement! Downstairs were a bar and a dartboard!

In the living room was a radio on top of what looked like a television. How do you turn this on? Where was the channel changer? There was this knob underneath the screen to turn the set on. But there was only one television station for the country of Norway!

Mr. Magnusen showed us where my father would work. It was only two blocks away. *Institut for Samfunnsforskning.* Institute for Social Research. Munthes Gate 31. He had also bought some food for us.

My parents asked about schools in the neighborhood. They would take us tomorrow. "Tomorrow? School already," I thought. "We weren't going to wait a week so we could adjust to the place. It wasn't even Labor Day."

Well, Norwegian schools had been open for two weeks already!

There was Majorstua nearby for Albie and me, but Wendy would have to go to Nissen *Gymnas* (High School). I guess our experience was beginning.

1 September 1969

The first day of school, maybe not as traumatic as kindergarten, was certainly anxiety producing. What struck me about the first day in Oslo and the new neighborhood was bigness and hugeness. There were long, big blocks along a busy street – *Kirkeveien* (Church Road). We – my mother, brother and I – passed a big park. We took a left down a side street and there it was: A gate in the middle of a stone overhanging structure. Above it, the sign: Majorstua *Skole*. There were three windows on each side of the entrance with metal bars. We walked through the gate. Wow! There was this immense cobblestone and cement schoolyard with trees scattered about and a statue in the middle. There were so many different entrances, labeled from A to F, or was it H? There was a tunnel-like walkway that wound from the entrance to the right, quite a distance, and then made an L-turn to the left and went farther until it met the side of the building.

Somehow we found the correct entrance – I think it was B – and found the principal's office. Mr. Sandersen was a very nice man, balding with white sideburns. He was set to retire at the end of the school year. I would be placed in one of the sixth-grade classes, my brother in third. I would have an advantage. English is taught as a mandatory language in Norwegian schools, beginning in fifth grade. The students in my class would have a year of English behind them. My brother's classmates would have none or TV English. As for how we would learn Norwegian, Majorstua would provide a tutor for us.

We went to our classes. My teacher was a nice man, who unfortunately would be leaving in several weeks. He told the class – which was all boys – to welcome the American student and make him feel comfortable. Norwegians start school a year later than Americans, so the boys in my class were 12- and 13-year-olds.

One immediate difference was that classes were 45 minutes long, and there was a 15-20 minute recess after each class, outside, rain or shine. This was a nice day. Soon, the schoolyard was full of students for my first recess. Beside the steps were water fountains with about six spouts. The Norwegians seemed to always be eating at recess, regardless of the time. They weren't eating "sandwiches." There was only one slice of bread with no top – open-faced. Salami or cheese (often goat cheese) seemed to be the popular food for the bread. The kids were eating enough of them, and with a recess at every hour, they must be full.

The "schoolyard" represents so much in a child's life. Sometimes it is more important than what happens inside the building. So many conflicts, interpersonal competitions, attitudes and friendships are developed. One's self-confidence can grow or deflate. The schoolyard was the arena of acceptance and rejection, belonging and alienation. For boys, much of that, as well as who you are and even what you may become, can happen at recess, and revolves around sports.

That was true for me back in Philadelphia. I was intensely interested in sports, but a great athlete I wasn't. Still, like many young boys, I harbored the dream of playing in the major leagues. In the schoolyard, I was in that category of being among the last picked for fistball. (Baseball, by hitting a rubber ball with your fist. We also called it handball, but I don't want to confuse it with the other forms of handball, particularly since I learned a new handball game in Norway during the year.)

There were loads of kids, and the weaker kids always got put at the bottom of the lineup and were lucky to "bat" before the recess bell. Interestingly, I became friends with one of the better and popular players. When I couldn't play, neither could he, nor would he. We got our own ball and a faction split off and created our own group.

Now, here I was in a schoolyard in a foreign country, not knowing the language, and there were new and different sports. It would be a miracle if I "cracked" these lineups.

At least my classmates knew some English – more than enough for us to find out each other's names. There was Jon, Jan Christian, Per Erik, Nils, Sven, Tony, Christian. I found Albie desperately trying to converse with a boy in his class. "I'm trying to find out his name," Albie moaned to me.

I tried, of course, with little success. The simple task of finding out a name was difficult on this day.

Then, I was *asked* by some of the boys in my class to play in the *fotball* game they were forming. A goalie stood in front of the open door of a fence. We all headed in the same direction and played with a tennis ball. I think I may have scored a goal! The game ended, and we returned to the classroom on the third floor of the D or B entrance.

As first days go, this certainly wasn't bad.

My father started his new job just two blocks from the house. His hours would be 8:30-3:30. No 9:00-5:00 in this country, it seemed.

For my mother, it turned out to be a struggle on the first day or at least in preparing the first dinner. She declared we should eat out. Of course, the question was where? We either walked or took a tram (trolley).

We also had one of our first cultural lessons in Norway. The Norwegians eat dinner – *middag*, literally, midday – early, between 4:00-5:00 p.m., which is why work ends at 3:30. Consequently, dinner in restaurants was also served early and then they close. We had quite a bit of trouble finding a place that was open. We finally found a cafeteria.

Afterwards, we walked around our new city and met an American couple vacationing from Minnesota. How about that – on our first day? We talked with them for a while. He was a big fan of the North Stars hockey team. Then we went our separate ways. They would be going back to the United States, while we were just beginning in our new world.

September 1969

For the first month, things went well, basically. Some time in that first week, there was a track meet against another school in the Frogner Stadium, a few blocks away, next to the Frogner Park. I can't remember if I barely won or lost my race of 100 meters – or was it the 60 meters? I also remember being part of a soccer game in the Park one evening. I seemed to be blending in well during the first week. Winning or losing wasn't important, but the chance to participate and feel a sense of belonging, particularly in a new culture, was important. My parents were surprised when I came home from school one day and sounded like I was speaking Norwegian. I had picked up the Norwegian accent and was speaking English with the accent.

There were still many new things to get adjusted to at school. The walk to school seemed so long, but we were small, and the streets were long and wide.

Among the changes for me was an all-boys class. There was another all-boys sixth-grade class in the room next to us. There was one all-girls sixth-grade class. My brother's class was co-ed. If the boys in my class weren't playing *fotball* or another sport, they would usually be talking and flirting with the girls.

There was also a *timeplan* – a schedule – of classes divided into the 45-minute segments. Sometimes, there were different teachers depending on the subject. The days were also staggered. One day, I might go to school at 9:00 a.m.; another, at 8:00 a.m.; and still another, at 10:30 a.m. One day, I might get out at 2:15 p.m. – the latest – other days, as early as 11:00 a.m. The same was true for my brother. Then, there was this extra day, which stunned us – Saturday! Regular school on Saturday! It was hard enough getting up for Sunday School back home, but Saturday for regular school? More on that endurance test later.

Of course, classes were in Norwegian. There was *Kristendom* (Christianity) class, which we were eventually excused from attending. At first, my mother thought we would learn something about another religion, but it was all in Norwegian anyway. The main teacher taught us Norwegian grammar, English, Geometry (which was hard enough a few years later in English, let alone Norwegian) and Algebra/ History/Geography/Social Studies.

Then there were the other *lærerene* (teachers), and each was something. What I remember most about the health teacher was that she was a woman with blonde hair, who, for some reason, screamed every time she entered the room. Maybe she was afraid of the class.

The entire physical-education program was a shock to me. Back home, the gym teacher was always blinking his eyes. It seemed more important to be dressed properly. The boys wore white: T-shirt, shorts, socks and sneakers. The girls wore blue jumpers with their name stitched in white across the top left-hand corner. There were these small circles on the floor, one for each of us to sit on. Everybody in a row. We did jumping jacks, squat thrusts, sit-ups, push-ups and chin-ups. For an activity, we might play some basketball, dodgeball or kickball.

Now came the gym class at Majorstua Skole on Thursday morning. The teacher was always dressed in a blue warm-up suit, and he must've been in his 70s. We did jumping jacks, too, but he led in such slow tones. He also didn't speak English. The jumping jacks were just the limbering up for what was to come. Out came the spring platform and the horse. Not the animal horse, but the pommel horse, the thing gymnasts in the Olympics spring and flip over with the greatest of ease on the way to 9.4 scores. We weren't Olympians.

Ready, set, go! One after the other, the boys in the class raced down the floor, jumped onto the platform, lifted themselves off the platform and over the horse. They must've been doing this for a while, like a few years. Spring! Spring! Screech! I'm supposed to jump over that? You expect me to jump over that? I've never done this before!

I don't think I ever did it. The teacher tried. The students tried. I think I got on the horse, never over it. From there, it was on to the rings! Though I laugh about it now, those classes were a time of discomfort and anxiety.

The second gym class of the week offered somewhat of a reprieve. We usually played basketball, more my game. I usually cherry-picked and waited for passes down court for lay-ups. Or handball, which is a form of soccer, except you can use your hands. It's an Olympic sport, and Norway and Denmark, particularly the women, have good teams. The problem with the second gym class of the week was it was at 8 a.m. on Saturday. There were times I just couldn't get up that early.

School on Saturday was an injustice in itself – which has since been corrected in Norway – particularly for Americans living in the country who expected to use the weekends to travel and be tourists. My class's longest day was Saturday. We started at 8 and left at 2:15. My class resented it. Meanwhile, my brother was in school for about two hours on the day of rest. When our class finally "heard the final bell" (I don't remember if there were bells), the rest of the school was empty. We were the last to leave.

The day ended with *kunst og skrivning* (art and handwriting). This teacher was feared. He also taught us *forming* (woodshop). It was said that if he got mad, he hit kids – with a hammer. That was even worse than my fourth-grade teacher who hit the students with a ruler. He was one of the few male teachers who dressed in a coat and tie. He, too, spoke little English. He would walk around the room mumbling so that you didn't know if he was talking to you or to himself. Considering I didn't understand Norwegian, it didn't matter.

Nevertheless, *forming* was a great new experience for me, and I enjoyed it tremendously. I don't know if I already liked wood then or that the experience sold me on woodcrafts. I had taken painting and clay classes at an art center near my home in Philadelphia. I made nice objects in wood shop such as a car and trays, which are still on display either in my parents' home or mine. I avoided any wrath from the teacher, too. Funny, I had the pastels from art class in one of my desk drawers for at least 25 years.

There was another striking thing at school. Any time the door to the classroom opened, the boys immediately stood up out of respect for the person entering. They were on their feet at the sound of the knob turning.

13

One of the first Norwegian words my brother and I learned was *slåss*. Fight. At almost every recess, there would be a fight, maybe two. From the far end of the playground, there would be the cry: *"Slåss!"* The students would run from all over the yard, form a circle around the combatants and watch them go at it. Finally, a teacher would arrive to break up the fight. While the fight might not have been interesting, the way everybody gathered at the sound of *"slåss!"* was amusing.

Another thing we noticed early was the students' – regardless of age – utter fascination with Donald Duck. There were always kids reading a Donald Duck comic book – translated into Norwegian. This fascination remains true today. My brother had a friend, who may've not known English, but was great at mimicking the Donald Duck voice.

We also had to adapt to the apartment, new neighborhood, scrounging for news, and for a while being without a car. My brother remembers going with Dad to mail a letter shortly after we arrived. We weren't used to the European 24-hour time system. The mailbox was an orange cylindrical box and under times of pickup were numbers like 14:00 and 16:00. "I said to Dad, 'We're in a different country. We're not in America anymore,'" my brother recalls.

Our block turned out to be Embassy Row. Brazil was next door, and each morning the smell of coffee would spread through the street. I think Turkey was also on the block, so our noses had a choice of Brazilian or Turkish coffee.

Shopping was different. There were many small grocery stores and specialty shops. At the corner, Frognerveien and Tidemands Gate, was the bakery where my mother (or we kids) bought fresh loaves of bread. Bread never came sliced. Farther down Frognerveien and down another street was the fresh fish store. One time, my mother bought whale beef, and it actually became a favorite.

There was a supermarket behind the school that was part of a shopping complex. It was called CC Coliseum, and in addition to the supermarket, there was a movie theater and stores for buying clothes. We bought our boots and coats there. The special feature of the supermarket was tables all over the store where one could sample food. For some reason, the "Dole pineapple lady" became a favorite of my brother.

Besides whale beef, food was different. We ate plenty of fish and in many different forms. My brother hated fish. I loved the cod cakes, although we could've done without fish balls. We ate more dry soups than canned. Hot dogs were replaced by *pølser*, which were more like long sausages. I felt like I was eating a skin covering, so I would peel the skin off of the *pølser*.

Chicken was not very common except as ready-made from rotisseries in stores. We never had turkey, but pork and lamb seemed plentiful in Norway. There was a hamburger-like meat, *karbonade*, which I liked. With all Norwegian dinners, there were boiled potatoes with parsley.

For lunch, we were soon eating like the Norwegians, open-faced sandwiches. There were many different varieties of salami – including black – and cheeses. The sandwiches were called *smørbrød*, which literally means butter bread. All the sandwiches had butter on them. There was a brown stone-wheat cracker – Wasa – which was actually Swedish and also used for *smørbrød*. Norwegian *flatbrød* (flat bread) was so thin it snapped easily in our hands. Breakfasts would sometimes include fish. Besides Norwegian sardines, there was mackerel or mackerel in tomato sauce – my favorite – in tins, and herring. *Gravlaks*, which was like lox, came from a tin. Hard-boiled eggs were popular in Norway, and the Norwegians would eat them from eggcups, which made it easier to peel, as well as to eat. Eggcups were sometimes nicely designed, made of wood or porcelain. We also had to learn about meal times. Dinner was between 4-5 p.m., and *aftens* was a light meal around 8 or 9 p.m.

Of course, the money was different, *kroner* and *øre*. The paper money, which was different colors, started at 50 *kroner*. Some of the coins had holes in the center. There were coins for one *øre*, 10 *øre*, 25 *øre*, 50 *øre*, one *krone*, five *kroner* and 10 *kroner*, so we could be carrying around a lot of change. One *krone* was worth 14 cents.

Then, there was doing the laundry. To dry the clothes, my mother had to hang them on rods that went into a heated closet.

I soon learned that getting news and sports from back home would be a challenge. The *Herald Tribune* contained excerpted news from the *New York Times* and *Washington Post,* and was a lifesaver, if we could get it. There was a newsstand down Frognerveien and one by the Majorstua *trikk* station near school. For some reason, the paper would arrive late in the day and sometimes not at all. We would make several trips to the kiosks. As it was, the information in the paper was a day late, and the news was brief. We finally learned we could get a subscription, which saved us a lot of trouble. We had to follow the pennant races – the first year of divisional play – from a distance, as the Chicago Cubs were blowing their first place lead in the National League East to, of all teams, the New York Mets.

Our ears also got well used. With the shortwave radio, we would listen to Voice of America each morning. In addition to the news, VOA had some other fascinating features: a running mystery and a series on Alexander Hamilton among them.

There was a NFL Game of the Week on Sunday nights on armed forces radio, but my father and I had to pin our ears to the radio above the TV to hear the faint signal. As luck would have it, the one Sunday when we got a clear signal was a game between the Philadelphia Eagles and New Orleans Saints from Philadelphia. With a six-hour time difference – we were ahead – I usually had to go to sleep before the games were over. That night I pushed myself to stay awake to the end. The Eagles won 13-10.

The *Tribune*, Voice of America and Armed Forces Radio made us feel a little less cut off from home across the ocean.

The Norwegian television was a revelation to us. This was before the age of cable in the United States, but we still had VHF and UHF. Here all you had to do was press the button underneath the screen and you had Norwegian television – just that one station. Broadcast times, like school, were also staggered. The day's visuals rarely started before 18:00 (6:00 p.m. by American time) and usually ended by 23:00 (11 p.m.). News was broadcast at 20:00 (8 p.m.). The weekly radio/TV listings would come with the Sunday *Aftenposten*, the major paper in Oslo. There were more radio listings than for TV. Each day's television schedule took up barely an inch. On the weekend, though, sports might be broadcast during the day.

However, except for the time and the one station, we could've been watching American TV. Most of the programming was imported from the United States, England, France or Germany. The programs were in the original language with Norwegian subtitles. With one station, it didn't take much for a program to become popular in Norway. *Gunsmoke*, which we had rarely, if ever, watched in the States, was a fixture on Saturday nights. The Norwegians loved the show, particularly after they found out that James Arness, who played Marshall Matt Dillon, was of Norwegian ancestry. They adored the Festus character played by Ken Curtis.

There were some other popular shows. At 20:30 on Friday evenings, there was *Detek-timen*, The Detective Hour. Each week they would run a different detective program from a different country. The American import was *Mannix*. England offered *Interpol* early in the year. Monday night was Movie Night, and we saw some classics like *Born Yesterday, Fear Strikes Out, The Fuller Brush Man*. And when there was nothing on the air, the screen would sometimes show an aquarium of fish with the time in the corner. This was 20 years before computer screen savers with fish swimming on the terminal screens. In addition, television was commercial-free. Commercials were left for the movie theaters.

September was also a month for my father to track down friends he hadn't seen in 21+ years and for us to meet new people. The first people we met were people he had stayed with in 1946. He knew their daughter, who had married a hero of the Norwegian underground resistance against the Nazi occupation (1940-45). I remember a lengthy ride on the *trikk* (combination train and electric cable car) to a woody area. I recall food, laughter and the "bathroom." It was a real water closet, an indoor outhouse, if that makes sense. Have a seat on the bucket.

Another couple was Per and Kari Hohle, who would become very special people to us. My father called Per on the phone and only said the name, "Per." The man on the other end replied, "Bob?" Per was my father's first friend in Norway. Per was a well-known mountain climber and naturalist, who had written books on climbing and nature. He had also been active in the Norwegian underground. They lived in a log cabin on a hill surrounded by trees, overlooking the city. I had played with Lincoln logs at home, but this was the real thing.

The house was warm and comfortable, as were the people, laughing and smiling. They didn't speak much English so that was a challenge. Kari took great care in preparing open-faced sandwiches. She also introduced us to a Norwegian specialty – *hveteboller* – rolls with raisins that have a very special taste. They were homemade. Kari always made the best *hveteboller*. Per showed my sister how to rock climb, and the first frames of our movies are of the two of them climbing up rock formations near the house. I remember Per's red sweater. They were "older" people, so on reflection, perhaps subconsciously, Per and Kari were my grandparents away from home for a year. After all, when you go to "Grandma's" house, there is sometimes a feeling of going into an old museum. And Grandma prepares food for you. This couple showed the same interest and warmth of grandparents.

There were to be many more months of meeting new people and experiences in our temporary home.

October 1969

October was full of activities – and changes. It was the month of my birthday, the birth of Wendell, the purchase of the new car, the World Series we didn't get to see, meeting the Bartons and some new people, starting Norwegian lessons, and the departure of my teacher. I think there was even a first snowfall.

One day at a recess, a boy in my class pointed to another boy in the schoolyard. "That boy is an American, too."

I walked up to the boy and introduced myself. His name was Roger Barton, and he was in the fifth grade. He had a sister, Linda, who was around my brother's age. His father worked for NATO. They lived on Gyldenløves Gate, which was around the corner from our apartment. "Home" was Austin, Texas, but that was a misnomer. His father's assignments had taken the family to North Carolina and Japan. Perhaps, our families' reasons for being in this country and our views were different, but I had found a "compatriot." I had found an American.

My 11th birthday certainly had to be a highlight, particularly since things at school were about to change. There were eight boys at the party. We all sat around the kitchen table eating *pølser* and cake. Curiously, all of the Norwegian boys were dressed virtually the same, with a dark blue sweater or sport coat. Only Roger and I, the Americans, were dressed informally. Nine of us and my family then headed down Tidemands Gate to Frognerveien, turned left and walked awhile to Bygdøy

Allè where we took the bus to the *Kon-Tiki* Museum on the Bygdøy peninsula of Oslo. Our family had visited the museums at Bygdøy, *Kon-Tiki*, *Fram*, the Viking Ships and the Folkmuseum. *Kon-Tiki* was the balsa raft Thor Heyerdahl had used on his voyage from Peru to Polynesia in 1947 to prove that rafts could've been used to cross the ocean in ancient times. That museum had struck a cord with me. The *Fram* was used on polar expeditions by Norwegian explorers Fridtjof Nansen, Roald Amundsen and Otto Sverdrup. The Viking Ships featured excavated ships from the ninth century. The Folkmuseum has old wood buildings from the 13th-19th centuries.

Now, the *Kon-Tiki* Museum was hosting my birthday party. All had a good time. To be able to have a birthday party with eight other boys in a foreign country was gratifying and made me feel really happy.

Shortly after that, we had a new addition to our family. When in Scandinavia, buy Scandinavian. My parents bought a navy blue Volvo station wagon. We loved that car. On the back window were horizontal lines and a windshield wiper. A rear defroster and certainly a rear windshield wiper hadn't become prevalent yet in the United States, but we had them. When we returned to America, we could brag about it. Dad was taken aback when the salesman tried to sell him four snow tires, but four snow tires are recommended in Norway.

Among the first people we visited with the car was my father's boss, the research director at the Institute, Erik Rinde. He invited us to dinner with his family. Erik had been active in the Norwegian Resistance Movement during World War II when Germany occupied Norway. He lived in an elegant house with his wife and two children in the mountains of Oslo. The son, Peder, was a year younger than me, but was very quiet, probably because he didn't know English. I remember real fine china, wonderful food – with boiled potatoes, of course – and as would become common, wonderful company. They shared an interest in sports, although Norwegian sports. All the Norwegians we were meeting were warm and made us feel welcome and accepted. I was a little less a stranger in a strange land.

October is an important month in American sports. It's time for the Fall Classic, the World Series, the championship of America's pastime – baseball. If there was any possibility that my father and I could see the World Series in Norway, we wanted to pursue it. That task, however, fell on my mother. She tried the American Embassy, who looked at her as if she was crazy. "We are not here to serve Americans," they said.

How about NATO? American servicemen would certainly be interested in the World Series. No luck. NATO made no provision for servicemen to watch the World Series. So, we followed the 1969 World Series by putting our ears up against the radio trying to pick up the faint signal on the armed forces radio. To make matters worse, the New York Mets won. To have a team, that since their inception just seven years earlier had been a laughingstock, win the Series before my Phillies, who had been in existence 80 some years without ever winning a Series, was too much for me. Thus, began my long-running contempt for the Mets.

Perhaps that was balanced out by the writing project I undertook in October. For a long time, practically since I first picked up a pencil, I wanted to be a writer. I started out with creative writing, both poetry and short stories. I was influenced by a friend of the family, who was an author of children's stories and taught in our Jewish Sunday School. She gave me my early direction in writing.

As my interest in sports grew, my interest in writing turned to sports writing and newspapers as a medium. I began to make up baseball, football, basketball, ice hockey and college leagues and write about the games, almost daily. This began my first sports-writing paper clutter. (In an ironic twist, my favorite team in the college league was *Rutgen*, whose bitter rival was Ivy. Perhaps, it was destiny, but I would attend *Rutgers* University,

21

whose bitter rival is Princeton of the Ivy League.) This was before computers; yet, I would try to write in different fonts.

During the year away, I acted out some of these games with my brother, which kept us occupied. I invented a different version of soccer – kicking – which we played outside. The most fun were the indoor hockey games played in the living room. I don't remember what we used for a puck, but we had plastic golf clubs for sticks. We would slide on the hardwood floors with our slippers. One goal was the dining room end, and the other was the little room at the other end, with the stairs that headed to the basement. If anyone hit the puck too high in the latter direction, it would fly down the stairs and into the basement. We would have to track it down.

The next logical extension of my writing – even at 11 – was a book. This, too, became a collaborative effort with my brother. So *Wendell the Football*, my first book – 82 pages – was born. I asked my brother, who was interested in art and architecture – and was only eight-and-a-half – to draw the illustrations. That caused interesting conflicts. He would say, "I'm the artist! I'll draw what I want!"

My response would be, "But, I'm the author, and I'll tell you what to draw!"

Who, what is Wendell? From the foreword: *"Wendell is a football. He looks like a football. He is just like a human being. He has all the senses like we do. He feels, moves, sees, hears and talks. I have decided to put it all in a book. In this book, it tells about him and his adventures in the various football games he participated in and the friends he made. All quotes or actions in the book are of course, untrue. Most of the games in the book were really played...I wrote this book while spending a year in Norway and have finished it two days before 1970 began. This was my first big effort in writing."*

The title page had drawings of the flags of Norway and the United States over "1969 * KLEINER PUBLICATIONS, OSLO." The names of actual NFL players and coaches were used. The book took the reader through muddy games; kickers and quarterbacks he did and didn't like *("Man those kicks hurt! My backside's killing me!..."; "It hurt so much that Wendell had no choice but to fly himself over the goalposts.")*; playing in two games in one day; a pick-up game; a rout where his cousin was on the other side; a football convention in which poor relations among the footballs were discussed *("...Tony V is Jewish and Randy is Catholic. Randy has been criticizing Tony V about his religion. Randy, take a pledge...")*; a game between the Minnesota Vikings and the Los Angeles Rams where Wendell was caught in between the sacks of Alan Page and Deacon Jones; a family reunion at The Footballs Pub, and then his retirement.

"...Wendell had lost a lot of air and had a leak. He had to go into the hospital to get more air and to get the hole fixed up. The leak couldn't be fixed up fully, so it was said that he couldn't be used ever again."

If I do say so myself, the content was clever for an 11-year-old and quite a successful collaborative effort. Wendell's retirement also showed the impact on me of the political climate of the time. Wendell's retirement announcement came at the Annual Football Peace Meeting, and he was surrounded by footballs wearing peace symbols, holding placards saying, "Bring Our Footballs Home" and "Bring Our Boys Home."

Politics and the Vietnam War began to creep into other writing I did. The *Herald Tribune*'s sports page was on the next-to-last page. Every other day on the back page were the columns of political satirists Art Buchwald and Russell Baker. I began to read them religiously and particularly enjoyed Buchwald. Soon, besides the sports stories, I was writing political satire. It is fair to say that the time in Norway also contributed to the development of my ideas and my writing.

A little outside of Oslo in Høvikodden, is the Henie-Onstad Art Centre, which opened in 1968. Sonja Henie is probably the most famous Norwegian athlete.

23

Henie, who died in 1969 of cancer at the age of 56, became a teenage darling, when at 15, she won the gold medal in figure skating at the 1928 Winter Olympics. She set the standard of excellence for the sport and followed up the 1928 performance with gold medals in 1932 and 1936, as well as winning 10 world championships. The record of three golds still stands. She then went to Hollywood and became a film star. Henie married wealthy Norwegian ship builder Niels Onstad, and they donated their art collection to the centre. More impressive to us than the art were the location and the building. It is situated on land surrounded by trees that look out on Oslofjord. I remember a ship being docked at the beach. The Centre can be reached by bus. The building is architecturally beautiful and includes a round glass elevator, which is what excited us kids. The museum is considered the center for modern art in the country.

The situation at school was not that peaceful anymore. My teacher left. When he left, it was as if the reins had been loosened on the boys. Some of it was teasing – and I can't even remember some of the barbs – and some of it was occasional isolation. The new teacher was nice, but I don't think he knew how to handle my presence in the class – an American who didn't understand the language. How does he include me? Now, instead of feeling part of things, I was beginning to feel lonelier, alienated, different and victimized.

At the same time, the administration provided a Norwegian tutor for my brother and me. Fru Hansen was a wonderful older woman and we learned much about the language. The first thing we had to learn was there were 29 letters in the Norwegian alphabet, with the addition of æ, ø and å at the end. At home, my father and sister helped me with my schoolwork, and we all studied the language. Our favorite book was a big children's picture storybook by Richard Scarry of Norwegian and English words.

November 1969

I don't remember when the letters first started arriving, but the first was a welcome surprise and then the following ones were anxiously awaited. When we left Philadelphia, we had not only left "regular" school, but also our Secular Jewish school. I had the textbook for that year with me – and though some people may think I was crazy – I read most of the book during the year, so I wouldn't fall behind. Ironically, the curriculum was "Jews in America," beginning with the suspicion that Christopher Columbus might have been a secret Jew and that many of his crew were Marranos from Spain (Jews who converted to Christianity but secretly practiced Judaism), and leading to Jewish immigration from Eastern Europe to America in the late 19th, early 20th century. Here we were, temporary Jewish "immigrants," so to speak, in Norway, and I was reading about the Vikings and someone named Leif Erickson, who supposedly discovered America in 1003.

The Sunday School teacher for that year would bring an aerogramme to class and have each student in the class write a note to me. I would receive these 10 letters in one. There were new students in the class, and they were writing to me, too. Then, I would write the class back. It was a wonderful idea conceived by my teacher, which kept the students in touch with me across the miles and allowed me to still feel connected to my class. By the time I returned, I knew the new students by handwriting and name, if not by face.

November marked the month when we finally searched out Oslo's Jewish community. It didn't take a long look. The community counted only around 831 Jews, including us, and only around 1,200 in the entire country. There was only one synagogue and center in Oslo, and they were situated on a hilly street. We rang a bell and were led upstairs to the rabbi's home. My brother remembers seeing a lot of musical instruments. I remember there were other people in the apartment. After talking for a while, we were taken for a tour around the center. We came to the auditorium where students were practicing the Chanukah play. I was startled when I noticed that one of the boys in the play was in the other sixth-grade boys' class at school. His name was Jakob Nusfeld, and he had a fraternal twin brother, Thomas. There was also an older brother.

Our families would become good friends. The father had been born in Lithuania and had survived a Nazi concentration camp as a teenager. He was proficient in many languages and after the war went to Palestine, later Israel. He met his future wife in Israel, and they returned to her native Norway.

This would be the beginning of a close connection with the Oslo Jewish community, as well as the beginning of our various experiences with Jews in Scandinavia and Europe.

The large discrepancy between the number of Jews in Oslo and Philadelphia would be cause for some humorous moments.

"How many Jews live in Philadelphia?" we would be asked.

"300,000," we would reply.

"No, not how many *people* live in Philadelphia, how many Jews live there?"

Two other Sunday visits in November would prove meaningful and special. In early November, snow provided a backdrop for our visit to the Saxlunds. I remember taking the train, and the station was close to their house. My father's brother lives in France and worked in the cosmetic business, as did Hans Petter Saxlund. The two knew each other, and my uncle had told my father to look up the Saxlunds when we were in Oslo. They were a pleasant family – Hans Petter; his wife, Ann; daughter, Ann Marie, who was about nine; and son, Tom, who was about five. The children were bright. Hans Petter's claim on our memory was he made his own beer. Of course, I was too young to try it. Ann prepared a nice spread of food, and we enjoyed visiting with them then and in future visits as well.

On another Sunday afternoon, we took a ride to Asker, a suburb of Oslo. My father had been told of a psychiatrist who was working on similar research. The two met and the man invited our family to visit him and his family.

The area where they lived was not completely "developed," as there were fields among the smattering of houses. We had to drive up a hill to get to the front of the house. It may have been more than just *forming* class that made me fall in love with woodwork. Wood and woodcrafts were so prevalent in Norway. This was a beautiful wood house with light wood. Outside above the front door were antlers and a wood nameplate: "Dalgards."

It may have been the first Norwegian home we were in that was built in the "traditional" way. The house was elevated on a stone base. We walked into a hallway on the first floor. But the bedrooms were on the first floor and the dining and living rooms and kitchen were on the second floor. We were told that this was to allow the heat to warm the bedrooms first, although my mother always thought it was because the views were better from the second floor.

After we entered, we were introduced to Odd Steffen, his wife, Ragnhild, and their two sons. Eivind, who had bright blond hair, was a little younger than me. Olav, who had these big, round eyes, was a little younger than my brother. The boys spoke no English; yet, we managed to play and get along. Odd Steffen was a tall man with brown hair, and he smoked a pipe. Ragnhild had dirty blonde hair and a bright smile. There was also a cat. My sister, who loved cats, started to play with it and suddenly broke out with an allergic reaction.

Upstairs was a big room that served as the dining room and living room, with a window that looked out onto a patio and the other side of Oslofjord. It was November, so Christmas decorations were around. My mother remembers Ragnhild lighting the traditional four candles in the window.

It was difficult trying to communicate with the boys, but neither family could predict how much we would mean to each other in the future.

It was an overcast, rainy and cold day when we visited the Munch Museum, which probably was appropriate. Edvard Munch is one of Norway's most famous painters. To my brother and me, he painted gloomy, depressing and scary stuff. My brother ran away from the famous "The Screech" painting. That was one museum the two of us didn't rush to go back to.

Only three weeks had passed since my first teacher had left. Then one day, the new teacher stopped me in the hallway. "I'm leaving. I got a job at IBM," he said. And, with that, I faced another adjustment, another new teacher. A similar thing had happened in third grade when one teacher had gotten sick and the substitute became permanent. This was a different country where I was just beginning to learn Norwegian words, let alone the language. My classmates were beginning to "test me," and a little over two months into this year in Norway, I faced my third teacher.

The first day with teacher #3 did not get off to a good start and it would take awhile before things smoothed out. I had the misfortune to show up late on his first day. I walked in, and as I took my seat in the right-hand row near the door, a classmate uttered, *"Han er amerikansk."* "He is American."

The teacher's first words to me (in English) were, "Are you always late?" I interpreted the question as an implication that I was always late, a judgment he could hardly make on his first day. I felt it was a strange way to begin, that this question should precede, "Hello, my name is...and I'm your new teacher. What's your name?"

Later, he called me up to the front of the room so he could become familiar with me. This would be an occasional occurrence during the rest of the school year. I'm sure he saw it as a way to bring me "into the class, to be part of the class," since I couldn't understand most things during the day. Maybe, it could've served a purpose if done in a positive way. Too often, these episodes were uncomfortable and embarrassing.

There I was on his first day in school, standing in front of the class.

"Where are you from?" he asked.

"Philadelphia."

"We're practically neighbors," he said. "I've been to New York nine times."

That's about all I remember from that conversation.

I was having enough trouble with the students. Now, the teacher would be a challenge, too.

Roger provided a refuge from this teasing, as we would usually hang out with each other at the recesses. Looking back now, that may have contributed some to my isolation from classmates. But Roger and I created our own tease and target – my brother and his sister. So much for "do unto others." We treated their friendship as a "romance" and would make up movie titles describing it. We called our "company" Marriage Productions! We thought it was harmless. It was certainly silly.

My brother and I were now taking our Norwegian lessons twice a week at school. There was also Norwegian grammar in regular class so we were getting a good fill of *norsk*. In addition, my brother was learning Norwegian cursive, which is quite different from American cursive. It would create great problems for him when he returned to Philadelphia. School homework was a challenge, as I would have to translate the Norwegian assignments and text to understand them in English and then translate answers into Norwegian. For compositions, I had to write in English and Norwegian. Even English class was an interesting experience because the students were learning British English. Norwegians distinguished between American and British English by saying we spoke American and the British spoke English. I would have to argue when I was marked wrong for spelling "color" with an "or" and not "colour."

My parents felt that my Norwegian education should be accelerated. So, they asked people if they knew of someone who would be interested in tutoring me. My father had hired two student research assistants, Berit and Torbjørn. Berit suggested a friend, Bodil, who was a student at the University of Oslo.

Most of the time, I would meet Bodil at the Blindern campus. I would go on my own, walking over to the Majorstua Station from school and taking the *trikk* to the campus. During the winter when the days were short, it would be dark by the time I got there around three p.m. and obviously darker when I returned. I would walk up the hill from the Blindern station and take a left down a street that led into a plaza of the campus. If memory serves me correctly, we met in the *Matematikk Bygningen* – The Mathematics Building.

Besides being a tutor for me, Bodil showed herself to be a concerned person. I rarely talked about my experiences at school. For some reason, one day, I mentioned my problems with the students. I remember the tears that welled up in her eyes. "I am so upset that these things are being done to you," she said. I was taken by her emotional reaction to my situation. This was the first Norwegian with whom I had personally shared my school experiences, and it not only felt good to see someone care so much, but also showed that our Norwegian lessons were a little more than helping me with the language. She was a friend. Obviously, that incident had a strong impact on me since I still recall it all these years later.

We quickly learned about the athleticism of the Norwegians and the value they put on enjoying their leisure time through the outdoors. Sundays didn't mean the National Football League. It meant taking a walk, and when the winter came, strapping on the skis or skates. November brought snow, not just a sprinkling, but a significant amount. We hit the sporting-goods stores to outfit ourselves. Cross-country skiing was and is most popular in Norway, so we purchased wooden cross-country skis. I also wanted to try skating, so I got skates too.

We were fortunate enough to have the immense Frogner Park around the corner from us, and we made like the Norwegians by taking advantage of it. There was no admission charge, and there were plenty of trails. We had heard the stories of Norwegian children learning to ski at three – if not sooner – without poles. There was evidence of that. People of all ages ski. The tennis courts in the park were also transformed into ice hockey and figure-skating rinks. In a corner of the park was a patch of ice for casual skaters – or those learning. Like the children on skis without poles, this ice had no railings. If someone wasn't interested in skiing or skating, which would be odd for a Norwegian, he or she could walk or bicycle and admire the interesting, although unusual, statues. Frognerseteren, near the Holmenkollen Ski Jump, is a popular spot on Sundays, as it has many beautiful trails through the forests.

You just don't ask a Norwegian if they ski. After all, it's part of the heritage. Norwegians invented and developed skiing – cross-country, ski jumping and slalom. Skis have been used by postmen to deliver mail and by doctors and midwives to reach expectant mothers. People ski to hunt and to attend church, funerals and weddings. Being snowbound is not a concept in Norwegian life.

Skiing in Norway is traced back 4,000 years. A rock carving of a skier was found in Northern Norway, and the oldest ski uncovered was 2,500 years old. Norway's name is derived from the god NOR, who legend says had to ski to get through a blizzard when he first arrived in the country. There are even gods of skiing and hunting (ULL) and a goddess of skiing (SKADE) in Norse mythology. Throughout Norwegian history, dating to the Viking period, skiing is prominently mentioned.

Skiing helped avert Civil War, with the most popular legend occurring during the war in 1206. Two skiers carried the two-year-old prince from Lillehammer in Gudbransdal to Rena in Østerdal and eventually to Trondheim. They had to ski through the mountains in the

31

dead of winter with only ice water to feed to the boy. Supporters of the royal family wore birch bark on their feet and became known as "birch legs" – *birkebeiner.* The boy later became King Haakon Haakonsen.

There has been an annual 35-mile Birkebeiner Race over the Lillehammer-Rena course since 1932, which draws thousands of competitors. The skiers must carry the same weight as the infant prince weighed.

Over the next 500 years, skiing grew in importance. Hunters became very adept on skis. There had to be restrictions placed on hunting to protect the animals. Soldiers were organized in ski units in 1716, and the first manual on skiing was authored by Captain Jens Emmahusen in 1733. Troops participated in competitions, including jumping and shooting while skiing downhill, beginning in 1767.

The first cross-country race was in Tromsø above the Arctic Circle in Northern Norway in 1843; while the first ski-jumping competition was in 1866 in the Telemark area in Southwest Norway.[1]

In the first 10 Winter Olympics, from 1924-68, Norway was the top medal winner six times, totaling 87 medals.[2]

While we were becoming involved in activities and elements of Norwegian culture, there were certain aspects or holidays from home we tried to retain. Certain Jewish holidays like Chanukah and Passover are universal, and you can find out how Jews in another country observe these occasions. My mother thought it would be wonderful to have Thanksgiving in Norway. She made a valiant effort to create it. Except she could not find turkey in the stores and went to Plan B – chicken. Most of the chicken sold in the stores was ready-made, off a rotisserie. Mom wanted the day to be special and wanted to prepare the chicken herself. She ended up buying a hen and that was only the beginning.

---

[1]Historical information from *The Holmenkollen Ski Jumping Hill,* by Jakob Vaage, Grundt Tanum Forlag, 1968.
[2] *Sports Illustrated 1993 Sports Almanac and Record Book.*

While my father, sister, brother and I went to the Park (they to ski, me to skate), my mother virtually killed the hen, or it must've felt that way. The hen still had hairs and feathers. We came home to a frustrated mother, who had been spending time plucking the feathers. Even after the hen was cooked, we could still see some hairs. So much for Thanksgiving in Norway.

I don't think my mother tried to cook chicken in Norway the rest of the year we were there.

December 1969

"There is no such thing as bad weather, only bad clothing."

-Norwegian proverb

Brr!! Welcome to Norway winters. The cold started to hit in December. There was a lot of snow. The white stuff would stay around until April. We can honestly say we trudged through feet of snow in below-freezing temperatures to get to school. Centigrade/Celsius degrees were another thing we had to adjust to. If Philadelphia and other areas of the United States were dumped with as much snow as Oslo got that winter, schools would have been closed for the entire winter. The kids laughed at us when we told them school in Philadelphia would be closed if we had a couple of inches/centimeters of snow.

When the weather was nice, the kids would ride bikes to school. The playground was full of blue bicycles. In the winter, it wasn't uncommon for students to ski to school. After all, cross-country skiing wasn't just a leisure sport, but a mode of transportation. And, "Neither rain, nor sleet, nor snow, nor cold, nor darkness would keep us from our appointed recesses outside."

As for skiing in, or rather on, the deep snow, it was a packed snow. In other words, people were skiing on top of the snow – and they just made sure they didn't fall.

We learned to deal with the cold. When in Norway, do as the Norwegians do. Dress warmly. Long johns, thermal tops, warm wool mittens or gloves were musts. I hated turtleneck shirts because I felt like I was choking. In Norway, I learned to wear them. I love Norwegian sweaters, particularly handmade ones. They provide great warmth. There would be kids who would wear a Norwegian sweater without a coat even on a day when I was bundled up. Thinking back, I'm trying to imagine a schoolyard full of kids wearing Norwegian sweaters and what a beautiful sight that must have been.

Then, there were the knickers, which I had only seen in pictures of George Washington and Thomas Jefferson and those guys from the 18th century. Knickers are pants that come to the knees, where they're met by long knee socks. This was common winter clothing and also warm.

In addition, they allowed for greater ease of movement when skiing or skating. The most popular colors were blue pants and scarlet socks. But, the Norwegians were as artistic with the knickers as they were with the sweaters. Similar designs were on the socks, mittens and gloves. In addition to hot chocolate, tea, coffee and bouillon, there was a warm berry drink called *solbær*. These precautions made us better able to *deal* with the cold. It doesn't necessarily mean we were completely warm. But to this day, I am better able to handle the cold in the United States because of that experience.

Thus, properly attired, we went out in the cold and snow and learned to enjoy it. Frogner Park was a haven, so easily accessible. I was becoming more frustrated with my skiing and started to devote more time and energy to skating. The TV exposed us to winter sports with which we had not been familiar and ones in which the Norwegians excelled. I might have seen some ski jumping on *Wide World of Sports* back home, but this was just one of the sports in Norway that replaced football, basketball and the National Hockey League for me. Cross-country skiing was featured, as was European ice hockey and speed skating. I had never seen speed skating before and I "fell" – no pun intended – for it. I was taken with the grace of the skaters, the ease with which they glided, and yet, they were going so fast. I also loved watching the winners cross the finish line, raise their arms and fall into the embrace of a teammate or a coach.

In 1969-70, speed skating was dominated by Norway, the Netherlands, Soviet Union, Sweden, Finland, Japan and probably some of the Eastern Bloc countries. Between 1924-68, Norwegian men won 16 gold medals in speed skating in the Olympics.[3] I liked one of the Norwegians who was good at the time, Dag Fornæs. And, so on my little patch of frozen water in Frogner Park, I began to copy his form and style (even though I didn't have the long blades speed skaters used). I began to glide back and forth with the arm behind the back. I would go to the Park after school or on Sundays. I was teaching myself how to skate.

There was another custom we learned. During the winter, when people visit someone else's home, they carry slippers with them. At the front door, the guests remove their boots and put on slippers, some of which are humorous looking. They walk around wearing the slippers or just socks, because it is rude to trample around the host's home with the mess from outside. This will happen at casual get-togethers or fancy dinner parties. Also, it is not hard to find the bathroom in a Norwegian home. There is a heart on the door, often with funny sayings.

Every month, we seemed to be meeting new people. In December, we spent time with some Jews we had met at the Jewish Center. We attended the Chanukah program, and it reminded me of the ones at our Jewish school in Philadelphia. We celebrated one of the nights of Chanukah at the Nusfelds, the family of the twins who were in the other class at school. They didn't live too far from us. They lived on the third floor of a small apartment building.

---

[3] *Sports Illustrated 1993 Sports Almanac and Record Book*.

There was a large room that was like a rec room. It was where we played. There was also a television in that room. The two boys became my Norwegian friends at school.

We were also invited for a Friday night *shabbat* dinner with the Demborg family. A traditional service was conducted. Mr. Demborg was Danish, and Mrs. Demborg was Norwegian. Both had escaped to Sweden during World War II and met there. Mrs. Demborg gave me a book, *Habibi's Adventures in the Land of Israel*, which I read, but never returned. We still have it. I remember there was much laughing and kidding about our name Kleiner. My father's father immigrated to the United States from Russia, but the word *kleiner* is German and Yiddish for "small." The people there couldn't believe we weren't German, and there was some joke about "small."

One man who was there was Oskar Mendelsohn, who had written a book on the history of the Jews in Norway, the culmination of 20 years of research in which he went through 25,000 documents for any citation of Jews. He had been a teacher in Trondheim prior to the war. His students warned him about a Nazi girl in the class. When his last day arrived, the students in the class surprised him by leaving flowers on his desk.

We had also met an Israeli couple, Simcha and Nava, at the Jewish Center. Nava was pregnant and gave birth to a boy on, of all days, December 25th.

Through his work, my father had come in contact with a couple of transplanted Americans. One was Sylvia Backer, who worked at the Institute. She was partially blind in one eye. Her husband, Finn, was a Norwegian judge.

Another was Morris Gardner. Morris had met his Norwegian wife, Liv, in the United States. They married and had a daughter, Rachel, who was now four. In 1968 or 1967, they decided to move to Norway. Morris and I shared a passion – potato chips. Norwegian *potet gull* are the best. We could have a big meal, but afterwards, the two of us would sit on the couch and devour a bag of chips! The Gardners came to our apartment for New Year's Eve. Without Guy Lombardo or Dick Clark and the falling balloons on Times Square, we welcomed in the New Year, a new decade. Although we weren't in the center of Oslo or outside at the "magical moment," we remarked at how quiet, unspectacular and anti-climatic the event was.

It was now 1970, and we had six-and-a-half months left in Norway.

January 1970

What better way to welcome in a new year than to welcome in a new life? January 1 was seven days after December 25 when Nava had given birth. That meant it was time for the *bris* or the Jewish ceremony of circumcision. We all went to the Jewish Center, and it was explained to me what would happen. But, all the women and young children were kept outside the room where the *bris* took place. So I have no idea whether a Norwegian Jewish *bris* is really any different than an American Jewish *bris*. And I hadn't been present at any American Jewish *bris* (except my own) either. Afterwards, there was food.

The *bris* happened to occur at the same time as an international incident among Israel, France and Norway. France had agreed to sell some ships to Israel, and then changed its mind. Israel sneaked the boats out of a French harbor under a Norwegian flag. The Norwegian newspapers reported the suspicion that an Israeli in Oslo may have aided Israel. It so happened that a good friend of Simcha's was a naval officer working in Norway. He came to the *bris* and was asked by people if he had anything to do with the French incident. He denied that he had. In addition, Simcha's father had to fly from Israel to Oslo through London. He was detained for a while in London under suspicion he might have been involved, when he was really en route to Oslo for his grandson's *bris!*

During the year, there were several special and unique trips. Wadahl, though, came first. The Royal Norwegian Council sponsored a weeklong trip in the mountains for the families of foreign academicians and researchers – in the middle of January. We had no idea where we were going; we just packed and got on a train for the three-hour ride.

My brother played a toy flute. To pass the time on the train, he took out his flute and music book. He began to play *Hatikvah*, the Israeli national anthem. Suddenly, a couple in front of us turned around. They were Israeli.

"Who would think that I would hear an American boy playing *Hatikvah* on a penny whistle on a train in Norway?" the woman said.

Mr. Davidson was studying folk music at the University of Oslo, and they had two young children. They, too, were going to Wadahl. We shared food, and she offered us a taste of avocado. Funny, after that, I always associated avocado with being Israeli.

Finally, the train stopped where we had to disembark. There was nothing there except snow and a bus. We got on the bus, which took us along the snowy mountain roads to the Wadahl *Høgfjellshotel* (high mountain hotel), situated atop this mountain on Peer Gynt *veien* with nothing else around. We were in Harpefoss in Gudbrandsdal (*dal* is valley), a popular resort area in Norway. The majestic and beautiful Jotunheimen and Rondane mountain ranges could be seen in the distance.

Gathered for this week were people from all over the world – Americans, British, Israelis, Czechs, Thai. A man from Thailand and another from Czechoslovakia taught me a card game similar to bridge. Grand smorgasbords were offered at breakfast and lunch in the spacious dining room that looked out on the slopes and mountains. Different fish, hard-boiled eggs, cheeses and meats were spread on the "cold table," (*kaldbord*) as it's called. Dinners were served at the tables, and boiled potatoes with parsley were always part of the dinners. There was a beautiful wood lounge – *stue* – with a fireplace, as well as a game room.

The first morning we stepped outside and was it ever cold! The temperature was -25°C (-13°F). There wasn't the additional wind factor though. The ski instructor asked who had washed their faces that morning. Everybody seemed surprised and somewhat indignant by the question. He told us that there are oils in the face that can protect it from the cold but are washed out by the soap. He told us to avoid washing with soap on such cold days.

There was another thing that struck us about the instructor. My father had a close colleague at Temple, Keith, who had died suddenly the previous summer. Keith was of Norwegian descent. The instructor looked just like Keith!

During that week, people learned or tried to learn to ski. I think I finally hung up the skis after that week. My father, of course, filmed us all. I tried to move around and fell several times before reaching the bottom of the hill. My sister was graceful going down the hill. Then, there was the shot of my brother skiing down the slope with my sister shouting to bend his knees. He reached the bottom, then fell!

At the end of the week, there was a children's competition. There was supposed to be age groups, and I think a different course depending on age. The instructor put me on the "easier" course, obviously feeling it was better to have me participate and try a course than sticking to the rules. It raised a slight protest from an American boy, but that didn't get too far. Then, again, neither did I, finishing last. However, everybody who participated received a Wadahl patch. We wore those patches on our coats proudly for a number of years until we grew out of the coats.

Despite the lack of "success" on the slopes, I did learn a number of things on the trip. I did learn the *fiskebein*, the fish bones method of walking up the slope, and walking sideways up and down hills. I use these methods now when walking in hilly or mountainous areas.

This was my first opportunity to be involved in an international cultural exchange, and it was fun and rewarding. Perhaps, Wadahl laid the groundwork for my future endeavors. In addition, the trip was paid for by the Norwegian government, and the notion that the government would go to such lengths to make foreigners feel welcome in their country, give them a taste of the culture and scenery, and create the forum and venue for foreigners to get to know each other had a lasting impact on me.

We also spent that week without any news, which caused my father and me some anxiety. The Sunday we left was Super Bowl IV. We had been picking the football games during the season and entered the Super Bowl tied in the overall standings. I picked Kansas City; he chose Minnesota. For a week, we didn't know the result of one of the biggest events in the United States. When we reached home – Oslo – we scurried for the *Herald Tribune* edition with the Super Bowl.

There was the headline: "Kansas City defeats Minnesota, 23-7 in Super Bowl."

That win certainly made up for my performance on the slopes.

Dad took a one-week trip to Philadelphia/Cherry Hill during January. He was sent armed with *Wendell the Football* for my writing teacher and others to read. He returned with favorable reviews from her and her son. Dad also told us how Pebbles jumped at his chest when Dad walked into my aunt and uncle's house.

February 1970

The last class on Saturday had finally ended, and I was walking down the stairs when I met my father on the way up.

"We have to hurry," he said. "Erik got tickets for the speed-skating championships!"

It was 2:15, and we had about a half hour before Erik Rinde and his son, Peder, would pick us up. We rushed home. I bundled up while my mother packed us a thermos of bouillon. We were ready in time.

The two-day world championships were being held at Bislett *Stadion* in Oslo. The stadium was packed by the time we got in. It seemed like a massive crowd. (In later years, I would learn Bislett's capacity is around 20,000, small for an outdoor stadium by American standards. Bislett is also the site where many track records, particularly the mile, are set.) All Peder and I could see were backs of people. The spectators didn't sit. They stood. Since we arrived just before the start, we were in the back row. The only way Peder and I were going to see anything was for our fathers to hold us up or find a way to get closer.

We chose the latter.

We weaved our way through the crowd of legs down the bleachers to the front row and then made one last move. We jumped the railing and were on the ice. The temperature was already below zero Celsius, and now we were standing *on* the ice. From where we had been to where we were now was unbelievable. Nobody else – except coaches and officials – had the view we had. From there, we watched skaters such as Dag Fornæs and Ard Schenk of the Netherlands, as well as the other racers. It was quite a thrill.

When we realized it was time to go, we weaved our way back up through the stands as people helped us along the way. Our fathers were waiting to grab us. By the time we reached the car, I was very cold and dying for something hot. I asked my father for some bouillon.

"We finished it," he said.

"You what? But I'm freezing. We were standing on the ice!"

Through the years, I've gradually forgiven him, and the incident has been remembered with good-natured ribbing.

The next day, I decided to defrost and watch the event on TV. My sister went with my father.

Geilo is another name that evokes special memories for us. In the middle of February, there was a mid-winter recess, a four-day weekend (which actually was three days off because of school on Saturday). We had been told Geilo was a nice resort area for skiing and relaxation. It was located midway between Oslo and Bergen.

Our British friend, Cissy, came to visit us, and she went with us to Geilo. My father drove through the snow to get us there. We stayed at the Geilo Hotel, which was situated right by the train station. It was a really nice place, which, like Wadahl, had wonderful smorgasbords at breakfast and lunch, and a sit-down dinner that, of course, included boiled potatoes and parsley. The food was wonderful.

Again, it was quite cold. Cissy borrowed Dad's parka. She vowed we would never get her on skis, but we have her on film taking some baby steps on skis, all the while saying, "You'll never get me on skis!"

Snow was plentiful and deep. My father, brother and sister did a lot of skiing. My father fell once and had trouble getting up because the snow was deeper than he was tall!

We found out where I might be able to skate. There turned out to be an oval nearby. I had never been on an oval before, except to watch the championships. Large drifts of snow had been piled in the middle of the track. Now, I could really mimic Dag Fornæs. I did the whole act. I glided around the oval – at no record-breaking pace – but when I completed the lap, I had crossed the finish line victorious. My sister came out on the ice to congratulate me, followed by the other "adoring fans."

The highlight of this trip, though, was when we met the Sami. They are an indigenous people to Northern Europe – Norway, Sweden and Finland – with a language and culture different than the countries they inhabit. The Sami are also known as Lapps or Laplanders, but that is considered a derogatory term by the Sami. It was unusual that the Sami were this far south. We saw an announcement inviting people to come to the Sami camp and learn about their culture. There were two ways to get there – by ski or reindeer sled. Dad, Wendy and Albie decided to ski to the camp. My mother, Cissy and I opted for the sled. It is hard to say who had more fun, the skiers or the sledders. The Sami put us in two sleds – my mother and I in one, and Cissy in the other. What lay before us was white tundra. Ready, set, go. Lurch. We were on our way. Nice reindeer, stay straight. Suddenly, Cissy's sled veered off course. Staying poised and calm, she summoned the famous lines from all those snow tundra movies. "Mush! Mush!" It must've worked because we all got to the camp.

My brother's memory is of a "walled camp," surrounded by skins draped over wood racks. We sat in the tent while the Sami, dressed in blue and orange outfits, showed us skins and crafts. It was difficult communicating because they didn't know English or much Norwegian, and our Norwegian wasn't that good. Still it was quite an interesting experience. There are Norwegians who haven't met Sami!

When we were done, we hopped on our sleds and my father, sister and brother on their skis.

"Meet you back at the hotel." Off we went, leaving the Sami behind, but never to be forgotten.

March 1970

It was the third weekend in March and that meant the "Festival" at Holmenkollen. A weekend event that one can't imagine without having witnessed it. The Holmenkollen Ski Jump is a distinctive site in Oslo because it can be seen from anywhere in the city. The white concrete slope protrudes from the mountains that surround Oslo proper. Holmenkollen is the area of Oslo where the jump is located.

On the third Sunday in March, the world's best jumpers gather for one of the world championship events, capping an exciting weekend. During the preceding

43

days, there are cross-country competitions as the competitors from different countries try to win the individual and team cross-country and ski-jumping titles. The combined event(s) is known as Nordic combined. As touched on before, ski jumping and cross-country skiing are two sports developed in Norway, and for a long time, they were Norway's domain in Olympic and non-Olympic years.

Norwegians won the first six gold medals in ski jumping in the Olympics from 1924-52. In men's Nordic combined, Norway captured the gold in seven of nine Olympics from 1924-64. Norway ruled the cross-country domain as well with golds in the 15 kilometers in six of 10 Olympics from 1924-68. The winners in the other years were Sweden three times and Finland once, giving Scandinavia the stranglehold on the medals.[4]

The first Holmenkollen competition was in 1892 on a slope of snow, with a wood jump being built in 1914 down the road from the current hill. The competition was limited to Norwegians until 1903 when Sweden sent jumpers. By 1914, seven countries, including the United States, had sent competitors. More countries became involved after World War II.

King Olav V jumped at Holmenkollen in 1922 and 1923 when he was Crown Prince.

Between 1918-69, Norwegians set 33 of the 40 record jumps. The longest jump in 1892 was 21.5 meters; in 1969, the record was set at 92 meters.

The length of the slope has been enlarged several times, up to 90 meters in 1969. The height from the ground has increased from 9.5 meters in the beginning, considered scary at the time, to the equivalent of a three-story building in 1969.[5]

The March weekend is called Holmenkollen Festival, Norway's version of "March Madness." We had visited

---

[4] From *Sports Illustrated 1993 Sports Almanac and Record Book.*
[5] Jakob Vaage, *The Holmenkollen Ski Jumping Hill*, Grundt Tanum Forlag, 1968.

Holmenkollen as a tourist attraction, but now we were going to be part of the Festival and the atmosphere. My father got tickets for Sunday's jumping competition for him, Albie, Wendy, Erik, Peder Rinde 'and me. (The tickets (*billetter*) cost 30 *kroner* ($4.28) for adults and 20 *kroner* ($2.85) for children.)

The Bislett crowd at the speed-skating championships was nothing compared to this. In fact, the Holmenkollen crowd was around *five times* the size. That comes to around 100,000 people, including the King. The largest crowd ever was 120,000 for the 1952 Olympics. Oslo's population is around 450,000 people. Therefore, the roads would be mobbed with bumper-to-bumper traffic, and the *trikks* crammed with Norwegian "sardines." If one drove, where would one park?

For Norwegians, though, there are practical alternatives. There are always the feet.

My father drove to Erik's house, and from there, we walked to Holmenkollen. We are not talking about leaving the car six blocks from the stadium to avoid the crowds. It was miles. We walked 1½ hours uphill in snow. What was neat and unique was that so many other people were walking, too. It's one of the things I remember most about Holmenkollen. Masses of people walking through the snow to get to Holmenkollen! Somehow I can't imagine Americans walking miles to the Rose Bowl. According to Jakob Vaage's 1968 book, *The Holmenkollen Ski Jumping Hill*, between 50,000-60,000 people *walk* to Holmenkollen. That is the outstanding memory, not whether I was tired or upset about walking.

At Holmenkollen, our seats were in the left bleachers. From there, looking up, we could see the end of the jump and then the jumpers lift off and fly with the greatest of ease – and with nerves of steel – and finally land on the runway, uh, circle below after a flight that lasts three seconds at a rate of 56 miles per hour (1969 standards). The side bleachers were steep. Bleachers also surrounded the landing pit area. Standing spectators ringed the area. Watching the jumpers was like a tennis match, where you turn your head from side to side to follow the ball, except your head moves up and...down.

In all those old pictures of people trying to fly, they always flapped wings like the birds. The ski jumpers figured out the secret. You don't flap your arms (although some early jumpers did) or even put "wings" on the arms. You wear skis on your feet, put your arms by your side and lean forward.

The Norwegian fans were dressed in red, blue and white, the colors of the flag, and brought along flags to wave. One section created the shape and colors of the flag. Of course, there were fans from other countries sporting their colors. The Norwegians cheered all the skiers.

A Norwegian didn't win the event, but that didn't matter much as compared to our experience of being part of such a special event in Oslo and in Norway. (Recently, I found the program from that Holmenkollen with my pencil marks where I had written the results.) We walked back to Erik's house, had hot cocoa to warm up (I was not denied this time), and then headed home to store away another special memory.

A couple of weeks later was Easter break, which gave us an opportunity to visit the two Nordic countries and capitals we had not seen yet, Stockholm, Sweden and Helsinki, Finland.

Before we take off for Sweden and Finland, it might be a good time to talk about the Moomintroll stories.

It is a bit difficult to explain what a Moomin is. From the simple drawings in the books, they kind of look like upright hippos. Finnish author Tove Jannson created them and wrote a series of books about the adventures of the Moomintroll family. The stories were translated into English. We first discovered them in the local library where there was an English language book section. The stories were delightful, and we all enjoyed them immensely. So, we bought the books.

The Moomintrolls became so popular in general that year that either the Swedes or Finns created a television program about them with actors dressed in costumes. The program was a disaster, regardless of the fact that we didn't understand the language. Now, we were heading to the "land of the Moomins."

We flew via SAS to Stockholm first. Stockholm was more of a metropolis than Oslo, and the high-rises reminded me a little of New York. The pace was also faster than Oslo. There was a charm about the city, which is composed of 14 islands. There were a number of amusing sites.

We visited the museum which houses the *Wasa,* a wooden man-of-war ship, that sank shortly after she left Stockholm Harbor on her maiden voyage on August 10, 1628. We were able to look around the ship. The ship was being sprayed to preserve it.

The *Wasa* museum is part of a larger complex called Skansen. The park opened in 1891 and is the oldest open-air park in the world. It includes a zoo, restaurants, open-air theater, museums and 150 buildings, representing different periods of history. There are concerts, folk dancing and demonstrations of glass blowing, baking, printing and weaving. For small children, there is Lil-Skansen, which features small animals.

It was quite an exciting place. I don't recall bars in the zoo. We loved watching the seals (maybe that's when Albie's and my fascination with seals began) and particularly the polar bears. They could care less about the cold air or water. They'd dive in the water and swim around. They would stand on their hind legs and beg for food from the visitors. The brown bears were cute, too.

The most amusing experience, though, occurred in *Gamle Stan,* The Old Town. Visiting there is a must when in Stockholm. The Royal Palace, built between 1700-1754 is located there. We toured the outside and inside of the Palace, which included many historic artistic artifices including classical sculpture and the King's silver throne.[6]

---

[6] Factual information is taken from *Fodor's Budget Scandinavia '85,* Fodor's Travel Guides, 1985.

The shops, houses and streets are just as they were in the 17th century. Cobblestone and narrow brick roads took us through *Gamle Stan*. This future History major loved this. *Gamle Stan* was also where we met the shoemaker. Coincidentally, the tongue on one of Albie's shoes had torn.

We were ambling along and came to a large square. A gray-haired man with a red face noticed us tourists. He decided to show us around and explain the history of *Gamle Stan*. "That's where they chopped (so-and-so's) head off."

The man was also very drunk. When he found out my brother had trouble with his shoes, he said, "I'm a shoemaker. Come to my shop and I'll fix it."

So we followed him to his shop. His wife worked in the store, but she never said a word while we were there. We watched the drunken shoemaker in this *Gamle Stan* shop work to repair the shoe. We wondered exactly what he was doing, and in his state, whether he knew what he was doing. He sewed the tongue to the shoe, but it worked, and we had a story to tell for all "time" about The Shoemaker of Gamle Stan. (Later, a shoe repairman said the man had done the right thing with the shoe – drunk or not.)

While in Stockholm, we also saw an exhibit of Paul Gauguin at the Museum of Modern Art on Skeppeshol-men Island. I remember the exhibit for a couple of reasons: the large Gauguin sign atop the museum which my father filmed from across the water from the museum, and that I retained the association of Gauguin and Tahiti. So, whenever I hear a question about art and Tahiti, I think of Gauguin!

We also found Sweden excited by the European Ice Hockey championship, which the Swedes were participating in with the Soviet Union, Czechoslovakia, West Germany and Finland.

And in Stockholm, we met Mr. Lansky, who provided us with a history lesson of another kind. It would become a pattern for us to find Jews, the Jewish community and

Jewish history in whatever city in Europe we visited. These experiences would have a profound effect on me in future years. We met Mr. Lansky at the Jewish Center, and he showed us around. Sweden, which served as a haven for fleeing Jews during World War II, had 14,000 Jews, half of whom lived in the capital.

We then sat in the lobby area by a staircase. Mr. Lansky had dark hair and a moustache and seemed anxious to talk to Jewish Americans. For most of the time, my mind wandered a bit because he didn't speak English. Mr. Lansky was Polish, so the common language was Yiddish. My mother communicated with him in Yiddish and then translated for us. He talked softly as he told us how he had been forced to leave Poland in 1968 when the government insisted that Jews denounce Israel for the 1967 Six-Day War. He had been a school principal and was well-respected among the teachers and students, who didn't want him to leave. The Lansky family had to leave their books behind and was permitted to leave without a passport. Mr. Lansky said he was writing a book about the history of the Jews in the Soviet Union, which his daughter would translate into English.

Our collection of Jewish history stories would continue in Helsinki. The language of communication was again Yiddish.

The door to the Jewish Center was locked, so we tried ringing one of the doorbells. We went to a floor that had about 20 rooms. It was a Jewish nursing home with 16 residents. A person took us to a small room where 84-year-old Mr. Gutvort sat. He welcomed us warmly and showed us the Yiddish newspapers that his tourist friends had sent him. Some were in English. Mr. Gutvort said Jews had first come to Finland in 1850, mostly as deserters from the Russian Army. There were now 900 Jews in Helsinki and 1,200 in Finland.

Mr. Gutvort showed us around, and we met Mr. Stiller, who was 85. Mr. Stiller's brother had discovered the actress Greta Garbo. Mr. Stiller showed us the synagogue, which was in remarkably good condition.

The Finns and Russians have historically been adversaries, and during World War II, Finland sided with Germany to fight the Soviets. We were curious why the synagogue had not been damaged during the war.

"Well, you see that man over there – Mr. Stiller," said another man. "He went to President Mannerheim (of Finland) and told him that he's going to have to do something for the Jews, because they had fought for Finland against the Soviet Union. He must protect us. When the Nazi boats came for the Jews of Finland, Mannerheim said, 'We are all Finns here, we have no Jews.'"

The boats left. Because of Mr. Stiller and Mannerheim's acceptance of responsibility, all the Jews of Finland were saved.

In order to get to Helsinki, we took an overnight boat from Stockholm to Turkü. Since we were leaving at night, Dad filmed us getting on the boat during the day. The boat was an ice cutter, and even in late March, there was plenty of ice. This was particularly grating for Dad. My mother and we kids bunked in one cabin, while Dad had a room near the hull. Every time the ship cut through the ice, he heard it.

When he tried to walk around the ship, he found the halls full of drunks, primarily Finns, who took advantage of the duty-free liquor prices onboard. There was a long line at the liquor store before the boat left Stockholm, and when the boat crossed international waters, the store reopened.

After arriving early in the morning at Turkü, which is called Åbo by Swedish-speaking Finns, we had to take a train to Helsinki, to the Finns, Helsingfors. Language would create a different problem in Finland. While Norwegian, Swedish and Danish are similar, Finnish is completely different. The Finns didn't speak much English.

Our time in Helsinki turned out to be extremely limited as we arrived on Easter weekend, and places were closed Easter Sunday and Monday. We ended up leaving a day early. The major attraction we visited was this beautiful new building, The Town Theatre, which contained several theaters. Afterwards, we walked across a frozen lake.

In Sibelius Park, we saw a beautiful profile steel statue of composer Jean Sibelius, next to a unique monument of welded steel tubes, which had been made by Eila Itiltunen. Sections of tubes were higher or lower than the next, much like the movement of pushing cords on a piano or organ.

Among other things, Stockman's Department Store offered the beautiful Arabia china and stoneware. Each set is made by an individual or team of artists. We brought a set back, which is still used for special occasions.

There was a boy in my class, Roald, who befriended me. I don't remember when it was, but he invited me to go see a Laurel and Hardy movie at the nearby *kino*, cinema. One time, I went to his home. Roald was also trouble and the problem kid in the class.

One weekend, I called the *kino* and learned the movie that Saturday was *Fårehunden Flash*. I invited Roald to go. After I got off the phone, I learned the translation was *Flash the Sheepdog*. At school, I endured teasing from classmates for picking a "children's" film. I considered finding a different film, but didn't. So, we went to the movie, and when we came out of the *kino*, we met two classmates!

Roald came back to the apartment. In my room, I had the stacks of my fictional sports stories and standings on a table. He asked what they were. My nine-year-old brother, who had endured teasing from Roger and me about him and Linda, answered, "These are his girl-friends, and the number of times he's kissed them."

On top of the standings was Tennessee. I became defensive, tried to tell Roald what my brother said wasn't true.

Some time after that, the teacher called me in front of the classroom for one of my sessions with the class.

These times in front of the class were uncomfortable because I don't feel they served the purpose they could have, such as learning about my life at home or cultural things. They were used to talk about "mundane" or "trivial" matters that at times I felt were intended to embarrass me. I felt as if I was onstage.

The teacher's question for this day was, "Do you have any girlfriends in Philadelphia?"

From his seat in the front row, Roald started talking with a sly smile on his face. The only word I needed to understand was "Tennessee." Anger and embarrassment gripped me. ˙ I don't know what was worse, Roald mentioning it, or what came next.

The teacher replied, "Tennessee? Is that Pennsylvania's rose?"

The whole conversation was ridiculous, and the teacher was falling in line with this and making things worse for me. I couldn't understand how something so stupid and untrue could be "believed" by Roald, passed on to the teacher, and was now out in front of the class, and the teacher was actually using it to continue the conversation.

Further, my writing was personal, and I always kept this fictionalized, fantasized sports writing particularly secret, even in America, fearing that would be cause for teasing and ridicule. It seemed much different than my normal creative writing. Now, that writing was being distorted in Norway. What was I to do, start explaining through the language barrier what the material really was? In addition, I was an 11-year-old who was still shy about interest in girls in a class with boys one to two years older than I was. All of these factors and the tone of the conversation hardly made for a comfortable position for me.

There was nothing much I could do or say. I was in shock that a silly thing a nine-year-old had said could reach this far and be believed!

Roald and I were no longer friends, and he became one of my worst tormentors. One day at recess, some of the other boys egged me on that I should fight him. I tried to resist, but they kept at it. The fight didn't turn out to be much. I landed a punch before it was stopped. It was the only fight I ever had in all my years in school.

April 1970

How appropriate, that after our Jewish experience in Stockholm and Helsinki, April brought Passover, the seven-day Jewish celebration of freedom from slavery to the Egyptian Pharaohs. I remember only a few things from Passover in Norway. We had to go to the Jewish Center to get Passover foods because they had to be imported. I had been raised on Mother's brand gefilte fish (chopped carp), and the gefilte fish we got was Rokeach brand. Since this was the first time I had the Rokeach brand, I always associated Rokeach as being a foreign brand!

Secondly, we invited the Davidsons for the first *seder*, the first night, when the Haggadah, the story of the liberation, is read. There are different interpretations, and long, short and edited versions. The reading must be completed before eating can begin. They came very late and insisted on reading the whole Haggadah.

Simcha and Nava, the other Israeli couple we met, left Norway in April. It was where they were going that was exciting. Simcha received a grant to study in Philadelphia. They rented our Philadelphia house while they looked for a home!

Things started to change for the better at school. I don't know whether it was due to meetings between my parents and the teacher. He also decided that I could provide help to the students learning English. During English class, I would sit with one of the boys, changing to a different one each day, until I had spent time with every one in the class. Then, there was my essay.

We had to write compositions for Norwegian class, every now and then. Earlier in the year, I wrote a paper on the Quakers in Philadelphia and Pennsylvania. As mentioned before, I would have to write in English and translate to Norwegian. For one assignment, one of the topics was "Majorstua School in 2070." With my English and Norwegian imagination, I wrote about a school not only with robots and futuristic equipment, but also with the same teachers that we had in 1970, including their idiosyncrasies.

The teacher read the Norwegian version of the composition in class, and the boys roared with laughter, not teasing laughter, but approving laughter of my writing and *Norwegian* sense of humor. And having my Norwegian composition read in class certainly beat having to stand in front of the class trying to explain about Tennessee. Ironically, it was my creative writing that had elevated me out of being a "victim" to a level of popularity. This would be one of the early instances in my life where this would be the case.

The weather was beginning to warm up. My brother remembers a day the two of us went downtown together and that our parents trusted us to go alone. We went to the *Rådhus*, the City Hall, and admired the mosaics inside the beautiful building.

We then crossed the street to the harbor. The shrimp boats had come in and were selling their catches. The shrimp came in a bag, and at that time, I think it cost 10 *kroner* ($1.40). The shrimp were a darker red than what we were used to in America. They were good just the same.

May 1970

May 1 is celebrated in Norway and much of Europe as a labor holiday. School was closed Friday and Saturday. We planned a weekend trip to the town of Lillehammer, leaving by car on Friday, May 1.

Along the way, we had to pull over to the side of the road in a small town because of the May Day parade, involving bands of children.

We stayed on a farm in Lillehammer, which was frequented by senior citizens. On the ground, in and around Lillehammer, there was still plenty of snow!

At the same time as our weekend holiday, critical events were happening on the American and world stages, with tragic events to come. On or around April 28, President Nixon ordered the invasion and bombing of Cambodia, accelerating the Vietnam War. On our first night at the farmhouse, we went to the living room where some other women had gathered to watch the news on television.

President Nixon's face appeared on the screen, as he made a speech explaining his decision. Dad was standing at the entrance to the living room. Finally, when he could take no more of Nixon's speech, he stormed out of the room. The women in the room looked at each other, and one whispered something about my father being an American.

But we went on with our weekend trip. The major attraction in Lillehammer is Maihaugen, an open-air museum similar to the Norwegian Folkmuseum in Oslo. It contains old wooden homes, shops and churches laid out among trees, woodsy areas, a lake and grazing cows and horses. Part of the uniqueness of the structures is that they are made without nails and metal, and many are elevated on stilts. They date from the 13th-19th centuries, yet have maintained the same architecture.

Many buildings have interesting carvings. The main attraction – the wood Stave Church – dates back to 1200. It is the largest building in the museum, and stretching out from the roofs are dragon heads. It was believed the dragon heads warded off evil spirits. There are old stave churches all over the country.

The beds in the Maihaugen houses were quite small. People of that time period were either tiny or curled up into a fetal position when they slept. Some buildings were small and had small doors.

My brother played for the camera, knocking on the doors, asking the "little trolls" to come out. Trolls are characters from Norwegian folktales. They allegedly have long hair and long noses. There are good and bad trolls – the bad ones are more silly than evil. The trolls live underground and under bridges. So, my brother tried to coax the little trolls out of their dwellings, but without success.

We enjoyed our weekend in Lillehammer, but when we returned to Oslo on May 3, my father was still upset about the American bombing of Cambodia. He talked with Morris Gardner – with whose family we spent New Year's Eve – and other Americans. They decided to draft a letter of protest. The purpose was to have as many Americans working in Norway sign it and submit the letter to the Norwegian papers.

Just as they were getting started, May 4, 1970 happened. National Guardsmen, who were trying to keep the "peace," had opened fire on students at Kent State University in Ohio, some of whom were protesting the War and the latest incursion into Cambodia. Four students were killed and nine wounded. It sent shockwaves through the house. The ultimate tragedy of campus protest had occurred. Students peacefully protesting a war had been shot and killed by the very people who were there to supposedly protect against outbreaks of violence.

I remember seeing the headlines in the *Herald Tribune* and the now famous picture of the student crying over a slain friend. To an 11-year-old, 18- to 21-year-olds still had the image of being much older, although some of my sister's friends at school were 18. Kent State had added significance when I went to college and was *their* age, and I realized how young the Kent State students really were. I felt a certain kinship to one of the slain students because she was from Pittsburgh. I had never been to Pittsburgh, and it was at the other end of Pennsylvania, but she was from Pennsylvania and so was I.

The Kent State incident also gave my father and Morris's petition more fuel. I remember they held a meeting at the Institute of Americans they had contacted. Sixteen people signed the letter, and it was sent to the Norwegian papers. *Dagbladet* translated the letter into Norwegian and printed it. Kent State will always have this Norway association for me.

The experience in Norway also pointed out some of the fallacies of the Nixon Administration's justifications of its policies. The President would always argue that America must carry out these aggressive actions to maintain our respect around the world. The sense we got from Norwegians was that they didn't respect America anymore for taking these actions; if there was any change, there was less respect. In Stockholm, one of the first signs we saw was "Fight U.S. Imperialism" in Swedish.

I don't remember when it was that a classmate came up to me in shop class and said, "Michael, you must not be a Nixon fan. You must be a Mao fan." I didn't even know who Mao was then!

Perhaps Norwegians, particularly in 1970, had long memories. On May 8, the 25th anniversary of the end of World War II, the Norwegian Resistance Museum was dedicated. It honored these proud people's resistance to the Nazi occupation from 1940-45. In 1970, the parents of many of my classmates may have been involved in the Underground during the War, and if not they, then their grandparents. War had been on their soil. Many people we had met had been involved in the Underground. This country is also the home to the Nobel Peace Prize.

There is no more special holiday in Norway than 17 *mai* or 17th of May. That is Norway's Independence or Constitution Day. The Norwegian Constitution was approved at Eidsvold, near Lillehammer, on 17 May 1814. What is curious about this is that Norway didn't become fully independent until 1905. Norway, being just north and across the water (Skaagerak) from Denmark, and west of Sweden, was a pawn in these countries' attempts for empires. Denmark ruled Norway from 1380-1814, which followed Swedish rule from 1319-1380. Denmark was forced to support Napoleon in the Napoleonic Wars. In the Treaty of Kiel, ending the war, Norway was given to Sweden.

The Norwegians were furious and hatched a plot. Despite a lack of roads, communications and experience in government, a call went out for elections of representatives to a parliament. The northernmost districts of Nordland, Troms and Finnmark were the only areas not represented among the 112 men who met at Eidsvold to draft a constitution. Clergy, officers, lawyers and landowners were among the delegates. The two most prominent men were two young lawyers, Wilhelm Christie, 36, and Christian Magnus Falsen, 32.

Time was of the essence as the Swedish Army was on its way from France. A constitution was drafted using American independence as an example. The delegates signed it on 17 May 1814 and pledged allegiance "so long as the mountains of Norway stand." They also gave the power of elections to farmers because "the free smallholder is the man who has best reason to defend his property and rights."

The Norwegians elected Danish prince Christian Frederick, King, but Sweden wasn't going to take these developments lying down.

Their own Crown Prince Karl Johan was an interesting person. He had been Field Marshal Bernadotte in the French Army and married Desirèe, Napoleon's "first love." He turned on Napoleon and resigned from his post in 1809. Sweden was in need of a leader so Bernadotte went there, changed his name to Karl Johan and led the Swedish Army against Napoleon. After the war, the Swedes turned to him as their King. Now, his first item of business was dealing with this upstart Norway. Karl Johan wanted to resolve the issue quickly. A compromise was reached. Norway accepted Karl Johan as King, and Karl Johan agreed to accept the constitution with some changes.

Things did not go smoothly over the next 90 years. Karl Johan, who ascended the throne in 1818, did not have a castle, so a *slott* had to be built. It now stands at the end of Oslo's main street – Karl Johans Gate – with a statue of the king upon his horse in front. After his initial attempts to subvert the constitution failed, Karl Johan relented and he became well-liked and respected. There was no parliament building until 1866, and that is situated a few blocks from the palace.

Christie and Falsen became even more admired in Norway's history. Christie, considered a "modest politician," outlined the constitution and was elected the first president of the *Storting* – the Parliament. He was considered the "Father of the Nation." Christie established the Bergen Museum in 1825 in the city of Bergen. A bronze statue of Christie holding the constitution in his hand, the first statue in the country, is in front of the museum.

Falsen is known as the "Father of the Constitution." He became president of the Supreme Court of Justice. Falsen was 47 when he died in 1830. He was also responsible for the abolition of the nobility in Norway, which was passed unanimously by the Parliament in 1821.

Much of the controversy with Sweden centered around Norway's persistence in asserting its independence and autonomy despite the union with Sweden. The issues ranged from which flag Norway would use to the kind of legislation to pass in the *Storting*. The King was permitted to veto a bill by the *Storting* twice, but after the third time, the legislation became law no matter how the King felt. At times, the *Storting* attempted to impeach the King's ministers if they opposed the Parliament. And in 1884, Johan Sverdrup, leader of the "Left" party (at the time, the only other party was the "Right"), declared, "All power shall be concentrated in this assembly."

Things came to a head in 1905. As Norway developed, it began to feel more confident that it could function independently of Sweden. Norway wanted to have its own ambassadors to other countries and the *Storting* passed the resolution three times over King

Oscar II's (reign 1829-1907) objections. Norway had two Prime Ministers, Christian Michelsen in Norway and Jørgen Løvland in Stockholm. Løvland advised King Oscar that the Norwegian government would resign over this matter, and the King would not be able to create a new government. For the King's laws to be enacted, he and a prime minister needed to sign the bill. Neither minister would agree to that because of the risk of being accused of disloyalty to Norway. In fact, Michelsen and the government did resign.

There were Swedes who wanted to go to war against Norway, but the King and Swedish Labour Party were more cautious. Europe sided with Sweden, but the Norwegian explorer and humanitarian Fridtjof Nansen was successful in getting an audience in England where he stated Norway's claim.

Sweden called for a referendum. Without a shot being fired, Norwegian men overwhelmingly voted for independence, with only 184 dissenters. Michelsen negotiated a truce with Sweden.

It is ironic that Norway turned to Denmark for a King, the Dane's Prince Carl. He called for a vote of the people to decide on a monarchy or republic. The results were overwhelmingly in support of a monarchy. Prince Carl became King Haakon VII, and he came to Norway in 1905 with his wife, Queen Maud, and baby son, Olav.

The last break with previous rule came in 1924 when the name of the capital was changed from Christiania (for Danish King Christian IV) to the medieval name of Oslo.[7]

Although Norway didn't gain full independence until 1905, 17 *mai* was always recognized as the Independence Day.

The focus of the holiday is on children. The parades feature children and are not meant to be processions of decorated military. In 1970, the holiday fell on a Sunday. In the morning, we walked to Kirkeveien to see the

---

[7] Information from Zinker Hopp, *Norwegian History Simplified*, John Griegs Forlag, 1969.

children in the Majorstua Skole band march to the school. They were dressed in white shirts, red vests and blue knickers. The neighbors, as well as the parents and relatives, were out to watch. The band proceeded into the schoolyard. The principal came out of the school to recognize the band, students and the holiday. My brother's friend, who was a member of the band, didn't know what to do for the camera, so just waved. Waving breaks all language barriers. A boy in my class was also in the band.

Next, we went to my sister's school. The high school graduates use this time to begin their celebrations. In Norway, the grads dress in red and dash white paint on their faces. They also wear red hats. They are called *Russ*. Many of my sister's friends were *Russ*. They carry bamboo canes, which they rap on the ground. They had elected my sister to carry the baton in the Nissen Gymnas procession. After some pictures at the school, my parents, brother and I headed downtown.

The day was just beginning. *Sentrum* (Center City) was a wall of people, carrying Norwegian flags, the blue cross and white border on a red background. The King's Guards started the parade, followed by the children. All the students from the Oslo schools paraded into *Sentrum*, along Karl Johans Gate, to *Slottet* (the Palace) and past the King's reviewing stand. Majorstua passed us again and then there was Nissen. My sister was holding the baton, which seemed too heavy for her, pushing it forward and back. The *Russ* made a circle, danced up Karl Johans Gate and pounded the pavement with their canes.

17 *mai* would be another special memory of our year away, which only had a couple of months left.

June 1970

June would be a busy month for us, and not just because we would be packing. We did much traveling and were hosts for American friends. School also came to an end.

As the weeks wound down, the situation at Majorstua seemed to improve, so that on the last day, things ended on a "good" note. I walked up to the front of the room one last time. This time, I was writing my name and address on the blackboard. I passed around a notebook to collect the boys' addresses. School let out. Two classmates, Frederick and Thomas, walked home with me. We reached Tidemands Gate 20 and said good-bye. I don't remember what we said to each other, whether we mentioned seeing each other again or writing to each other. I opened the gate and walked up the driveway. They went their way. I wondered if I would ever come back and see them, or anybody else in the class, again.

In early June, we made "the trip." Bergen, the second largest city in Norway, is on the west coast; Oslo is on the east coast. The journey should not be taken by plane, unless it's one way. There are other options: trains, boats and buses (which are described later in the book). Then, there is the option to drive.

My father chose the latter, and we are indebted to him for the experience and getting us there and back safely. The trip *to* Bergen is the experience, which includes some nerve-racking moments, but also the most dramatic and beautiful scenery one will ever see, earning the journey the reputation as the most beautiful in the world.

We traveled on narrow roads through the mountains, which still had snow. We have postcards of snowdrifts in June that towered over cars. The roads were barely wide enough to hold one vehicle, let alone two-way traffic. There were hair-raising turns and no guardrails on the side, just a steep drop into the valley. It reminds one of the cartoons where the characters are driving on narrow mountain roads with the car jumping up and down. For long stretches, there was not a word spoken in the car. We had heard stories about the Danes, who don't have mountains in Denmark, getting stuck and offering the car to the Norwegians who live in the mountains, if they got them down!

My father stuck it out. At one point in the journey, we came around a turn, only to be confronted by cows relaxing in the road. We just had to wait until they decided to move. In many areas, there were sheep and lamb grazing alongside the road.

The trip continued along the fjords. We had to take two or three ferries – which allowed cars – across or around the fjords to get to the next roadway. On the trip west, we took the long, scenic route, heading north, then coming south and west. We crossed at Revsnes and Balestrand. At Vangsnes on the other end, we stayed over at a *pension*, an inexpensive bed and breakfast hotel, before picking up the trek again. There was another ferry crossing, but I don't remember where. Finally, after two days, we arrived in Bergen.

We had heard and read the stories of the rivalry and good-natured ambivalence Oslo and Bergen have for each other. For example, Oslo doesn't consider Bergen really a part of Norway because they talk in a dialect, and, besides, it always rains in Bergen.

It rained during the weekend we were in Bergen. We stayed in a nice hotel near the harbor. Our stay seemed "water" related. Not only did it rain, but also we visited the fish market and the aquarium. My brother and I loved the aquarium.

Then, we had to make the trip back to Oslo, again through the mountains and around the fjords. The ferry crossing at Kinsarvik is one of the most beautiful of the fjord rides. We went through the beautiful Hardanger-vidda valley. The midpoint of the trip was Geilo, so we had the opportunity to stay at the Geilo Hotel again. Actually, one of my memories of this second stay at Geilo was the 1970 soccer World Cup. Even though Norway was not playing, Norwegians were glued to the TV sets. It was the year Pelè led Brazil to the championship, and I had the opportunity to watch this master magician play the game and to witness how hooked Europe was on soccer.

I must also mention another important element of these May and June trips. As I said previously, Norway had one television station for the entire country. Obviously, this meant that whatever came on was your only choice. That also meant it was easy for a show to become popular. The Friday night feature was *Detek-timen*, The Detective Hour, which imported shows from the United States, England, France and Germany. One of the programs from England was a captivating 13-episode mystery, *The Gold Robbers,* about a conspiracy to rob gold. Each episode was written by a different writer and described how a different member of the ring was caught.

The series so captivated the country – and us – that everything stopped on Friday night so people could watch *The Gold Robbers*. The show was winding down during May and June, so on every weekend trip, we set conditions: We had to reach a *pension* with a TV by 8:30 in order to watch the latest installment. We never missed a show.

Torbjørn, my father's research assistant, had a summer house near Kristiansand, on the southern coast of Norway. It was his wife's family home. He invited us to visit them. We had to drive four hours or more to get to Kristiansand, and we stayed overnight at a *pension* – getting there in time for the last episode of *The Gold Robbers*.

The next morning, we had to drive to a dock and park the car. All that lay ahead was water. Torbjørn met us with a small brown boat, the size of a rowboat, except he steered it from the back. What we will always remember about the boat rides is the water. It was dark blue and clear. We could see the bottom! We wore raincoats or windbreakers to protect us from the spraying water. It was a windy day.

We arrived at the island, which was occupied only by their small white house. In addition to his wife,

Torbjørn's father and brother were there. His father was the principal of a school.

Later in the afternoon, Torbjørn took us fishing. He showed us how to wrap the tackle and hold it in the water. We all had an opportunity. As luck would have it, Albie, who hated fish, was the only one to catch a fish. When he got the tug on the line, he was so surprised that he didn't know what to do. So, he ran to the other end of the boat, and the boat wasn't very big. Torbjørn pulled the fish in, and it turned out to be a small salmon. Torbjørn gave us the tour of the area, driving us through narrow openings between rocks. Again, we were impressed by blue water.

We returned to the house. On the dock, Torbjørn's brother was fishing for crabs, which came right up to the shore, and he showed us how to get them. Then, dinner was served. I thought we were eating the salmon Albie caught. But, it was from another fishing trip, and it was eel! It was delicious. Unbeknownst to us, this would start the tradition of never knowing what Torbjørn would serve at his house!

As our days in Norway were winding down, we were hosts to friends from America. We awaited these arrivals with much anticipation – the opportunity to see some familiar faces.

First to arrive around June 18 was Seymour, my father's colleague from the University of Utah, with whom he had written a book. For our weekend trip, we went to the lower Jotunheimen Mountains, a popular vacation spot for hikers and campers – another majestic and beautiful mountain range. We went to the areas of Valdres and Bessheim. There was still snow on the ground. Seymour, a lover of snow, enjoyed himself by picking up some snow and pretending to shave his beard, hamming it up for the camera. I remember the irony that we were dressed for spring-like temperatures, while being surrounded by the remnants of snow. In Valdres, there was a stave church from 1125!

It may have been with Seymour that we made one of our trips to Drammen. The town is about 45 minutes away from Oslo, and the main attraction is Spiralen, another example of Norwegian technology and engineering. Spiralen is a tunnel built into a mountain, but not just a tunnel; it is a tunnel built in the form of a spiral. The road winds through the mountain, winding its way up and up, curved steeped incline after curved steeped incline. Finally, we exit, and there we are at the top, overlooking a panoramic view of the valley. Like at many Norwegian sites at the top of mountains, there was a cafeteria and a place to enjoy the views.

A few days later on June 23, we excitedly welcomed the Stubs. They were from "home," Philadelphia, our only guests from home. Holger worked with Dad at Temple. He and his wife, Elin, were of Danish descent and had grown up in Iowa. Their daughter, Lisa, was around my sister's age, and their son, Peter, was about my brother's age. Holger and Dad interviewed for positions at Temple on the same day, and they became immediate friends. During the mid-to-late '60s, camaraderie in the Sociology Department developed through weekend camping trips. The Stubs were one family with whom we had developed a real closeness as a result of those trips. Now, they were all traveling this distance to see us.

Their arrival was perfectly timed. June 23 is the longest day of the year, when there is 24 hours of light. There are many celebrations. First, however, we walked around Frogner Park; showing off the statues. Later, we went into the mountains to a spot where there were crowds of people celebrating the Land of the Midnight Sun. At midnight, it was still light, and we watched the bonfires along the shore of the Oslofjord.

Over the next day or so, I'm sure we gave them the tour of Oslo, the Kon-Tiki Museum, Vikingship Museum, Folkmuseum and Holmenkollen. Though they stayed for a short time, we realized we would be in Copenhagen at the same time in July and arranged to see each other then.

Believe it or not, we squeezed in one more small trip in June. It may have even been early July. The town of Fredrikstad is about a two-hour ride south of Oslo. I had been there on a class trip in May. You can also cross over into Sweden from there, which is what our class did. I believe our family had also made a previous trip there during the year.

This time, it was our "bon voyage" trip with the Gardners. We piled into the Volvo with Morris, Liv, who seemed ready to give birth any day, and four-year-old Rachel. Fredrikstad is an ancient town surrounded by the huge 17th century Kongsten Fortress in the Old Town. Frederikstad is the oldest preserved fortress town in Scandinavia (from *There's Only One Place Like It: Scandinavia*, produced by Scandinavian Tourist Board). We had great fun walking around the stone fortress, which was built in 1685. There were these big cannon in front, which we all took turns pretending to fire. There were many grassy, hilly areas where we walked. We also visited a garden in Fredrickstad. Within the fortress are restaurants and craft shops.

Our return to Oslo marked the end of our travels in Norway. It was time to prepare to go home. We would travel across Western Europe toward London, and then take the ship *Queen Elizabeth II* across the Atlantic Ocean. It promised to be exciting. For now, we had two weeks left in Oslo, time to pack our clothes and our memories.

July 1970

Our final night in Oslo was July 14. The Dalgards invited us to their house for a farewell barbecue. We drove out to Asker one more time to the beautiful wood house. I remember we went swimming in a lake nearby. We had only seen the Dalgards a few times during the year, but had become friendly. Albie and I had somehow communicated across the language barrier with Eivind and Olav. Here, we were spending our last evening in Norway with them. Who could know this would also begin a tradition? One of our last pictures of Norway is a blond-haired Eivind munching on a *pølse*, while staring at the camera.

The next day, we started loading up the Volvo. Berit showed up, beaming with exciting news. She and Torbjørn had received money for a conference they would attend with my father in Bulgaria later in the year. In between Berit's excitement and the commotion of our leaving, my mother was trying to get rid of things. She gave a broom to Berit, who amidst her joy began dancing with it. All of this was captured on camera.

One of my brother's friends came over to say good-bye. The two shook hands rapidly and smiled for the camera. Again, they had found a way to communicate through the language barrier.

Then, it was time to close up Tidemands Gate 20. After my father filmed each of us walking down the steps, he locked up the house, and we got in the car. We drove away and headed to Oslo*havn*, the harbor. We were to take an overnight boat to Copenhagen to begin our trek across the continent. We stood on the deck as the boat pulled away from our home-for-a-year. Dad filmed the last shots of Holmenkollen, always standing majestically out on the horizon, and the dual-towered *Rådhus*. I suppose our emotions were tugging at us. It was good to be heading home; yet, we were full with the many experiences of the year. There were people we met, places we saw. They had been part of us for a year. Would I ever return?

Eventually, the harbor and sites disappeared from view. Norway was officially history. We were now heading into the future. The next two weeks would become an odyssey, mixed with fun, learning experiences and Murphy's Law, that anything that can go wrong will go wrong.

Upon arriving in Copenhagen, we drove to the hotel, the Renaissance, which seemed aptly named, since it looked like it was from that era. We walked around the neighborhood, which could be a dangerous situation. On the pavement, there were pedestrian and bicycle paths. The walker is crossing unchartered waters if he or she breaks that plane. You are met with derisive comments.

Looking at signs and stores, I noticed the slight differences between Norwegian and Danish, such as a "g" in Danish is a "k" in Norwegian and *Bog* instead of *bok* for the word book.

We were to meet the Stubs in Copenhagen, and the plan was to get together at the palace at a given time. Through the years, our wait has become a joke. We waited for maybe an hour or so. We had nothing to do, so Dad filmed us waiting: my mother and sister on a bench, my brother sitting on a lion statue, me on steps. So, every time that film has been shown, it's described, "We waited, and waited." Then the frame switches to the changing of the guard at the palace. "We finally found them."

The changing of the guard at the palace was not supposed to be as good as at Buckingham Palace in London, but better than Oslo. There were more people than when we saw the routine in Oslo, but it was less exciting than London. Then again, you begin to wonder how people can get so excited about seeing soldiers changing shifts.

There was a visit to a museum with ancient prehistoric stone art. Of course, we had to go to Tivoli Gardens, with its bright lights, amusements and entertainment. This time, I wasn't sick!

Just as there is a Norwegian Resistance Museum, there is a Danish Resistance Museum. As we entered the museum, we saw plaques on the wall from Jewish organizations and congregations from around the world, thanking the Danes for protecting and smuggling Jews out of the country during the German occupation. There were pictures of the heroic Danes putting Jews on small fishing boats that would take them to Sweden. Denmark ferried 7,220 of its 7,800 Jews to Sweden and lost "only" 60 Jews to the Holocaust (Mary Morris, *Wall to Wall: From Beijng to Berlin By Rail*).

Danish legend has it that during the war, the King of Denmark wore a yellow star to protest the Nazis edict that Jews must wear a yellow star. This has never been confirmed (*Rescue in Denmark* by Harold Flender). The museum was quite an emotional experience.

We walked around the area and stopped at a store. My parents decided to buy something, but when they reached for the travelers' checks, they were missing. We went back to the hotel and couldn't find them there either. So started the agony of traveling across Europe with half the money we started out with, and trying to catch up with our refunds in every city. Our itinerary called for us to leave within the day and drive to Amsterdam. This didn't give the Copenhagen American Express office time to refund the money before we left. But, we'd be able to get the money in Amsterdam – so, they said. First, we had to get to Amsterdam.

Getting to Amsterdam meant driving through (West) Germany. Even as an 11-year-old, I had some fear about that prospect. It was 25 years since the war, but only 25 years. I knew of the Holocaust before we left for Europe, but during the year, we had visited two resistance museums, heard heroic stories in Sweden and Finland and been part of the small Jewish community in Oslo. It was my father's intention to get through Germany quickly by driving through in one day.

He took the crazy Autobahn, with cars driving at whatever speed they pleased. It rained heavily. As the trip wore on and the weather didn't change, we were going to have to stop for dinner. There seemed to be nowhere to stop on the Autobahn, until after hours of driving, there appeared one restaurant. Of course, being the only restaurant, it was very crowded.

Our family of five went into the restaurant. We were finally seated at a table in the far corner by a wall. I don't remember if we received menus at the time. For this large restaurant, there were only a few waitresses. We sat and waited, and waited, and waited. She never came to our table. Others seated after us were served first and had left.

Something had to be said. My father did not know German, nor did my mother. She knew the closest thing to German – Yiddish. It was left to my mother to call attention to us.

She walked up to the waitress in the middle of this crowded restaurant. I had never seen my mother so angry, nor have I seen her that angry again. She doesn't remember what she said, but out came the Yiddish. Her face was red, as she followed the waitress. It was as if my mother was not just defending her family, but spewing out 25 years of Jewish anger at Germany through this waitress.

The flustered waitress understood enough, and she finally served us. The menu was in German, and we waded through it. We finally ate and left with our first taste of Germany.

My father's plan to get in and out of Germany in a day wasn't going to be feasible. The continuous rainfall hindered driving, and combined with the long wait in the restaurant, we had lost considerable time. It got late, but we didn't know where to stop or what would await us when we crossed into the Netherlands. In addition, because of the stolen travelers' checks, we were traveling on limited funds.

We finally pulled into the port town of Bremen. It was hard to see anything because it was dark and rainy. We couldn't find anyone to ask where an inexpensive hotel or *pension* was because many places were closed. Finally, we stopped at a Good Samaritan place that looked like a fire station. There, again, my mother's Yiddish became important. This time, there didn't need to be anger. There was a young man with black hair – who my mother said reminded her of the actor John Garfield –

who smiled and helped us. The people at the station were friendly and found us rooms above a bar.

For our day in Germany, we had experienced the Autobahn, rain and two extremes of German "hospitality."

The next day was much nicer as we left Germany behind and proceeded into the Netherlands toward Amsterdam. The city was different than anything we had ever seen, mainly because of the canals at every street. We felt that immediately when we stopped a person on the street to ask for directions to our hotel.

"Three canals down, turn left," was the reply.

Three canals down, turn left, took us onto a small, narrow street, which hardly looked like a hotel row. The buildings on the right were small, connected buildings, like Philadelphia row houses. The Davidsons had recommended the hotel to us. The parents of Mr. or Mrs. Davidson had stayed there. It was just another one of these homes that had been converted into a rooming house/hotel. We entered down a long hallway. On the right side, there was a dining room, where the hotel manager's wife served tremendous meals at breakfast and dinner. She said little to nothing during our stay. Meals were included and so was history. Her job seemed to be the meals; the manager's job was the history lessons.

He sensed immediately that we were Jewish. He was half-Jewish on his mother's side. It appeared that he felt it was his obligation to pass on the story of what happened to the Jews of Amsterdam and Holland in World War II to other Jews, but he didn't speak English. Once again, my mother's Yiddish came in handy.

At every meal and each time he saw us, he told us another chapter. We learned that we were in the old Jewish neighborhood. Prior to the war, he had gone with a boat of Jewish refugees to England, but the British wouldn't let them in. They were sent to Africa. His own son worked in the Dutch underground, but a neighbor gave the Nazis his name. He was arrested and killed.

A rabbi had once lived in this house. A German woman moved onto the block and became an informer. She gave the Nazis the names of the Jews on the block, and all 142 Jews were arrested. Approximately 100,000 of Holland's 140,000 Jews perished in the war (*Wall to Wall*). He told us that the Nazis in Holland, Austria and Romania were even harsher to the Jews than the Germans.

Around the corner from the hotel was a monument. A taxi driver told us it was a memorial to all the Dutch Jews who went to concentration camps and never came back. Across the street from the memorial was a square where three synagogues once stood. Only one, a beautiful Spanish-Portuguese synagogue from the 17th century, was left standing by the Nazis. The mystery remains as to why this synagogue was left unharmed.

Staying in this neighborhood with such a harsh history, gave me a tense and chilling feeling.

In another part of Amsterdam, on Prinsengracht, is the building that served as the hideout and home for eight people, the young Anne Frank, her family and four others. This house was immortalized in her *Anne Frank: Diary of a Young Girl*. I remember little about the visit to the Anne Frank House. It was situated along a canal. When we entered, there was a steep, narrow staircase going up to "The Secret Annex" as it is referred to in English. Off to the right from where you enter was a room with wood floors. On display were copies of the diary in different languages. (It would be many years before I would read the diary or see the movie.) I remember the annex looked very small for living.

Amsterdam was one of the most enjoyable places we had been. While it was filled with a recapitulation of sad times in history, that also made it educational. The city seemed exciting and cultural as it is a city of art. This trip was also exasperating, for every day, my father – sometimes I would go with him – made a trip to the American Express office to see about the travelers' checks, without success. Dad had also wired his brother in France for money.

In between, we visited the museums of the Dutch master artists, first the Rembrandt Museum, then Van Gogh and the Rijksmuseum (the Modern Art museum). This was influential in my tastes in art. I liked Rembrandt less because his dark colors seemed gloomy to me. I was much more "impressed" with the impressionists and modern art. Van Gogh and the other Impressionist artists used brighter colors that I liked. It's interesting that the brighter colors made me feel better, considering Van Gogh's troubled life. The Van Gogh Museum was a beautifully laid out facility. There was an outdoor café by a pond that had ducks and geese.

Speaking of eating, the Rijksmuseum introduced me to an unusual "custom" I had never encountered before or since. As do many museums, the Rijks had a cafeteria, where we decided to eat lunch. Yours truly, lover of salt, picked up the container with the white stuff in it and poured. I tasted the food and suddenly I was reaching for water. The white stuff was white pepper! So, I offer this warning to you if you're ever in Amsterdam, beware of the white containers on the table!

We stayed in Amsterdam about four days before we resumed our trip west, still without the travelers' checks or the money from my uncle. Our journey took us through Belgium and a brief stop in Brussels, where my sister's high school French tried to get us directions. Then, we crossed into France on our way to Calais.

Our overnight stop was in Dunkirk, another famous name from World War II history. The invasion of Europe took place here toward the end of the war. It seemed no matter where we traveled in Europe, we couldn't avoid World War II history. It followed us, or we followed it. Talk about scars? When we walked around Dunkirk in the evening, we found buildings – churches – that still had bullet and shell holes. I suppose we got an understanding this year of what the term *world war* means.

The following morning, we headed toward Calais. We took a ferry across the English Channel heading toward Dover. As we neared Dover, we saw the famous White Cliffs of Dover. From Dover, it was on to London to see the Sussmans again – to the place where our European tour had started 11 months before. We still had the five-day cruise aboard the *Queen Elizabeth II* ship to look forward to.

This whole journey seemed destined to have bad things happen. When we reached London, the long-shoremen went on strike! No one of course could predict when it would end. Our return was in a state of flux. We could still take the boat, but we would be crossing a picket line. In addition, we would have to drive to Southampton and load our stuff on the ship ourselves. Then, we would have to store all the luggage in our rooms. The prospect of living five days amongst a year's worth of stuff didn't sound like fun on the high seas. So, we rearranged our plans to fly to Philadelphia, which would at least eliminate driving from New York to Philadelphia.

We arranged to ship the car and loaded it with many boxes. (To top off the trip, when we eventually picked up the car in the United States, the knobs on the radio and some other items had been stolen.) Naturally, the strike was settled the day before we left.

The end of the travelers' checks story was that we only received half of them back and never received the money from my father's brother. A couple of years later, Karl Malden started doing commercials about how easy it was to replace AMEX travelers' checks. We would always snicker when we saw the ads.

On July 31, 1970, we boarded a TWA flight for "home." We said good-bye to the Sussmans, the people who we had said hello to when we first set foot in Europe 50 weeks before. Fifty weeks! How the time went!

Again, I got a little airsick on the flight, but the TWA attendants involved me in helping them, and I was fine the rest of the trip. Some seven hours later, we touched down in Philadelphia. We were met by my aunt and uncle(s). Again, we loaded into the turquoise station wagon and only this time drove to Cherry Hill.

The first one to greet us at the house, of course, was Pebbles. Now, seeing us for the first time in a year, he went bonkers. Welcome home! Later that night, friends came over to welcome us home. I was upstairs, and my friend came running up. We sat as I began to talk about the year, every detail, school, the experiences, the things we did. It was beginning, the first telling of Norway. But, the year in Norway and Europe was over. It would now be film reels and postcards, photographs and brochures in shoeboxes. That would keep Norway part of us always, but it was just memories, now.

Chapter 2
January 9-16, 1986

Going Back

It took almost 16 years before I finally returned to Norway, to a year of my childhood. As time goes by, the images stay with you, but the time gradually becomes vague and distant. Even the memories of school, though good and bad, stayed with me. There was still an attraction to Norway, something strongly positive that our whole family took from that year. After we returned, my sister tried to maintain her Norwegian. There were years when my brother hung the Norwegian flag outside his bedroom window on 17 *mai*. For a couple of years, I wrote to Jakob Nusfeld, and he wrote back. My father and I would root for the Norwegians in the Winter Olympics and scour for results and coverage – without success – of Holmenkollen.

Of course, there is Kodak. We had the films to keep our memories alive and fresh. The films (of course) recaptured, to quote Kodak, "the good times of our life." We rolled them often, it seemed, like every chance we got – for friends or relatives. I know I was one of the enthusiastic ones, who offered to show them and run the projector.

I returned to Philadelphia and two new schools in the next two years, requiring more adaptations to different situations. After a year of feeling isolated as a minority in a school in a foreign country, I now found myself in a predominantly Black junior high school. Whereas in Norway I was subjected to verbal teasing, now my white classmates and I were verbally and physically harassed. This was a rude awakening for me, as I had been raised not to hate anyone. I had spent a year living in another country learning about another culture, and heard World

War II survivors' stories while traveling in Europe. Now, I had spent two straight years in rough situations at school.

The following year, I advanced to a Quaker private school, Germantown Friends School, which I attended for 8th-12th grade. There was a diverse student body with no overriding tensions. While most people were friendly, the fact that students came from all over the metropolitan area created difficulties in getting together outside of school. Still, it was a better environment than the previous two years.

While life went on, Norway also appeared occasionally in other ways, as in Norwegian guests. My father's colleagues would visit. Odd Steffen Dalgard came to work with Dad, occasionally with Ragnhild. Torbjørn would visit to work.

Most important was when the Dalgard family lived in Philadelphia in 1972-73, in our neighborhood. One of my strong memories of the 1972 Summer Olympics actually revolves around them. They arrived either the day of or day before the killing of the 11 Israeli athletes by Arab terrorists. Eivind and Olav were anxious to watch the Olympics, and I remember trying to explain why the Olympics were halted.

The Dalgard boys were already sports fans, but we got them hooked on baseball, American football and Harvey's Pizza, the local pizzeria. We had met them just a few times in 1969-70, but we became best of friends in 1972-73. My brother and I were always with them.

My father returned to Norway numerous times, at least once or twice a year. My mother accompanied him occasionally, and my sister went back once. Dad would bring news and sometimes gifts. He brought me at least two Norwegian sweaters. One was blue and white. I wore it so often during college, friends said when I graduated, they were going to retire the sweater and hang it from the rafters in the gym. Perhaps, on a trip, my father attended Holmenkollen, and he would tell me about it or bring me the programs.

During high school, my journalism ambitions began to take off. I was in the group that founded the high school paper, when I was in ninth grade. Although I started out by writing news stories, I quickly steered toward sports, and in my senior year was Sports Editor of the paper. At the same time, I was a sportswriter for the local weekly newspaper for three years, covering my high school's games. This afforded me great popularity at school, earning me the nickname "Scoop."

The moniker stuck in college at Rutgers University, where I again immersed myself in working for the newspaper, which was a daily. I worked my way up the ladder to Associate Sports Editor as a junior and Sports Editor as a senior. I was responsible for significant changes in the sports section.

After graduating in 1980, I worked in the publications office at a hospital, before becoming a sportswriter at a suburban newspaper chain.

Norway made an appearance in a big way in 1982 or 1983. Olav Dalgard was "attending" The Traveling School in Norway. Students were to select a topic to study together and the world was the classroom. He was in Central America studying water and energy and decided to visit North America and, specifically, Philadelphia. He showed up with five other boys. We found enough room in the house to accommodate them. We spent the next several days having a wonderful time. I remember one thing in particular.

After we had all stuffed ourselves with a spaghetti dinner, Olav decided he wanted to have Harvey's Pizza again before he left. My brother and I (who had long since stopped going there) and the six guys walked to our old pizza hangout and wolfed down pizza together once again.

I can't quite remember what finally made me decide to return to Norway in 1986. Perhaps, it was just time to see it again. I have a feeling my friend and apartment mate, Andy, pushed me the last step to finally decide to go. I know it was he that wanted to go in January to see the winter wonderland. He has commented that I had been saying that it was a long time since I had been there. I wanted to see what had changed and to see my father's colleagues. So, I finally went back. I had no idea what to expect.

9-10 January 1986

My father, Andy, and I had to fly out of JFK Airport in New York, so we drove to New York and parked the car in the long-term lot. The plane would land at the old military airport, Gardermoen, situated 25 miles outside of Oslo (where my father had been stationed in 1945), rather than at the main airport, Fornebu, in Oslo. We were to take a bus in the early morning hours to the city before finally reaching the Dalgards.

The first word of advice when traveling to Norway or Scandinavia is to try to take SAS (Scandinavian Airlines System) because the Scandinavian hospitality begins with the flight. The staff was courteous. The food was good; they continually offered warm rolls. Later, they offered warm washcloths (something more airlines are doing, but this was the first time I encountered it). To top it off, the plane arrived 30 minutes early at 6:35 a.m.!

Our first shock was when the pilot announced the temperature was -10°F! Gardermoen, being an old airport, didn't have tunnels, so my first step in Norway in 16 years was from the plane right outside into the cold! The moment we stepped out on the steps our nostrils froze. We walked across a tarmac that had enough snow to close Philadelphia International Airport. Snow was quite abundant during this stay, as was darkness.

Getting through customs was a breeze, and we stepped out into the cold and darkness. There is only about six hours of light during the winter. Of course, that is reversed in the summer. We waited for a bus to show up, but none was in sight. Suddenly, a woman attendant came outside and approached us. She was all bundled up and said in English, "Did you just come in on the plane from New York? Well, because the plane was early and there is no transportation into the city at this hour, we are paying for a taxi into the city."

Gee, when did that ever happen in the United States? The three of us got into a cab, which took us to the *Sentral Stasjon* (the Central (Train) Station). Since the Dalgards' apartment was nearby, we had the driver take us there and paid for that end of the fare.

The Dalgards now lived on Thomas Heftyes Gate in the same neighborhood my family had lived in 16 years before. They had lived in the suburb of Asker in 1969-70. Ragnhild and Odd Steffen lived in an apartment on the fourth floor at the end of winding stairs, an exercise in breathing, particularly with luggage. It's a beautiful, large apartment. From the dining room window, there is a good view of the Holmenkollen Ski Jump in the mountains.

Eivind, now about 26, and his girlfriend, Angela, lived in the apartment with them. The younger son, Olav, now about 25, was living in another town, I think Lillehammer, helping to run a hotel.

The plan was my father would stay at the Dalgards, and Andy and I would stay at the Grünfelds. We were waiting for Gunhild Grünfeld to pick us up. I had met Bert Grünfeld a few months before when he, Odd Steffen and another man visited Philadelphia to discuss a possible project with my father. He is the preeminent sexologist in Norway and since he is Jewish, and the Jewish population of Norway is so small, he is one of the country's preeminent Jews. As we waited, I started to try to take things in. Ragnhild was already at work. She works as a nurse in a cancer ward at a hospital.

Odd Steffen tried to wake up Eivind. I waited in anxious anticipation. What would he be like? Would we get along? Like a mystery guest, a tired, blond man entered the living room. He had gotten taller. Soon, a small blonde German woman joined us – Angela. She seems never to be without a smile or laugh. She was studying social economics at the University of Oslo.

81

Eivind and Angela had met when they were 17, when Angela came to Norway as a student and they were in *gymnas* (high school) together.

It took a short time before the four of us – Eivind, Angela, Andy and I – were involved in pleasant conversation and on the way to becoming and resuming being friends.

I believe it was sometime in the afternoon when Gunhild Grünfeld finally picked us up. She had a small red car. First, she took us to the *Rådhus*, the City Hall, where the tourist office was located. We wanted to buy the Oslo Card, which would get us reduced admission to the museums and on transportation. It cost 75 *kroner* for a two-day card. The Rådhus is across the street from the Oslo Harbor. Rådhus is a beautiful brick building and is distinguished by its two parallel towers.

The Grünfelds live on Bygdøy, a peninsula of Oslo. This was actually an ideal spot for us. Most of the major museum attractions of Oslo are located on Bygdøy. It is also an area where housing is expensive. Theodor Loustads Vei, where the Grünfelds live, is a road hidden away from the peninsula's "main road," Bygdøynesveien. Our first day was to be the coldest day of the week. I think it also snowed that first day.

Snow would be a common sight. What would amaze us was how the Norwegians handled it. Then again, we were Americans from the East Coast, where a couple of inches sends the city into a panic and may even close schools. Here, there were several inches, maybe even a foot or two in some spots. Since there was so much snow – and it would snow three times during the week we were there – there was only so much space where the snow could be dumped. So, the streets were plowed to a minimum, leaving significant enough snow on the roads. Yet, cars, taxis and even the buses drove on the streets without a problem. Cars are equipped with four snow tires.

The *trikks* (a combination electric train, trolley and cable car) and *trams* (trolleys) didn't seem to have a problem running, like our trains do when there is snow or bad weather. Norwegians must take a driving test on snow in order to get their license. This snow-packed praise is coming from someone who panics when there is a forecast of snow in Philadelphia. Another thing about the snow in Norway – and this probably won't be the last word – is it's white and beautiful and does wonders for the already scenic landscapes. And, of course, this snow is in Norway and not Philadelphia.

Like many Norwegian homes, the bedrooms in the Grünfeld house were on the bottom floor, and the kitchen, dining and living rooms were on a higher level. This is to allow the heat which rises, to reach these rooms first. It's neat to feel the heat coming up from the floor in the bathrooms.

Andy and I each had our own room. There was a living room with a fireplace on the lower floor near the bedrooms. It was very cold that night, and we tried to get warm by the fire. Then we tried to get some rest, as I absorbed my first day back in Norway.

11 January 1986

I woke around 8 a.m. and immediately reached for my camera. Light was slowly trying to make an appearance. I had a beautiful view from my window of Oslofjord through trees and across snow-covered roofs. A little later, I took pictures from the Grünfeld living/dining room area.

Andy and I would soon find out our biggest obstacle on the trip – getting away from the hospitality so we could maximize the day. A winter trip to Norway means less light and reduced hours at the museums and stores. In some cases, museums like the open-air Norwegian Folkmuseum and indoor exhibit of the *Fram* polar ship are closed. Our hosts were so hospitable, that it would take Andy and me a while to get out of the house.

We finally started out on our mission for the day: to hit the museums on Bygdøy (except of course the

83

Folkmuseum and *Fram*). We also decided to walk. The snow on Theodor Loustads Vei covered our ankles, about three to six inches. It was quiet on Bygdøy. I think we got slightly lost, but I got us there. Along the way, we saw a Norwegian girl, about eight years old, using skis as her mode of transportation.

At the end of Bygdøy, situated by the water of Oslofjord, are three museums in a small plaza. You can see the distinctive towers of the Rådhus in the distance from the pier at Bygdøy. A look in the other direction shows views of the water and mountains. There were snow-covered benches planted in about six inches of snow, where at other times of the year, people relax and take in the views.

The location of the museums by the water is perfect, because this peninsula is a maritime lovers' dream. There are four museums dealing with different times, modes and theories of navigation. The three museums in the plaza are the *Kon-Tiki/Ra*, the Norwegian Maritime (*Norsk Sjøfartsmuseum*) and the *Fram* Polar ship. The Maritime museum details the maritime history of Norway. The *Fram* is closed in the winter, which in some ways is ironic, considering it was used on polar expeditions to Greenland, the Arctic Ocean and the South Pole by Norwegian explorers Otto Sverdrup, Fridtjof Nansen and Roald Amundsen. You can tour the *Fram*. The *Kon Tiki/Ra* houses the raft and papyrus boat used by Thor Heyerdahl and his crews on their journeys to Polynesia and Barbados, respectively.

I remembered the Kon-Tiki Museum well, at one point better than I realized. This is where I celebrated my 11th birthday. At that time, only the Kon-Tiki, the raft, was in the museum because the *Ra* expeditions occurred in 1970. For the first time, I was seeing the *Ra II* papyrus boat.

What is interesting about the Norwegian explorers is they were great humanitarians. Heyerdahl's *Ra* Expeditions had nautical, historical and social purposes. He wanted to show that papyrus boats could have been used by ancient Egyptians to cross the Atlantic Ocean. *Ra I* left Morocco for Barbados on May 25, 1969, but had to be aborted 54 days later. Almost a year after *Ra I* departed, *Ra II* was launched. Heyerdahl and crew reached Barbados in 57 days.

But, Heyerdahl, an anthropologist, also had a higher purpose and goal: to prove people from different countries and cultures could cooperate toward a common goal. In addition to the Norwegian Heyerdahl, the *Ra II* crew consisted of Norman Baker of the United States, Santiago Genoves of Mexico, Yuri Senkevitch of the Soviet Union, Carlo Mauri of Italy, Georges Sourial of Egypt, Kei Ohara of Japan, Madani Ait Ouhanni of Morocco, Safi, an ape, and Sinbad, a duck. Abdullah Djibrine of Chad participated in *Ra I*. So, the *Ra* expeditions proved the nautical and social theories. They also discovered that pollution of the sea was worse than believed.

Twenty-three years earlier in 1947, Heyerdahl had undertaken the *Kon-Tiki* Expedition. The *Kon-Tiki* raft was made of balsa by Heyerdahl and six others and sailed from Peru to Polynesia, proving peoples from both countries could've sailed to each other, since similar artifacts have been found in both places. The 4,300-mile journey took 101 days. Surrounding the *Kon-Tiki* are descriptions and pictures of the building of the raft and samples of the findings on Polynesia. Notably, these were large rock and bronze statues, possibly representing idols. Downstairs, people can see the underside of the raft and what the ocean and sea life would look like.

Then you come to a cave-like exhibit. For some reason, suddenly the memory camera clicked. I remembered this part of the exhibit as if I had been there yesterday. It was eerie and weird.

Nansen, who took the *Fram* to the Arctic Ocean, and skied across Greenland, received the Nobel Peace Prize in 1922 and the Nansen Office for International Refugees won the Nobel Prize in 1938. He became active in the refugee cause after World War I, serving as the League of

Nations High Commissioner for the aid of refugees and prisoners. A passport with his name on it could secure some civil rights for displaced persons.[8]

About a 10-minute walk from the three museums is the Viking Ship Museum. Along the way, I would unknowingly be involved in *a deja vù* type of experience. I innocently took a picture of the sea and mountains in the distance with a house on the left side in the foreground. One night, after returning from this trip, I was going through a box of pictures from the year in Norway. I came across a Polaroid shot my father had taken. It looked strikingly familiar. I went through my photos from the recent trip and found it was the same as the picture I had taken on the walk on Bygdøy. Different seasons, same shot, 16 years later!

The Viking ships in the museum date back to the 800s A.D and were excavated in the early 20th century in Tønsberg, two hours south of Oslo. The Oseberg ship's hull was rebuilt from the original timber. The boat is 22 meters long and has the distinctive Viking curl at the top of the front and back of the boat. It is the ship in the museum that seems the most intact. The Gokstad ship is 24x5 meters. There are remains of a third ship that couldn't be rebuilt. During the Viking periods, people were buried in their boats with their possessions. A small house was built as the burial chamber and the deceased's small boats were also buried with him/her. These small boats and the chambers were also excavated and are on display. In addition, exhibits included tools, wagons and textiles found with the ships, and "animal head" sculptures from the Oseberg ship.

We returned to the Grünfelds' house, which was a couple of blocks from the Vikingship Museum, and prepared for our evening. My father, Andy and I were invited to Torbjørn's for dinner. Torbjørn lived 45 minutes to an hour outside of Oslo. He was going to pick us up at

---

[8] Zinker Hopp, *Norwegian History Simplified*, John Griegs Forlag, 1969.

the Dalgards. Andy and I were about to embark on an adventure where it would have been helpful to have a Nansen or Heyerdahl to navigate.

Norwegians are a prompt people who scorn lateness. Even public transportation is on time. We walked to the bus stop. The ride to the Dalgards was not supposed to take a long time. I asked the bus driver to let us know when we reached the stop. The announcement never came. And the bus ride continued. We finally realized something was wrong and got off. I had no idea where we were. We figured we'd catch a taxi and went to the taxi stand. None were coming. Finally, we were able to get a cab. The driver was from Iran. The taxi slid around on the icy roads. He got us to Thomas Heftyes Gate but the wrong end. He kept going up and down this one end, before finally crossing Bygdøy Allè. Thomas Heftyes Gate is uphill, narrow and two ways. It was also snow-covered.

We finally reached the Dalgards and explained the predicament. Torbjørn, now divorced, drove us to his home, which appeared to be in a forest, which may have been because it was dark. We met his girlfriend, Debbie, who was an American from Chicago. Berit, my father's other student research assistant from 1969-70, was there, as were colleagues, Tom Sørensen and his wife, Inger, and their newborn. It was a wonderfully pleasant evening, full of warmth, fun, humor and good food. I just don't remember whether we ate something Torbjørn had hunted or caught fishing.

After pictures were taken in the six-inch snow, we headed back to Oslo.

It had been a full first day, but more full days awaited us.

12 January 1986

It snowed again during the night. The Grünfelds' patio had a foot of new snow. Large amounts drooped on branches and covered small bushes. Outside, the snow was piled on the sides of the small road, and there was hardly a pathway to the Grünfelds' door. There were six inches on the roofs of the houses and six to eight inches on Gunhild's car.

Again, we had a leisurely breakfast with the discussion more like a psychiatric seminar. The topics were "Is Depression Biochemical?" and "How Do We Raise Children?"

Bert was to take my father, Andy and me to Frognerseteren, a favorite Sunday spot in Oslo, no matter what season of the year. It is the highest point overlooking the city. On a clear day, there are beautiful views. It is near the Holmenkollen Ski Jump. This was not the clearest day, but it was still not a bad day either, particularly if you wanted to see snow, Norway as the winter wonderland, and how the Norwegian people spend their leisure time.

Frognerseteren is a forest with many trails, about 20-25 minutes from the center of town on the *trikk*. During the spring, summer and fall – and I suppose in the winter, as well – people hike around Frognerseteren. In the winter, people of all ages, from the very young to senior citizens, cross-country ski there. There was almost as much traffic of skiers as cars. As much as two to three feet of snow were piled on the sides of the road, making the road even narrower than it was. Of course, the road was covered with snow. There was two-way traffic, and the drivers didn't experience too much difficulty negotiating the road.

I don't know which "Norway" trees they were – spruce, pine, fir or birch – but they all looked like Christmas trees and they were completely white, making for beautiful scenery. We walked some and came across a picnic area – of course, used in seasons other than winter. It would have been quite difficult to use these tables. Not only had the tabletops accumulated about six inches of snow, but also the snow on the ground was just about reaching the tabletop!

A trip to Frognerseteren isn't complete without a stop at Frognerseteren Restaurant, from where there are beautiful views of Oslo. The restaurant is a beautiful wooden building with the famous Norwegian mythological dragon heads coming out from the points of the roof. Inside are traditionally designed tapestry, a woodcrafted clock and staircase, metalwork and a warm fireplace.

The restaurant is also known for its apple cake with whipped cream. So, we stopped for *varm sjokolade og eple kake med krem* (hot chocolate and apple cake with whipped cream). It was amusing to see the skis parked in the snow outside the restaurant. This also showed the Norwegians lack of concern about theft.

From Frognerseteren, we went to Frogner Park. The two should not be confused with each other. Frogner Park is also known as Vigeland's Park or in some cases, "The Park." If anything was to evoke nostalgic thoughts for me, it would be The Park. We lived around the corner from Frogner Park in 1969-70 and spent a lot of time there. It is the main tourist attraction in Norway.

There is probably no park like it anywhere for all the things it offers. It is huge and expansive (320,000 square meters/350,080 square yards). You walk in through sculpted gates and down a tree-lined path. You come to a bridge over a pond. Along both sides of the "bridge" are sculptures, some bizarre, but all fantastic, all displaying great emotion and detail. The most popular statue is a little boy having a temper tantrum. Some figures look like they're running at you. One has a man holding children on his feet and in his hands.

You reach a fountain. In the middle, tremendous statues of men are holding an enormous bowl, from which water flows over the figures holding it. Around the rectangular base are little plaques with sculptures enclosed, and on stands around the fountain are statues of trees with figures in them.

Finally, there is the Monolith, a tall, imposing structure of bodies on top of each other. Around the base of the Monolith are statues, showing elderly people with children, or parents with children, or children relating to other children. The statues in The Park are in a sequence that represents the "cycles of life."

Back below the bridge and surrounding the pond, are more statues of little newborn children and toddlers in different positions. They look so real, you want to touch them, and people of all ages are always doing so. All the statues were given an added touch with the snow covering them.

A waterfall flows from the bridge. Live ducks and geese were scavenging for food, and some young people were obliging them.

All the statues, gates and even the layout of the park were done by the amazing Gustav Vigeland (1869-1943), who made an agreement with the city, that in exchange for a studio (which also served as his home) and food, he would donate the statues to Oslo and place them in the park. The studio is across the street from the park and is now the Vigeland Museum. The Park was a life's work – 40 years – and Vigeland never lived to see his project completed.

The Park is more than the statues. Next to the entrance gates are tennis courts in the spring, fall and summer. In the winter, the courts are transformed into ice hockey and figure skating rinks. I'm not aware if there is a charge to use the courts. There are trails throughout the park for walking, cross-country skiing, biking. There are swimming pools (there is a charge for use). The Park is used by people of all ages.

This is where parents take their young children – at three years old, maybe younger – to teach them to ski. We saw at least one child around that age in The Park on skis. Often the children learn without poles. It is a place where children can go alone. And this is where our family in '69-70 went to learn to ski.

I turned to skating, on a patch of ice in a corner of this park, which was used by learning skaters, even though there were no sides. I guess, like the young Norwegians learning to ski without poles, the skaters learned without sides. Sometimes, my father, sister, brother and I would go to The Park together; they would go skiing and I would skate. Sometimes, I would go on my own after school or on the weekends. The Park was free and accessible.

When I returned to America after that year, I was never able to continue skating. Rinks weren't easily accessible. There were specified hours for leisure skating, and you had to pay to join a skating club. As I took in Frogner Park on this wintry day, 16 years later, all those memories – that "free-dom" – were remembered.

That evening, dinner was at the Dalgards with Odd Steffen, Ragnhild, Eivind and Angela. Ragnhild prepared a Norwegian delicacy.

"Should we tell them what it is or let them guess?" she asked, piquing our interest. It was obviously some meat dish in a cream sauce.

About three bites into it, Andy said, "Is this reindeer?"

Indeed, it was. It was tasty, a little gamey, but I kept thinking of Rudolph. Refusing seconds when offered is discourteous in Norway. I ate, and the company was great.

During these first couple of days, warmth and humor were shown from all the people we were seeing, despite the cold outside. I felt welcomed and accepted, as if the time had not passed.

13 January 1986

Monday provided us with a clear day, which meant a trip to Holmenkollen to catch the views we missed out at Frognerseteren the day before. Holmenkollen is below Frognerseteren but no less dramatic. The ski jump provides added drama and excitement. The trip there is an experience.

Andy and I went by *trikk*. The older, brown wooden rickety ones have a certain charm to them. There are hooks on the side of the *trikk*, where people attach their skis. Children bring sleds and toboggans on the *trikks*.

Other people take bikes on, too. Despite the snow, the *trikk* navigates the tracks. It winds upward and around curves through the mountain. You feel yourself rising higher and higher, with the views on the left getting more and more spectacular, as the *trikk* heads toward Holmenkollen. At each stop along the route, the sign for the station includes the meters above sea level, noted by the initials m.o.h. (*meter over havn*).

After getting off at the Holmenkollen stop, we turned right, walked up a snowy hill, to the left, across the road, uphill past the Holmenkollen Restaurant. We came across four tall skis side by side planted in the ground with a sign "Holmenkollen *Riksanlegg* (Public Park)" at the entrance to Holmenkollen Park. In the distance to the left, the top of the jump could be seen.

A little bit more walking through two feet of snow brought us to the office building. If you walk straight past the building, you get a side view of the jump. On the left and right of a downhill slope under the jump were the snow-covered steep bleachers. The jump gives the impression of almost coming out of the sky. It is 90 meters long. The nerves-of-steel jumper(s) ski down the slope – *sans* poles – crouched with the upper body almost touching the knees. The jumper reaches the edge of the jump, raising his body as he takes off. He then leans forward, at about a 45° angle to the skis. He flies over a snow-filled slope of ground, with the views of Oslo around him, and wants to land in the round mound of snow below, reaching the farthest distance he can. He wants to land with knees bent, left ski in front of right. He is graded on distance and style.

The "stadium" is like a bowl stadium. In addition to the bleachers on the side of the slope, just below the jump are steep bleachers surrounding the landing area. Auxiliary bleachers are against the building.

The jump is used for one of the world ski jumping championship sites on the third Sunday in March. As many as 100,000 spectators attend. Sixteen years before, we had been here, for "The Festival," walking miles with thousands of people to be part of one of the biggest events in Norway.

There are other views of the jump and surroundings from different angles. From the side of the bleachers, you can continue to walk to the right and get a head-on view of the jump, then continue around until you reach the top of the bleachers.

You can walk down through the bleachers to get to the bottom and look up.

You can walk up the side stands to get to the top of the bleachers and look down.

Or you could choose, probably the easiest, although strenuous, safer way. You can walk back toward the building, continue uphill, around the curve to the right, past the unique looking Holmenkollen Hotel and on to the underside of the jump.

We took the first option, stopping to pose for pictures with the jump as a backdrop, and us leaning forward as if we were the brave jumpers. From the vantage point at the top of the bleachers, you look out to the right at views of Oslo and Oslofjord. Straight ahead are forest and trees. Looking down, well, uh, if you're faint of heart, watch how you look down. It's the bleachers and landing area below. If you're not faint of heart, you can take an elevator to the top of the jump and see the view as the jumpers do before they leave the tower!

Underneath the jump is the Fridtjof Nansen Café. Next to the jump is the *Skimuseet*, a museum of skiing history. We posed in front of the closed museum, with snow-covered boulders on each side of us. If you are fortunate enough to be in Oslo, but are unfortunate to only have a couple of days, Vigeland's Park and the Holmenkollen Ski Jump are absolute must-sees!

We walked back down to the Holmenkollen Station and caught the *trikk* into *sentrun* (Center City). Karl Johans Gate is the main road in *sentrum*. A large portion of it is for pedestrians only.

At one end is the *slottet*, the King's palace. There are side streets with peddlers' stands. The walkway was wet and snowy, the roads slushy. Many shops and restaurants are along Karl Johan's Gate, but as in most city centers, these are among the expensive souvenir stores. But, the crafts and clothes, particularly the Norwegian sweaters – most of which are handmade – are beautiful.

Later that evening, we met my father. The evening's hosts were very special people to our family, Per and Kari Hohle. Per is the well-known Norwegian mountain climber and author of several books, who we had met in 1969-70, and my father's "first friend in Norway." An outdoorsman, he "lives" that way. The Hohle's house is situated on a hill among trees overlooking the city. The house is a log cabin with much traditional wood furniture. There is such warmth from the house and the people in the house.

Kari had prepared open-faced sandwiches and, of course, *hveteboller* (rolls with raisins that are a Norwegian specialty). She always made the best *hveteboller*.

As older Norwegians, they didn't speak English well, though they understood some English. This would be a challenge. These situations can be fun, communicating through language barriers. I had bought a Berlitz *Say It in Norwegian* book before I left on the trip. There were also words, bits and pieces of Norwegian that were still stored somewhere in my head. But, since Norwegians love to speak English, I had not needed the book that much.

Tonight would be different. For one, Per and Kari wanted to hear me speak Norwegian. They wanted to see what I remembered. We had such fun trying to communicate.

Per was wearing a red sweater, and I remembered he had worn a red sweater 16 years before. I joked, "Was it the same one?"

It was another in a series!

Kari looked at the Berlitz book and the pronunciation section. "This isn't right!" she exclaimed.

Then it was slide time. They had recently climbed in the Matterhorn in the Swiss Alps. Per was so taken by the Matterhorn that he took a large number of pictures of the mountain. Since his English was not that good, he couldn't explain everything we were seeing. At every picture of the mountain, he would say, "Matterhorn." Soon, we were all saying it and laughing with him. It would be what Andy and I would always remember from that visit.

(In 1993) a strange coincidence occurred when I first wrote these passages in the book. When I was writing about Nansen, I went to my bookshelf, where I had two books about Nansen, to check for the date when he won the Nobel Peace Prize. I had no idea where I had gotten the books. One is in English and includes articles about different aspects of Nansen's life. The other book is a biography in Norwegian. I flipped through the English book to see if I could find any mention of the year when Nansen was nominated. I couldn't find the information, but in flipping through the book, I found an article by Per Hohle, appropriately about Nansen as an outdoorsman.

A couple of days later, I went to the shelf again to get the English book out so I could show my parents the article. I had stopped writing before this last section about the visit to the Hohles. I took out the Norwegian book to see if I could find the information about Nansen. I opened it, and there was an inscription: *"Til Michael med de beste hilsener. Fra Per."* "To Michael, with best wishes. From Per." There was no date. Per may have also given me the English book. He must have given me the books on this visit.

When I write of that visit now and look at the photo of Kari, Andy, my father and Per, there is a hint of sadness. Over the last few years since 1986, when my father has traveled to Norway, he has called the Hohles. But, Per has felt ill and does not want visitors. Oh, how they would revel (or to use the Yiddish word, *kvell*) at hearing my improved Norwegian. They would swell with pride like proud grandparents. Our 8mm movies from 1969-70 begin with Per showing my sister how to rock climb. I didn't get involved in climbing, but it did not take away the special feeling that Per and Kari extended to

95

our family. As I look at that picture from 1986, I can't help but wonder that we're missing out on a special piece of Norway for us. Then again, I'll always have that visit.

14 January 1986

Snow again! The weight of the white stuff sagged the trees in front of the Grünfelds' house. The snow reached the halfway point of the small trees. There was about a foot of snow. Still this didn't confine us to the house.

The destination for Andy and me today was *Norges Hjemmefrontmuseum*, Norway's Resistance Museum. It is a museum dedicated to the Norwegian resistance movement against the Nazi occupation from 1940-45. I look back at the year our family spent in Norway and Europe as very important in developing my knowledge of not just the Holocaust, but of World War II. It also contributed to my compassion for peoples' suffering during that war. For in Europe, it is hard to find an adult, Jew and non-Jew, who was not touched and affected by World War II.

During that year, we had heard many personal stories about the experiences of Jews in Europe, and seen the remnants of the war in some cities. Through my mother's Yiddish, we communicated with these people.

In Oslo and Copenhagen, there are resistance museums. It is an important learning experience to visit these exhibitions because it enables you to step back and realize the meaning of occupation. In some cases, the non-Jews helped the Jews of their countries escape. They themselves suffered injustices, were stripped of *their* human rights, were sent to camps or died through torture and execution. They resisted the Nazis.

As one goes through the Oslo museum, he or she might wonder, when will we get to the section on the Jews? It takes a while, but the Jews are not ignored. The section is small, but it must be remembered again, that this was an entire country that was subjugated, and the Jewish population was small. The museum is a monument to an entire country's courage and survival, and just as Jews use the adage, "Never Again," so, too, the museum ends its exhibit with the same words.

I think it is no coincidence that the Norwegian Resistance Museum is located within the Akershus Fortress and Castle. Akershus, which is situated by the harbor, was built in the 1300s to protect the city. When the Nazis took control, they first raised the swastika flag above Akershus. At the site of the museum is where "Norwegian patriots were executed."[9]

The Museum being within Akershus is a statement that Norway took the country and fortress back. The exhibit begins with pictures of Nazi planes descending on Norway outlined against the copies of official documents describing the invasion of April 9, 1940. Denmark was invaded the day before. There is a map of Norway indicating the location of British troops, the resistance forces and the German bombing raids. Sweden, which was neutral, permitted the Germans to March through its country en route to Norway.

Germany considered Norway critical to their cause. The southern part of the country had heavy water needed to make the atomic bomb; the north imported iron from Sweden and also provided a route to the Soviet Union. But, more important, perhaps, was the Nazis hope that the Norwegians would share the Aryan philosophy of superiority, since Norwegians were predominantly blond and blue-eyed, and create a united front. But, Norway never fell for the propaganda in large numbers.

The Germans did have a friend in Vidkun Quisling, a former foreign minister of the Norwegian government, who was a Nazi. He was put in charge of the occupation government, but the Norwegians refused to pay attention to Quisling, who made himself Minister-President. After the war, Quisling was hanged for treason, and his name became synonymous with traitor in many languages.

---

[9]From *Norges Hjemmefrontmuseum,* Norway's Resistance Museum, Norges Hjemmefront Museum, 1983.

The family of King Haakon VII was smuggled to England, from where he sent encouraging messages to the Norwegian people through the underground radio. The King and the Government, who flatly rejected German demands for surrender, exercised Norwegian authority while in exile.

The Norwegians' commitment to resistance is spelled out in this statement from the exhibit:

"Open resistance was the natural reaction of a community based on law. Norwegians, however, were soon forced to the conclusion that their struggle against a ruthless enemy would have to be organized in secret if it was to prove effective. This resistance was labeled 'illegal' by the Germans. The resistance movement proudly adopted this term: From now on, in the eyes of all patriotic Norwegians, 'illegal' received the cachet of legality."

An example of extreme resistance occurred in the summer of 1941, when the Nazis held a sports/track festival at Bislett Stadium to empty stands!

As we walked downstairs, the exhibits became more and more dramatic. Above the stairs is a picture of the Eidsvold Building where the Norwegian constitution was drafted on 17 May 1814. There are bars in front of the picture, "...symbolizing the setting aside of law and order." Below is a poem entitled: 17 May, 1940:

"Today no flag at the masthead
on Eidsvold's greensward is seen.
But, now we know, as never before,
exactly what freedom can mean.
A song that is truly triumphant
is sung by a million folk,
though whispered by lips that are sealed
'neath an alien tyrant's yoke."

Bars follow you throughout the museum to give the feeling of imprisonment and occupation. Downstairs, there is a map of Norway, with a swastika imposed on it and bars in front of the map. The exhibits deal with the *underground* activities, so there is symbolism having this part of the museum *downstairs*.

There were numerous underground newspapers, which were distributed, along with other materials, hidden inside the logs of trees. Among the titles: *The Norwegian Times; All for Norway; The Norwegian Woman: Campaign for Patriotic Women.* The caption to the newspaper exhibit said:

"The clandestine newspapers were the answer to the Nazi muzzling and control of the press. Their importance was greatly increased when all radios were confiscated in the summer of 1941.

"By the autumn of 1943, five thousand men and women were employed editing, printing and distributing over 60 clandestine newssheets. Some of these had a circulation of several thousand and appeared twice or three times a week.

"The Nazis feared free speech and an uncensored press. In October 1942 the occupying powers decried the death penalty for the production and distribution of illegal newspapers.

"The underground press suffered heavy losses: one thousand men and women were sent to prison; over two hundred lost their lives."

Of course, the Nazis attempted to recruit Norwegians and incorporate Nazism into Norwegian institutions such as education. One recruitment poster on display read: *"With the Waffen SS and The Norwegian Legion Fight the Common Enemy...Fight the Bolsheviks."* There was some success as indicated by pictures of Norwegian children in Nazi uniforms.

The attempted Nazification of the schools, however, was met with incredible resistance:

"With ruthless efficiency the Nazis had set out to create a new type of citizen, by political indoctrination of children both at home and in various youth organizations.

"...in the autumn of 1940, NS (Norges Samling, the Norwegian Nazi Party) set about copying their masters, demanding their right to carry out propaganda in the classrooms. The teachers refused to cooperate.

"In 1942 a decisive struggle took place. Quisling, in February, decreed that everyone aged 10-18 years was to serve in the NS Youth Organization. At the same time, he introduced compulsory membership for all teachers in a NS organization and demanded that they should teach the principles of Nazism.

"In defense of the ethics which had always guided teaching in the Norwegian schools, Norwegian teachers resisted this pressure almost to a man.

"In the struggle that followed, the teachers were supported by the Church, the University and hundreds of thousands...throughout the country.

"Quisling then closed the schools, and every tenth teacher was arrested. When they still did not yield, a great number were sent to a forced-labor camp in Kirkenes." (in the far North of Norway, near the border with the Soviet Union)

Gunhild's father was one of the teachers sent to prison for disobeying his Nazi boss.

Just as impressive was the staunch opposition of the Church to the Nazis, as all Christian denominations joined together. "On February 24, 1942, the bishops resigned...a pastoral letter, 'The Church's Foundation' was read from the pulpit in practically every church in the country. Of a total of 858 incumbent clergy, 797 resigned...these had the support of their congregations...The bishops and 55 clergy were interned, and 127 banished from their parishes." (From the book, *Norges Hjemmefrontmuseum.* Norway's Resistance Museum, 1982)

In that letter to Quisling, the bishops stated that Quisling had promised the party would protect basic Christian values, and the commandment to 'love thy neighbor,' the most elementary legal right for any human being, was being endangered.

"The Church has God's call and full authority to proclaim God's law and God's Gospel. Therefore, it cannot remain silent when God's commandments are being trampled underfoot. And now it is one of Christianity's basic values which is being violated; the commandment of God which is fundamental to all society...Stop the persecution of Jews and stop the race hatred which, through the press, is being spread in our land."[10]

The space devoted to the Norwegian Jews is surrounded by barbed wire. There is a picture of a Polish Jewish boy with Nazi guns at his back. There are pictures of defaced Jewish stores. There is a sign: *"Jüdishes Geschäft/Jødisk Forretning* (Jewish/Forbidden, as in forbidden to shop there)...*Palestina Kaller/Jøder Tåles Ikke i Norge* (Palestine Calls/Jews Are Not to be Tolerated in Norway)." How ironic that the Nazis "recognized" Palestine/Israel as a place "to send" Jews, and the Germans' Arab collaborators have taken so many years to recognize Israel's existence. Of the 700 Jewish deaths, 74 were children ages two months to 16 years.

Bert Grünfeld was a small child, who was smuggled from Czechoslovakia to Norway, and then to Sweden. He never saw his parents again. To this day, he suffers separation anxiety when he leaves his wife and family. Oskar Mendelsohn, who our family had met in 1969 and wrote the history of the Jews in Norway, had come from Trondheim to Oslo after losing his teaching job. He

---

[10] From *Norway's Response to the Holocaust* by Samuel Abrahamsen, Holocaust Library, 1991.

brought along a young child. The child was Bert Grünfeld.

Bars and barbed wire cover pictures of the prisons and labor camps. There is a sample of a solitary prison cell. There are also articles from British newspapers about the teachers' refusal to teach Nazism.

"While the prisons and slave camps in which Norwegians were confined in their own country witnessed untold suffering, conditions in German camps in Norway especially constructed for Russians and other East Europeans, were far worse. These contained some 100,000 inmates. After the war, 17,000 bodies were found in mass graves."

There were 9,000 Norwegians who were sent to camps in Germany, France, Austria, Poland and Czechoslovakia; 1,400 died, 700 of whom were Jews.

The exhibit further discusses rationing, attacks on the University of Oslo and the Gestapo's attempt to stamp out the "illegal" press.

"In the autumn of 1943 there was trouble at the University in Oslo; new rules for admission gave priority to NS students. Resistance leaders among students and teachers were arrested. A fire on the premises, the work of a Resistance group, was used by the Germans as an excuse for closing down the University and arresting students. On November 30, the campus was surrounded by German troops. Some students were arrested, as well as a number of teachers, but others escaped, thanks to a tip-off...

"...the Gestapo set on foot (for) a wholesale round-up in private homes and on the streets. The result was one of the most terrifying days in Oslo throughout the occupation. Some 700 of the arrested students were sent to German internment camps. The University remained closed for the rest of the war."

With the closing of the University, the resistance movement was the victor because it succeeded in not allowing Nazism to be taught.

Despite the German crackdown on the underground press, the resistance survived there too.

"...Never had the underground press flourished as vigorously as in the spring and summer of 1943, when its total circulation was estimated at half a million.

"After long and secret preparations, the Gestapo struck. In November 1943 the office of the largest radio newssheet, London Nytt (London News), was blown up. In February 1944 the Gestapo struck again, uncovering the majority of the most widespread underground papers, and arresting more than 200 people.

"The damage inflicted was patched up in a relatively short time; in a matter of months, clandestine papers were once again in circulation."

As you leave the exhibit, there is a picture of the Nazis leaving Norway (which made me think of my father being part of the Allied liberation forces in Norway) with the caption, *"Five Years of Foreign Rule and Occupation at End – Never Again."*

Then there is a wall with three white towers. Each tower features a flag of one of the major Allied powers – Great Britain, the United States and the Soviet Union. Below are the words:

"In the skies above London
In the African desert
In the ruins of Stalingrad
And on the Normandy beaches
Norway was given back to us."

Walking through the museum is a chilling and emotional experience. Narrow walkways guide you through the exhibits. We marveled at and gained respect for the magnitude and levels of resistance, such as no one showing up at Bislett for the sports festival; the unity of the teachers and church. Staying with people personally affected by the war as Bert and Gunhild brought the reality closer to home for us.

After that strong dose of history, we visited a piece of my Norwegian history – Tidemands Gate 20, my family's home in 1969-70. Snow was falling again in the afternoon darkness. The brown apartment house looked the same. The little yard, the porch. I didn't go inside, but the light was on in "our" first-floor living room. Home for a year. Memories of a year. All I could do was look and remember. It was 16 years later, but I was lost somewhere and jumping around in time. I took a couple of pictures, and we moved on.

My father had worked two blocks away at Munthes Gate 31, the *Institut for Samfunnsforskning* (the Institute for Social Research). Torbjørn was now the research director of the Institute. My father was meeting Torbjørn there, so Andy and I agreed to meet them. Andy and Torbjørn had talked about playing ping-pong. There was a table at the institute. Torbjørn is quite a player. While they played, I sat in a chair and dozed off.

Among my impressions on the first days were the perspectives of things. Buildings seemed smaller than I remembered as a child, and that walk to school really wasn't that long.

That evening, Eivind, Andy and I went out to a bar near the American Embassy. Angela was working the night shift at her job, so couldn't join us. We walked there because of the strict drinking and driving laws in Norway (and also I gather because Eivind likes to walk). As we walked down Thomas Heftyes, we were struck by an amusing sight. A Cadillac, symbol of American luxury, was stuck across the narrow road in the snow. Here in Norway, small cars are better. The three of us laughed at this sight. We debated. Should we offer help? I believe we finally did, but were turned down. Oh, well.

At the bar, we talked some and listened to music. Andy and I had remarked during the week how we had never seen so many blondes before and how attractive all the women were. Andy spotted two blonde women at a table and decided to talk to them. (They were Swedish.)

This turn of events was a blessing in disguise because it afforded Eivind and me a chance to be alone and talk.

"So what have you been doing for the last 13 years?" he suddenly asked me.

Wow! Thirteen years had passed since I tried to sneak away in the Dalgards' Dodge Dart as they left Philadelphia to drive across the United States, and then to travel on back to Norway, following *their* year abroad. Thirteen years is a resumé.

I began to mention what I did in high school and my jobs: working on the high school and local community newspapers at the same time; how I graduated from high school in 1976 and college in 1980. I wrote for the college daily newspaper and went up the ladder as sportswriter, assistant sports editor, associate sports editor, sports editor, building up my resumé for my journalism career. I worked at a hospital doing medical writing and as a sportswriter for the last four years at a suburban Philadelphia newspaper chain. Sportswriting is always what I wanted to do, even back in the year the Dalgards lived in Philadelphia. However, I found long working hours, low pay, equally praised and criticized. Yes, I had a modicum of success, but define success. For what was lacking in my answer, and during those years, was much of a social life. Even to take this week off from work at this time of year was risky.

In 13 years, though, how many friendships had come and gone? I'm 11 months away from my 10th high school reunion. How many of my classmates had I seen since June 1976? Six years removed from college. How many of those people had I seen or talked to? How many of these people had talked *to* me? Time passes. This whole trip seemed to be about time, the past, history and friends.

Thirteen years. I was 14 then. Eivind was 12 or 13. Eivind and I had gone from wolfing down pizza on Tuesday's all-you-can-eat night at Harvey's Pizza Den in

Philadelphia with his brother, Olav, and my brother, Albie, to sitting in a bar in Oslo. Little to no correspondence for 13 years. Yet, here we were.

Roll the film reels back to the last frames before the Kleiners left Oslo in 1970. There we are with the Dalgards at our farewell barbecue at their Asker house. A young Eivind and Olav munching on *pølser* (hot dog, sausage), staring at the camera. They could speak little English; we, little Norwegian. We communicated somehow. We did not see them often during the year because they lived outside Oslo, but this family friendship has endured.

And here we were, 16 years later, 13 years later. Adults. Speaking English. Catching up on lost time. Separated by 4,000 miles, 13 years and money for a flight that takes only six-and-a-half to seven hours. Back together again. And...still friends.

It was around one or two a.m. when we finally left the bar. Women were walking alone on the streets. People did not seem worried about walking at that late hour. We walked back to the Dalgards' apartment and crashed there. Perhaps the impact of that evening is still having effects on me. It's a question and time I won't forget.

15 January 1986

This was our last full day in Oslo. That meant getting all the last-minute items done, like shopping and getting Andy on skis.

Eivind went shopping with us earlier in the day. We stopped in a bookstore. I had decided I wanted to relearn Norwegian and wanted to look for a good book to help me. Eivind found one, flipped through it and thought it would be good – *Learn Norwegian* by Sverre Klouman.

We were not going to leave Norway, and I certainly wasn't, without a sweater. My father met Andy and me at a great store, Husfliden, on Møllers Gate. It is an expensive store, but has sweaters, mittens, hats, scarves, woodwork, pewter, candlesticks in wood and pewter, dish sets, placemats, etc., etc. All are beautifully crafted. Most of the sweaters are handmade.

I bought a handmade white sweater with red, white and blue at the top with the traditional X patterns. Norwegian sweaters are made of heavy wool and are very warm. Some Norwegians will go out in the cold wearing the sweater, but no coat. To deal with the cold, Norwegians follow a simple philosophy. "There is no such thing as bad weather, only bad clothing." In other words, if you go out wearing a T-shirt and a jacket when the temperature is 15°F, chances are you'll be cold. But, if you wear a *Norske gense* and a down coat, chances are you'll be warm. I usually am when I wear that combination. If there's anything that makes me "feel" Norwegian or close to Norway, it's the sweater.

Andy also bought a beautiful sweater, except he was "traitorous." He bought an Icelandic sweater!

That evening – the last – brought us together with the Dalgards again – just like our last night in 1970, and their last night in Philadelphia in 1973 – and Bert and Gunhild. We ate at a restaurant across the street from Majorstua *Skole*. Feelings and thoughts were beginning to well in me. The hours and minutes of this trip were winding down. I knew it would be too short. I was just getting to know people again, and now I would be leaving. When would I see them again? Where? In America? In Norway?

Ragnhild asked me if I enjoyed the trip because it could've been a disappointment for me since I had a past here and a certain image. I talked about the people and how hospitable they were, how nice it was to get to know Eivind again and meet Angela. Having Andy there gave me someone to share the experience.

Before he left, Andy wanted the opportunity to try cross-country skiing. Darkness doesn't stop Norwegians. It can't since there's so much darkness in the winter. Eivind and Angela took us to Sognsvann, near *Studenter-byen* (literally Students City), off-campus housing for students at the University of Oslo. Eivind helped Andy on with the skis. Andy inched his way along, and then the two of them went on the trail for a little while. It wasn't something Eivind had to do, but he extended himself to a stranger in order to give that person a Norwegian experience. After the trial run, Eivind drove back to the apartment.

Andy and I took the bus back to the Grünfelds. By now, we knew the bus stops. We were both deep in thought, but thinking somewhat similar things. The trip was over. It was like no trip I had ever taken, for similar, but different reasons than Andy. My thoughts were taking me back and forth from an 11-year-old child to a 14-year-old teenager to a 27-year-old adult. I was going from childhood memories and emotions to adult retrospection and emotions. I was overcome by the friendship, compassion and genuineness of all these people I had remet that had transcended through time and the "ages." We were now adult friends. I was overcome by the hospitality of people I didn't know.

For Andy, too, though, the trip was like no other he had ever taken; he asked me on the bus what I would remember, and I talked of the people. When I asked him the same question, he also mentioned the people. Imagine this was his first trip to Europe, so short and compact, but not only did he see so much, but he was also able to experience the warmth and friendship of the natives.

Thoughts and emotions were swirling in me. We reached the Grünfelds, finished packing and went to sleep in preparation for the trip home. Sleep, perchance to dream.

16 January 1986

I don't think I got much sleep that night. Around nine a.m., I took another picture from the Grünfelds' dining room window, showing the light starting to squeak into the day. We had breakfast with Bert and Gunhild.

When Bert had to leave for work, he couldn't seem to say good-bye. He kept coming back to say good-bye to us. I thought of how he had told us about his separation anxiety that dated to his life as a child during the war. Was he experiencing it with us? Like many Norwegians, the Grünfelds drink a lot of coffee. When we returned to Philadelphia, Andy and I bought them a coffeepot and sent it to them as a thank-you gift.

Interestingly enough, this day was much like the day we arrived – very cold. In between, the weather had been in the 20s°F and manageable. Excited about my new sweater, I wanted to wear it home. I dressed for where we were and not for where we were going. I was overdressed.

We met my father at the Dalgards. Dad and Odd Steffen worked to the last minute. Meanwhile, my emotions were building up even more. I took a picture of the apartment building; my dad and Odd working; and the view from the dining room window with the street, buildings and Holmenkollen on the mountain in the distance.

Soon it was time for us to catch the bus to Gardermoen, a 45-minute ride. Norway passed us by as we rode on the bus. I took my last pictures of the white-covered landscapes.

On the plane, I had thoughts and feelings swirling in my head. As a writer, I needed to get them down on paper. I wrote furiously. I got hot because of being overdressed. I was tired, and my emotions had taken over. There were some tears in my eyes and a lump in my throat. With the plane ride, the combination made me sick. But the Scandinavian hospitality continued. The attendants on the SAS flight took care of me and when we landed, they wheeled me off the plane. Once they finished their duty, it was welcome back to New York and America.

There was the noise, the hustle and the bustle. Andy and my father took care of customs. Now, we had to get back to long-term parking. Immediate aggravation. With me sick, should we take the bus or a taxi? We took a cab, and there was a problem with which cab to take. Then, the driver could not find the long-term parking lot. Somehow, we got there. My father drove back to Philadelphia as quickly as he could. I slept.

I could not sleep off the effect of the experience in Norway. The comparison of the atmosphere in Norway to when we arrived back was not lost on me.

So, I wrote.

"It is not many people who can return to a place 16 years after being there, having crossed a childhood-adult timeline. Perspectives should be put on my trip to Oslo, 16 years after living there in 1969-70.

"The school I attended in Oslo goes from first to eighth grade. With the possible exception of the current eighth graders, none of the students now attending Majorstua Skole were born when I went there.

"None of the students I have taught in Sunday School were born.

"Perhaps Eivind Dalgard unknowingly put it best, when in one of our rare moments alone, asked, 'So, what have you been doing the last 13 years?' I realized that during the last 13 years, I had worked untold hours in developing my journalism career, had graduated from high school and college, and spent five years in the 'real world.'

"I approached this trip with great excitement and anticipation, although I'm not quite sure what I expected, except that I knew a week would be too short. Was I trying to recapture something, and what was that something? What could be recaptured from a year of childhood, by a now 27-year-old adult?

"My school days in Oslo were not my fondest memories and that was where I spent a large part of that year, so, maybe, it was just as well I didn't take a picture of the school.

"What drew me back to Norway? And in January?

"To see a beautiful country? Yes. To show my friend, Andy, this beautiful country and show him where I spent a year of my life? Yes. To see what was familiar and different? Yes.

"Throughout the first few days, I had a strange feeling that is hard to describe. For one, I found it hard to believe I was there. Things had a familiar, but strange, look. They were being seen through an adult's perspective, rather than a child's. Walking into the *Kon-Tiki* and Vikingship Museums, I was struck with a feeling like I had been there yesterday, remembering exhibits clearly.

"There was something else that soon became evident. It was in the relationship with my father's friends and associates, some of whom I had seen on their visits to the states. There was togetherness, no longer a child-adult separation, but an adult-adult relationship. Now, 'everybody was my friend.' Everybody was warm, friendly and hospitable.

"Bert and Gunhild Grünfeld, who hardly knew us, openly welcomed us into their home and engaged us in topical conversations.

"The Dalgards were their consistently, pleasurable selves.

"There was a warmth and "fun" atmosphere at Torbjørn's.

"And, Per and Kari, who seemed to revel in our being there, loved to hear me try to speak whatever Norwegian I could remember. They enjoyed when I joked about whether the red sweater Per was wearing was the same one I remembered him wearing 16 years earlier. Actually, it was another in a series.

"Everybody had a sense of humor. Everybody so readily welcomed and accepted a total stranger in Andy. (In a way, so was I.) It was relaxing to be with these people.

"The most important people though were Eivind and his girlfriend Angela...It was slow at first, but soon the four of us were engaged in great conversation. And in the space of a few days, we established a friendship that seems stronger than has seemed possible with (some) people here in America. Angela was so impressed by two 'non-typical Americans' that she began asking Eivind when they would go to the United States.

"...I realize that I have taken few trips where there was not someone to visit, a relative, a friend or someone to look up. A city may be worth visiting, but the people make it enjoyable.

"While there are many inviting things about Oslo, the trends, particularly among young people, seem to be whatever is American is 'in,' especially (yuppie) materialistic things. None of us were that way, so that is why we were special to Eivind and Angela, and they to us.

"Perhaps, this trip was a type of rite of passage; a sort of final crossing between childhood and adulthood. I know it won't be 16 years before I go back again. Now, when I go back, it'll be because of this trip. Sixteen years ago was the impetus, the ground breaking for this trip.

"As we headed back to the Grünfelds on the last night, Andy asked what I would remember from this trip. I repeated the same sentiments as I mentioned before. Then, I asked him, 'What will you remember? I was here 16 years ago.'

"Yet, he mentioned the same thoughts.

"He said, 'I'll come back. It may be without you. In one, two, three years. Maybe with a wife.'

"I wondered whether that was satisfactory for me. A year, two years from now. This trip was so special, that I feel I want to see these people sooner. They revitalized us, restored a faith in the potential of human kindness, which had its opposite effect as soon as we arrived in New York to immediate aggravation.

"That created a greater resolve. 'I shall return to Norway.'"

Chapter 3
June 5-14, 1990

Waiting for "Soon"

"Soon" did take longer than expected. The flight to Oslo is only six-and-a-half hours, but it's amazing how many months and years can pass between trips. Different obstacles get in the way – money and the spare time to travel being the major ones.

I would write to these friends, but "soon" would turn out to be four years. I returned to Norway with a cousin, a new convert-to-be to this country. It would be another significant trip.

The 1986-90 years were periods of great change for me. I left the newspaper in August 1986 and was unemployed for six months before settling in as sports information director at a small college in Philadelphia in 1987.

I enjoyed success there and was surrounded by good people. However, I was soon to find out this would be a place of constant personnel turnover, particularly in the College's public relations area and athletic department. For a four-month period in 1989, I served as interim director of college relations and sports information director.

In January 1989, I moved to an apartment closer to the college, in West Mt. Airy, an area known for maintaining stable integration and progressive politics.

By 1990, I was ready for a trip to my Norwegian "family." My father was planning on going in June, and I checked into fares. There was a bargain rate if reservations were made by March 31, and it was about March 23, forcing me to quickly find someone to accompany me. I didn't have any success. I made the reservations anyway for my father and me, leaving from Newark, New Jersey.

Then, in April, I visited my cousins, Steve and Adrienne, and their father, Marty, in Boston. We had not seen each other often in our lives, but through bar mitzvahs and weddings, I had become friendlier with Steve, 26, and Adrienne, 28. I brought my photo album of the 1986 Norway trip with me.

Prior to my leaving for Boston, Steve asked me if I was interested in going to the Boston Bruins-Montreal Canadians Stanley Cup playoff game at Boston Garden. I said I was, which set him in search of tickets.

Steve's searches don't end until he's tracked down the best bargain·or exhausted all possibilities. He found hockey tickets at an agency in Chelsea. We had to go to Chelsea to pick up the hockey ducats, but we would come back with more than we expected. Steve had shown an interest in traveling to Norway. The ticket agency wasn't open yet when we got there, but lo and behold, next door was a travel agency that was open.

I suggested, "Why don't we see what prices we can get for Norway?"

Prices were what we intended to investigate. I virtually booked the trip. First, I realized the agent was calling the wrong number for SAS. Even with the right number, it still took awhile to get through. Eventually, we had two agents working on the deal. I somehow remembered the seats my father and I had on the plane, and Steve was able to get a seat right next to us!

Then, I remembered I had heard once that Continental Airlines ran a free shuttle to Newark. One agent called Continental, who quoted a $145 price to Newark. Meanwhile, another agent was trying to reach SAS again to check on the shuttle. SAS said there was a free shuttle. There were 1:30 p.m. and 3:30 p.m. flights from Boston to Newark with the flight to Oslo leaving at 6:45 p.m. SAS insisted the 3:30 flight was the only one Steve could take if he wanted the free shuttle. The agents ended up working about a half-hour of overtime on this deal, but Steve walked out with a ticket for Norway, and I, with a partner for the trip. (By the way, the ticket agency next door was now open, and we picked up the hockey tickets.)

We headed into Boston to a map store down the block from Boston Garden. We bought a map of Norway. We raced to Steve's father's house for dinner.

Steve announced, "Guess where we're going? I'm going to Norway with Mike in June!"

His father was stunned. "Is it safe to go there? I think you should take El Al (Israeli airlines)."

"I don't think El Al flies from Newark to Oslo," I said.

"Then go to Israel first," he said.

Six weeks later, we were en route on a trip that Steve – whose father had been a victim of my father's 1948 goats' milk scam – and I would never forget. The ride to Chelsea and the hassle in the travel agency would prove to be worth it in more ways than one.

4-5 June 1990

The three of us worried up until the last day about the possibility the shuttle would be late. SAS kept assuring us it would make the connection. An agent told me on the phone that if Steve missed the flight, they would put him on a 7 p.m. plane to Stockholm, where he would change to a plane to Oslo, arriving, of course, at a different time than we would. Since this shuttle was supposed to be timed to meet these flights, you'd think they might delay the 6:45 p.m. flight until they knew the shuttle passengers were aboard.

You'd also think they'd put the gates closer. The SAS flight was at Gate 82, while the Continental flight was arriving at Gate 111! My father and I, who had driven to Newark, were at the airport in plenty of time. We began our "vigil" at Gate 82, asking the agents, "What if the shuttle is late?"

They kept insisting everything would be fine. A little later, I took a stroll to the television screen, and sure enough, the Boston flight was delayed. I pestered the agents again, and they continued to insist Steve would make it, and they would have a representative at the gate to meet Steve.

Well, the boarding for the Oslo flight was announced. No Steve. We were in the plane. No Steve. The seats were in the upright position and carry-on luggage was stored under the seat in front of us or in the overhead compartment. Seat belts were fastened. No Steve. We sent another alert to a steward on the plane, who said he would check into it. Steve barely made the plane. Our worst fears were almost realized. Finally, at about 6:30, Steve came quickly down the aisle. He didn't know if there was an agent at the gate to meet him. He was so worried about missing the flight; he just took off for the SAS gate. Then again, he did make the plane as SAS said, and the trip was on its way.

We arrived in Oslo at about eight a.m. – early – with little sleep. Still, it was amazing what we accomplished on the first day. We spent the first day marveling that we were here.

Odd Steffen Dalgard met us at the airport, and we went back to his apartment.

Steve and I then took a walk. There was some nostalgia tripping for me as I saw the Majorstua Skole once again. I had not bothered to visit it in 1986, and now, I did. I felt more comfortable making the connection to that part of my Norway past this time. I even took pictures.

There was a statue in the middle of the schoolyard, which I did not remember. The water fountains with the six spouts were at one of the entrances. Right now, the schoolyard was big and silent; the memories buried there. Steve took a picture of me at the "B" entrance of the building where I used to enter to go to class on the third floor. I went into the building, but it was very quiet and eerie. School had probably let out for the summer, or the students were being attentive in the classrooms, students who had not yet been born when I walked these hallways and played in the huge playground.

We walked down toward Frogner Park, but stopped in a photo store so Steve could buy some film. On the plane, Steve had asked if you could bargain with Norwegians. My father had said that Norwegians did not like that. Now, just a couple of hours later, Steve haggled over the price.

The salesman then said to him, "How long have you been in Norway?"

I said, "He's been here two hours. I've been here before."

As we walked toward The Park, we found ourselves just ahead of a group of young, beautiful, blond, Norwegian children. We could not pass up this photo opportunity and photographed them as we walked backwards.

In front of The Park was a statue of Sonja Henie, which I had not noticed before. The Norwegian figure skater won Olympic gold medals in 1928, 1932 and 1936. She had died in 1969, during the year we lived in Oslo.

Frogner Park is the home to the amazing statues by Gustav Vigeland. The statues depict the various cycles of life from infancy to adulthood to old age. Though some people have criticized the sculptures because of their nudity, they capture people's attention because of their realism, detail, expressiveness of emotion, activity, shapes and uniqueness. In statues that include more than one person, Vigeland captured the emotional relationship between the characters.

It was different being here in the spring. In 1986, it was winter; the day was overcast. The snow that capped the statues provided a unique artistic impression – into that "cycle" of the year. Most of my memories of The Park from 1969-70 were skiing and skating there in the winter.

Now, it was a bright, sunny, spring day. You could see more, with the statues unveiled. The frozen waterfall underneath the bridge now flowed with water. The walkway leads first to a huge fountain sculpture. In the middle is a statue of men holding the Tree of Life from where the water pours into the fountain. Around the sides of the fountain are small tree sculptures with sculpted people inside, while around the base are individual "plaques" showing stages of life and astrological signs. Then from the fountain you go up steps and come to gates and then to the Monolith, a 60-foot sculpture tower of bodies on top of each other, each one sculpted with great detail. The Monolith is supposed to depict the struggles of life. I lay on my back and photographed the Monolith, looking up to grasp the height of the sculpture.

Around the Monolith are statues, many dealing with old age, such as joyful children with parents or grandparents. In all, there are 192 sculptures with 600 figures and 15 cast-iron gates in The Park.

Even though I had taken a number of pictures four years before, I couldn't stop taking pictures now, and neither could Steve. Was there a statue or pose I missed? I had gone through changes in four years. The statues are supposed to be about the cycles of life. Had the statues changed, even an inch? And not just because they had shed the snow of four years ago for the bright sun of this early June spring day.

There was sereneness about The Park. There was an outdoor café, pools and a sports stadium, where I had played soccer and run in a track meet the first week of school back in '69. We watched a group practice *A Midsummer Night's Dream* for the summer theatre. The cross-country skiing trails of the winter had become the walking and bicycling trails of the spring and summer, and the ice hockey and figure-skating rinks had become tennis courts. The ducks and geese that had scavenged for food in the winter of 1986 were still scavenging in the spring of 1990.

I realized the statues imitated life because people of all ages were using the park – and it's free. They're biking or walking. The children we had seen on the street were playing and laughing, just like in some of Vigeland's statues of children. I couldn't pass up taking pictures of the live children. One of the women watching them asked, in Norwegian, why I was taking pictures.

"Turist," I said. "Tourist."

The Park is down the block from where my father had worked and a couple of blocks from where we had lived in 1969-70. We passed both on the walk back to the Dalgards.

Tidemands Gate 20 was still a two-story brown apartment building on a street that we called "Embassy Row," because of the number of embassies on the block. I remembered how we would smell Brazilian coffee in the morning.

I walked up the driveway of "our" old house, around to the right. Here my brother and I had played soccer. I opened the front door. Though I didn't go up the steps to the apartment, I saw the MAGNUSEN nameplate on the door. They were the people who rented us the apartment, and the name was still there. Steve and I left and walked back to the Dalgards' apartment. It amazed me how I had retained my sense of direction through these years.

We accomplished all of these activities between 10 a.m. and 12:30 p.m. We had lunch at the Dalgards. The youngest son, Olav; his girlfriend, Florence; her daughter, Siri; and their adorable five-month-old son, Joachim, joined us. I did not see Olav in 1986 and had not seen him for about eight years since he had stopped in Philadelphia.

Later, Angela, now Eivind's wife, came by. Eivind, who is studying to be a doctor, is doing his internship at the hospital in Skien, while Angela is studying social economics at the University of Oslo. She invited Steve and me to go with her to Skien, a town of about 40,000 people, two hours from Oslo, and known as the birthplace of playwright Henrik Ibsen. It didn't seem to matter that our presence might infringe on her own limited time with Eivind.

Parts of the ride were scenic as we drove up and up through mountains. Parts of the ride were rainy, and parts of it were taken up sleeping. Eivind lived in a complex of apartments for hospital staff. Keeping with family tradition, there were winding stairs leading to Eivind's apartment, except it wasn't four flights. There were some artifacts around the apartment from their trip to Nicaragua, when Eivind went there to study its medical service system.

We visited a Norwegian supermarket, where we shopped for dinner. After dinner – fish, naturally – we sat around and discussed various trips or cruises Steve and I could take from Skien and the environs. At about 9:45 p.m., we took a walk in the area, through woods and past several well-groomed soccer fields, an equestrian training ground and a small ski jump. It was still light out with no hint of it getting dark – or wanting to get dark. When we went to bed just after 11, the streetlights were on, but the sky was still light! We had a full day, but at a slow pace. It was relaxing and exciting being reunited with friends.

6 June 1990

We got off to a late start because we slept late, particularly Steve, as jet lag hit us. In Eivind's words, he's a "slave doctor" now. He had to work a 24-hour shift, so he left early in the morning. Angela was our hostess for the day. She drove us to Kragerø, a small resort, shopping town of 11,000 people on the Southeast coast. Our intention was to catch a ferry to Jutland Island, but we didn't make the proper connections. It didn't matter because the ride to and from was captivating and scenic with plenty of photo opportunities. We crossed bridges over blue water, with mountains and fjords all around. We were captivated by the greenery, red houses and tunnels that were constructed through mountains. Angela, with her ever-present smile and good humor, helped make it a delightful day.

The town was very quaint with narrow streets, interesting alleyways and views of the blue water and mountains. In this small town, there was a Chinese restaurant that served both Chinese and Norwegian food, which is where we ate lunch. Steve wanted to learn some Norwegian, so Angela and I tried to teach him the days of the week and counting. This was interesting, a German (who was fluent in Norwegian now) and an American, who's Norwegian was dated by 20 years, teaching another American. Steve tried, but (naturally) had trouble with pronunciation.

It was a clear, sunny day and a bit cool. I wore a sweatshirt and jacket. We were here prior to the heavy summer season, so we enjoyed the peacefulness as we walked around. Steve was intrigued by the parking signs. He set up his tripod and the self-timer on his camera, so he could get a picture of the three of us in front of the sign. We all looked "stylish," wearing sunglasses.

We wound our way through the small streets and alleyways, coming to a square where there was a fountain and young girls jumping rope. On another street, there was a restaurant perched atop rocks. We walked by the dock where many boats were anchored. A beautiful 17th century church with a tall steeple was the centerpiece of the town.

Eivind and Angela had sold Steve on the two of us taking one of the cruises. For most of the day, Angela and Steve worked to convince me. I hesitated because I didn't know if I had brought enough travelers' checks from Oslo, and we didn't know when Torbjørn would be taking us to the mountains. I placed a call and managed to reach Dad in Oslo, who hadn't heard from Torbjørn.

After all the prodding and twisting of my arm, I agreed to the trip.

"Of course, it took 12 hours of coaxing," laughs Steve.

We would take an overnight boat ride to Frederik-shavn in Denmark, spend a few hours there and take a three-and-a-half hour boat ride to Gøteborg in Sweden, spend the night there and return to Oslo Friday morning via train. We could then say we had set foot on Danish, Swedish and Norwegian soil on this trip.

We rushed back to Skien to grab our luggage and Angela then drove us to Larvik, about 30 minutes from Skien, to catch the first boat. The boat left about 8:30 p.m., but the sunlight made it feel like 5 p.m.

The boat was just like a cruise ship – *Peter Wessel* of the Larvik Line. We enjoyed a wonderful smorgasbord dinner of cold fishes like lox, pink salmon, mackerel, different shrimps, crab and different herring salads. (About the only time I felt the boat rock was when I had to reach for one of the herring salads.) There were also salads, roast beef, various vegetables, hot dishes and desserts.

We ate by a window, as piano music played in the background. We continued to marvel at how late it stayed light. I took pictures of the sun starting to go down at about 9:45 p.m. From the deck at 11:25, I took pictures of the moon reflecting in the water.

Steve played some blackjack. The dealer was excited to hear we were heading to Gøteborg because that was her hometown. We played the slot machines, winning some money, but losing it back again. Most of the passengers were senior citizens, and the young people were too young, so dancing in the disco never developed. But we enjoyed each other's company.

The cabin was small with just two beds, but we had our own bathroom. We went to bed at two a.m. At that time, we couldn't see out the porthole, but by three a.m., we could.

7 June 1990

The *Peter Wessel* docked in Frederikshavn at eight a.m. and after much searching, we found a place to eat breakfast. They served a mini-smorgasbord of meats, cheeses, breads, hard-boiled eggs, coffee and tea. Frederikshavn is a small, pretty town with interesting streets. The main road includes open-air shopping. Frederikshavn is a resort town during the summer, and is the largest fishing port in Denmark. It is also an historic town, with a 700-year-old fortress. We didn't have time to see the fort, so we took pictures by a big anchor in front of one of the newer buildings, a church from 1892.

Our time was limited, so we decided to go to the Bangbo Museum and Park. It was becoming obvious that we were drifting away from our "safety net" of Norway. Fewer people talked or were willing to talk English. Danish – and Swedish – is similar to Norwegian, so between my broken Norwegian, sign language and the Danes' broken English, we did well. We caught a bus – which are like coach buses and run promptly – to Bangbo. While waiting for the bus, we noticed the preponderance of bike riders of all ages – riding on simple bikes. At one point, three riders going in different directions converged at the intersection.

At Bangbo, we took a quick, but relaxing, nature walk. Besides having old buildings dating to the 19th century, the Bangbo grounds are very pretty with flower gardens, a pond with various ducks inhabiting them and walking areas. It was another example of a calm environment within a city. We caught the bus back to the center of town where the open-air market was now hopping. We grabbed a quick peak before returning to the harbor for the boat ride to Gøteborg.

The cruise was three-and-a-half hours, but we spent most of the time sleeping in the lounge. I woke up in time to photograph some views as we entered Gøteborg. These turned out to be our only shots of the town because we disembarked to a few unusual adventures.

The ship docked at four p.m. The banks were closed, so how were we going to exchange our money for Swedish *kroner*? Fortunately, we found a post office that was open until six that exchanged money. That adventure out of the way, we moved on to the next one. We intended to stay at a youth hostel, but we didn't have a name, address, telephone number – or a map of the city. The steward on the boat had told us we could take the tram to the tourist bureau, but since we had no clue where we were, we called the tourist bureau. It was closed. We could not find youth hostels in the telephone book or figure out how to call directory assistance from the information on the telephone.

Steve spent an hour-and-a-half trying to use his AT&T card to call the Oslo Youth Hostel so they could give us the number for the Gøteborg hostel. He was trying to get through to an American operator through the Swedish operator. After this didn't work, we finally found the number for directory assistance on the phone. There were five hostels and, naturally, we called each one to compare prices, find which one was closest to where we were and get directions. With the clock nearing six, and knowing that in Scandinavia – or at least in Norway – places, even restaurants, close earlier than in the United States, I suggested we also ask where we could eat.

At this point, naturally, it began to rain, but things picked up. We had a wonderful meal and a nice waitress. Without our asking, she called her daughter, who was visiting from the United States, to see if she could suggest where Steve and I could go in Gøteborg that evening!

First, we checked into the hostel. Finding it was yet another adventure. The woman from the hostel told us the tram stop, and to then go over the bridge and look for "the big house." It became a perfect example of how things can get confusing in translation. When we got off the tram, I thought we should go right. There was a hill and a "big house" in the distance. To the left would take us over an expressway, and there didn't seem to be much in the distance. First, we went right, but that didn't take us to the youth hostel. The only option was to head in the direction of the expressway. There were no signs – or maybe no signs that we understood – so we asked a bike rider. "I'm going there. Follow me," he said.

He then drove on. We finally found "the big house" – a 12-story youth hostel! We never expected the "big house" for a youth hostel to be such a tall building. After checking in, we fell asleep and woke up around 11. *Then*, we hit the town.

Gøteborg was jumping with young people, many dressed in white with sailor hats. I recalled that in Norway, high school and college graduates celebrate wearing red clothes and hats. In Sweden, they wear white. (There is also a festival in Sweden, Valborgsmässoafton, that welcomes the spring and is popular among high school and college graduates. That is another reason the students wear the white caps.) We went into a bar and talked with a couple of women (yes, in English).

When we went to catch a cab, around one or one-thirty a.m. to go back to the hostel, there was a long line at the taxi stand. The drinking and driving laws in Scandinavia are very strict. A person can have their license revoked if they are caught driving after *one* drink. People take cabs or have designated drivers. There is still much drinking in Scandinavia, but people don't drive afterwards. This is not a "new" policy. It was true 20 years before when my family lived in Norway.

"They had a very organized system where everyone took taxicabs after the night out," observed Steve. "It was normal. This is what you do. Nothing unusual about it. It was like you were at a supermarket checkout counter. The only way to get food is to wait in line. There was a sense of camaraderie among the people in the line. There was no feeling that this was a restriction on their rights. The delay, the wait, didn't really bother many people."

To add more excitement to our Gøteborg adventure, the taxi driver got lost looking for the big house.

8 June 1990

We caught an early morning train back to Oslo, a four-and-a-half hour scenic ride, the last leg of this spontaneous adventure. Steve and I spent the time talking about family. He was amazed that I knew the birthdays of so many of our relatives. He jotted them down in his calendar book.

Again, we didn't stay in Oslo long.

Torbjørn picked up my father, Steve and me for the trip to his home in Rauland in the mountains of Telemark, three hours southwest of Oslo. It took longer because of the traffic getting out of Oslo. Torbjørn and Debbie had a two-year-old daughter, Ingrid. Debbie is a Jewish-American woman who has lived in Norway for 17 years. Torbjørn works during the week in Oslo, while she works in a town near Rauland. His two sons from the previous marriage were with him, Are, 14, and Audun, 9.

The scenery leaving Oslo is pretty, but it was to get better. Once out of Oslo, we drove onto narrow mountains roads. Torbjørn, already known to us as a bit daring, handled the roads with no problem, going around 55-60 miles per hour. Are and Audun sat in the back of the station wagon, reading their Donald Duck comic books. After 20 years, Norwegian children still loved Donald Duck.

At one point, Torbjørn stopped, so we could take pictures of some dramatic sites. There was this dominating mountain with splotches of snow overlooking a deep green valley. (After I returned home, I enlarged the picture to poster size, and it now hangs on my living room wall.)

We were going into the county of Telemark, a very historical area. It is where modern skiing developed, thanks to Sondre Norheim (1825-97), who lived in Morgedal in Telemark. What Norheim simply did was invent tighter binding for the feet. He used shoots from birch roots and twisted them to fit around the feet. This became known as "osier binding." This gave Norheim and "...the competitive...young farm boys from Morgedal..." flexibility as they skied down the mountainsides, twisting and turning around obstacles and jumping off hills and ledges. Norheim invented the Telemark and Christiania Turn, which is also known as The Christie.

At the same time, he invented slalom and ski jumping. Slalom is derived from a Norwegian word, *"slålam,"* which literally means, "slope," and "track in the snow."

The popularity of skiing with the new bindings spread throughout the country, hitting the capital of Christiania (Oslo) in 1868. Crowds marveled at Norheim's ability on skis. Huseby Hill was built in 1879 just outside the capital, and jumping competitions were held there until 1891 when the first Holmenkollen jump was built.

The skiers from Telemark were the show. As opposed to the contemporary styles, the Telemarkers lifted off the jumps with their legs tucked underneath them. They traveled only about 20 meters, but at the time, jumping still seemed death-defying to spectators.

By 1881, 5,000 Norwegians were competing in jumping, and 50,000 were involved in skiing. Some of the Morgedal skiers opened a ski school in Christiania for children and adults, male and female. Excursions were taken to the countryside. Trophies were awarded in competitions, notably The Royal Cup. The Telemarkers were so dominant that the Ladies Cup was established for the "Most Gallant Skier from Christiania." Two of the most notable Telemarker instructors were brothers Torjus and Mikkel Hemmestveit, who later immigrated to the United States and pioneered skiing here.

Despite the fact that Norheim invented slalom, ski jumping became more popular in Norway. It was left to an Englishman living in Switzerland, Sir Arnold Lunn, to further develop and popularize slalom.[11] Norwegian Stein Eriksen won the first giant slalom gold medal at the 1952 Olympics in Norway, the country's only Olympic gold medal in downhill skiing.

Telemark was also a critical area during World War II, and skiing played a major role. Telemark had heavy water, which was needed to make the fusion for the atomic bomb. The Germans wanted the heavy water and used the Vemork hydro plant in Rjukan. Three hundred Nazi soldiers were stationed in the valley, but Norwegian resistance was successful because of their knowledge of the terrain. The

---

[11] Jakob Vaage, *The Holmenkollen Ski Jumping Hill*, Grundt Tanum Forlag, 1968.

story of the Norwegian band of saboteurs who blew up the plant in February 1943 – and altered the future of the war – was made into a movie, *The Heroes of Telemark*, and starred Kirk Douglas. In a Norwegian-produced film, *Kampen om Tungtvannet (The Battle over Heavy Water,* or *Heavy Water Film,* as it became popularly known), one of the heroes, Knut Haukelid, played himself.

Along the way, Torbjørn told us the story about a hero of Telemark, Claus Helberg, from an interview with Helberg on television.[12] Torbjørn punctuated the tale with the words "our hero" throughout his telling. First, he told about the preparations for the attack on the hydro plant.

"Our hero trained in the mountains of Scotland during the summer of 1942," related Torbjørn. "He and other Norwegian boys were trained for sabotage against industries and ships. Our hero says they eagerly undertook this training because it was to help the home forces. Professor Leif Tronstad was responsible for planning and organizing the mission. Not only did he have scientific expertise that contributed to many Allied efforts, but he also had been involved in the building of the hydro plant as a chemical consultant for Norsk Hydro in 1934. As our hero said, it was now Professor Tronstad's responsibility to figure out how to destroy the plant.

"Our hero, Claus, with Jens Anton Poulsson, Knut Haugland and Arne Kjelstrup met with the professor in London in August 1942. Only Kjelstrup had not grown up in Rjukan. Poulsson was designated the leader for the mission and he was the only one who received the information about the importance of the mission, to avoid the plans from leaking out to the Germans. 'The rest of

---

[12] This narrative is a recreation based on an article by Claus Helberg that he wrote for *Den Norske Turistforenings Årbok* (The Norwegian Tourist Association Yearbook) in 1947. I translated the text from Norwegian into English. Used by permission of Den Norske Turistforeningen (The Norwegian Mountain Touring Association) and Helberg's widow, Ragnhild.

us,' says our hero, 'knew nothing of the reasons for our attack.'

"The attack was planned for the winter, so our heroes had to pack winter clothes, anoraks, skis and boots. As our hero points out, 'London in August was not the right place to search for these types of needs.' It took two months before our heroes could arrive home. Our hero, Claus, says the weather was the worst enemy for the next six months. Bad luck did not help. The first time the band tried to land in their homeland, the airplane's engine burned, and they barely made it back to England. The second time, they had to turn back because of radio messages about fog in England. Finally, on the 18th of October, they returned home, parachuting into the snow-covered Hardangervidda (*vidda* is plateau).

"'The terrain was bad, with large stones and dirt,' our hero said. The band was all safe, though, and they had their 12 containers with food, equipment, weapons and ammunition.

"The leader, Poulsson, called the group together and told them that the story they were instructors for the resistance was camouflage. 'We were to destroy the heavy water plant at Vemork,' said our hero. 'Two English gliders with 40 Royal Engineers were to join us. We had to find a place for the gliders to land, and it couldn't be too far from Vemork because the Englishmen weren't coming with skis. The Skolandsmyrene (forest, marsh), five kilometers west of Møsvassdammen, was chosen. We had four weeks to carry out the operation.

"'Unfortunately, we had landed 15 kilometers farther west than planned, in Fjarefit in the mountain range east of the Songa River,' our leaders said. 'To Skolandsmyrene was 100 kilometers. Under normal conditions, it was a difficult journey, but now with snow and 300 kilos of equipment, food, sleeping bags, skis, a radio with a storage battery, weapons and ammunition, it was even more difficult. It took two days to pack everything we were taking, and we left everything else at a depot. On the third night, it snowed heavily, nearly burying the tents.'

"On the 21st October, our heroes began the march toward Møsvatn. For over 14 days, they traveled on bad terrain and in terrible snow conditions along the Songa River, past closed farms, up through Valasjaadalen (*dal* is valley) and down Bitdalen and in on the road between Rauland and Møsvatn. A good skier would have taken a day to complete this trip. The ice was bad on the rivers, so our band of heroes twisted themselves along the steep birch mountainsides, each carrying 30 kilos on their back, which was only half of their provisions. The food was only enough for four weeks, so strict rationing was necessary."

As Torbjørn related the story, we drove through these mountain roads, past these beautiful massive mountains toward Rauland. One had to wonder if we were on the same route that the heroes of Telemark had taken?

Torbjørn continued.

"Rationing was difficult because the four heroes needed more calories than normal to withstand the trip. So, as our hero, Claus, said, 'We had to cut down on how far we traveled each day. One day we only went two kilometers. There were many *hytter* (cabins, cottages) in the Songadalen and Bitdalen, so we stopped at Sand-vasshytta, about 10 kilometers from Skolandsmyrene on the 10th of November. We would stay here until the gliders arrived. We couldn't communicate with England because of a bad battery, so I went to a contact, Torstein Skinnarland. He gave us the food we needed, fixed the radio and provided information about Vemork. Two of us went to spy on Vemork, so we would be better prepared for the operation.'

"Our hero said, 'The bad weather continued with harsh winds. It wasn't until the 19th of November, that it subsided, the same day we received word from England that the gliders would arrive that night. So we went to the landing area and set up our reception lights. The winds increased and we heard on the radio that the drop was delayed an hour. At 11 p.m., we heard the hum of the planes, so we lit the lights. It was quite an achievement that they had found us. The next day, we heard that only one of the planes returned to England.

"'We stayed in the *hytta* at Sandvatnet, but didn't feel particularly safe because the Germans' camp at Møsvass-dammen was only five kilometers away. We headed northwest toward Saura, which was between Mogen and Kalhovd because there was a hunting *hytta* there, which was not marked on the map. We stayed there for three months.'

"There were many difficulties and worries, namely the location of the Germans. Our hero went to Møsstranda to get the latest information from their contact, Torstein. He heard that Torstein had been arrested. There had been German raids in Rauland, Møsstranda and Rjukan with many people arrested. Every house in Rjukan and Vestfjorddalen was searched, and people were asked if they had seen any Englishmen.

"Our band knew that the Englishmen from one of the downed gliders had been captured and killed. The Germans found maps and information about the Vemork action in the glider. They knew there had to have been radio contacts between the Englishmen and people in the area. The Nazis suspected Einar Skinnarland, the brother of Torstein. Einar was not at home when the Germans came, so Torstein was arrested.

"Torstein's arrest made the heroes' food situation quite dire. Our hero, Claus, said that for two weeks, they survived on rolled oats, a little margarine, sugar and moss, which they dug up from under the snow and cooked. 'It didn't give us much nourishment,' says our hero, 'but we used our imagination and that helped some.'

"The lack of food made them susceptible to disease. At one point, everyone but the leader was bedridden. Our hero says, 'The leader was dreaming of reindeer steak, and that's what kept him going. He had shot many reindeer in these mountains before the war and assured us that the animals would eventually come to the region, and we would have plenty of food. The rest of us had rarely seen wild reindeer, so were much more skeptical.'

"Fortunately, the group had maintained radio contact with England and learned that six more men who had trained with them in England would soon be joining them. This would give them 10 men against the 200-300 German guards at Rjukan and Vemork.

"Just before Christmas, the reindeer had come west from the Vidda. However, the leader, the reindeer hunter, had no luck until Christmas Eve. For two months, they lived only on reindeer steak. To prevent scurvy, they ate the contents of the stomach mixed with blood and suet.

"It was a fierce winter and sometimes they could barely step outside, let alone hunt. In addition to fighting frostbite and hypothermia, our hero says they had to fight against becoming enemies. So they created a study circle, and each night, a different person delivered a lecture. The theme did not matter, Claus said, because it diverted the attention away from the problems.

"Our hero took occasional trips to Rjukan or Møsvatn to get information about German movements. The word was the Nazis were preparing for an attack on Vemork, bringing in additional guards and setting up floodlights. Our heroes sent these notices to England and our hero, Claus, had to carry the radio and battery with him on these trips, often through storms.

"It wasn't until the end of February that the weather cleared enough for the six other men to be dropped into the Vidda. Eventually, the new party – leader Joachim Rønneberg, Knut Haukelid, Kaspar Idland, Fredrik Kayser, Hans Storhaug and Birger Strømsheim – met Claus and the others.

"They discussed the best ways to penetrate the factory and return alive. One of the new men was inexperienced on skis. When the group informed him he would have difficulty getting to Sweden after the action, he said he had not counted on returning alive. As our hero said, 'This wasn't particularly encouraging.'

"There were two alternatives to reach the factory. One was by the bridge over a steep gorge, but our heroes knew this was well guarded. If they tried to blow up the bridge, it would create noise and possibly result in losses to their small group. The other was to ski down through the gorge under the bridge and come up unseen to the building. The contact at Vemork said it couldn't be done, but our heroes also knew that the Germans wouldn't expect anyone to come this way.

"The day before the attack, our hero, Claus, went into the valley to investigate possible ways to cross the river gorge. He went on a highway past Våer and down toward a cliff. After some climbing, our hero reached the river ice and also found a serviceable road around the side of the factory. He determined this would be a difficult road to take in the dark, but better than engaging the guards on the bridge.

"Our hero returned to the group, and at nightfall, they set out for Vemork on their skis to scout the route and plans.

"The plan was that the lookout party would alert the others if the Germans sounded the alarm. If all was quiet, they would man their posts until the explosion was heard. If the alarm went during the advance on the factory, the lookout party would attack the guards. When the explosion was heard, they would wait for the demolition party outside of the factory area. Orders would then be given for withdrawal. The password was 'Piccadilly? Leicester Square!'

"The demolition party was to destroy the heavy water building in the cellar of the hydrogen factory. First, they were to look for an open door, and if that failed, to crawl through cable tunnels. As for the retreat, there was disagreement. It was impossible to try the mountainside on the south side of the valley. The path along the water was mined, and the mountain was steep. The majority felt they should take the same road back over the river gorge and up onto the Rjukan-Vemork-Møsvatn highway. However, going up toward Fjøsbudalen meant they

133

would have to pass a bridge over Våerbekken, which would surely be guarded by the Germans. Going up the mountainside was too steep. The only way was taking 'Kraftledningsveien' (power line road), a closed-down road, which led to Krosso and paralleled with the main road, about 50 kilometers above. From Krosso, they could follow the zigzag below the cable track to Gvepseborg.

"The minority preferred a retreat over the bridge at Vemork. The Germans on the bridge could be surprised by two of the lookout party before the explosion. The minority of the heroes believed there would be little resistance from the bridge and up through Fjøsbudalen, and this would be less dangerous than Kraftledningsveien. However, most of the party felt if the attack on the bridge guards failed, they would all be prisoners. The majority prevailed even though the leaders were in the minority."

It was time for Torbjørn to take a breath, and we stopped at a store briefly before he continued the exciting adventure.

"Naturally, on the night they began the march, it was cloudy with strong gusty winds. They were dressed in British uniforms and on skis with packs. Our hero says the ice on the road was slippery and shiny as a skating rink. Climbing the cliff went better than expected, but the water in the river overflowed. They were able to get across and to the train lines at the other side.

"They were now 500 meters away. They reviewed the plan. At midnight, there would be a changing of the guard. The guardroom was right by the building, and they decided to allow a half hour for the (departing) guard to fall asleep before they advanced on the building.

"Our hero was part of the lookout party, which watched the guard room and entrances to the factory. During the time they were covering, they saw one German, but he did not see them because they were leaning against the wall of the factory.

"The demolition party found the doors locked, and the cable tunnel was not easy to find in the dark. They were separated from each other, and only two men found the opening. They had the explosives so they decided not to waste time by waiting for the others. The tunnel was just wide enough for them to crawl through. They came to a room by the side of the heavy water building, and the door was open. They walked in and found a worker there, who became frightened by the sight of them.

"The two men began to lay the charges, which they had practiced and learned in London. To prevent the charges from being removed, the men cut the fuse as short as possible. The leader lit the fuse. The worker went up the steps to the top floors, while the demolition crew jumped out the cellar doors. Thirty seconds later, the room blew up.

"It was only the instruments that were blown up, so the building was still standing. This resulted in a slow reaction by the Germans. One guard stuck his head out the door of the guardroom, shined the light, saw the building was still standing and lied back down.

"This gave our heroes a head start and it wasn't until they were on the highway on the north side of the valley that the first (cable) cars with Germans started pursuing from Rjukan. The heroes found their skis and packs and headed toward the city. They discussed whether they should go toward the wooded mountainside. Those of the group who were familiar with the area said it would be too steep and that they would meet the Germans. The (cable) cars were coming uphill toward Vemork on the road under the saboteurs. None of the group had considered going down toward Rjukan in the opposite direction as the Germans. At five a.m., the saboteurs reached Gvepesborg and looked toward Vemork, satisfied with the commotion they had created.

"The heroes then separated. Five men – Idland, Kayser, Rønneberg, Storhaug and Strømsheim – skied to Sweden. This included the inexperienced skier. Poulsson went alone to Oslo and eventually to Sweden and England. Haukelid and Kjelstrup went west and established headquarters for the resistance forces in the Vinje regions. Kjellstrup returned to England at Christmas, while Haukelid remained in Norway until the end of the war. Haugland and Skinnarland operated a radio station in Hamrefjellene (*fjell* is mountain) by Møsvatn.

"But, it was our hero, Claus Helberg, who had some exciting adventures following the sabotage.

"First, our hero went to Fjøsbudalen, and the intention was to meet the others again by Langesjø (*sjø* is sea) inside Rjukan. Because of the bad weather, he was delayed and ·never met them again. Claus went by himself to Geilo and took the train to Oslo, leaving his uniform in the mountains.

"The Germans had not set up some inspections in the Vidda, and three weeks after the heroes' action at Vemork, our hero, Claus, went inward toward the mountains again. He was to get the weapons and explosives, which had been left.

"Our hero found the *hytta,* where the fellows had lived, to get some food. When he saw a pigsty there, our hero figured the Germans had been there and might be nearby. Our hero ran out of the *hytta.* Four or five men on skis came running toward the *hytta.* Our hero got on his skis quickly and ran away. His only weapon was a Colt 32, which wasn't much for a battle. Our hero had to rely on his skiing ability. He was a good skier, but one of the Germans was better. After a while, some of the Germans began shooting at Claus. At a great speed, our hero headed west, so the evening sun would be in the Germans' face during the shooting. Fortunately, there was only one German who could maintain the pace, but he was like a gadfly. The German got close, but he also had a pistol, making the chances equal. The best shooter would win. The German became so frightened when our hero began shooting at him, that the German emptied his whole magazine. And missed. He threw his weapon down and ran back toward the other Germans. Our hero raced after him. Each second was valuable. The German's comrades could emerge from over the hill at any time. At 30 meters, Claus shot at him, and thought he might have hit the German soldier.

"Our hero turned around and went further. The sun was going down. The ski tracks were a problem because, even in the dark, the Germans would be able to follow them. He knew it was shiny white down at Vråsjøen, so set out for there. It was starry and quiet, but dark, and unlucky to go over the cliff at Slettedalen, directly north of Vråsjøen. There was aircraft traffic, and his left arm was broken. Our hero had to continue. He had yet to meet any Germans. But, they swarmed the area. Earlier, the Germans had started raids. With a broken arm, our hero could not go back to the mountains, but had to get to a doctor.

"He came to Hamaren tired and hungry. Our hero knew people there, but couldn't stay because the Germans were inspecting every farm at Møsvatn. After eating and resting a little bit, our hero continued, broken arm and all, toward Rauland – (where we were heading now). He had been on his feet for 36 hours and covered 16 (Norwegian) miles (99.2 American).

"In Rauland, there was much confusion, and our hero could not have chosen a worse time to be there. Terboven and Rediess, the German commanders in Norway, had just been there inspecting the troops, which numbered 300 men. Then, there was mild weather with snow and sleet. It was impossible to continue his journey. Our hero knew a village shopkeeper at Austhø and was taken in there. He had to sleep on the kitchen floor because the Germans had the other rooms! During the course of the night, our hero invented the story that he always wished to serve the Germans, and they were tricked! He said that he was someone familiar with the area, who was working for the Germans in the hunt for the Vemork saboteurs and had broken his arm during this service. The Germans believed that our hero was a brave fellow. A German doctor in Rauland examined our hero and sent him by ambulance to Dalen, where he could travel to Oslo on his own. In Dalen, he said *'Auf Wiedersehen'* to his helpers, and they made a show of being good friends.

"Our hero was to take a boat the next morning but wanted to rest a little. The tourist hotel was inviting, so he stayed there. Then Terboven and Rediess and their staff came to the hotel and took most of the rooms. Our hero remained. All the doors were locked, and there was no possibility to run. All the guests, about 30, were interrogated – their name, address, age, purpose for being in Dalen. Our hero's identity card, which had been made in London, was closely examined and found to be in order.

"The next morning, 18 guests, including our hero, were arrested for 'impudent behavior' against the Reichcommissioner. Our hero did not know what to do and decided it was less risky to go with the prisoner transport and look for an opportunity to escape. He put his pistol under the waistband in the ski blouse.

"A large bus came in front of the hotel and they all entered one by one. Our hero made sure he was last, so that he could be near the exit. A German solider kicked him in the back, and our hero stumbled on the steps. The pistol came out of the ski blouse and fell down between the legs of a German. Certainly, our hero thought, his trick had been discovered! But the Germans followed orders that everyone should go on the transport.

"A German sat guard in front of the bus, and four others in motorcycles created a convoy, one 10 meters ahead, another 10 meters behind the bus. Our hero was on the floor in the way back. Beside him sat a young woman from Oslo. They began to talk and had pro-ceeded quite nicely. The German was envious, and they exchanged places. Our hero was now in front by the exit door.

"They had driven two hours, and it was getting dark. Our hero saw his chance, opened the door and jumped out. He went over the end of the road and came to his feet just before the Germans on the motorcycles began to pursue our hero. Exploding hand grenades followed our hero as he got into the forest. He was thankful to be in the dark away from the pursuers. The Germans must've given up and gone on without him. After our hero received treatment at Lierasylet and a three-week stay at Drammen Hospital, he traveled to England by way of Sweden.

"The television interviewer asked our hero if he ever had nightmares about all the experiences he endured. Our hero's instant reply was, 'No.'"

Torbjørn was finally finished with this remarkable and educational story. Here we were now traveling through these mountain areas of Telemark, where it was so still and quiet, isolated, with very few homes dotting the landscape.

Nearly 50 years before, it was an area of great danger and activity. The Germans restarted Vemork following the explosion, but Allied planes bombed the plant. The Germans decided to try to transport the heavy water to Germany, but Haukelid blew up the ferry. Helberg was among nine men who parachuted into Ugleflott on the 5th of October 1944. Poulsson, Kjelstrup and Major Leif Tronstad were among the other men. They were to train resistance forces in Øvre Telemark to prevent the Germans from destroying the factories. Helberg trained an elite troop of boys in weapons and field maneuvers in the mountains of the Tinn-Rjukan district. The war ended before the men and young boys had to engage in combat. Tronstad, however, was betrayed by a traitor and killed and never saw the Norwegian and Allied victory. Helberg writes that Tronstad's death was a great loss for Norway, not just for his knowledge, but because he had become so popular among the people in the rural areas through his humor and optimism. He earned their respect, and there was great sorrow. The efforts of Claus Helberg and the others in this isolated region helped significantly change the outcome of the war.

Finally, *we* reached Rauland. It took about a minute to pass a few stores, before Torbjørn turned right on another road. There were few homes, buildings, cars or people, contrary to the scene of 50 years before. On the left were lakes and fjords and all around were mountains. Finally, Torbjørn reached an "intersection," that had a store on the left. He turned right, drove around 100 meters until we reached a dead end at their house. We had definitely reached getting away from it all.

They live in a beautiful wood house in this village. There are a few other homes on their road. Otherwise, you can see miles of views devoid of "civilization." Their neighbors are the mountains.

9 June 1990

We had a variety of things to choose from for breakfast – cheeses, salamis and "tubes." Caviar, shrimp and bacon flavor, shrimp and cheese, usually in a mayonnaise mix, are among the delicacies to be found in tubes. You squeeze it out of the tubes, just like you would toothpaste. Actually, the mixtures are quite good.

We relaxed for a little while after breakfast. Dad read to Ingrid and Audun outside, along the side of the wood porch. From the front of the house, you look left and face a huge neighbor. There is this massive mountain staring at you from down the road. The tracks of the slalom trails can be seen, as well as the wires for the ski lifts. Are and Audun ski there when they visit during the winter.

Then, we were taken into the "center" of town, which is 150 yards long. Seriously. Despite Rauland's small size *Fodor's '90 Scandinavia* devotes a good deal of space to the village. It notes that the Rauland Hotel is 3,300 feet above sea level and that this is an excellent area for fishing, hunting, hiking and learning about rural culture. Only the Oslo Folkmuseum has a greater concentration of the old wooden storehouses on stilts than Rauland. Dyre Vaa, who sculpted the Swans Fountain in the courtyard of Oslo's City Hall (the *Rådhus*), and *Myllar-*

gutten (The Miller Boy), one of the most famous country fiddlers in Norway, hailed from Rauland.

After stopping in a store and post office, we went for a ride. Everywhere we looked, forward, to the sides of us, in back of us, there were breathtaking, captivating views. We didn't know what to take a picture of because we didn't know what would be around the next bend. There's unspoiled land, water and mountains that go on for miles. You have the feeling – or hope – it won't ever be spoiled. We're hundreds of miles away from "urban civilization" and McDonald's.

One stop became our favorite picture. Across Lake Totak, running down the middle of a mountain was a streak of snow, cutting a curving path to the water, with the sun reflecting it on the water. Steve and I each photographed the scene through bushes along the side of the road and had outstanding pictures. It was remarkable to think that here we were in June on a bright sunny day, and there was snow "rolling down" a mountain.

Torbjørn then drove on, but couldn't drive as far as he wanted, because there was too much snow ahead! So, we stopped at the foot of this mountainside. There was snow on some large rocks, and we played with the white stuff.

We all climbed up the side of the mountain and parked ourselves. After settling in our spot, we ate. Debbie picked leaves from birch plants, which she uses to make salad dressing and tea. It was great to be surrounded by nature's beauty and the atmosphere was so quiet. In the distance were continuous mountains with snow along the top, and green, with some brown areas below.

Torbjørn had brought his air rifle with him, and we took turns – except for Ingrid and Debbie – shooting at bark. Are was particularly adept. After about an hour-and-a-half, we headed back down the mountainside.

While we were eating, Steve panicked because he suddenly realized he had left his camera bag at the bottom of the mountain. When we reached the bottom, it was still there. Then again, who was around to take it?

Torbjørn is a hunter and fisherman. His latest catch was grouse. Steve watched him prepare it for dinner, taking step-by-step photographs. The rest of us relaxed. Audun had fun blowing bubbles with those toy liquids.

We sat down to the grouse dinner. Even Steve, a vegetarian, tried it. In the evening, we watched the Italy-Austria World Cup soccer game on TV.

Around midnight, my father, Steve and I decided to take a walk. It was just getting dark. We walked down to the corner and turned left down the road. We were taken with the site of the store at the corner all lit up. It was about the only light in the area. Steve set up his tripod, while I just shot the photo. We walked on. Once again, it was peaceful and nobody was around. Hard to believe, here we were walking after midnight, without fear, relaxed, and miles away from the hustle and bustle of the city.

10 June 1990

Sunday was a workday for Dad and Torbjørn. Debbie was excited about an orienteering program in the area. Orienteering involves "finding one's way around" by following markers and a map. She is athletic and teaches children with disabilities to swim.

Debbie took the three children, Steve and me to orienteer. We piled into the station wagon, and she drove on narrow, dirt roads. Once again, we were surrounded by greenery and mountain views. At one point, there were sheep alongside the road. Finally, there was no more road to drive on, and we parked.

Now, we had to find the "meeting place." We followed yellow markers tied to trees. All six of us, including Ingrid, walked on the mountain trails, through marsh and swampy areas to the gathering spot. Of course, when we reached the swampy areas, Ingrid wanted to be carried. Along the way, we didn't know what we'd miss if we looked one way or the other. Everything was so strikingly picturesque. Finally, we reached the "meeting place."

At the gathering, there were several families – yes, indeed, other people lived in the Rauland area. Free coffee, juice and cake were available. An orienteering trail had been mapped out for children by a woman, who had been a national orienteering champion in Denmark, and now lived in the Rauland area. She explained to the children that they were to follow the map and look for the green markers. Then, the children were off, with some adult supervision.

Other parents stayed behind. Steve, Debbie and I remained to rest and relax. We ate and talked with the others, including Debbie's British friends. There was also a German shepherd at the top of this grassy hill, who seemed to be guarding the area, and wouldn't let anyone get close. Seeing a challenge, Steve worked on becoming friends with the dog. With patience, he proved successful.

The children emerged from the woods, and Audun was the first to cross the finish line, and Are and Ingrid, who was on Are's shoulders, were three-four.

"(All) The kids were adept at finding their way around," says Steve. "What really impressed me was that the adults conducting the orienteering were in their 20s, maybe 30s, 40s, but active. It was a good time. The kids weren't afraid. They were very comfortable in their wilderness. I saw a definite connection between the serenity of nature and the serenity of the individual in nature in Norway."

On the way back, Debbie stopped by the lake where they usually swim. It was too cold at this time of year. A fjord and mountains surrounded us.

Later that afternoon, Torbjørn grilled char (fish) in back of the house. Again, from the backyard, all you could see were mountains, valleys and the lake. Danish friends of theirs joined us, and we had another fine dinner before heading back to Oslo. In addition to his camera, Steve had brought along a few Kodak disposable wide-angle cameras. The friends took a picture of Torbjørn, Debbie, Audun, Are, Ingrid, my father, Steve and me sitting together on the back porch.

We then said good-bye to Debbie and Ingrid, got into the car and headed back to Oslo.

We spotted a McDonald's in Drammen, 190 kilometers (118 miles) from Rauland, a disappointing indication we were returning to "civilization."

11 June 1990

We were finally in Oslo for more than a couple of hours. We took a two-hour boat tour of Oslofjord. The guide was dressed in one of the regional dresses. Norwegians' versatility with language was again evident as the young woman guide spoke English, German and Norwegian. It was interesting that many of the houses on the islands were summer homes of Oslo residents. They're as close as a 15-minute boat ride.

An unexpected sidelight to the ride was a school group of seven- to eight-year-olds. It was a small boat and they began to get unruly to the dismay of the tour guide, who later apologized to us. Steve and I tried to talk to the kids. Steve showed them some games, like whistling through a straw. I counted and said the days of the week in Norwegian and taught the English to the kids. I talked to them in my broken Norwegian. Gradually, it got quieter on the boat because a number of the children had turned their attention to us.

The boat conveniently dropped us off at Bygdøy, the peninsula in the Oslofjord, where the major museums are located and a maritime lover's delight. We entered Bygdøy from the other end, than I had in 1986, right in the plaza where the *Kon Tiki/Ra, Fram* and Norwegian Maritime History Museums are located. We did the Bygdøy tour run.

First, we saw the *Fram* ship, used by Fridtjof Nansen on his expedition to the Arctic Ocean, by Otto Sverdrup to the areas northwest of Greenland, and by Roald Amundsen to the South Pole. The wooden boat, which was built in 1892, is housed in a triangular-shaped building. You can board the ship and tour it, walking along narrow stairways and paths, and see the cramped quarters of the crews. Clothes, weapons, a doctor's instruments from the voyages are on display. During the course of walking around the boat, we found an unlocked drawer with valuable documents. Steve briefly debated whether to take them. We informed the museum officials about the documents and unlocked desk. They were very appreciative and disturbed that the drawer was unlocked.

We then went to the *Kon-Tiki/Ra* Museum and the Norwegian Maritime History Museum, next door to the *Fram*. There was a beautiful smorgasbord at the Maritime Museum restaurant, but it was too expensive for us, so we ended up eating at the outdoor cafeteria. It is noteworthy that even at places like small museum cafeterias, the food is well-prepared and good. After lunch, we made the five- to 10-minute walk to the Viking Ship Museum, which features excavated ships from the 800s A.D. No, I didn't take a picture of the scene I had photographed in 1986, which my father had photographed in 1970.

Next to the Viking Ship Museum is The Norwegian Folk Museum. It is Norway's largest open-air museum with 140 buildings from different parts of the country, and dating from the Middle Ages to the 19th century. They are distinctive by the wood construction, preservation and height. Women in traditional regional costumes serve as hostesses. There are even cows, horses and sheep grazing in pastures by the buildings. During the spring and summer, there is a folk dancing program on Sundays.

The most famous building is the large Telemark Stave Church from 1200 A.D., built with wood and without nails. They are unique-looking buildings, and it is amazing how they've withstood time. They are artistic with carved dragon heads coming out from all sides of the roof – believed to ward off evil spirits – and beautifully designed doors.

When Christianity was established in Norway a thousand years ago, it created a clash of European and Norwegian culture, according to Haakon Christie, principal inspector at the Central Office of Historic Monuments and Sites in Oslo. The clash is reflected in some of the church buildings. The dragon heads may be one example. The inside of the churches are dark, and some of the carvings on the interior posts resemble Roman columns.

There are 29 stave churches still standing in Norway today, but they all postdate the arrival of Christianity in the 11th century. However, the architecture of the churches resembles the earlier period. The earliest ones were built of wood and had walls of upright posts and planks. However, the posts were embedded in holes in the ground. This gave them sufficient stability to function as the constructive framework of the building, but it also caused their bases to rot, according to Christie. Apparently, the first-generation churches did not stand for more than about a hundred years. In the 12th century, the need for more solid constructions became obvious. The problem was solved by introducing sills, upon which the planks and staves rested, thus raising the walls above ground level and protecting them against rot. The method proved so effective that churches built in the 12th century are still standing today.

It is this method of construction that has given the stave churches their name. A stave wall consists of vertical planks with their bases in a groove in the sill beam, and their tops in a groove in the wall-plate.[13] At each corner is an upright post connected to the sill below and the wall-plate above. Thus, a stave wall has a solid

---

[13] Haakon Christie, principal inspector at the Central Office of Historic Monuments and Sites, Oslo. From Royal Norwegian Embassy web site (1995).

frame consisting of sill, wall-plate and two corner posts. This sill is filled with vertical planks. The sills of the four walls form a solid horizontal frame on which the whole church rests. The wall-plates form a corresponding horizontal frame at the top. Many different types of stave churches have been built, but they have one shared feature in that all have stave walls.

The doors are completely decorated with carefully crafted artistic carvings, a reflection of the Viking period. Dragons predominate, some carved intertwined with vines, making "...the stave church doorways...among the most distinctive works of art to be found in Norway."

That night, we went to dinner at Olav and Florence's apartment. Odd, Ragnhild, Eivind and Angela, Siri and Joachim – were also there. It was another long, relaxing, multi-course dinner with stimulating conversation.

12 June 1990

Steve and I took the *trikk* to the Holmenkollen Ski Jump. The jump can be seen from all over Oslo, but nothing beats going there to grasp not only the magnificence of the jump, but to question and admire the daring (and sanity) of the jumpers. Once again, I remembered how me, my father, brother, sister and Erik and Peder Rinde walked from the Rinde house and were part of that event 20 years before.

It was unusual to see the jump in the spring since I remembered seeing it in the winter. There was a pond where the jumpers land, except it's covered with snow in the winter. There was a shell being built for summer concerts.

There was one picture we couldn't get. There is a long steep hill under the edge of the jump. Because it is dangerous, people are not permitted on the hill. However, there was a woman working there. Steve asked if she would take a picture for him of the jump from that angle. She complied, and we are the owners of one of the few pictures of Holmenkollen, looking up at the jump from that hill.

We rode the *trikk* to Frognerseteren, one of the highest points overlooking the city and enjoyed the famous *eple kake med krem* (apple cake with whipped cream) at the artistic Frognerseteren Restaurant. It was a nice day, so we ate at a table outside. Our waitress, an attractive brunette, proved there weren't just blondes in Norway. We were shocked to learn she was 20 and engaged!

Berit, my father's other research assistant in 1969-70, met us there and took us back to her apartment for lunch. She had always bragged about having the best view of the city from her balcony. This claim was verified. Obtaining this view took some "upward mobility." She had started living on other floors and worked her way up. We had a delightful time.

Afterward, we met Dad in *sentrum* and made the required stop at Husfliden, my favorite store for sweaters and crafts. It's also one of the more expensive stores, but it's still a great place to browse and shop.

"The city itself is really not a city," observed Steve. "It's an extension of the wilderness, just more tightly compacted. The ratio of city blocks with buildings to a batch of trees, or grass or a park is very nicely proportioned. When you're in the city, you haven't left the country. I've been in many countries in Europe, and I don't know of another city like that."

It was our last night, which meant the traditional farewell dinner with the Dalgards. My father, Steve and I treated the whole Dalgard clan to dinner at an Italian restaurant, which of course was nothing short of special. We sat at a long table that was in an enclosed porch that gave us a view of the outside. I had to take several steps back to get everybody into the farewell picture.

13-14 June 1990

Our flight was delayed three hours leaving Oslo. To us, it was more like a reprieve. SAS was extremely apologetic. They provided vouchers for lunch without our asking; let people call the United States, and on the plane gave out the headsets without charge. Steve and I raced around the airport for final souvenirs – naturally comparing prices. Olympic souvenirs for the Lillehammer Games in 1994 were already being sold. We bought identical T-shirts.

The delay naturally messed up Steve's connecting shuttle to Boston. He had difficulty rescheduling the flight and thought about going to New York. We then suggested he return to Philadelphia with us and work out getting home the next day. He agreed to the idea.

As we drove back to Philadelphia, we couldn't stop talking about the trip and the special experiences we had over the previous seven days. We talked about the meaning of friendship. I had returned to Norway twice now after long absences and little correspondence, and not only was I quickly reunited with friends, but I also felt a closeness to them. I knew their sincerity was genuine. At times in America, it seems if people don't contact each other for a couple of months or even a few weeks, there's a feeling the friendship is over.

We reached Philadelphia and had dinner with my mother and exchanged information about the trip. After Steve made several phone calls to airlines, trains and his girlfriend in New York, it was finally decided. There was a local train he could take from my neighborhood to Trenton, and from there take another local train to New York.

So, Steve came back to my apartment. We couldn't stop talking about the trip and when we could go back. Steve was hatching business ideas that might get him to Norway.

The next morning, we both dressed identically – our white Lillehammer T-shirts. I drove him to the train station. While we waited, he set up his camera again, this time with the self-timer. He wanted to chronicle every step of the trip until the end. After all we had done together, we needed a picture of us together to close it

149

out. There we were by the Mt. Airy train station, arms around each other's shoulders, smiling and wearing Lillehammer T-shirts.

This perhaps was one of the most important things to come out of this trip. Steve and I became closer as cousins, and friends, as a result of the trip. No matter what we did on the trip, Steve threw himself into it with great enthusiasm and laughter. He made the most of the activities. When we talk on the phone, Norway is never far from our minds and hearts and is sure to come up in conversation. We are forever linked by Norway.

Chapter 4
December 13-28, 1990

Tilkyntting and the Olympic Dream

My strong feelings and connection – *tilknytting* – to Norway were becoming strongly established and evident. My excitement – and slides – from the June trip made me want to share that with as many people as possible. I "created" the Michael Kleiner Norway Promotions Bureau. I put that on a flyer I sent to friends at work inviting them to a screening. Debbie Rieser's cousins, who live five minutes from me, also came to the screening.

By a pleasant set of circumstances, it would take only six months before I would return to Norway. At the same time, several seeds were set in motion for the future.

I began making plans "to get back to Norway." The 1994 Winter Olympics were to be in Lillehammer, Norway. When we arrived in Oslo in June 1990, there were Lillehammer posters on the walls of the airport, and souvenirs were already being sold. In 1982, I had applied for an Olympic research position at ABC-TV and was turned down because I didn't know German or Russian, although I was told I had one of the best resumés. Since that was two years before the 1984 Games, I concluded that there would be at least two years of advance work to be done on the 1994 Olympics.

That made 1992 my "target date," although there would be winter and summer Olympic Games in 1992. My Olympic dream began to take shape. If I could work on relearning Norwegian "by" 1992, I figured I could enter the Olympic job searches in the United States and/or Norway with the combination of sports public relations/journalism experience and knowledge of the host country and the language.

About a month or so after I returned from Norway, I was in Houston for a conference and stayed a few extra days to spend time with my relatives. My Aunt Bevy had to show me this unusual bookstore, which was inside an old movie theater. I strolled down the language aisle and found books on Norwegian. I bought *Norwegian in 10 Minutes A Day*. When I returned to Philadelphia, I opened the *Learn Norwegian* book I had bought four years before in Oslo, for the first time. I spent more like 20-30 minutes a day with *Norwegian in 10 Minutes A Day*. I began to teach myself the language, and I started to write letters in Norwegian to our friends.

I talked to the United States Olympic Committee, but they kept telling me that people – sports information directors like myself – land Olympic assignments by first being selected to work at the U.S. Olympic Festivals. Once, I called and obtained the name and address of the communications director of the Lillehammer Olympic Organizing Committee. Twice, I wrote to him. I also wrote to CBS-TV, the network that would be televising the 1994 Games.

The opportunity to go to Norway presented itself sooner because one of the reasons my father went to Norway in June was to work with his colleagues on obtaining a grant to establish a special social psychiatric program at Ullevål Hospital. The purpose of the Center for Social Network and Health was to determine if there were factors in the community and in people's networks that increased the risk of mental illness. If there were such risks in the community, then what changes could be made in the community and among those networks to prevent the development of mental illness? They were successful in obtaining the grant, and my parents left in October to spend seven months in Oslo.

My brother, Albie, and his girlfriend, D.X., who had lived in San Francisco for five years, came to take care of the house and Buddy, the dog, for that period.

The possibility of a visit to Norway seemed ideal. At another showing of the June slides, my neighbor and friend, Seth, was quite impressed by the pictures and what I had to say about Norway. He began to express interest in making a trip together to Norway.

We were both members of the same Jewish organization. Seth, a computer programmer, is soft-spoken, laid-back, with a quiet sense of humor. Like Andy, he is socially conscious. It would be interesting to see how he would react in a country of laid-back people, who freely talked world politics. Plus, it gave me another chance to show Norway to yet another friend. Seth didn't mind a two-week trip in December, so we began to make plans.

After some problems with the reservations – losing out on the bargain rates – we still ended up with the dates we wanted in the first place, December 13-27. We would have the chance to spend Chanukah *and* Christmas in the North.

But, we would have to be prepared for the winter in the north. Seth knew of an Army/Navy store in the neighborhood, so we went there. We loaded up with long johns, socks for Arctic freeze, hiking shoes, which could double as boots for the snow. We were now set.

For me, of course, December 13 couldn't come soon enough.

13 December 1990

There was definitely more packing done for this trip than the other two. I couldn't forget to pack the *Norske gense*, the down coat, gloves and scarf. In addition, after traveling to Norway with two different cameras, I decided the third trip deserved a new lens to capture those dramatic scenes even better. Albie helped me with the project to shop for the lens.

I also wrote to the man at Lillehammer to tell him I would be in Norway and would like to meet with him, if possible. I never received a reply to my letters.

I also decided that T-shirts from the college I worked at would be nice gifts to bring everyone and ordered 13 shirts through the athletic department buyer.

That was only the beginning of the gifts. I had asked Debbie Rieser's cousins if there was anything they wanted to send along with me. The message from Norway was that Debbie liked kosher salami.

A couple of nights before I left, two kosher salamis, books for Ingrid from Debbie's uncle, along with other items, were delivered to my apartment. It had occurred to me that I might not be able to bring the salami into Norway. If I could, how should I pack it?

I called SAS.

The agent asked, "Why do you need to bring salami? Norway has the best salami in the world."

"Not kosher salami," I said.

He advised that I wrap the salami in foil and carry it on the plane with me.

A colleague of my father also dropped off material and data that had to be given to my father. I also decided to bring my slides from the June trip, which meant transporting slide trays. Since we would be there for Chanukah, I brought my menorah.

Somehow, I found room for the clothes, too, but had to also take a box with all the goodies.

Finally, December 13 was here. The limo van picked us up at about 1:30 p.m. to take us to Newark International Airport for the daily 6:45 p.m. flight.

It took the van quite a while to make all the other pickups. The driver was quite talkative. He had an opinion on everything, and when some of the other passengers tried to have conversations with each other, he chimed in. But, it was door-to-door service, and he got us there on time. You take the good with the bad. Coincidentally, almost all of the passengers were taking SAS. We were the only ones flying to Oslo; the others were flying to Stockholm.

We went through the airport procedures and stopped at the duty-free shop to buy liquor as gifts (since liquor is so expensive in Norway). More to carry. As we waited for the plane, I saw Rune, the goalie for the Drexel soccer team, who was from Norway. He was returning for the

Christmas break and ended up sitting in the row behind us on the plane. We chatted a bit.

As the plane flew to Oslo, the hectic pace of work was fading away.

14 December 1990

We arrived at around 8 a.m. Once we were through customs – I tried talking in Norwegian – the doors swung open, and there were my parents to greet us. How strange to be in a foreign country and be greeted by your parents. We piled into a cab and went to their apartment on Drammensveien, which is a long street that goes all the way into *sentrum*, the center of the city. The airport is about 15 minutes from the apartment, which was in the same neighborhood as the Dalgards. The Mexico embassy was nearby. Living on an embassy street, just like 20 years before.

My parents' apartment had a master bedroom, an office/storage room, dining/living room, kitchen, powder room and bathroom.

The day took much the same form as the first day of the June trip. The trick in dealing with the jet lag going to Europe is to force yourself to stay awake after arriving to get used to the new time zone. So, being in the same neighborhood as The Park, it was a relatively simple thing to walk to The Park.

I also stopped in the same photo store where Steve had bargained on our first day in June. I shot a test roll with my new lens and left the film there – *Time Photo* (One-Hour Photo Developing) on Kirkeveien. I tried to talk Norwegian, but didn't hear the salesman's reply. So, he said in English, "What language?"

Once again, it shows the Norwegians' proficiency and versatility in language. If I said German, he would've spoken German.

Time Photo was around the corner from Majorstua Skole, so we took a peek there, too.

Norwegians had been complaining about the lack of snow during the previous winters. A conversation among Norwegians that winter might be: "I hear it's going to snow," says one.

"Optimist," says the other.

There was snow, particularly in Frogner Park. The steps in the park had snow, and the streets were icy. Everything seemed to be in place at the park. The ducks were still there scavenging for food. The same bird seemed to be perched on top of the same statue as in June. The statue of the boy having the temper tantrum. Across from him, the little girl who you weren't sure was smiling or crying. There was the statue of the man juggling two children on his left arm, one on his right and one hanging upside down on his left toe. Etc., etc.

As we walked up the steps leading to the Monolith, Seth spotted two snowball-packing kids.

"If you throw those things, you're dead," Seth shouted in English.

We made it safely to the Monolith and the statues surrounding it.

On the way back, we were suddenly face-to-face with those kids. Perhaps, they did understand Seth's English. They started to pelt us with snowballs. Ah, a cycle of children's lives Vigeland didn't sculpt!

We had to try to defend ourselves – and life, liberty and the American way? We did the best we could. After all, we were suffering jet lag, right? The snowballs kept coming our way. This event became an attraction as other people with cameras stopped to take pictures of these American adults being pelted with snowballs by two 10-year-old Norwegian boys. Tourists, go figure!

At one point, I had to leave Seth on his own, so *I* could get in position for a picture of the kids throwing at us. Then a friend of the two boys came by looking for his comrades, only to find them engaged in this exciting snowball fight. Naturally, he joined in. At this point, I started shouting at them in Norwegian about the unfairness of this situation.

"Tre mot to!" "Three against two!"

Finally, we got close enough to them and made a truce. I tried my Norwegian.

"Går du til Majorstua Skole?" I asked. "Do you go to Majorstua School?"

"Ja," they replied. "Yes."

"Jeg gikk til Majorstua in 1969-70," I said. "I went to Majorstua in 1969-70."

They seemed a little confused at this, and one asked the other what I had said. For all I know, I might have said I went there in 1979-70.

We asked them their names, and they us.

"Michael," I said.

They had an immediate frame of reference. "Mike Tyson," they said, putting up their fists.

Then, dancing, they said, "Michael Jackson."

"Seth," said Seth.

"Seth?" they said, looking puzzled.

Well, what an eventful first few hours in Norway. A snowball fight in The Park!

My parents had bought tickets for the Oslo Symphony for that night. We decided to go. We took the tram (trolley) from the corner of their street into town. For 60 *kroner* (@$10), you could buy an eight-ride ticket. Two people can ride on the same ticket (for two punches), and a transfer to any tram, *trikk,* or bus line within one hour is free. Or you can get back on the same line within the hour.

There is great dependence on the honor system. Buses, trams or *trikks* can be entered in the middle, and passengers insert the ticket into a machine, which stamps it with the time. You don't need exact change and can buy tickets from the driver. You can purchase monthly and weekly tickets, as well as paying for each individual ride.

The concert was in the beautiful Oslo *Konserthus* (Concert Hall) and was wonderful, although at points I began to drift off with exhaustion, even though the music was Beethoven's ninth symphony.

This was a major musical highlight of the Oslo concert season. The government heavily subsidizes the arts, making concerts, theater and cultural activities accessible to all. The *konserthus* was packed with people of all ages and classes, dressed informally and formally.

For Seth, it capped a big first day, because he hadn't been to many classical music concerts.

15 December 1990

The itinerary was taking shape. The first week would be filled with traveling.

First, however, tonight we were invited to the Dalgards. Tomorrow, Sunday, there was a Chanukah program at the Jewish Center, and that evening my father's colleague, Elsa, had invited us to her daughter's Christmas concert and then for *aften* (a small evening meal around eight or nine p.m.).

On Monday, Torbjørn would take us to Rauland, where we would spend a few days. The next weekend we would take the train ride across the country to Bergen. My parents had found out that the Gardners, old friends who we hadn't seen in 20 years, were living there.

Today, Seth and I decided to visit the *Hjemmefront-museum* (Resistance Museum), the tribute to Norwegian resistance during the Nazi occupation from 1940-45. It was again a touching tour, and Seth was impressed.

"It shows another perspective on the war," he says. "Jews are not particularly numerous in Norway, and this museum showed a country's resistance to foreign occupation."

Seth had also made it a mission to find compact discs of British singer Billy Bragg, which he hadn't been able to find in Philadelphia, and he thought might be available in a foreign market.

Akershus Fortress and Castle, where the Resistance Museum is situated, stands at the harbor and across from the Rådhus (City Hall). Across the water from Akershus is Aker *Brygge* (*brygge* means wharf), an area built up with

158

shopping areas and restaurants modeled after the Baltimore Inner Harbor. Right by the harbor in the spring and summer are stands selling fresh fish, vegetables, T-shirts and other wares. So, we went to Aker Brygge to scout out the music stores. We also ate some shrimp *smørbrød* (open-faced sandwiches), which Seth grew to love on this trip.

By the time we walked over to Aker Brygge, it had become dark, yet it was only around three p.m. We were taken by the simplicity of the Christmas decorations. They didn't overwhelm us, like the decorations Stateside. Lampposts were adorned with small "lighted trees branching out to hold three stars." Stores displayed holiday scenes in the windows. Trees weren't adorned extravagantly.

From there, we made our way to the Dalgards. Odd Steffen, Ragnhild, Olav, Florence, her daughter, Siri, and now 11-month-old Joachim were at Odd and Ragnhild's apartment with my parents. Eivind and Angela couldn't make it, although we had arranged to check with them on Sunday about getting together.

We had a wonderful meal together with the Dalgards. It didn't take long for the discussion to turn to politics. Saddam Hussein, George Bush, Kuwait and the possible impending Persian Gulf War were popular subjects at the time. Opinions differed, but Seth easily participated.

However, the Dalgards told us about the disturbing rise of right-wing factions in Norway.

We stayed quite awhile, but despite the hour, my parents, Seth and I walked the approximate six blocks back to the Drammensveien apartment.

16 December 1990

I called Eivind in the morning to see if we could get together with him and Angela. He was no longer working in Skien as a "slave doctor," as he had put it in June. He was now in Kviteseid, southwest of Oslo, while Angela was still in Oslo, continuing her studies at the University of Oslo. Eivind was in town for the holidays. They had dated for 12 years before getting married, and since getting married, were now living even further apart.

Eivind said they were thinking of walking around Holmenkollen and Frognerseteren, which sounded great. We agreed on which *trikk* Seth and I would take to Angela's house. Eivind said he would "pick us up." The emphasis is on "pick us up" because the connotation that has for us Americans.

Seth and I took the bus to Majorstua station and caught the *trikk*. We got an earlier one, which is possible since public transportation is pretty prompt, and they run much more frequently than at home, even on Sunday. We got off at the right stop. Since we were going to be "picked up" and I had no idea where we were going, we waited at the station, which was just a platform.

At Majorstua, Seth had bought the newspaper, *The European*, so he passed the time reading. I looked at the scenery. Eventually, Eivind came walking down a road toward us to "pick us up." To Americans, that usually means picked up in a car. It turned out Angela lived a block away! Eivind walked over to "meet us." The three of us walked the short distance to Angela's house.

She lived in a beautiful two-story wood house with four other women. I think it was part of University housing for graduate students and/or married students. We sat around in the living room, talking over tea and coffee. I had copies of Steve's pictures from June. I showed the photos as I reminisced and laughed with them about the June trip: Angela taking us to Kragerø; and the whirlwind Larvik-Frederickshavn, Denmark-Gøteborg, Sweden-Oslo journey.

Then we decided to head toward Frognerseteren. We walked down to the station to catch the *trikk*. There were plenty of children with sleds, toboggans and skis on the *trikk*. It was a perfectly clear day. When we got off at Frognerseteren, we had a beautiful view of the forest, the Oslofjord and the city in the distance. Evident in the distance through the trees was a view of the top of the old Holmenkollen Ski Jump.

Frognerseteren is the highest point overlooking the city, so when you get off the *trikk*, you have to walk downhill. The kids poured out of the *trikk* with their sleds and toboggans and began hopping on them to challenge the hill. Three girls adorned in Norwegian sweaters crowded on to one sled.

We walked. There was plenty of snow and ice up there. We followed our leaders and eventually came to Frognerseteren Restaurant. *Eple kake med krem* called, so we stopped.

From there, we walked through the forest toward Holmenkollen. Views of either the old or new jump were never far from sight. We came to Holmenkollen from an angle I had never used before. On the last two trips, I had come from the Holmenkollen Station side. This was just the opposite end. There was not as much snow as in 1986, but there was enough to cover some of the bleachers and the landing. We saw cross-country skiers in their knickers and what looked like a father and son riding a toboggan.

As we walked, Seth engaged Eivind in a discussion about Norway's support for Israel. Eivind said, that 20 years ago, support for Israel was 90 percent. Now, particularly since the Palestinian *intifada* in 1987, support for Israeli policies was down to 30 percent. I talked to Angela.

Eivind couldn't remember where the *trikk* station was, but I did, resulting in some joking about my knowing the area better than they did. I asked why Holmenkollen wouldn't be used for the 1994 Olympics. Eivind's answer was that Lillehammer wanted to have all the events provincial. He said Norwegians thought it was a joke when Lillehammer bid for the 1994 Games and never thought it would receive the Games. Now, Norwegians are wondering what's going to happen after all these arenas are built in this small town and the Games are over.

We caught the *trikk* into *sentrum*, from where Seth and I would find our way to the Jewish Center. In *sentrum*, the city's Christmas tree was in front of the Aula, the auditorium at the old campus of the University of Oslo. Again, though it was impressive in stature, the tree was decorated simply with lights. We ended up taking a cab to the Jewish Center.

It should be noted that this is the *only* Jewish center and *only* synagogue in Oslo. The Jewish population is very small, around 1,000 or so in Oslo now, and 1,400 in Norway, compared to 1,800 prior to the Nazi occupation. The other major Jewish community is in Trondheim on the northwest coast, around eight hours from Oslo.

Yet, the Jews are accepted. Norwegian Jews contend that Norway is one of Europe's friendliest countries (*The Jewish Traveler: Oslo*, by Phyllis Ellen Funke, *Hadassah*, April 1991). Jews were finally allowed in Norway in 1851, thanks to the efforts of non-Jewish poet Henrik Wergeland, who began his advocacy for that in 1839. There is a Jewish cemetery and monument to Wergeland in western Oslo.

After Kristallnacht, a night of violence and destruction of Jewish stores and neighborhoods by Nazi soldiers in Germany and Austria in November 1938, the Norwegian government and other organizations helped Jews escape from Germany and Czechoslovakia. There were 300 refugees in Norway by 1940, the year Germany invaded Norway. Norwegians, including the state church, protested anti-Jewish legislation in 1942, but to no avail. It is believed that 900 Jews avoided arrest, with many finding refuge in Sweden, thanks to the efforts of the Norwegian Resistance. Sixty Jews were imprisoned in Norwegian camps, and of the approximate 800 Norwegian Jews interned in European concentration camps, only about 25 survived.

The efforts on the part of the church and/or its members were quite laudable and remarkable. My parents had met a man, who as an infant was hid in his mother's knapsack, as a theologian walked them across the Swedish border.

In Trondheim, the Methodist church hid the sacred artifacts from the synagogue, and a pastor officiated at funerals in the Jewish cemetery during the occupation.[14] The deportation and treatment of the Jews drew reaction from many corners. Prime Minister Johan Nygaardsvold, who was with the Norwegian Government-in-Exile in London, wrote in *The* (London) *Jewish Bulletin*, 1942:

"...in democratic Norway, there was never any question of distinction between the class, race, or creed of Norwegian citizens. But when the German hordes forced their way into our peace-loving country, they had to find a Jewish problem. Anti-Jewish demonstrations were staged by the Germans, windows were smashed, and insulting remarks were painted on the walls and windows of Jewish properties. Their livelihood was taken from them, their citizenship revoked; they were oppressed and starved. But they still fight on as staunchly as other patriotic Norwegians. All these wrongs will be righted when Norway is once again a free land."

Even in some Nazi quarters, the "Jewish problem" was debated. The following is excerpted from the Norwegian Nazi Party *Månedshefte* (National Union Monthly Journal), December 15, 1942:

"...we must not forget that this Jewish problem is not only a racial one, but also a national and, above all, a human one. The Norwegian people have never regarded Jews as countrymen...since our people is too healthy-minded for that, but they have always been regarded as human beings, and, at that, as unfortunate human beings. Our movement must be held responsible to the Norwegian people for the way it solves the problem.

---

[14] *The Persecution of the Norwegian Jews in WWII*, by Oskar Mendelsohn 1991.

Above all, we have to guard ourselves against the destruction of feelings of justice within ourselves. It does not help to win the world if one harm's one's own soul. "

Bishop Lars Frøyland of Oslo, a Quisling appointment, but not a member of the Nazi Party said in 1943:[15]

"...our behavior toward people of another race and another belief within our own borders (is a disgrace). I feel bound by conscience to say this. And I do this even if it shall cost me ever so much. Is it correct to judge everyone the same way, and to punish the innocent with the guilty? We are, after all, Norwegians! We are, after all, Christians!"

Sweden, which remained "neutral," in the War, but allowed the German troops to march through Sweden en route to Norway, now became a haven for the Danish and Norwegian Jews. From the church and the press, Sweden protested the treatment of the Jews.

Theologian Natanael Beskow told a large protest in Stockholm:[16]

"A ship that left Oslo Harbor had a freight of anguish on board. We cannot imagine how much these human beings, men, women and children, are suffering...We cannot call them back. They go to their death or to slavery...If we can do nothing else we can try to be the voice of the condemned...let them through us call forth their anguish and accusations..."

Domprost Olle Nystedt, Gøteborg Cathedral, Sunday, November 22, 1942:[17]

---

[15] *Norway's Response to the Holocaust*, by Samuel Abrahamsen, Holocaust Library, 1991.
[16] Ibid.

"...the churches in Sweden cannot remain silent when such things happen on our borders. If we are silent the stones will cry out. We are shaken to our innermost, thinking of the suffering of the unfortunates. This is a breaking of God's law and a violation of the basic values of our civilization...The Swedish government should increase efforts to rescue Norway's Jews."

The Swedish press was nearly unanimous in condemning the treatment of Norwegian Jews. Swedish women's organizations also protested: *"...Persecutions of people belonging to another race is against the Nordic concept of justice and has, until now, been unknown in Nordic countries."*[18]

After the war, Norway was one of the few countries willing to accept displaced Jews, although it took several months before they were allowed to return. Many refugees opted to stay in Sweden, or go to Britain or North America. However, because Oslo's refugee population had begun reorganizing itself in Sweden, the synagogue was rededicated on August 31, 1945, with Crown Prince Olav present. There were 559 members of the Oslo Mosaic Jewish community in 1946. In May 1947, 392 Jews from displaced person camps came to Norway, followed by 150 during the next two to three years. It wasn't until October 1947 that the Trondheim synagogue – which had been used by the Germans for barracks – was reopened.[19]

The synagogue, Jewish community center and Jewish senior citizen home in Oslo are all on the same small, hilly block. Though Orthodox in orientation, the community recognizes that there is diversity in Jewish observance, and theirs is a small community, so they try

---

[17] *Norway's Response to the Holocaust*, by Samuel Abrahamsen, Holocaust Library, 1991.
[18] Ibid.
[19] *The Persecution of the Norwegian Jews in WWII*, by Oskar Mendelsohn 1991.

165

to accept and integrate different approaches. Many of the Jews are immigrants or Israelis who married Norwegians. About 60 percent of Oslo's Jews are over 60 years of age. The most prominent Jew in Norway is Jo Benkow, the President of the Parliament or *Storting*.[20]

Nevertheless, there has been vandalism and some tension with the large Muslim immigrant population. Security is tight when you come to the center. Police cars are stationed outside, and we had to identify ourselves to people at the door of the synagogue and Center. Once inside, Seth and I went downstairs for Chanukah in Norway, as our family had done in 1969. There were a significant number of adults and children. It was interesting to think that here was about 20-25 percent of the Jewish population of Oslo. Imagine, 20 percent of New York City's Jewish population is 600,000, which is greater than the entire population of the city of Oslo.

Paper dreidels hung from string connected to the walls, as did "Happy Chanukah" streamers in English. There were also drawings posted on walls. As with Chanukah here, the holiday is for the children. There were plenty of beautiful blond children. A student choir sang Chanukah songs, and then to our surprise, a teacher read a Sholom Aleichem story in Norwegian, which she had translated into Norwegian from the English transla-tion of the Yiddish story.

"There were a number of Sephardic Jews as opposed to the Ashkenazi Jews I'm familiar with," said Seth. "I was struck that there were people from Morocco and elsewhere, not just the United States. It was a multi-cultural celebration."

After Chanukah, we were then off to get a taste of *Christmas* in Norway. My father's colleague, Elsa, invited us to the *Julekonsert* (Christmas concert) at a church near Akershus. Her oldest daughter played in the orchestra of the Lysejordet *Skoles Musikkorps* (the Lysejordet School's Music Choir), a prestigious choir that won competitions

---

[20] *Haddassah*, April 1991.

in Norway. There was a very competitive process to get into the choir. There was a major and junior choir.

The hall was packed and the choir was very good. It felt like an American event in different ways. First, it was long. The concert was interrupted with recognition of parents who sold the most tickets, raised the most money or sold the most raffle tickets. The musical selections included *Parade of the Tall Ships, Sophisticated Ladies, Just A Closer Walk with Thee, The Magic of Sammy Cahn, Feelings, Cute, Hooray for Hollywood, Strike Up the Band, The Trombone Rag, My Kind of Towns* and *They Went Thataway.*

During the course of the concert, Seth and I got hungry, so we slipped out. Somehow, we found our way to Karl Johans Gate and found a pizza place. The pizza wasn't bad and not too expensive. When we got back to the concert, we found ourselves in a little predicament. The concert was not yet over, and in the hallway was the next act, which included children dressed in a horse costume. While they waited for their cue, they sat down in a chair. How were we to sneak our way back in without causing a distraction and ruining the entrance of the Wild West show? If we waited to follow them, it would look like we were part of the act. We worked it out, by slipping in after the grand entrance of cowboys and horses, and sitting in the back of the auditorium.

After the show, we joined Elsa, her husband, Bjørn, and two daughters for *aften* at their home on the outskirts of Oslo center. They were extremely pleasant and also lived in a beautiful home. They served open-faced sandwiches of cheese and meats, and cakes. We learned that Norwegian children were now learning English in third grade, but the staggered hours of the school days were still a problem for Norwegian parents. Elsa and Bjørn also emphasized the importance of the children knowing English. Many of the college textbooks are in English, and if Norwegians travel or study abroad, people in those countries will not know Norwegian. English enables Norwegians to study and travel.

We had been impressed by the quality of so many homes. Norway discovered oil and gas in the Norwegian part of the North Sea in 1968.[21] When the profits came in during the early to mid '70s, the government decided to use the money to provide loans to Norwegians for home improvements. Many people made use of the loans. This freed up money for Norwegians to spend on improving other areas of quality of life from summer cottages to clothing to cars to boats.

It was quite late when we walked to the corner and caught a bus that took us a couple of blocks from my parents' apartment.

17 December 1990

Another colleague of my father's, Ragnhild Sætre, had a brother-in-law who was a sportswriter for the newspaper in Lillehammer and was working on press relations with the Olympic committee. I was given his number to see if I could arrange an appointment to go to Lillehammer.

I was successful in reaching him. I expressed my interest and desire to visit Lillehammer. He said he would call someone at the Olympic Center and that I should call him back. I explained I would be traveling and would have to try tomorrow.

Step one was accomplished. No stonewalling, no discouragement, just an effort to help and to be cooperative.

Torbjørn was to pick us up later in the afternoon to take us to Rauland, so there was time to do a few things.

I had to show Seth the *Kon-Tiki/Ra* and Viking Ships Museums. We wouldn't be back in Oslo for almost a week, which would then be Christmas, and the museums would be closed. We took the bus from Bygdøy Allè to the museums.

---

[21] Arne Selbyg. E-mail Correspondence related to his book *Norway Today: An Introduction to Modern Norwegian Society,* Norwegian University Press, 1987.

Torbjørn's sons weren't with him this time, but his dog was. The dog was sick and wore this funnel-shaped, lampshade contraption around his head.

The route was the same as the spring trip, but there wasn't as much to see because it was dark. There was snow, and it was cold.

Along the way, we stopped at a store. Seth found the best souvenir, a *Calvin and Hobbes* comic book in Norwegian, except it went by the name *Tommy and Tigern*. Seth and our family love the cartoon.

Seth bought it and said to me, "Now it's your job to translate it."

I started to.

We arrived at Moum/Rieser around seven p.m. I could now empty the "Santa Claus" box of presents I had brought: the kosher salamis, the children's books and the T-shirts. The T-shirt for Ingrid was more like a full-length dress or night gown/shirt. Regardless, she was thrilled with the gift and wore it proudly.

Dinner was Debbie's homemade pizza, and then we settled in for a relaxing evening. Few better places to do that than Rauland.

18 December 1990

Phone calls two and three to Lillehammer highlighted the morning. I called the sportswriter. True to his word, he had called the Olympic Committee. He gave me the name of a woman at the Committee who would set up an appointment for me.

I called her. Again, I explained my interest. I had yet to speak to the person to whom I had written the letters. There really was only one day for me to visit them. This was a Tuesday; we were heading back to Oslo Wednesday, and Friday we were leaving for Bergen for the weekend. Next week was Christmas. It would have to be Thursday.

"I don't have a train schedule here," I said.

"That's okay," she said. "I have one right here."

She listed some times and the return schedule as well. I decided on the 8:30 a.m. train, which would get me in around 11:30.

"How do I get to the Center from the train station?" I asked.

"Don't worry. We'll pick you up," she said.

"How will we find each other?" I asked. "If it wasn't cold, I'd wear my Lillehammer T-shirt."

"We'll find you," she assured me again.

I was going to Lillehammer – for an interview. To meet with people at the *Olympic* Committee. They were going to pick me up at the train station (by car or by foot as Eivind had?). This was hard to believe. It was arranged so simply and pleasantly. They didn't know me from 'Adam,' and they did this for me.

One of the pleasures of Rauland is the peacefulness of the area, and its isolation, which allows for relaxation. There is no noise, commotion or bustle of a city or even a small town. Although, I don't know if I could handle it for long stretches of time, it's nice to be in a place where you don't feel you have to rush somewhere, and are surrounded by picturesque, snow-covered mountains and snowy evergreen trees.

There was snow on the ground, but still complaints from the hosts that there wasn't enough. As a matter of fact, I myself was anxious to see some snowfall. While it had snowed three times in the week I was in Norway in January 1986, we had yet to see the white stuff descend since my arrival. No "luck" today.

The day was virtually a repeat performance of the June trip – *dejà vu* all over again. This time what I had seen in the spring I was seeing in the winter. We went into "town." We looked in a handcrafts store and another clothing and souvenir store. Seth had been looking fruitlessly for a sweater for his girlfriend, Gwynne, and it was here that he finally bought one.

Torbjørn took us on the same ride he had in the spring. This time he stopped by a wood building similar to those seen in the Folkmuseums. On the side of the building was a wood post with carvings of people.

Again, the ride took us along Lake Totak, which was mostly covered with ice and snow, and surrounded by fjords and mountains. Ice hung on the mountainsides. We came to the spot where Steve and I had taken pictures of snow flowing down the middle of a mountain, meeting the water and causing a reflection in the blue water. Now, it was a beautiful view of contrasts. In June, it was a sunny day with a clear blue sky and white clouds. The picture was shot looking through green trees. And, yet on that spring day, snow was splattered in the mountain and greenery surrounded this snow that flowed down the middle of the mountain.

I was seeing the counterview. It was an overcast December winter day. It was not clear and cloud formations were hard to detect. There was snow on the mountain, but not the clear white of June. In the distance, one could hardly make out the images of the trees on the mountains, the ones that had been so green six months before. Gone was the smoothness of the appearance of the mountain, now replaced by a stark roughness. And, where in *June*, snow had cut a path through the mountainside, there was little evidence of the path and snow. It was an interesting perspective and contrast, an interesting view of nature.

That evening the house was full of people. Torbjørn and Debbie invited the British couple and their children for dinner. Steve and I met them at the orienteering event in June. They were very nice people who now lived in Rauland. He was British and she Norwegian. He had been a university professor in England. They met and married in Africa. Her ill mother lived in Rauland, which brought them to the area.

Dinner was reindeer in a traditional cream sauce. Torbjørn had hunted the reindeer in the area. There was good food, company and conversation.

19 December 1990

We were to leave for Oslo later in the morning. Debbie was rushing out of the house with Ingrid. Debbie pleaded, "You must come to the day-care center for the Christmas program, before you leave, and see Ingrid."

The prospect of experiencing a children's Christmas in a small village in Norway was hard to pass up. After loading up the car, we took pictures of my parents, Seth, Torbjørn and me in front of the house. It was snowing! Hooray! The first snowfall of the trip.

Torbjørn drove to the day-care center, located a short distance up a road from the "center" of town. Torbjørn explained that more than Santa Claus, the central figures for Norwegian children are *Julenisse* (pronounced *Yula neesa),* Christmas elves. There are good and bad elves. The good elves are dressed in red. Fairy-tale legends claim that *nisse* descended from trolls, who moved from living underground to becoming "house gods" in Norwegian homes. They took care of the cattle. The Norwegians fed the *nisse* well to keep them happy. Porridge was placed in the barn every Christmas Eve (*Trolls and their Relatives,* by Jan Bergh Eriksen, Dreyer Bok, Aase Grafiske, Stavanger, Norway).

We walked into the day-care center, and there were all these children dressed in red, wearing what looked like red crepe paper hats tied at the top in a cone shape. The beautiful children, mostly blond, sat at tables eating porridge, drinking juice and listening to the story of the *Julenisse.* Most of the parents and teachers also wore some red.

Ingrid was shy and tried to avoid our looks and the camera. Everybody then went into another room to sing, listen to music and dance around the Christmas tree. One young boy, who we were told would be appearing on national television later in the week, sang a solo. One young girl in the audience crouched for a long time with a blown-up balloon in her mouth. The British man, who had visited with us the night before, played the flute, performed magic and a puppet show for the intensively attentive children.

Soon, Christmas in Rauland was over for us; it was time for us to say our good-byes and head back to Oslo.

20 December 1990

"The main thing in life is not to be afraid to be human."

–Pablo Casals

I was up early for another trip – one that would be one of the most special experiences of my life. The train to Lillehammer was leaving from Sentral Stasjon around 8:30 a.m. After breakfast, I caught the tram into town. I had some problems finding the train station in the darkness of the morning, but finally got there.

The ride took between two-and-a-half and three hours. I quickly learned about the train system in Norway. It is advisable to buy a reserved seat. There is an extra charge, about 15 *kroner* (@$2.50 at that time). If you don't have a reserved seat, you can find yourself continually changing seats because someone getting on the train along the route may have your seat reserved. I didn't realize this when I left Oslo.

The train trip to Bergen awaited the next day, but this journey was beautiful. The winter wonderland – one of the many in Norway – was found. Snow was on all sides and covered the trees. Here, there was definitely a white Christmas.

Finally, *toget,* the train, pulled into Lillehammer. Here was the town where the Olympics would be held – two tracks, a small depot (there has been much renovation since then) in a town with a charm all its own. The population is about 22,000 people, and hundreds of thousands will descend on it from February 12-27, 1994. I remembered visiting Lillehammer with my family in 1970, but the memories were staying on a farm, visiting *Maihaugen,* Lillehammer's Folkmuseum and being in a bad mood.

This time was different. I was anxious and excited. I walked to the door of the station with the other passengers, looking around. A man around my age, maybe younger, was at the door.

"Are you Michael Kleiner? I'm from the Lillehammer Olympic Organizing Committee," he said. "My name is Frode Nielsen."

Again, another person, another name to know. Who was Frode Nielsen? *Prosjektleder, Redaksjon*; Project Manager, Editorial Office. Actually, it couldn't be more perfect.

We got into the Volvo, and he drove to the Olympic Center. There were many Volvos in the parking lot. I asked him if Volvo was the "official" car of the Olympics.

"Sweden was upset they didn't get the Olympics, but they gave us their Volvos anyway," he joked.

The Swedish towns of Östersund/Åre bid for the 1994 Olympics. Norway was under Swedish domination from 1814-1905. Norway likes to poke fun at its neighbor.

The Lillehammer Olympic logo was prominent as we walked into the lobby. We went upstairs, and he introduced me to other people. Wherever I could, I said, *"Så hyggelig å møte deg."* "So very nice to meet you," which is a very courteous greeting in Norwegian.

People were impressed. *"Snakke du norsk?"* "Do you speak Norwegian?"

I finally met the man to whom I had written the letters. (His title and position had changed.) Whether or not he remembered my letters or was reacting to the introductions, he said, "We appreciate your interest and aggressiveness."

Then came the gifts. Frode gave me a folder with magazines, newsletters and newspapers produced by the Olympic Committee, as well as brochures about Lillehammer and the Oppland region where Lillehammer is located. Some were in Norwegian and some in English. There was more. He gave me picture negatives of Lillehammer; Gerhard Heiberg, chairman and C.E.O of the Lillehammer Olympics; Henrik Andenæs, president of the 1994 Games and Petter Rønningen, president of the LOOC. Then, there were posters, stickers and lapel pins with the Lillehammer Olympic logo.

"Do you have brothers and sisters? Here take some more pins," said Frode.

Nothing seemed too much!

After showing me his work area, Frode took me to the Center cafeteria for lunch. I started to get in line, but Frode said, "I already ordered for us."

I was overwhelmed. We hadn't even talked about me yet, and I had already been showered with gifts, friendliness, hospitality and treated to lunch. We sat at a table toward the back, but there were windows on the sides for views of the town and area. I showed Frode my brochures and talked about my job and my affection for Norway. So far, all of these conversations had been conducted in English.

With lunch over, we returned to the Volvo. It was time for the tour of Lillehammer. Along the way, I learned a little about him and the Games. He had worked in public information at NATO prior to coming to the LOOC. He was married with two children, and he pointed out his house in the distance during the ride. Frode had been to the United States. Atlanta would be hosting the 1996 Summer Olympics, and Atlanta and Lillehammer have a "sister city" relationship. So he had been to Atlanta, and I believe to New York and California.

While Eivind may have talked about Lillehammer wanting a provincial Olympic Games, Frode called it "The Compact Games." Lillehammer is situated at the northern point of Lake Mjøsa, the largest lake in Norway. The Gudsbransdal valley and the famous Jotunheimen Mountains are picturesque and favorite tourist and resort areas. There are three towns that create a triangle, Lillehammer, Gjøvik and Hamar, where all the Olympic events will take place. Gjøvik is 45 kilometers (@28 miles) south of Lillehammer at the left point of the triangle and will host some of the ice-hockey games.

Hamar is located 58 kilometers (@36 miles) south of Lillehammer at the right point of the triangle. It will host the speed-skating events at an indoor arena, as well as some of the ice-hockey matches. Lillehammer is at the top of the triangle and will host cross-country skiing, ski jumping, Nordic combined, biathlon, freestyle, figure skating, bobsledding, luge and the balance of the hockey games. Alpine skiing will be conducted at Kvitfjell (*fjell* is mountain) in Ringebu, 50 kilometers (31 miles) north of Lillehammer, and at Hafjell Alpine Center in Øyer, 15 kilometers (nine miles) north of Lillehammer (*Newsflash, Newsletter for the XVII Olympic Winter Games*, June 1990). An obvious question is: Since Oslo is three hours away from Lillehammer, will people be able to get to Lillehammer?

Frode said he had been to Albertville, France, where the 1992 Winter Olympics were to take place and said it's harder to get there. Oslo's Fornebu Airport is 180 km (111 miles), while Gardermoen Airport is 150 km (93 miles), and the Fagernes Airport (probably for small commuter-like planes) is 100 km (62 miles) from Lillehammer.

Frode drove along a narrow road with snow-covered trees on the sides. On the right side was a view overlooking Lillehammer. He stopped, so I could take pictures, but said the panoramic view was among the pictures he had given me in the packet. We then went to the Hafjell Alpinesenter. Trees surrounded the steep course. People were using the slope, including a young boy. Frode mentioned that near the top of the mountain were the cross-country trails. The ski jumps would also be nearby.

On the way back, he pointed out where the press center would be, the International Broadcasting Center, the Olympic Village and the bobsled run. Frode said he had promised himself he would try the downhill ski course and the bobsled run. He wasn't quite sure though if he would follow through with the bobsled. Much has been said about the building going on in Lillehammer and what would happen to the structures after the Games were over. Frode explained that some of the Village accommodations would remain as dormitory space for the local college. Some of the other buildings were being constructed, so they could be dismantled afterwards and taken to other parts of the country as housing, probably for senior citizens.

We came back to the Olympic Center, and he dropped me off at the information center next door. He had some calls to make and would meet me back here in a little while. He introduced me to the woman at the information desk who would show me around. While the building was not completely furnished, I was shown where the computer rooms would be and where the media would work. The computers will be programmed with records, and the history of the Olympic Games and people will be able to come and find the information. She showed me an exhibit about the planning and building in Lillehammer. The information center also maintains community relations with the people of Lillehammer. She explained that if construction was being done on a road, people could come to the Center and find out about alternate routes or could find out when the construction would be taking place.

I asked, "Suppose people can't get here because of the construction?"

She looked at me somewhat incredulously and re-plied, "We are Norwegians. We walk. Everything is 10 minutes from here."

Silly me.

I was then shown a magnificent slide show – six simultaneous projectors – but I caught the "slip," as would any Norwegian. The slide show was trying to show what a perfect area Lillehammer was for the Winter Olympics. Since there was no ski-jump hill in Lilleham-mer, yet, the ski-jump shot was of Holmenkollen!

Frode returned, and we walked from the information center down a small street, which had Lillehammer Olympic flags on both sides, to *Storgata*, the Main Street. To the right on Storgata was the main square with the town Christmas tree, with little decoration. In the distance was a mountain. The decorations on Storgata were simple – green pine with a star in the middle strung from one building or post to another across the road. The left side of the square was for pedestrians. The only vehicle was the Thomas Toget, the Thomas Train, a small row of cars similar to what you sometimes see in zoos. Santa Claus drove it, one of the few images of Santa Claus I had seen in Norway.

We went into a record store, and I looked for Billy Bragg for Seth, and asked Frode who were some of the popular Norwegian musicians. He mentioned a jazz artist, Jan Garbarek, and a singer, Steinar Albrightsen. I did not buy anything.

We continued to walk along Storgata, stopping at a money machine so he could get cash. He commented that Storgata had so many stores incorporating American names; one might think it was an American street.

"You would not be able to tell this was Norway," he said, dismayed.

We went back to the Center. He wanted to see if the personnel director, Ragnhild Staff, was available.

"Staff, funny name for the personnel director," he said.

She wasn't there, but he gave me her card as well as his own.

"To inquire about jobs, write to her," he told me.

We headed back to the Volvo. In the car, he talked about Christmas in Norway. It was an important holiday with an emphasis on children. Gifts were bought mainly for children, but even those gifts were still usually simple and not lavish. Frode stopped at a *vinmonopolet*, wine monopoly or state store. He had to buy a bottle of wine for his father.

"For the parents, that is good enough," he said.

We went to the train station, but it was still early for the train. He advised me to buy a reserved seat on the train. We sat in the car and talked. By now, I was attempting Norwegian and not doing too badly. He also told me two things regarding the Olympics.

"Go back and try to become more fluent in Norwegian," he said. "I know that outside of Minnesota, there are a number of Norwegians in Pennsylvania. Marketing of the Lillehammer Olympics outside of Norway cannot begin until after the 1992 Olympics are over because it would interfere with the marketing of those Games."

It was time to depart. I had spent four hours here in Lillehammer. This man, who didn't know me before this morning, had treated me royally. The Olympic Committee, which didn't know me from 'Adam,' gave me a chance to meet them, see the operation and the town. I was loaded down with "gifts" (simple, but special).

We shook hands.

"Så hyggelig å møte deg," I said.

"I hope to see you again," Frode replied.

I purchased my reserved seat ticket and waited for the train. Many soldiers were taking the train to Oslo, returning for the holidays. Once on the train, I tried to digest all that had happened, as I flipped through some of the reading material I had been given. I had been wined and dined. Nothing like this had ever happened to me before. And this was the *Olympics!* They hadn't made it so large that they couldn't make room and time to host an American for a day. I understood what good public relations truly meant.

For me, this experience further proved the goodness of Norwegians. I walked away from my time spent with Frode, not just as if I had simply met someone, like two ships passing in the night, a chance meeting that didn't mean more than introductions in relation to a job. I met a real human being, pleasant and kind. I felt I had made a new friend in Norway. By his saying, "I hope to see you again," perhaps he felt the same way. How many times can you say that after a job interview?

I walked into my parents' apartment. They were all anxious.

"Well, did you get the job?" asked Seth.

I told them the story of the day. I passed out some of the pins. I shared with them the experience I shall never forget.

21 December 1990

It was early to rise again for the ride to Bergen. I had wanted to take this trip because it has always been advertised as one of the most beautiful, if not *the* most beautiful train ride in the world. It is worth doing both in the winter and summer. I was also interested in seeing Bergen again. Twenty years ago, we were brave; actually my father was. He drove us through the mountains on hairpin curves and narrow roads from Oslo to Bergen and back, taking a break for the ferry rides.

This trip would have added significance. My parents reported to me, before I came, that they had located Morris Gardner, an American we had met during our year in Norway, and my fellow potato chip aficionado. He was now divorced, but all the Gardners lived in Bergen. Rachel, the oldest daughter, I was told, remembered me. How much she could remember was debatable, considering she was a four-year-old at the time. The younger daughter, Rebekka, was about to be born when we left Norway in 1970. We could look forward to seeing the Gardners again.

First, there was getting there. How beautiful was the trip! I took 28 pictures on the seven-hour ride, even though virtually every time I lifted the camera, we went through a tunnel. I got my timing down enough to get the 28 photos. You never knew whether to look left or right. One view would surpass another. There was plenty of snow.

If you think you can catch up on reading during the ride, you're mistaken. There is just too much to look at. Besides, I charted the trip on a map, marking every stop of the route, along with the picture number.

It was amazing to see the solitary and isolated homes, and wondering how these people manage out here.

There were a number of shots between Hønefoss and Nesbyen in the early part of the trip, including nice reflections of the sun on the mountains. There was the interesting-looking house by the station at Gol. As the ride progresses, the train is going higher and higher in the mountains. The tracks are on narrow roads, winding around curves and through the tunnels. The tunnels are to protect against snow avalanches. One marvels at the engineering that went into building the rail line.

The halfway point of the journey is Geilo (pronounced Yilow), and the train goes right past the Geilo Hotel, which brought back fond memories. Here we spent a long weekend in February 1970, when Cissy came to visit from London, and where we stopped in June 1970 when we drove to Bergen. It is that winter trip that I remember most. Geilo is a resort area, so it attracts many people. Somewhere in those snowy mountains I was now photographing, Cissy, my mother and I took a reindeer sleigh ride to the Sami (sometimes called Laplanders, although that is a derogatory term) camp, while my father, sister and brother skied there.

Flashback.

("Da familien min bodde i Norge i 1969-70, reiste vi til mange steder. Vi tenker tilbake på en spesiell tur med særlig varme tanker. Vi besøkte Geilo. En britisk venn ble med oss. Min far, bror og søster gledet seg til å gå på ski og jeg gikk på skøyter. Jeg prøvde å etterligne Dag Fornæs, en norsk mester på skøyter.

"Men en dag så vi et oppslag. Samene hadde tilbud på kjøring med reinsdyrslede og en sjanse til å lære om samiske kultur. Min far, bror og søster gikk på ski til samenes leir. Min mor, vår britisk venn og jeg tok reinsdyrsleden. Vår britiske venn kjørte sin egen slede. En gang gikk reinsdyret kjørt av vennen vår forskjellig vei, så vennen vår sa, 'Mush, mush!'

"Endelig kom vi alle sammen til samenes leir. Jeg husker blå og oransje samiske klær. Vi satt i teltet og så på skinn og håndverks gjenstander. Det var vanskelig å forstå hva de sa fordi de ikke snakket norsk eller engelsk

181

og vår norsk var ikke så god. Men det var en hyggelig tid."

"When my family lived in Norway in 1969-70, we traveled to many places. We think back to a special trip with very warm thoughts. We visited Geilo. A British friend was with us. My father, brother and sister enjoyed going skiing, and I went skating. I tried to imitate Dag Fornæs, a Norwegian skating champion.

"But one day, we saw an announcement. The Sami had offered rides with reindeer sleds and a chance to learn about Sami culture. My father, brother and sister went on skis to the Sami camp. My mother, our British friend and I took the reindeer sled. Our British friend drove her own sled. One time, the reindeer driven by our friend went a different way, so our friend said, 'Mush, mush!'

"Finally, we all came to the Samis' camp. I remember blue and orange Sami clothes. We sat in the tent and looked at skins and handcraft objects. It was difficult to understand what they said because they did not speak Norwegian or English, and our Norwegian was not so good. But it was a nice time."

Written August 3, 1992)

In a blink, we were past Geilo and history. The deeper and higher we got into the mountains, the more spectacular the sights became. At Ustaoset, virtually the entire scene was white snow; while at Finse, it was all white. Finse is the highest point along the ride at 1,232 meters above sea level (4,040.96 feet). The station building had a two-tiered roof, and the snow just about reached the first roof!

We passed by the beautiful snow-covered valleys with just a few houses sticking out. There was Voss, another popular spot and the birthplace of legendary Notre Dame football coach Knute Rockne. There is a statue of Rockne in the town. At Voss, the ride begins to level out, as we come down from the mountains and travel along the water of the fjords. Snow covered some of the fjords, more pronounced on some than others, and you feel cold looking at the water. One of the last towns before reaching Bergen is Dale, which is one of the major producers of Norwegian sweaters.

Finally, the train pulled into Bergen. We disembarked and walked down the platform. It was a small station. Somewhere near the end of the platform, we recognized Morris. With him was an attractive blonde woman. This was Rebekka, who we had never seen.

"How are you for walking? I don't have a car," Morris said. The walk gave us an excellent chance to look at the city. How different Bergen is from Oslo. This is not a city of skyscrapers dotting the skyline. The second largest city in Norway is on the West Coast, and therefore closer to the rest of Europe. Bergen was founded by Olav Kyrre in 1070. It was an important port city in The Hanseatic League in the 16th century, a trading collaboration of European countries. It was also the capital of Norway at one time. They speak a dialect of Norwegian, and there has always been a rivalry between Oslo and Bergen about who are really Norwegian. Bergen has maintained the old historical look in some of the buildings, stores and homes around the *sentrum*. We walked along some cobblestone roads past old churches, small stores and old buildings. If you looked left down alleyways and streets, you could see the harbor. We wound our way uphill on slippery cobblestones and along Støletorget. Morris lives above a market area (*torget*) – up winding, narrow metal stairs – in a two-story condominium.

He is a psychologist who operates a private practice out of his home. In the hall on the first floor, there is a life-size aquarium on the right. Upstairs, he had a large-screen TV, with a "super VHS video cassette recorder," just about every cable station in Europe, a unique state-of-the-art top-of-the-line turntable with huge triangular speakers.

Morris was well-prepared and well-stocked for my arrival. He had bought six different varieties of *potet gull* (potato chips). It wasn't long before we were all grabbing at the bags, including plain, paprika/barbecue, dill, sour cream and onion (new from America!). Rebekka had also followed in the family tradition.

Eventually, Liv and Rachel joined us, and we all walked to Peppe's Pizza. We pigged out on pizza with shrimp, fish, meat, veggies, etc. Pizza didn't exist in Norway 20 years before. Now, there were Peppe's located all over the country. The pizzas were huge and came in a rectangular shape, rather than circular. They also cost about $20 each.

Afterwards, Liv suggested we take the funicular, a cable car on tracks, up to Fløien, to see a panoramic view of Bergen. Morris and my mother begged off, but the rest of us went. We waited for the funicular along with Norwegians who were going to Fløien for some night skiing.

There was a man standing near us with children. He overheard us speaking English, and said to us, "Where in the United States are you from?"

"Philadelphia," we said.

"I played soccer at the University of San Francisco and was an All-American," he began. "We won the championship in 1978 and 1981, and there was a team from Philadelphia there, Philadelphia Textile."

We were stunned.

"I work there," I said. "I'm the sports information director!"

He began to mention some first names of players from that period, and though I wasn't there at the time, I knew who the players were from my research. We shared names of Norwegians playing soccer in the United States.

Here we were 4,000 miles from home and meet a Norwegian, who knows Philadelphia by Philadelphia Textile, and he meets not only someone who works there, but works in sports there! The world becomes small again.

The funicular takes about seven to 10 minutes and goes up a steep incline. At the terminus, you get off and can see different panoramic views of the city. It was quite dramatic at night. Other people were taking advantage of the skiing trails.

After returning, Seth and I left with Liv, Rachel and Rebekka. My parents were staying with Morris, and we were staying at Liv's house. The four of us walked downhill along some cobblestone streets to a bus stop carrying the luggage. They lived on the outskirts of the city in Sandviken.

There was a little apartment at the side of the house where Rachel stayed. But for these two days, Seth and I would stay there. We stayed up for a while. Rachel and Rebekka were both pretty and very quiet. Liv was also somewhat reserved. These were the first Norwegians I knew who came close to "fitting the stereotype of the reserved Norwegian." There was still the graciousness. After all, Liv was opening up her house to us.

Rachel was studying political science, and Rebekka, economics at the University of Bergen. Liv, a lover of books, worked in a library, and Rachel worked there part-time. Rebekka was interested in studying in the United States, but the only school she had read about was Wharton at the University of Pennsylvania. Seth, the Penn graduate, started to push Penn, while I tried to play up Textile's MBA program.

Seth went to bed, but I stayed up and watched a German detective program that was a favorite of theirs. I was pleased, and they were impressed at how much I was able to understand from reading the Norwegian subtitles. I was also guessing by assuming what would be happening at certain points in a detective show.

Soon, fatigue from the long day overtook me, and I retired for the night.

22 December 1990

One of the needles Oslo prods Bergen with is that it always rains in Bergen. For the most part, this is true. It would pour for the next two days, and I would come away with postcards, but no pictures of Bergen.

Nevertheless, under such circumstances, you must persevere and see what you can see. Seth and I were to meet my parents at Morris's and spend the afternoon. We were all invited to dinner at Liv's that evening.

Rebekka had been having trouble with her computer, and since Seth is a computer programmer, he did his utmost to try to diagnose and cure the problem. As hard as he tried, he couldn't figure it out. He enjoyed helping, as he was in his element with the computer.

When it was time for us to leave, Rachel walked us to the bus stop. The bus took us back into town, and we met my parents and Morris. The five of us slogged through the downpour to the *fisketorget*, the open-air fish market by the harbor. In addition to stands selling shrimp, salmon and other fish fresh off the boats, there are peddlers selling other wares like skins, T-shirts and other souvenirs. We stopped in a shop across the street from the market for a brief respite from the rain, as well as to check out the souvenirs. I bought a few things for people at the office.

Across the street there was a second-story café, which Morris recommended to us for something hot to drink and a quick bite. Again, we went there to get out of the rain. We then checked out some more music stores. Seth's search for Billy Bragg CDs continued.

My parents left Seth and me and headed down the street where we were to meet them later. About a minute or two later, my mother came looking for us and said, "Dad had an accident."

He had walked onto a manhole that had a loose top. A couple of people had helped lift him up out of the hole. My father is not skinny. He said he was all right and didn't think anything was broken. But there was a big bloody scrape on his right leg. Getting him to a hospital seemed to be a good idea, except there was a problem. We found out about Norwegian strikes. The taxis chose that hour to go on strike. For one hour! Gee, if Dad had only fallen an hour earlier or later.

The alternative was to find a pharmacy where we could get some bandages, gauze, medicine and towels to clean his wounds. Fortunately, we were with a native. Morris thought of a place, and we walked in the rain with my father limping to this store. Actually, the store was perfect, with a chair for him to sit on. The man at the store even took a look at the wound. The store specialized in bandages and stuff for the legs.

After that excitement, the evening was pleasant and special. I asked Rachel what she remembered of us 20 years before. She said two boys (my brother and I), a car and a trip, which probably was the Fredrikstad trip before we left Norway.

We enjoyed a good dinner. Liv was quite active in politics in the city and planned to run for the town council. Seth was quite impressed by her commitment. (After we returned to the States, Liv sent Seth a sticker of her party.)

We retired to the living room, which had a decorated Christmas tree. We never expected what happened next. Liv had bought gifts for each one of us! I received a book *Trolls and their Relatives*, which had been translated into English. Seth received an audiocassette of Jan Garbarek, ironically the musician Frode had recommended to me in Lillehammer.

The moment was quite overwhelming for us. If any of our Norwegian friends fit the "stereotype" of the reserved, quiet Norwegians, it was Liv and her daughters. Underneath, there was still the sociability, generosity and graciousness. It was seen in Liv hosting Seth and me at her house 20 years after I had seen her, and then giving us gifts. She would answer my later Norwegian letter(s), sending them back with corrections. So much for the so-called "typical" Norwegian, whatever that means.

23 December 1990

It was raining again on our last day. I had to get some pictures. Liv, Rachel and Rebekka finished breakfast before Seth and I did and went to the living room. As we ate, we were suddenly taken by the sight of them in the living room. They were not watching TV. Each was engrossed in reading a book. It was an interesting commentary (even though Liv is a librarian) and a picture I had to try to take. I even got them to smile together for the picture.

Back at Morris's, there was still some *potet gull* to finish off. I just had to have a lasting memory of the two potato chip kings munching the stuff that brought us together so many years before.

We hung out there for a while. Morris walked with us to the SAS Hotel, where we took the bus to the airport for the plane ride back to Oslo. We took Braathens SAFE, the domestic airline in Norway. The Bergen trip was now another pleasant memory of Norway. After a week of traveling, Seth and I would now spend the last three or so days in Oslo.

24 December 1990

Christmas in Norway was upon us. Ragnhild Dalgard warned us that *everything* closes down from 1 p.m. Christmas Eve through December 26. Everything meant everything: stores, restaurants, museums. So our second week would be improvisational. It meant that any shopping for souvenirs or food would have to be squeezed into the early part of Monday the 24th.

I had succeeded in discovering some of the Christmas food of Norway. A colleague of mine had read an article in a magazine that said there are seven different kinds of cake served on Christmas in Norway. My assignment was to bring the seven back. Our Norwegian friends told me the tradition of the seven cakes wasn't as common as in the past. In the bakeries, however, I did notice the popular pyramid ringed cake with the finishing touch of a small Norwegian flag on top (which was not edible). Most, if not all these cakes, were sugar coated.

Another concern was that the public transit would be reduced for the holidays. We had to be sure to get the revised schedule. The holiday schedule was every 15-20 minutes instead of every 10. Quite a setback, when holiday schedules in Philadelphia might be every hour or two!

Given the early closings on Christmas Eve and the complete shutdown the next couple of days, it meant we had to search out Billy Bragg one more time. Seth and I went to a music store on Karl Johans Gate. The music stores in Norway allow you to listen to a tape or compact disc with headphones before you purchase it.

I found a Jan Garbarek disc. Some of the music was influenced by the Sami. I also listened to a disc by Steinar Albrightsen. He was a Norwegian singer who sang in English. The selection I listened to was nice, although when I returned home, much of it sounded like country music. Seth finally found a Billy Bragg disc and a couple of other things. The discs were expensive, about $20 each.

On the way back, we stopped at RIMI, a market chain in Norway, and bought a few items for the house. One of the few places open past one was the 7-Eleven! We spent a quiet evening in the apartment, as Christmas descended on Norway.

25 December 1990

What could we do with this blank day? Nothing open. I suggested that we had not seen where my father worked, and it would also be nice to show Seth the university campus. They were two places we knew we could get into.

The Ullevål *Sykehus* (Ullevål Hospital) is an amazing complex. It is the size of a college campus and bigger than some. The hospital is a multi-purpose facility. There are the medical wings, cancer wards, research centers and psychiatric/psychological care facilities for in- and outpatients. Ullevål is impressive in other respects as well.

You enter the grounds at a stone fence, past a security office. You turn left and walk a short distance past the taxi stand and wind to the right. On the left is a building with a food store, post office, hair salon and bank. It provides a convenience for the hospital employees. My father often took advantage of the services, particularly the post office.

Next to the building is a playground and day-care center for the employees' children, right there on the grounds!

A couple of blocks down on the left were another of the brown brick buildings of the complex. There was a sign on the building: *Senter for Sosialt Nettverk og Helse, 4 etg.; Hudavdelingen.* Center for Social Network and Health, 4th floor; Skin Department. Obviously, the skin department was in the same building, but had nothing to do with the center where Dad worked. My father unlocked the door, and we walked up the four stories and through these large, heavy doors to the center. His office was spacious. Seth immediately tested out the computer on the desk, again relishing in his element.

After a little while, we walked downstairs. Blindern, the site of the University of Oslo campus, was about five to 10 minutes away, but we weren't sure how to walk there. We caught a cab. The driver was an American from Minnesota, who had married a Norwegian and moved to Norway.

At Blindern, we walked around and into the main plaza. This held another nostalgic memory. Twenty years before, at age 11, I would take the *trikk* by myself up to Blindern for Norwegian lessons with a student at the University. As Seth, my parents and I walked around, we came across another playground and day-care facility on the campus.

We found our way to the *trikk* stop. First, we stopped at the 7-Eleven. I bought potato chips; Seth, another Freia chocolate bar. After returning to the apartment, we took a rest. Seth and I wanted to take my parents to dinner to thank them for their hospitality, and we found out Peppe's Pizza was open. Peppe's was located around the corner from where we lived in 1969-70, but it had not been there then. Afterwards, we went home and watched Danny Kaye in *The Secret Life of Walter Mitty* on television.

It had been interesting to see the city so peaceful and silent, and so many stores and restaurants closed.

26 December 1990

The movie theaters opened, and Seth and I searched for a movie to see. The best offering turned out to be Mel Gibson in *Air America*. We headed to a *kino*, cinema, downtown. The price was 36 *kroner*, comparable to $6 in the United States. The ticket entitled you to a reserved seat, which was something different. The movie wasn't bad. I tried to read the Norwegian subtitles to catch the translation. I found it interesting that when a character talked about "intelligence," as in spying, it was translated as CIA. Virtually all films are imports. They have subtitles and no dubbing. One of the fun things for English-speaking foreigners is that we laugh before the Norwegians.

That evening, Odd Steffen, Ragnhild and Eivind came over for dinner/my parents' wedding anniversary. A trip to Norway isn't complete without the last dinner being with the Dalgards. As usual, it wasn't anything but warm and pleasant.

27 December 1990

The two weeks were over already. There were few or no direct flights during the week from Oslo to Newark. So, we had to catch an early morning flight to Stockholm, followed by a three-hour layover before the eight-hour flight to Newark. The Stockholm airport was a good distance from the center of town; so despite the three hours, it still wasn't enough time to look at the city.

The cab came quickly. We said our good-byes to my parents and were on our way. At Fornebu, we found the perfect souvenirs to bring back. Huge long bars of Freia chocolate – some plain, some with nuts. They came wrapped in sets of threes. It hadn't taken long for Seth to fall for Freia, the best chocolate in the world. It was a great gift for others, and us, particularly at work. It was a taste of Norway and could be shared among many people. It certainly placated our pallets. We bought several three-packs.

The flight to Stockholm took about 45 minutes. The layover was tedious, and the flight to Newark seemed like it lasted forever. I probably have never been on a plane that long. The line was long at immigration, and they refused to take us as a pair. After we finally passed through immigration, picked up our luggage and cleared customs, we called the limousine service.

When the van arrived, it was full of people going in opposite directions to us. There was a snowstorm on the way, so they radioed for another van to pick us up. Panic was in the air, and the ironies were starting already. We had just been in Norway, where the people were anxious *for* snow, not anxious *about* snow. This was our lucky day. We were the only ones on the van. Snow was starting to fall as we arrived in Philadelphia.

28 December 1990

We woke up the next morning, and 9-11 inches of snow had been dumped on Philadelphia. It created a paralysis in the city. I was stranded. Obviously, there was virtually no food in the house. Seth called and advised against driving because it was slippery. Eventually, I walked in the snow to the store.

Just a couple of days before, I had walked to and from the store with snow on the ground. My mother was doing that every day. There was little thinking about it.

Why now, I wondered, did it seem like an effort and a problem? I realized I should be walking to the store more often when the weather wasn't so bad.

A few days before, we wanted to see snow. Now, we had been dumped with more snow than had fallen in the two weeks in Norway, and we dreaded it. Of course, now we had to deal with it.

A few times over the next year, I would walk the approximate two miles to work in the snow, and some people would laugh. Yet, Norwegians wouldn't have. The feet are a means of transportation, too.

The year 1991 would be important and eventful, not just at work, but also in relation to Norway and the pursuit of *my* Olympic dream. And, 18 months later, I would arrive in Norway again.

Chapter 5
Summer 1992

The Puzzle Beginning to Come Together

The trip to Norway in the summer of 1992 cemented and reinforced my feelings for the country and people. It was quite a different trip than the others. I spent eight weeks in the country, the longest time since 1969-70, allowing me a special opportunity to study the language.

However, the time leading up to that visit was filled with anxiety, changes and excitement. The year 1991 started off with international tension, the outbreak of the Persian Gulf War. I never realized that the conflagration would have a Norwegian connection. When I was in Norway in December 1990, Eivind had been debating how to fulfill his Norwegian military service. If he went the regular route, it was a one-year commitment; if he chose the conscientious objector status, he would do community service for 18 months.

I received a letter from my father, dated January 14, 1991, in which he said that the Norwegians had set up a military hospital 300 kilometers from the Saudi Arabia-Kuwaiti border. *"Eivind is starting his military service as a doctor next week. He told us that the army is asking for volunteers. If they don't get enough, they will have to send personnel there. As you can imagine, he is very concerned...Ragnhild told us that the top staff at Ullevål Hospital had a meeting to plan the care of military personnel that are chemical warfare victims..."*

Two days later, on January 16, the war, with all its complexities, began. I woke my parents up with a one a.m. Norway-time phone call. Eivind was never called to Kuwait.

In January, I also began my search. Following Frode Nielsen's advice, I sought a Norwegian who could help me become more fluent in the language. It proved difficult, but the search finally took me to the linguistics department at the University of Pennsylvania and then a German language teacher. She knew a Norwegian student who might be interested and gave me the young man's telephone number. During the course of my search, I had found a woman who was also looking for a Norwegian teacher. When I located the student, I telephoned her.

One evening, we met at Nicolai's apartment. It was his feeling that I was beginning at a different level than she was, so teaching both of us would impede the progress of each. He *offered* to find another teacher for her.

Nicolai and I, however, got right down to business. I had begun a draft of a letter to Frode in Norwegian and English, and we worked on the Norwegian. As he went over the letter, he gave me tips on how to approach a job search in Norway. "Norwegians are a laid-back people. You don't have to be as aggressive in your letter(s) as in the United States."

At the end of the session, I made a comment about sending both the English and Norwegian letters.

"Why would you want to send the English letter?" he asked. "It'll be more impressive if you send the Norwegian one."

He sent me home from the first session with copies of Norwegian papers to read.

Over the next year, I committed myself to working with Nicolai to learn Norwegian. It was not easy, considering my heavy schedule. Usually, on days when I didn't have games to cover, I would ride the train to Penn after work. We would meet at the Wharton School – where he was studying – and search for an empty room or space to work. Sometimes, we would buy soda and junk food, and spread out at a table.

He would bring *Nytt fra Norge* (News from Norway), a paper for Norwegians in foreign lands. It's like the *Herald Tribune* for Norwegians, except it's more biased.

Nevertheless, *Nytt fra Norge* was my learning tool. I translated articles and gained Norwegian perspectives on certain issues. Soon, we were conversing with each other regularly. I would write letters to friends in Norway and occasionally to Frode and the personnel director at the Lillehammer Olympic Organizing Committee. Nicolai would review and correct them.

Between our sessions, I somehow squeezed in the study time. Sometimes, it was at 11 p.m., after a 14-hour day with double-header basketball games, or in a hotel room on a road trip. I also had my own motivational tools. The poster with the Lillehammer Olympic logo that Frode had given me was framed, and on the wall. Next to it was a poster I had for a number of years with a quote from Langston Hughes: *"Hold fast to dreams for if dreams die, life is a broken winged bird that cannot fly."*

I would play David Foster's *Winter Games*, the theme song from the 1988 Games, and other Olympic-related music to keep me focused on my goal.

When Nicolai returned to Norway during the summer of '91, I tried as best I could to keep up with my studies. We resumed our meetings in the fall of '91, and I was feeling better about my command of Norwegian.

In December 1991, I received the most pleasant surprise, a Christmas card of Olympic artwork from Frode! I was overwhelmed. I would display it in my living room for years. It is not often one can say they received a Christmas card from someone they met on a job visit.

In December, Nicolai graduated, meaning I would need a new instructor. He left for Norway before he could give me the name of a Norwegian friend at Penn. I tried to track Nicolai down, finally reaching him at a party in Oslo. He got on the phone and said, "I'm here with a lot of Norwegians. You should be here. You would have plenty of opportunities to practice your Norwegian."

He assured me he would get back to me. By January 1992, I had not heard anything and got anxious. I decided to contact the Norwegian soccer goalie at

Drexel, who I knew from Drexel-Textile games and had met on the plane to Oslo in December 1990. Rune was interested, and we began the lessons – he, too, received *Nytt fra Norge*. (Of course, the day after I talked with Rune, Nicolai called.) The meeting place just moved down the street from Penn to the Drexel campus in West Philadelphia.

One of the highlights of our work was when Rune gave me a compact disc of a popular Norwegian singer, Jahn Teigen, who was from his town. I translated the lyrics into English.

In January 1992, I received a booklet on my desk at work about the International Summer School at the University of Oslo. I never found out who sent it to me. Six weeks of study, touring and meeting people from around the world. The school offered many interesting courses, but most notably, for me, was the intensive study of Norwegian. It seemed perfect, studying the language daily and being able to be in Norway at the same time.

The previous September, I had started dating a woman, Alice. She taught English as a second language to Cambodian children in a public school. She was interested in other cultures and expressed interest in attending the school. We both applied. The problem for me would be to get the time off.

Change was amiss again at work. Yet, another public relations director came aboard and another athletic director left. In the latter case, the associate athletic director moved up. The new public relations director seemed on a mission to clean house and finally suc-ceeded. In May, after six years, I was no longer part of Textile. It was right at the deadline when we could inform the International Summer School of our decision to attend.

In many ways, I was relieved to be free of the pres-sure at work of the last several months. I could now also look forward to school, a significant amount of time in Norway, and being with people from different countries.

In addition, I had been in touch with the personnel director at the Lillehammer Olympic Organizing Committee, who told me to call when I reached Oslo. The Olympic dream was still alive.

Maybe, the pieces of the puzzle would be coming together.

Monday, 29 June 1992

"Travel is fatal to prejudice, bigotry and narrow-mindedness."

-Mark Twain

We made it! We went through the first day of class still tired from the long two-day trip – some 31 hours awake. The flight over was okay on British Airways. The food was good, and our seats were on the second floor of the 747.

We had a four-and-a-half-hour layover in London before our flight to Oslo. We were sitting in the cafeteria in Hearthrow when a woman turned to us and asked, "Would you like the rest of this sandwich? I'm full."

"Where are you from?" Alice asked.

"I'm going to Norway," the woman answered.

The three of us spent the next four hours together. She was a deaconess in the Lutheran church, returning from a conference in Canada. She talked about having rented a bike in Canada, which delighted Alice, a bicyclist herself. Ana suggested a place in Oslo where one could rent bikes, and the name of an old friend to ask for. She lived near Maridal, and talked of swimming in a lake nearby. Alice brightened again, since she likes swimming in lakes.

Ana grew up in Tolvsrød, the same town where Rune, my Norwegian tutor lives, about a half-kilometer from him! She is 32, married, with two sons, six and a year-and-a-half.

Alice found a travelers' Scrabble game in an airport store. We laughed as Ana tried to use Norwegian words and struggled with the English ones. I had a chance to experiment a little with my Norwegian. Though we were at different ends of the plane, we saw each other when we got off. Alice and I said to Ana: *"Så hyggelig å møte deg."* ("So nice to meet you.") Ana invited us for dinner some day after she returned from her vacation. At the baggage claim, there were hugs before we separated. Alice had met her first nice Norwegian, and made her first Norwegian friend.

The second was on the other side of the hall. Eivind met us at Fornebu (with a car). The plane landed at 4:45; we were outside shortly after five. We dragged the luggage to his illegally parked car and managed to cram all the luggage into the small car. Alice and I went back into the airport to exchange money, which took a couple of minutes, while Eivind moved to a legal spot, never telling us where to look for him. He came inside to look for us, while we waited outside. We finally met again.

When Alice saw the fjord surrounding the airport, she said she would love to swim in it. Eivind offered to take her. He invited us to Olav's birthday party, but we told Eivind we needed to check in at Blindern. The opening ceremonies were that night. He drove us to the campus. On the way, I practiced my Norwegian with Eivind. At one point, he replied in Norwegian that I had a good grasp of the language, but I didn't follow all that he said. He responded in Dalgard humor, "I take that back."

We checked in and met JoAnn Kleber, the North American administrator for the Summer School, who knew who we were right away. Eivind helped us with the baggage. The room, located in the main dormitory building (*studenterhjem*), had a beautiful view of the courtyard and the Oslofjord. Alice and I went downstairs for a quick dinner before going to the program, which was being held at the Aula auditorium on the downtown campus. At dinner, we sat next to a young man, who started to talk to us. He was from New Jersey! Imagine that, the first person we meet is from a neighboring state!

Tuesday, 30 June 1992

The school had rented four buses to transport us to the Aula, the auditorium at the University of Oslo campus in Sentrum for the opening ceremonies on Sunday. The transportation system is on strike on the weekends after 5:30 p.m.

The Aula is a beautiful hall with a large Edvard Munch painting of blazing rays of the sun on the wall. There were paintings on the sidewalls, but I don't know who the artist(s) were. We were entertained by a quartet that sang music by Norwegian composer Edvard Grieg, as well as other songs. There were some speeches, mostly repetitious; the best speech was by the rector of the University. Because of all the fatigue, I can't remember much of what he said. The ceremony concluded with the singing of *"Ja vi elske"* (Yes we love), the Norwegian national anthem.

There was a reception back at Blindern, but I spent much of the time facing one of the great challenges of Norway – using the pay telephones. I lost many *kroner* trying. I was calling Torbjørn, and we could barely hear each other. Finally, a woman at the reception desk showed me how to use the phone. You have to lay two one *krone* coins at the top of the phone, rather than putting them in coin slots. They fall in only when the connection goes through, so there is a delay after the person picks up the phone on the other end. There is one phone where you deposit coins in the slot and can use one, five or 10 *krone(r)* coins. Anyway, I finally reached Torbjørn, and we arranged our visit to Rauland. He, Debbie and the two girls (there was a new child) were leaving for the United States the next day, so it was important to reach him.

I found Alice talking to an older Norwegian gentleman. I had a conversation in Norwegian with him. It was gratifying to be able to have Norwegian conversations and understand signs on the first day in Oslo. After learning Norwegian through newspapers and some conversation, it had made me wonder how well that could be "translated" to the real country.

Our first full day yesterday showed that a tape recorder should always be handy because you never knew who you would meet. There are 490 students from 71 countries here.

It's a weird feeling that we're really part of something international. A requirement of the program is to have some knowledge of English. But you see people in different attire, with different color hair, with different skin color and hear English spoken with so many accents. This is probably as diverse as Norway will get, or many other countries for that matter.

At breakfast yesterday, we sat with four women from Mauritius, Bhouten and Bangladesh. Later, a man from Russia, Sultan, sat down. He was studying Peace Research at the Summer School, and was interested in conflict resolution.

Yesterday morning, class rosters were posted outside the administration building. As I walked into the main courtyard of the University and past the fountain, memories came back. I had walked here on my last visit to Norway. Here I was, going to a Norwegian class at Blindern 22 years after I made the trip by *trikk* to Blindern as an 11-year-old to take Norwegian lessons with Bodil. I got a lump in my throat as I reflected on the memory.

There were 17 students in this class, and we sat around rectangular desks set up in a "semi-circle" side-by-side. There were eight men in the class. "Most" of the students were American, but 11 nationalities were represented. An Iranian and an Iraqi sat next to each other. This was unusual, considering their countries had recently been at war with each other. To my left, sat women from Lithuania, Estonia and Latvia. Also represented were Rumania, Canada, Germany, Portugal and Italy. A Portuguese student was a woman studying the Science of Sport at the University in Lisbon.

For me, the class was easy, the basic "My name is..." (*"Jeg heter..."*). The teacher, Gunnar, at one point split us into pairs making sure there were not two people who spoke the same language. We were to ask questions of each other in Norwegian. My level of Norwegian was higher so that when I asked what was a simple question to me, the Estonian woman didn't understand.

There was another Mike in the class, from Minnesota. He was a sportswriter who quit his job to attend the ISS and also had an interest in working at the Olympics. Eerie.

The Norwegian test to be placed at a higher level was given again at one, an hour after the class ended. The test included dictation, writing an essay and filling in blanks.

30 June 1992, 12:52 p.m.

Still trying to finish yesterday's activities. I wrote the essay on the placement exam. Dictation was okay, but the woman spoke faster as she went on and didn't mention periods or commas, so I hope I put them in the right place. The dictation was about care for the elderly in Norway, and I would be interested in knowing more about the subject. The "fill in the blanks" was difficult because I didn't understand everything in the text.

Alice is taking two classes – "Elementary Norwegian" and "Norwegian Culture and Society." The latter class is taught by a Kenyan sociologist who has lived in Norway for 25 years.

Wednesday, 1 July 1992

I was moved up to Intensive Intermediate Norwegian, and it was quite different. I went from being one of the best, if not the best in the class, to being confused. The entire class is conducted in Norwegian, as was most of the elementary class. But I was going from *"Hva heter du?"* ("What is your name?") to trying to understand exercises. Students must talk in Norwegian. Questions must be asked in Norwegian, and the teacher replies in Norwegian. I was confused about the first exercise. We were split into groups. I was with a woman from Slovakia and one from Japan, neither of whom seemed to speak much English. As the class went on, however, I understood more.

Back on Monday, there were economic and political lectures in the evening, as part of an "Introduction to Norway" series for the students. The economist caused somewhat of a stir. He talked about market economics; how Norwegians should take on more responsibility for themselves, such as contributing something toward health care; and about looking at the U.S. model.

An American student questioned his use of an American model pointing out the statistics on unemployment, homelessness, etc., in the United States. The economist's answers were glib.

One questioner said, "Isn't a little unemployment good to make people appreciate having a job?" That didn't sit well with me.

The political speaker said it's not easy to use Norway as a model either because it is such a small country. However, by the same token, it is hard to look positively to the U.S. model with all the problems we have.

As Alice and I discussed the lectures while we were walking back to the dorm, a man suddenly turned to us and asked, "Have you ever been to a Communist country?"

Angel was from Bulgaria. He told us of some of the hardships in Bulgaria. He was a secondary school teacher, but he said students were not very motivated because they were not optimistic about the future. The girls were interested in finding the guy with a car. People could be shot for dissent. "A group of old men decide what people should like and dislike," he said.

However, it was mutual education because he was surprised to hear from us about the situation in America. He was surprised to hear about the unemployment and health-care problems.

Alice mentioned she liked Bulgarian music. Angel said the older people knew the ethnic dances and music, but the young people were more interested in American pop music. He said he had a tape of Bulgarian folk music if we were interested in listening to it some time.

As we walked toward the entrance of the *studenterhjem*, Sultan, the Russian we met earlier in the day, was sitting on a bench. He invited us to sit down. He's not comfortable with his English and tries so hard to communicate with us, but has a hard time understanding us. I thought I understood he was from Moscow. He was an ethnographer at an academy of technology and anthropology, studying nutrition in the tradition of the people. He invited us to hear him play Russian music on the guitar. We said we'd love to, but at another time. We settled on tomorrow night.

Tuesday night's long lecture was on Art in Norway. I was extremely exhausted. We had gone full throttle since we arrived, with little time to rest from the trip. I haven't felt well and have had trouble eating. Food is okay, but there's little choice.

We walked in Frogner Park Monday, and on Tuesday around the harbor. At Frogner Park, once again, I was visiting the statues. How appropriate! The Vigeland statues represent the cycles of life. There are statues of children and adults. My trips to Norway spanned cycles of my own life. I played here amidst the statues as a child; as an adult, I admired them as art. Since then, I had been through many emotional peaks and valleys, just like the representations in the statues.

To create the statues took a large part of Gustav Vigeland's (1867-1943) life, 40 years worth. There are nearly 200 sculptures with 600 figures over 80 acres of the Park. On the bridge are 58 copper figures. The Monolith, with its tower of sculpted bodies, stands 17 meters high and took 14 years for the stonemasons to finish. There was a team that did the stone carvings. Vigeland donated his works to the city for a home, a studio and a salary. His home and studio is now the

Vigeland Museum across the street from Frogner Park. He first discussed the idea in 1900 when he submitted a sketch of six men holding a fountain. Vigeland never lived to see the completion of the Park.[22]

The statues impressed Alice.

The Park was, of course, near Majorstua Skole, and we took a quick look at the schoolyard.

I have never seen anyone in my class again. I never wrote to them, or they to me. Sometime through the years, I lost the notebook with their addresses, probably not even thinking I would ever get back to Norway. Since I have returned to Norway, my curiosity is piqued about what it would be like if I met some of them again. I remember many first names, but not many last names of the boys in the class, so it would be hard to find them. They would have their memories, just as I have mine. But also time has passed, and as the cliché goes, "Time heals all wounds." Perhaps, it is time to forget some of the bad episodes. Optimistically, I think things would be different, probably awkward at first. The years have passed; we are adults, and we are no longer on that playground.

I took a bus tour today with those who missed Saturday's tour. Alice missed it because of a class field trip. The tour made me feel a little better, and I got something of a "rush" seeing familiar sites, particularly Holmenkollen and Frognerseteren. I tried to add to the guide's talk. I knew which *trikk* to take to Holmenkollen while she didn't.

Tonight, we visited with the Dalgards – Odd Steffen, Ragnhild and Eivind. It was a pleasant stay, as per usual. We talked about the lectures we had heard the previous evenings. Odd Steffen told us the economist was from the conservative wing of the Labor Party.

The weather has been somewhat cool with some rain during the last couple of nights. Rain is serenading us

---

[22] *Scanorama* (magazine of Scandinavian Airlines System), August, 1992.

tonight as opposed to the previous nights of guitar-playing students on the steps outside.

Tuesday, 7 July 1992

It's been almost a week since I last wrote some notes. There was difficulty adjusting to the first week, and the food has been unimpressive. Berit called Sunday night, and we had a pleasant conversation. She wants to invite us for dinner. The problem with making plans is working things around class schedules, the meal times, study time and recreation. Alice has a lot of homework in both classes. She seems to have more Norwegian homework than I do.

9:40 p.m.

I never thought I'd say "Thank God for 7-Eleven," least of all in Norway. There's one down the hill from the *studenterhjem*, at the *trikk* stop. It's been a great study break the last two nights. I craved Maarud (Norwegian brand) potato chips last night and made a run to 7-Eleven. Tonight, I finished my homework, and I went for a Freia (Norwegian brand) chocolate bar. Nothing like something good to eat to make you feel more at home – in Norway – and to make you feel better. It's a piece of "home" in two ways! Seeing an American store with my favorite Norwegian junk food! Like the 7-Elevens at home, the prices are high.

Class is getting better, although it is still complicated trying to understand everything being said. The workbook finally came into the bookstore today, so now I'll be able to do the exercises and keep up better. The translations we have to do are, at least, interesting to me. We've been translating text about the immigration problems in Norway, racism, cultural conflicts, and whether these immigrant groups should give up their cultural identities and assimilate into Norwegian society.

Yesterday, Audun, the teacher, split the class up into two sides to debate cultural identity in Norway, with another group of students serving as judges. I was one of the three who were supposed to be "judges." It really ended up as a discussion rather than a debate. But everybody spoke in Norwegian.

For today, we had to translate a story about the Vikings. Two women students, Erica from Vancouver, B.C., and Shayna, from Miami, acted the story out in class, using tennis rackets as swords and a paper cup as a helmet. It helped to lighten up the atmosphere of the class.

The first day I came to the Intermediate class, the teacher began the session by having the class sing a song they had learned in a previous class! On Friday, he taught us to sing *Happy Birthday* in Norwegian because it was a student's birthday. Audun brought in cookies to celebrate the occasion.

On Friday night, Alice and I walked to Sognsvann with a woman from Hungary. Sognsvann is a beautiful lake north of the campus. People can swim in the lake. It was almost an hour's walk. But there was plenty of light, and it was an energetic walk. Originally, Sultan and his friend were to join us but somehow they got lost in translation after dinner. It would have been an East-West walk (Eastern bloc-Americans).

Norway has laws to preserve the trees. I think 75% of Oslo has trees and/or forests, earning it the nickname as "The Country Capital." Approximately 25% of Norway is forest area.[23] Sognsvann was surrounded by trees, including small islands of green-leaved trees. A 1957 law established the right of anyone to use mountain and forest areas for leisure activity, even when they are private property. Hiking, putting up a tent, making a bonfire for cooking, picking a few berries for personal

[23] Arne Selbyg, *Norway Today: An Introduction to Modern Norwegian Society*, Norwegian University Press, 1987, and a 1995 correspondence with Mr. Selbyg. Used with permission 2005.

use are all permitted. There are also laws governing forestry, protecting areas of nature, establishing zoning regulations, requiring government permission before buildings can be put up and establishing natural and national parks.

By the lake was a geese family, which we closely observed. An older goose seemed to stand guard, which we assumed was the father. The other adult therefore had to be the mother. There were three babies. It was interesting to watch the mother and children as they nibbled and pecked at the grass. There were also birds, which looked like gulls, except they were brown and white.

We took the bus and *trikk* back to Blindern and went to the "disco party," where they raffled off travel tickets and played loud music.

On Saturday, Alice's "Culture and Society" class went to Rygge in the *kommune* of Råde, and Moss. I tagged along. In Rygge, we met with farmers. First, we visited Ole's family farm.

He was married with four kids. His wife's mother was also there. His farm was about 40-45 acres, one of the smaller ones in Norway, but one of the larger ones in Rygge. This was one of five farms in the area that had milking cows. We got to meet them "up close and personal."

Our guide was Tor. As self-conscious Norwegians will often do, he said, "My English isn't so good. I speak it only once a year."

Our Norwegian once a year should be as good as his English! We then went to his farm, which was about 60 acres. He grows oats, barley and wheat. His wife and 15-year-old son were there. She had prepared lunch for us – open-faced sandwiches, cakes – which was unexpected.

After lunch, Tor discussed farming in Norway. There are 100,000 farmers in Norway, a country whose land is only three percent agricultural. As of 1991, only 5% of Norwegians worked in farming. There were 672 farms with 125 acres or more of farming area in 1989.[24] Almost all of the American farms are larger than 100 acres, said Tor.

The average size in Rygge is 30 acres; 25 for the rest of the country, according to Tor.

Norwegian farming is very much a family business. There are few, or no, hired hands. (In 1989, only 10 percent of the work was done by hired hands.) The oldest child can purchase the farm, but it is getting more difficult for the next generation to do that. For 23 percent of the farmers, 90 percent of their livelihood comes from farming, Tor told us. Among the other produce of Norwegian farms are beef, pork, mutton, chicken, eggs, potatoes and vegetables. They earn 140,000 Norwegian *kroner* (@$24,960) per farm. That includes 16,000 NOK (Norwegian *kroner*) from the government (@$2,560). This is in return for certain "advantages" the farmer has. One is the lack of travel to work. Tor said the government sees working on holidays and weekends as an advantage, whereas the farmers don't necessarily agree. The government has some good and bad policies, according to Tor. Fifty percent of the food is imported. There are heavy restrictions against spraying and artificial colorings. However, the government tries to limit the amount of milk produced in Norway. Farmers are paid four NOK (@64 cents) per liter of milk for only the first 100,000 liters per year. Above that is 30 *øre* (@five cents) per liter. The 16,000 NOK subsidy is paid to all farmers regardless of the size of the farm, according to Tor.[25]

The two families were quite hospitable, and we had collective photos taken. We then went to Moss where there was an art museum with an exhibit of Russian icons. The museum was next to a lake with pretty Norwegian scenery.

Alice ventured into the water but it was too cold.

---

[24] Arne Selbyg, *Norway Today: An Introduction to Modern Norwegian Society*, Norwegian University Press, 1987, and a 1995 correspondence with Mr. Selbyg. Used with permission 2005.
[25] Ibid.

Sunday we finally got out to Bygdøy to see the Folk-museum, Vikingship and Fram. The *Kon-Tiki/Ra* Museum closed before we could get to it. We took the ferry from Rådhus to Bygdøy and back. We saw the Norwegian folk dance exhibition at the Folkmuseum, and I took many pictures of the colorfully dressed dancers. Everything had been rushed these first days and were not the usual introductory days – or food – I was used to on previous trips. I had been moody, but now that I was seeing some familiar sites and getting off campus for a while, I was feeling better.

We ate dinner at a vegetarian restaurant in town, which was quite good, and a change of pace from the stuff we were getting at the cafeteria. Then, it was back to Blindern to do homework.

There are numerous activities – maybe too many – organized by the ISS and the students. There is the Continental (although it should be the Intercontinental) Football Cup, a soccer league with teams representing the United States, Africa, Norway, Asia, Western Europe, Eastern Europe/Baltic States. The opening game between USA and Africa was advertised around the *studenterhjem*. It was played yesterday on an overgrown grass field behind the main *studenterhjem* building. One goal has netting, the other just posts. Africa dominated, winning 11-1, but no one tore the place down. And it didn't seem to matter that a Lithuanian played for the Americans. When I wasn't taking pictures, I sat with Sultan, and we broke chocolate together. Now, there's going to be a "Wimbledon" tennis tournament.

We missed a trip to Frogner Park tonight led by the art history professor because of homework. Will miss tomorrow's tour of *Stortinget* (the Parliament) because Alice's "Culture and Society Class" has another field trip.

The weather has been nice, so people will study outside, play games, or hang out by the steps in front of the main building, talking or playing musical instruments. We studied at the picnic tables by the building last night. A Belgian woman sat down to talk with us. Then her roommate, who was from Croatia, joined us. It doesn't take much to evoke responses from students from some of the Eastern bloc countries. The Croatian woman was quite bitter about the war. "The Serbs attacked us...This Communism was the silliest idea ever come up with."

She tried to avoid tears.

Alice is motivated by her classes, but overloaded with homework. The field trips have been disruptive to other activities. Tomorrow, she'll not only miss the tour of the *Stortinget*, but we had plans to meet Eivind and Angela at the Munch Museum and then have dinner with them and the Dalgard family. Fortunately, we were able to reschedule it for Thursday. The work is also cutting down on socializing with the other students outside the cafeteria and class.

We've met a nice German couple from Manheim, Matthias and Astrid, who have attended ISS before. They helped us with our Norwegian homework last week. I hope to play some tennis with them.

Wednesday, 15 July 1992, 8:36 a.m.

Another attempt to get a couple of quick thoughts down.

We had a "real" Norwegian meal of salmon, potatoes, cucumber salad, strawberries and ice cream at Eivind and Angela's. We spoke some Norwegian, but the family talk was too fast. It was amusing trying to pick up words here and there.

All the Dalgards have a sense of humor, and there were some funny moments.

Olav had trouble opening a bottle of cognac. Odd sat confidently in his chair, saying, "Give it to me. Let me try it."

Olav was trying to resist. "He beats me in tennis. He beats me in cross-country skiing."

But, Olav finally handed the bottle over to his father. Twist, snap, open!

Ragnhild, a nurse, discussed the strange case of a 49-year-old woman, who tested positive for being pregnant. But, it was believed that she might have a tumor instead. The bizarre part was it was thought that the woman was pregnant "in the liver!" Well, at the table were one doctor (Eivind), one almost doctor (Olav) and a psychiatrist (Odd). Dr. Eivind made his diagnosis; then (almost) Dr. Olav chimed in with his, and also Dr. Odd.

"You tell a story and get two medical opinions and the psychological," I said to Ragnhild.

"It's worse when Florence (Olav's girlfriend) is here, because she's a doctor, too!" she said. "Odd is just interested in what they say. I come for support, and I get diagnoses!"

Somewhere along the line, the conversation became a little more serious as we discussed memories of World War II. I learned that Odd's father had been a political prisoner during the war.

After dinner, Eivind, Odd, Olav, Alice and I took a walk around the East side of Oslo, supposedly the bad side of town because that's where most of the Asian immigrants live, particularly the Pakistanis. One of the few similarities to an American "bad" side of town – that was evident to us – was some graffiti. We walked through a park area and by a stream. The neighborhood was not rundown, like an American slum, and still seemed to have a high standard of living.

"I like a variation of people," Eivind said.

Eivind and Olav said the buildings had been torn down in certain sections and rebuilt. Higher rents were charged, forcing the people living there to move to rural areas. Over the last 10 years, there has been an increase in immigration to Norway because it has been open to accepting immigrants. While the government has attempted to create special-language programs, the mood among Norwegians is mixed. If you talk with people like the Dalgards or Berit, who we saw today, they are going to be open to a "varied" population.

"Norway has been in an isolated situation for a long time," said Berit. "The people feel that the Norwegian way is the best."

There is an undercurrent of racism and prejudice among segments of the populace who feel unemployment will increase; that too much money is being spent on special programs for the immigrants; that the immigrants should give up their culture and completely assimilate into Norwegian society, and that Norway should be for Norwegians. Then again, the immigrants are not required to learn Norwegian and tend to cluster with each other. Curiously, these issues are included in some of the material our class has translated.

Last year, I translated an article from *Nytt fra Norge*, about a demonstration by 10,000 Norwegians against racism, which outnumbered those attending a rally calling for restrictions on immigration. The anti-racism demonstrators forced the others to abandon the site.

Earlier that day (July 9), I walked to Ullevål *Sykehus* (Hospital) to meet with people who work with my father. I spent most of the time with John Ivar, who was very friendly. We spoke mostly in Norwegian. I also met Ragnhild (Særtre) briefly; Mette, the secretary, and a younger man whose name escapes me.

The highlight of Friday (the 10th) was when I went to a travel bureau in *Sentrum* to arrange our trip to Bergen. We were closed out of the school's excursion. I arranged the whole trip speaking Norwegian, which made me proud. Later, the bill didn't look "right," probably because it looked so cheap. In a country where everything is so expensive, 570 *kroner* for two people to take a train to Bergen and fly back is pretty good. That's approximately $95 plus 132 *kroner* for the boat from Flåm to Gudvangen and a bus from Gudvangen to Voss. Also, we got 50 percent off as students. *(Note: When I got my VISA bill when I returned home, the airline tickets were on the statement along with the 570 kroner. They were billed separately. The airline tickets were 390 kroner each or @$67.25. The ferry was 43 kroner each at half price and* *the bus 43 kroner with no discount. So the total was 1,522 kroner for two, still a bargain at @$262.41.)*

The highlight, Saturday (the 11th), was going to the Holmenkollen Ski Jump and then walking to Frognerseteren Restaurant. It was a perfectly clear day, providing excellent views of the city below. Alice was impressed by the immenseness of Holmenkollen, but it's hard not to be. Then, we enjoyed the walk to Frognerseteren. At Frognerseteren Restaurant, we had the obligatory *eplekake med krem* (apple cake with whipped cream). Alice was overwhelmed by the view and the quiet, serene atmosphere.

We walked down to the road to inspect these old-style wood Norwegian buildings, similar to the ones in the Folkmuseum. We asked a couple if they knew what the buildings were for and if they were still in use. They were buildings that had been part of a farm that used to be there. The next thing we knew, the man was driving us around the area, showing us different views. He was a bridge engineer. After the tour, he dropped us off at the *trikk* station.

On Sunday (the 12th), we visited two museums I had never been to – the Oslo City Museum in Frogner Park and the Vigeland Museum. The City Museum details the history of the city through geography, athletics, education, transportation, fire companies, police and housing. The museum is in an old converted barn. It was one of the few museums that didn't have English descriptions, but I was able to understand many of the Norwegian captions.

Across the street is the Vigeland Museum, which is just as impressive as the statues in the park across the street. The museum was the studio and home of Gustav Vigeland, where he worked on the statues to be put in the park. You see models of the figures that are in the park and realize he did these immense figures many times. There's a real impact when you see the figures of the men holding up the fountain, up close and life-size;

when you see up close the objects within the tree figures that are in plates around the fountain in the park.

What is also impressive is realizing the famous Norwegians who were alive at the same time as Vigeland: Edvard Munch, playwrights Henrik Ibsen and Bjørn Bjørnsen, composer Edvard Grieg. What geniuses! And Vigeland made a statue of each of them!

I was intrigued by one of poet Henrik Wergeland, with figures hanging onto Wergeland. The non-Jewish poet fought for the rights of Jews to live in Norway, and I wondered if these figures represented the Jews.

It's interesting that the pictures on Norwegian money at one time were of these cultural heroes – Ibsen, Bjørnsen, Wergeland.

We walked down to Peppe's Pizza for a different meal, and the two of us actually devoured a huge one (about 158 *kroner*, @$26).

Earlier in the day at breakfast, we wound up at a table with two men from Mozambique, one from Tanzania, one from Vietnam and a woman from Ireland. They were talking about Mozambique politics. It was just another experience of the diversity of people here.

On Monday night (the 13th), the political committee sponsored a talk about apartheid, presented by four South African students (actually one, with a panel of three others) attending ISS. It was impressive and attended by almost 100 people! The room was decorated with posters and South African flags (African National Congress).

Today, we visited Berit, and it was a delightful time. She lives down the road from Sognsvann. We took the bus this time. She served us lunch – much more inviting than the *studenterhjem* – on her terrace, which has the best view of the Oslofjord. Breathtaking and relaxing. Alice hit it off with Berit, who works in child development and teaches teachers how to deal with kindergarten students.

We also discussed the status of women in Norwegian society. Berit said many women come from households where the mother was a central figure who worked in the house while the father was away fishing (to support the family). Berit had taken the data dealing with my father's first Norwegian research in 1969-70 when she was his research associate and found a correlation between the level of education of the mother and the aspirations and self-esteem of the male children. She also said women are more accepted or taken for granted as being part of the workforce and government. A large percentage of the Parliament are women (59 of 165 as of June 1991[26] and 36 percent in 1992[27]), and the country's prime minister and the Mayor of Oslo are women.

Yesterday, I was able to arrange an interview with the personnel director at the Lillehammer Olympic Organizing Committee for 23 July. It was quite an achievement with the pay phones. The phone cut us off the first time the personnel consultant got on the line, and I had no more *kroner*. I must have spent 20 *kroner* on the call. I tried to speak Norwegian, but it was hard with the phone problems. She spoke very fast. I understood enough to know the appointment was for 11:30 a.m. on 23 July.

Tuesday, 21 July 1992, 12:30 p.m.

Well, what do you know, *another* week has passed since the last entry.

The highlight of the week was the long weekend to and in Bergen. Classes were cancelled Thursday (the 16th) and Friday (the 17th) for the ISS trip to Bergen. As mentioned previously, we were closed out of the school trip because of numbers and arranged our own.

I can best relate the trip by translating my composition for class from the **Norwegian** – minus the grammatical mistakes – and then add some other details.

"It can be good or bad that Bergen is at the end of the trip from Oslo. The trip is so special, exciting, beautiful

---

[26] *New York Times*, June 1991.
[27] Arne Selbyg, 1995. Used with permission 2005.

and dramatic that Bergen can be anticlimactic. But, Bergen itself is a charming city with historic buildings and mountains. So, it is good to know that Bergen awaits at the end of the trip.

"On Thursday, we traveled 12 hours from Oslo to Bergen. First, we took a train to Myrdal, then another train down to Flåm, winding around the mountain on the descent. From Flåm, we traveled by ferry to Gudvangen, then by bus to Voss, and then by train from Voss to Bergen. One sees the most beautiful views in the world on this trip – the mountains, fjords and waterfalls!

"The Norwegian workers on the trains and buses were courteous and humorous. At the beginning of the trip on the first train, the driver welcomed us by saying, 'Have a nice day traveling through the mountains with us!' He told us when the train approached the highest point in the mountains. The views get better as the trip continues. We even saw snow as well as green landscape, and the most remote houses. We thought, 'What do the people do who live here?' The trees grow out of the mountains. It was natural beauty; the water was clear and unpolluted.

"On the next train, we saw many waterfalls. Some began at the top of the mountain, and the water flowed down to the base. The engineer stopped the train by a large fall so the passengers could take photographs. (At Flåm, we took the ferry.) The boat moved around the fjords, and at one time, we went near a pretty fall so people could take photographs. It was windy, and if one stood up from the chair, the chair blew along the deck. From a distance, the fjords seemed to be together, as one, but when the boat moved nearer, it was two fjords and the boat went between them.

"The bus trip from Gudvangen to Voss can be a nervous, harrowing experience because the roads are narrow and uphill with steep views down the mountain. At one point, the driver drove around the curve, and another bus was coming from the other direction. Another time, the driver said, 'The back of the bus is now two meters lower than the front of the bus.' But, we came to Voss, and took the train to Bergen.

"The planning and building of the railroads and roads are a tribute to Norwegian science, knowledge and technology. In Friday's *Bergen Tidene*, there was an article about a book about the building of the Flåmbanen.

"Bergen is a charming city which has maintained its old flavor with historical buildings. We visited the open-air fish market by the harbor and bought fresh shrimp. We went to the Bryggen Museum, which has historical material from the Middle Ages that was discovered during the archaeological digs in Bergen from 1955-72.

"På lørdag tok vi banen til Fløien, hvor man kan se en utsikt over byen og området. (When I write the Norwegian, I slip into English; now I'm writing English and slipping into Norwegian!)

"On Saturday, we took the funicular to Fløien where one can see a view over the city and the surrounding area. We went on a hike to the top of the mountain, and saw a view of the fjords *men ikke byen* – (oops!), but not the city. It took almost two hours going uphill and only 30 minutes to go down. Later, we went to the aquarium and enjoyed watching the seals.

"We stayed in the home of friends. There were beautiful views to the water and fjords from the windows."

The technology of the railroads and roads through the mountains is a marvel. The Flåmbanen has four levels of tracks in the mountain. From the article in the Bergen paper – what I've translated so far – it was believed to be technically impossible to build. Flåmbanen took 20 years to complete, from 1920-40, and cost 20,000,000 *kroner*.

Alice was nervous on the bus – "I've never been on a trip like this and don't ever want to be again!" she said, echoing a refrain uttered by many other tourists who have traveled on this route.

After arriving in Bergen, we walked from the train to Morris Gardner's. Using the map, I remembered from the 1990 trip how to get to his apartment. He welcomed us and offered us some eggplant for dinner before sending us on our way. His mother was visiting from the United States. He apologized for being busy the next couple of days, but said, perhaps on Sunday, we could take a walk together. It rained Sunday morning, so we didn't see Morris again.

From Morris', we walked to Liv's house, a walk of about 45 minutes to an hour. Liv and the youngest daughter, Rebekka, were away and the oldest daughter, Rachel, was in and out. We had breakfast with her on Friday.

Alice enjoyed Bergen. She particularly liked the hikes. One of the wonderful things about Norway is that, within the city limits, nature, in the "form" of mountains, forests, parks and water exists and is accessible to the people. And the people take advantage of the surroundings, both in the city and in the rural areas we passed on the train. People on the train(s) had large backpacks, and there were families with young children. From the window of the train, you could see bike riders and hikers of all ages, and they waved at the train as it went by. Walking in the forest was the same story, seeing bike riders and hikers. And you see it in Oslo as well. A Sunday activity can be a four-hour walk in the mountains.

The studies are still high-pressured. I'm unsure about my progress. Different days bring different results. I write my compositions at my English level in Norwegian, which may improve my vocabulary, but I make other – or the same – grammatical mistakes. It is hard to keep track of all the rules, and then they throw the curve ball – the exception to the rule – at you. While others may seem to do better in class than I, others are having trouble, too. Audun, our teacher, wants us to discuss problems with him, which is good, and I met with him last night. He was particularly taken with my essay about my grandmother's immigration experiences to America.

By chance, we also had dinner together. Alice had gone back to the line for seconds. Audun walked by our table, and I wanted to ask about meeting with him. Alice returned, not knowing he was my teacher, and asked if he thought the Norwegian social welfare system worked. She is learning about it in the "Culture and Society" class, and is intrigued by a system that seems to take good care of its people. She's interested in different opinions.

In my class, we had just discussed the Norwegian system after translating a text. Earlier in the day, Alice and I met a British saleswoman who was working for the summer at William Schmidt (a major souvenir and craft store), and said the Norwegian system was "crap."

Looking at the people peddling their wares on Karl Johans Gate, Alice wondered, "Does the system work for them? Are they struggling?"

Audun sat down with us. This was the most English I had heard him speak! Whether the system works, he said, depended on who you asked and what you compared it to. The wealthy would like to privatize some of the health care, so they could have easier access to it. There are Norwegians who left Norway to make money in the United States. They didn't like the Norwegian system. But, there hasn't been an exodus. There are proposals to have Norwegians pay part of their hospital bill, perhaps for food.

A little later, I ran into Angel, the Bulgarian man we met the second night. I asked if Bulgaria had retained any of the social net, such as national (free) health care, from Communism. He said no. Angel seems to play devil's advocate, a little bit of both sides. He felt there should be some controls on the system. If a drunk driver gets into an accident, he said, why should the state pay for his care because of his mistake? It was an interesting point, but because of the drunk driver, should there not be coverage for others? His answer to these discussions seems to be "There's good and bad in all systems."

Indeed, there is. Perhaps, all of us become clouded by the negatives we see in our own systems.

Monday-Thursday, 27-30 July 1992

The main highlight of the previous week was my interview at Lillehammer on 23 July with Ragnhild Staff, the personnel consultant at the Lillehammer Olympic Organizing Committee.

Dad's colleague, John Ivar, had offered to drive me to Lillehammer, his hometown. The night before the interview, I received a call from him saying his 18-year-old daughter, who apparently had recently received her license, wanted to drive me. Would I mind? The next morning, John Ivar picked me up at Blindern and introduced me to "my beautiful daughter." Turning to her boyfriend, he said, "This is the bodyguard."

We dropped John Ivar off at Ullevål Hospital. As he got out of the car, he said to me, "I hope to see you again."

She negotiated us out of Ullevål, which is quite a feat because Ullevål is a huge complex. The question was, Could she get us out of Oslo? We reached a street, and she said, *"Venstre eller høyre?"* ("Left or right?") She made the right – correct – choice by turning left.

About 30 minutes into the ride, I realized I didn't know their names. Her name was Marit, and his, Andreas. They had just finished high school, but did not know what they were going to do. We mixed Norwegian and English conversation on the trip, and Andreas helped me to phrase a few questions in Norwegian for the interview.

The interview was conducted entirely in Norwegian and lasted about an hour and 15 minutes. Talk about intensive Norwegian. (My teacher had said to do the best I could.) At one point, Ms. Staff said I could ask a question in English, but I didn't want to. I tried not to look flustered. She would explain something in a different way if I was having trouble, and I would say in Norwegian, "If I understand you correctly..."

She began by explaining the flow chart of the LOOC, and that was a bit complicated. What I understand is that after Barcelona (the 1992 Summer Olympics), 80-90 jobs are expected to open up, about 25 in marketing and public relations. A certain number of the positions have to go to Norwegians. Proficiency in Norwegian is important now because of writing and communicating with the town's residents. They have a timetable for having publications completed by the summer of 1993. So aptitude in Norwegian is important now.

She asked about my background. I discussed my experience and my media campaigns – all in Norwegian! Ms. Staff felt I had a better chance through CBS-TV in America, which is broadcasting the Olympics. Since the LOOC is in close contact with CBS, she was going to tell Norwegian Broadcasting (NRK) to talk to CBS. Nothing was ruled out about working with the LOOC.

Unfortunately, Frode was on holiday, and I couldn't see him. Again, I was sent home with a folder of information and the latest lapel pins. I wore the pin Frode had given me. She noticed and said it was worth a lot of money now. She gave me a few extra of the latest pins for Marit, Andreas and Alice.

Afterwards, Marit, Andreas and I had a quick lunch and then went to Maihaugen, Lillehammer's Folkmuseum. John Ivar had given her money to treat me. Maihaugen is more of a forest than the Oslo museum and has a lake in the middle. A centerpiece is the 13th century *stavekirke*. But, overshadowing this area of buildings, dating from 1200-1700, are cranes building structures for the Olympics. A hundred years from now, people will be taken to see the 1994 Olympic buildings. On the way back to Oslo, we played Norwegian Trivial Pursuit.

That evening, there was a student talent show at school, a real multicultural event of music, singing, dancing, poetry and storytelling. We finally heard Sultan sing and play the guitar, as a man from Azerbaijan danced. The highlight was an American student's tribute to the cafeteria food, *Deja vù Café*, a song he had written.

JoAnn Kleber, the North American administrator for the ISS, had mentioned there was another Philadelphian on campus besides the two of us. The woman worked in the administration office and would be leaving Thursday 23 July. I met her on Wednesday, and we talked in Norwegian. She lives in Manayunk, 10 minutes from me! She had attended the ISS as a student and came back to work in the office. Her mother is Norwegian and works at Drexel, the university Rune attends.

We returned from Noresund at about 8:30 last night, the 26th. There has been a different excursion each weekend, and students choose one trip, which was included in the ISS expenses. Noresund was our choice. Enjoyable, but a mixed bag of some strange events. Fortunately, we were there for two days. About 40 students went on the trip, which was a more sociable way of getting to know people than just at meal times and in class. Three other students from my class were on the trip.

Noresund is in the central part of Eastern Norway in Central Buskerud, if that makes sense. It is on the old route to Bergen. The mountain range is Norefjell. Noresund is about 1½ hours from Oslo. And as with any part of Norway, there are stupendous views. The area of Krødsherad, Modum, Sigdal and Øvre Eiker is advertised as a fairy-tale region. Jørgen Moe, who along with P. Chr. Asbjørnsen collected the Norwegian fairy tales and put them on paper for the first time, was from this area. There were two famous artists from the region, Christian Skredsvig, whose house we visited yesterday, and Theodore Kittelsen, who is credited with developing the trolls and gnomes in art.

As one brochure puts it: "...where else could you visit one region and experience fjords, mountains, woodlands, valleys, lakes...salmon fishing, a mountain climbing paradise, a motor sports arena and water sports...rock carvings, Norway's first paved road, industrial artifacts from the 1700s, a hunting lodge from the 1800s and World War II memorabilia...within the same geographical area?"

Saturday was somewhat of a fairy tale – somewhat hard to believe. We left Blindern shortly after 8 a.m. on

Saturday the 25th, and arrived at the Sole Hotel around 9:50. The hotel was very nice. Rooms were small, but with a refrigerator, a shower and toilet! The hotel was situated by a lake.

At 10:30, we took a boat – *M/S Kryllingen* – from the lake to Ringnes where the bus met us to take us the few minutes to the Ringnes (Farm) Manor. The day was overcast, so the views weren't accentuated. Then again, it would be hard to match the boat ride around the fjords on the Bergen trip.

After the bus driver inched his way on another narrow road and bridge to reach the farm, we were greeted by a beautiful blond boy and puppies. The shy boy went and hid in a hole that led from the house to the dog pen, holding a puppy. Most of the ISS students were immediately attracted to the puppies.

The Ringnes Manor has been in the Ringnes family since 1325. Ellef Ringnes, who is about 66, now runs the farm. He read from an English script about the farm's history. He stood in front of a house built in 1812 that had a door with woodcarvings. This had been the house of some of the Ringnes family and was now a museum with artifacts, including kitchen and dining ware and bedrooms from the different historical periods.

Ellef's great-great-grandfather had lost his money on the farm and had to sell it to another relative. Ellef's great-grandfather, Ellef, and his brother went to Christiania (Oslo) where they made their fortune in Ringnes beer, Norway's most famous brew. They were able to buy the farm back. Ringnes also helped support the polar expeditions of the *Fram* and the building of the museum at Bygdøy. Among the visitors to the farm have been Fridtjof Nansen, Otto Sverdrup and Roald Amundsen, the leaders of the three *Fram* expeditions. Part of a film about the South Pole expedition was filmed at the farm. The most famous visitor came in 1947, Crown Prince Olav, later to be the revered King Olav V. King Olav died in January 1991.

We ate our *matpakkes* (lunch packets) at the farm, and then headed toward Villa Fridheim for what was advertised to Guro, the ISS excursion manager, and then to us, as an example of a traditional Norwegian country wedding.

At Villa Fridheim, there were hundreds of people sitting on a lawn in front of an impressive looking building, which was a fairy-tale museum. The lawn backed up against a lake and the setting was in a forest. Beautiful Norwegian children ran around. Families were on a weekend outing together with the children and dogs, a common sight we have noticed.

A man gave an introduction, saying something about history, but it was in Norwegian, and it was hard to follow everything. A boy dressed in traditional clothes came out onto the porch, which was serving as the stage, and played the horn. One figured this was to herald the wedding procession. But the procession didn't appear. The boy played "contemporary wedding" songs and something seemed strange when he played "If I Were A Rich Man" from *Fiddler on the Roof.* Was this a Norwegian Jewish country wedding?

A man and a woman seemed to act as emcees, cracking Norwegian jokes, which we didn't understand, much less get. The procession finally arrived with the bride and groom in a horse-drawn carriage. Children from the crowd ran up to the horse. No one seemed to mind. The bride and groom sat in two chairs at the foot of the steps of the building. They sat there for virtually the whole program doing nothing. There was a parade of people to the porch where they displayed the designs on the back and front of the traditional outfits (*bunads*). The emcees explained about the patterns. There was some fiddle music with two men dressed in the traditional knickers (also known as *bunads*), and the other six players wearing ordinary clothes.

Meanwhile, children played with the pebbles in front of the steps, and one tried to climb the steps. Finally, a parent who happened to be part of the show grabbed him and set him with the grandparents. They should've left the kid there. He was better than the show, which was very slow. Hope for the better sprouted with a folk-dance exhibition. The last straw, however, came when after the dancing, a woman wearing black leotards appeared on the porch and lip-synced to a Michael Jackson song, followed by a mixture of other songs. At this point, the ISS students looked at each other and smiled, thinking in all languages, "What are we watching?"

It was 3:15, and we had to be back on the bus at 3:30. There was a museum to visit. Half the group got up and went inside. The museum featured artwork and photographic displays of fairy-tale themes such as the trolls. We were given extra time to tour the museum.

"Let me try to explain what happened up there," Guro said on the bus. "The program was actually a community talent show around the 'country wedding' theme."

It was not what she expected either or what had been explained to her. She said it was boring in Norwegian. She added, if nothing else, we got an anthropological look at country community life. We returned to the hotel to rest before a very nice dinner of salmon, boiled potatoes, cucumbers and fruit cocktail.

We sat at a table that included two classmates of mine, Erica from Vancouver, British Columbia, and Denisa from Slovakia. After dinner, people moved to a lounge for tea and coffee. We spent the next few hours in pleasant conversation with Guro, Lena, the other tour guide, who was delightful, a student from the University of South Carolina (who would be studying at the University of Oslo in the upcoming year), and David, a student from Ohio State, who was in my class.

It was nice to socialize and relax outside the school cafeteria and class.

The next morning it rained, which put a damper on the scheduled five-hour hike. The bus climbed steep roads, and I wondered if there would be any more space to walk once we reached the destination. Guro and Lena decided to change the route because of the weather. When we got off the bus, we could see the clouds practically touching the mountaintops. The weather began to clear.

The "leave the umbrella home and it rains; bring it and it doesn't" proverb came true regarding my camera. I left it in another bag, thinking the rain might continue, and it would weigh my backpack down. So, I missed photographing all the views. The uphills were strenuous; the inclines toward the end of the route up were full of stones and pebbles. When people tired, others waited for them.

Everyone – people from so many different countries – made it to the top of Høvegarde, 1,340 meters above sea level. On the way, we saw herds of reindeer and sheep. The sight from the peak was absolutely beautiful. The clouds seemed so close to the top of the mountain. People took plenty of pictures. How exciting to have group shots with people from the United States, Slovakia, Nepal, Benin, Norway, Slovenia, Canada, Italy, France, Germany, Philippines, West Bank! Walking down took only an hour and fifteen minutes, less than half the time it took hiking up.

We were then taken to the home of author and painter Christian Skredsvig. The home, called *Hagan* (garden), overlooks the valley in Sigdal. Skredsvig lived here from 1894-1924. His life encompassed the same period as other Norwegian creative talents mentioned before like Vigeland, Ibsen, Bjørnsen, Grieg. According to the Sigdal brochure: "...He turned the barn into a studio and the rooms added to the house later all contribute to the very special atmosphere of the house...the true home of an artist...the house stands there unaltered, inside as well as outside. This authenticity is part of its charm...personal and charming rooms with furniture and equipment, all intact. Paintings, his as well as others, decorate the walls."

He painted the landscapes, as well as the people, of the area. There were some sketches he had drawn as a young child, and you could see the burgeoning talent. One of the guides was his great-granddaughter.

From there, we went to Blaafarveværket, which had crafts in buildings that had a German architectural feel to them. Located in Åmot, Blaafarveværket was founded in 1776, and by 1830 was the country's largest cobalt mine, producing the cobalt blue used in 80 percent of the world's glass and porcelain. Indeed, there was a shop selling blue glass and porcelain. In addition, there are art exhibitions, the Haugfossen waterfall, workers' cottages and a farm with livestock. At one time, 2,000 people lived and worked around the mines (from brochure for Krødsherad, Modum, Sigdal, Øvre Eiker).

We ate dinner in a beautiful room. The vegetarians sat at two tables and received lettuce for dinner, which, unfortunately, necessitated another apology from Guro. The non-vegetarians got a bowl of meat and beans. Dessert was *lefse* (a tortilla-shaped with sugar) according to Lena. After dinner and some walking around, we headed back to Oslo.

On Monday (the 27th), there was a reception for the entire school – students, teachers, administration, staff – with the Mayor of Oslo, Ann-Marit Sæbanes, at the *Rådhuset*. We were taken on a tour of the building, which has tremendous murals on the wall, and in some cases artwork on the ceiling. We had a very good guide, although she disagreed with another guide about the origin of the name Oslo. Much of the artwork showed the history of Oslo and Norway, including World War II. The guide remembered being a child during the war. Afterwards, a local bar hosted the school for dancing.

On Wednesday (the 29th), Alice and I were invited to the house of Finn and Sylvia Backer, who live in a community along the route to Holmenkollen. Sylvia is an American, who had worked at the Institute for Social Research with my father in 1969-70. She is blind in one eye, with limited vision in the other one. Finn is Norwegian and a judge. Except for a brief visit they had made to Philadelphia a few years ago, I had not seen them since 1970.

We were invited for 7 p.m., which I figured was *aftens* or dessert, so we ate something before we left. I misread the *trikk* schedule, and we arrived late. They were leisurely about everything. First, we sat and talked some. Then, they served dinner!

Conversation centered on South Africa, Norwegian politics, the debate on membership in the European Community and the problems of and with Pakistani immigrants. Finn had presided over cases involving Pakistanis, some of them murder cases. They leaned toward supporting Norway joining the EC.

The Backers were very happy to have our company. As it got later, we got concerned about the *trikk* schedule. The evening moved to the living room for dessert, where the conversation turned to Alice and my Norwegian lessons at school. They insisted we couldn't make the next *trikk*, but we ran to the station, only to have the *trikk* come late.

Once again, we were caught up in Norwegian hospitality.

Friday, 31 July 1992, 10 p.m.

We are now in Rauland with Torbjørn, Debbie, four-year-old Ingrid and seven-month-old Anja. Both children are adorable and smile a lot. I read Ingrid *Hansel and Gretel* in Norwegian. She put her head on my arm. She also corrected my pronunciation. Another time, she was playing with block letters, trying to spell her name. She came across "A" and said, "Audun!," one of her stepbrothers.

I asked, *"Hvem er Audun?"* ("Who is Audun?")

"Brørene."

I looked at Torbjørn, and asked if the pronunciation was part of the dialect of the area.

Then she piped in, *"En er bror; to er brørene!"* ("One is brother; two are (the) brothers!") The other stepbrother is Are, but she had not mentioned him when she saw the "A" block. She was explaining singular and plural to me! Four years old! (When I told my teacher about it, he was quite impressed.)

Ingrid gets along very well with Anja.

Saturday, 1 August 1992, 9:35 a.m.

Ingrid is very funny, if you hadn't gathered. When she had taken the block letters out (yesterday), I asked, *"Kan du stave navn?"* ("Can you spell your name?")

And she said, "Yes."

Typical Norwegian, answering in English.

She mixes English and Norwegian. They had just returned the previous Sunday from the United States where they had visited Debbie's family.

I tried Norwegian again: *"Liker du Amerika?"* ("Do you like America?")

I kept asking her.

Finally, Torbjørn asked what she liked about America. She thought for a while and said, *"Kylling!"* ("Chicken!")

Ingrid brightened up when she found out we were staying until Sunday. One time, I was holding Anja, and Ingrid was running around my legs. Another time, Alice and I were sitting on a couch and Ingrid took running starts, moving farther back each time, and leapt into our laps.

She also remembered that I had brought the T-shirt in December 1990, and wore it around the house.

Sunday, 2 August 1992, 10:35 a.m.

Yesterday was a special day in Rauland. Around 1897, there were no roads in Rauland. People would bring horses from Hardanger in Western Norway down to Rauland to a market. This would take them over mountainous terrain, and the trip would take about a week. At the market, people could sell the horses and buy other wares. Someone came up with the idea of reenacting the trip using the old route, which goes along the road at the end of the Moum/Rieser block.

Torbjørn went out shooting, but Debbie, Alice, Ingrid, Anja and I walked down the "old new road" to await the horses. "Never" were so many people seen in Rauland at one time. Anja was very happy to be riding on Mommy's back. Ingrid was walking along, occasionally holding our hands. She found a friend, and we met Debbie's friends. Then the horses arrived with people dressed in traditional costumes. Music was being played. People joined the procession to the site of the old market. We were treated to fiddle music. A reporter from *Hardanger Folkbladet* interviewed Debbie. The Moum/Rieser clan are becoming media celebrities. Anja was born on January 1 during a snowstorm. It took three hours to get to the hospital. She was Telemark's (region) first New Year's baby. It was front-page news in the local papers!

Wednesday, 5 August 1992, 3:04 p.m.

First, let me finish up with the trip to Rauland.

After the procession of horses was over, Alice and Debbie went to an Academy to see the crafts. Torbjørn had to pick up Are and Audun in Høvden. Ingrid and I went with him. We went to the Høvden *Badeland*, an indoor swimming pool. (It had to be indoors because it was too chilly outside.) The place was decorated with fake trees surrounding the big pool. There were many slides that kids could ride into the water. The pool, which was circular, had jacuzzis and faucets, which provided a whirlpool feeling. It was nice to get into a pool. Ingrid loved the water.

That night, we ate homemade pizza, watched some of the Olympics, and Alice and I did some homework. Final exams were coming up this week. Are helped me.

On Sunday, Alice and I took a bus back to Oslo, a ride of about four hours. Rides in Norway are seldom boring because of the beautiful scenery, but this ride felt tedious. Because we got back to Oslo close to seven p.m., we had to eat dinner in *sentrum*, which is rarely cheap. What is cheap in Oslo?

Whew! I just finished my Norwegian oral examination. The oral was to last 15 minutes and include questions on one of the texts we had translated from the book or additional material. Papers were placed face-down on a table, and we had to pick one. So we had to be knowledgeable about 17 topics in Norwegian. A few of us studied together last night – interrupted by a program on the Israeli-Palestinian conflict presented by an Israeli and Palestinian student with an Egyptian translator and Peruvian moderator.

The teacher and another examiner, or censor, are present in the room for the oral exam. Audun, the teacher, mentioned to the class this morning that Tina Lindstrøm would be the censor. My parents took Norwegian two years ago with Tina Lindstrøm at the University! I had gone to her office several times during the summer to send *"hilsen"* (greetings, regards), and she was never there. Now, the examiner was Tina Lindstrøm! I told Audun of the coincidence. I figured this would provide a great opener and a way to stay relaxed. During the exam, Audun tried to make the atmosphere comfortable. It was *he* who started the session by asking me, "Don't you have greetings from your parents for Tina?"

I was asked my name, what I do, where I'm from. Then I picked the fateful paper. *Hvalfangst/miljøvern/ naturnvern.* Whalehunting/environment/nature. The questions concerned my opinions on the renewal of whaling in Norway, which we had discussed in class; whether there are active environmental groups in Philadelphia; litter in Philadelphia; what I'll do for the environment; whether there are parks in Philadelphia; what I do with my free time; what I did in Norway; how many times I've been to Norway.

Audun remembered topics I had written about for class. He had particularly liked my essay about the experience with the Samis in Geilo.

"Didn't you have a nice trip to Geilo once?" he asked.

I recapped the story.

I don't think I was in there for 15 minutes.

I feel such a sense of relief getting that part done. There's been so much studying and saturation of material the last few weeks, and there's a feeling of such fatigue and exhaustion. Now, there's a three-hour written exam tomorrow. There's so many rules and grammar to remember.

The other news is that, after much heartache, we've been able to change our reservations for the trip home. The student travel agency said that they couldn't do anything for us, even though – oh never mind! They eventually did, and we're returning to Philadelphia on August 19. First, we're going to the Lofoten Islands above the Arctic Circle! Tom Sørensen and Inger Sandanger, colleagues of Dad's, have been inviting us to come during the whole summer. Ragnhild Dalgard had told me the Lofoten Islands was one of two places in the world people should visit before they die because of the Islands' beauty.

We finally changed our plans. I call Inger, and everything is fine. She gives me the ferry times and says she would be driving back to Oslo later in the week, and we could go with her. Ten minutes later, she calls back to say she had to pick up her kids on the West Coast on the 10th, and she and Tom wouldn't be in the Lofotens. However, a friend of theirs was willing to put us up. It was unfortunate we wouldn't see Tom and Inger, but Inger had still arranged a place for us to stay.

The trip will take 23 hours, 2½ days, and we'll travel on two trains and a boat. We got a 50% student discount on the train fares.

Friday, 7 August 1992
Who We Were and The Good-byes

Last night, there was a farewell party – the first sign that this experience was ending – at the *Ingenørings Hus* (Engineer's Hall) near the National Theatre. There were some encore performances from the talent show, including a "deja vù" rendition of *Deja Vù Café*, a song written by an American student in honor of the Blindern cafeteria.

A man from Zimbabwe came on stage, somewhat nervous, and said, "There are two things I hate: meeting people and leaving." He then gave three stirring orations, the last one about how African women should throw off the yoke of male chauvinism.

There were singing groups made up of people of different nationalities. Awards were presented to the tennis champion, who was also captain of the championship soccer team from Western Europe. He then presented a special shirt to Mattias. The Student Council presidents, a man from Kenya and a woman from the United States, presented a special card to the retiring managing director of ISS.

The woman president acknowledged the cultural, political, social and sports committees and listed all the events they had organized. I realized how many activities we/I missed out on that could've made it an even fuller experience for us/me: e.g., Polish, German films; Argentinean, Indian cultural programs; discussions on topics like "Women's Rights Around the World."

Still, there was a special feeling during the last week. There was a bonding with the students in class with whom I experienced six weeks of learning Norwegian. But, also with teachers, administrators and staff that made up our community. Maybe exams had something to do with it. I studied for the oral exam with Shayna from the United States and Denisa from Slovakia. During the pauses in class, Denisa would sometimes go and buy chocolate. When I signed her directory/yearbook at the farewell party, I teased her about her chocolate-aholism. (Who could blame her with Freia chocolate available?)

We had assigned seats in class. On my left was a woman from Estonia; to my right was Beatriz, and to her right was Erica. Beatriz was from Spain, but had spent many summers in England, so she spoke English with a very British accent. She was married to an American, and they had moved from New York to Oslo because her husband got a job with Den Norske Bank. During pauses in class, we would often talk. She had invited us, along with Erica and Shayna to dinner the week before, but we had to back out because we were so tired from running around trying to rearrange our travel plans. Anyway, Alice met Bea at the farewell party and had an opportunity to talk Spanish. Later, pictures were taken of Bea, Erica and me.

An Afghan woman commuted two hours to class from her home outside Oslo. She asked me to sign her directory/yearbook. There were two Japanese women in the class. They didn't know each other before they came, but sat next to each other for the whole course. When they would try to talk Norwegian to me, they would talk so fast it would surprise me, and I couldn't understand. We would always laugh. One wants to be a Japanese-Norwegian translator. She and Denisa were the two women with whom I had trouble communicating on the first day of the Intermediate class and now...

Audun, our teacher, made us talk to each other in Norwegian. Some of us knew about each other's goals and reasons for learning Norwegian. So, our lives, in a way, became intertwined. It will be interesting if we ever find out how we did. Denisa was studying Swedish and was interested in languages, as was a student from Belgium and a man who attended the same college as Denisa in Slovakia. The Belgian and Slovakian guys seemed to rarely study, but did well. They good-naturedly ribbed me during the last few days when I was studying. In the class, there were four Americans, two Czechs, two Japanese, two Spaniards, one Dutch, one Austrian, one Belgian, one Canadian, one Afghan, one German and one Estonian.

I grew to appreciate and respect Audun even more during the last few days. On the evaluations, I don't think too many students were critical of him as they were of the text. I heard complaints about the other Norwegian classes, but Audun wanted us to talk Norwegian. For example, he broke us into pairs to talk about what we did on the weekend. We laughed in class. David, from Ohio State, may never forget his birthday in 1992 because Audun taught us to sing *Happy Birthday* in Norwegian and brought in cookies. He was available after class for questions. He helped Alice with her homework. We sat with him at the farewell party program.

He was patient and interested in the students. The night before the written exam he told a few of us, "Don't study past 12 because you need a good night's sleep."

He made it comfortable in the oral exam, beginning by asking me, "Don't you have greetings from your parents for Tina?"

I talked with him and Tina at dinner later. I ate a few meals with Audun during the six weeks.

Another unique aspect of the ISS was that the students ranged in age from 20-60s. There was some intergenerational mingling. At lunch yesterday, we ate with a retired couple from Minnesota. Delightful. His grandparents had emigrated from Norway to the United States. His father was one of 10 children; his mother, one of 12. He talked about how his grandparents and parents struggled. He was the first of his family to get through high school. He worked as a mechanic in his father's plane business, and then decided to become a Lutheran pastor. St. Olaf College asked him to teach theology. He joked, "I never applied for a job."

I asked how St. Olaf felt about the TV show *The Golden Girls* and the character Rose, the not-too-swift character from St. Olaf played by Betty White. He had never seen the show, but said White had visited the town and college several times. The show's producers and writers had asked permission to use St. Olaf's name, although the college is located in Northfield, Minnesota. The show uses St. Olaf as the town's name. He says the college enjoys the notoriety. The College choir was in Hollywood and had a chance to watch a rehearsal of the program. He admitted that people in Northfield do some funny things. (*St. Olaf College is the North American administrative center for the ISS.*)

When they heard I was involved in sportswriting, they said their nephew wrote sports books for children. They gave me his name and address.

They had lived in South Africa last year, working at a Lutheran seminary. Pastors were considered dangerous, he said, because they give people ideas of self worth. He said pastors were arrested, and it was known there were informers in the seminary. He said the Blacks had a greater faith than he did, showing great courage in attending the seminary.

10:11 p.m.

Wow, it's really over now! After six weeks, we finally got to sit out on the steps. Every evening while we sat studying, we could hear the chatter, the laughter, the singing. One night, we would join them. It came down to the last day.

The place was emptying out of people; some people were coming back because of the SAS strike. How strange closing down and partings can be.

The mail baskets were taken down. No more announcements were on the bulletin boards. The reception area was set up for checkout.

The school allowed people to stay through the weekend at 165 NoK per person per night, without food, to accommodate different travel plans. We are taking advantage of it before leaving for the Lofoten Islands tomorrow. There are several people hanging around. It's eerie because there is virtually no one on the floor. There is no staff on duty.

As difficult as parting can be, this was one of the nicest days we spent here – certainly the most relaxing. It helped add perspective to this experience. Despite some regrets, it is a teary good-bye. There is no way to meet every single person at the summer school. So you hold onto the memories and experiences of the people you did get to meet, even if it was for a few minutes at a meal some weeks ago.

There were enough people around today that we knew, either staying or on the way out, that we could spend time with. Then there were people we met for the first time. In one of the ironies, I never met the Israelis, but met some Palestinians. And I found that some of the nicest people were the German students, notably Matthias and Astrid from Mannheim. They were also in Intermediate Norwegian, but in a different section than me. We shared a common shower. I would shower around 8 a.m., and Matthias would joke that was his wake-up call. I'd often have breakfast with them. They had been at ISS in 1989. They're studying law in Germany. Matthias is studying environmental law and wants to do graduate work in England.

He had an eventful last few weeks. Right after promising me we would play tennis, he dislocated his shoulder in the "Wimbledon" tournament. Then this week, he had a cold and could hardly talk. We had our picture taken with them at the party last night, and they gave us a ride back in their car. This morning, there were hugs. This experience may help reduce my previous strong feelings against visiting Germany.

Students, most faculty, administrators and staff were so nice, and it was evident today.

While Alice got a haircut this morning, I sat on the steps and talked to Mike, the sportswriter from Minnesota (from my Elementary Norwegian class) and a couple of others. I had a picture taken (for me) of me with the two women receptionists, Kari and Inger (who helped us with our Norwegian homework, answered the phone and gave me change for the pay phone); the night watchman, who was Yugoslavian and had come to ISS for 37 straight summers and would let me know about the availability of the *Tribune*; Kaare, a law student who worked in the administration office and always had a pleasant smile; my classmate, Shayna, from Miami; and my teacher, Audun.

While Alice was at the hairdresser, Shayna and I went to the cafeteria in Fredrike (a shopping area on campus that includes a supermarket, hairdresser, kiosk, computer store, record store, cafeteria and El Paso Mexican fast food, which was not open during the summer). It was only the second time I'd been to the cafeteria. In the afternoon, after Alice and I returned from shopping, I sat on the steps and wrote the last postcards. I talked to a man from Bangladesh and a Palestinian woman. It was a beautiful day, warm, similar to when we came. It was also ironic that we were the last to arrive, so we didn't see everyone arrive. Now, we were one of the last to leave and watched all the taxis arrive; the luggage in the courtyard; the good-byes; the hugs and the departures toward everyone's *hjemmebaner* (home bases, home places).

We joined a group that was going to a vegetarian restaurant, Krishna, at Majorstua for dinner – all you can eat for 55 NoK (@$9, a bargain in Oslo!). Twelve people walked over to the restaurant (about 20 minutes), and six others met us there for a total of 18. There were some new people we hadn't met before, and a Norwegian student organized the dinner. We talked to three Germans – a pleasant, young woman from Würzburg that we had talked to before, her friend who had just arrived, and a German friend of Matthias who was from Tübingen. The woman from Würzburg is so thin, and we had seen her around campus with a backpack that looked bigger and heavier than she is! She will be studying sociology at the University of Oslo during the next year. Matthias' friend and Alice compared notes on how the Elementary Norwegian classes were taught. The three of us walked back together.

It was still very early – about 6:30. For the first time since playing in Heathrow Airport, we played Scrabble. We invited an Irish young woman to join us. She was stranded by the strike. Her face reminded me so much of my cousin Sharon when Sharon was younger. It was a tight game between Alice and the Irish woman, with

Alice winning. The game provided spectator sport for the others gathered on the steps.

Erica came out ready to depart. It was her birthday, and she was being picked up by Norwegian relatives. We said our good-byes. She said she would try to contact an old friend of mine or her father, who lived in Vancouver.

Astri, the housemother, had her car all packed up. She hugged us good-bye and wished us luck.

Later, Sultan came out ready to leave. He was leaving with a man from Azerbaijan, who gave Alice and the other women flowers. Sultan insisted, "...we must write...continue to be friends." He is impressed that I am a journalist, who could be a contact for him to publish some of his material (he is an ethnographer). For the last couple of weeks, he had been saying what a wonderful person I am. Then we had a picture taken of Alice, myself, Sultan, another man from Moscow and someone we didn't know. Who would've thought a couple of years ago this could happen?

Earlier in the day, Angel from Bulgaria gave Alice a tape of Bulgarian folk music, something we had discussed when we met the first time on the second night. Alice cried when she listened to the music because it sounded sad. We had hoped to see him during the day to return the tape. As we sat on the steps, he returned from *sentrum*. We went over to return the tape. Angel said she could keep it.

"Perhaps we'll see each other again," he said.

We had disagreed on some issues, but it didn't mean we weren't friends.

We spent most of the rest of the evening talking to Kaare.

Alice took a picture of me with a man from South Africa, Kaare (Norway), a woman from Switzerland, Matthias' friend, the woman from Würzburg and her friend (Germany). We were holding the flowers the Azerbaijanian man had given out.

Saturday, 8 August 1992, 9:47 a.m.

We are on the train getting ready to leave for Trondheim, the first trek of our journey to the Lofoten Islands. We ate some of our provisions this morning for breakfast. To save money, we went shopping yesterday afternoon for food for the trip. So we're loaded down.

We woke up this morning in time to say good-bye to JoAnn Kleber, the North American administrator for ISS from St. Olaf College, a delightful, pleasant person. She knew every North American student and what course(s) they were taking without consulting the book. She knew who we were the first night we walked in the door. She listened to our complaints and offered advice. Her husband was here for the first few weeks, and we used to scour the campus for the *Herald Tribune* to look for the baseball scores; in his case, the Twins.

Said good-bye to Terje, the housefather; the woman from Malibu, California (who knew Alice's friend's family); a man from Alice's Norwegian class, and a few others. Took a few last looks at the view of the fjord from the room. Walked down toward the *trikk* stop, took a couple of backward looks and continued on.

As I think about these six weeks spent with people from all over the world, I can't help but reflect on my answer to the essay question on the Norwegian written exam, which may have put the summer experience together for me. The last part of the written exam was to choose among three selections and write a 200-word essay in Norwegian on it.

"1-Children are our best resource. How do we provide a better world for them?

"2-What would you do if you won 1,000,000 *kroner* in the lottery (@$160,000)?

"3-My candidate for the 1992 Nobel Peace Prize."

I looked at 2 and didn't know if I could get 200 words out of my answer. I looked at 3. Who? Couldn't think of anybody. Then, it occurred to me: The International Summer School. Corny? Then, again, why not? I will try to recreate the essay from memory, translating it into English.

"It is difficult to choose a candidate for the Nobel Peace Prize in the world today. There is a war in the former Yugoslavia. There is conflict in the Middle East and Eastern Europe. The world is not peaceful, as President George Bush in the USA believes.

"My candidate is The International Summer School, which meets in the city where the Nobel Prize is presented. The goal is friendship between people from different countries.

"For six weeks, I have met people from different countries, some nations I didn't know existed. I have met people from Russia and other Eastern European countries. Who would've thought a few years ago Americans and Russians could meet and be friends? I am Jewish and have become friends with Germans. People from different countries have talked, laughed, played and sang together. Palestinians and Israelis discussed their conflict without weapons (with an Egyptian translator and Peruvian moderator).

"On our excursion to Noresund, people from USA, Norway, Canada, France, West Bank, Benin, Nepal, Philippines, Germany, Slovakia, Slovenia, Italy, to name a few, hiked and reached the top of a mountain together. And hiked back down. People speaking different languages learned Norwegian together. Some people studied Peace Research. People from different countries have become friends. My candidate for the 1992 Nobel Peace Prize is the ISS."

But, one of the toughest things, about leaving a situation like this, is the word "Maybe" in the sentence "Maybe we'll see each other again." Without the school as a backdrop, what is the realistic possibility of seeing some of these people again? I anticipate being in Oslo again, and Beatriz gives me another friend to look up. What are the chances of seeing some of the people from some of the more "remote" places? And from the hotbeds of unrest? Then again, you never know. We were talking about coincidences at dinner last night. There are so many that make the world smaller. I know that when I hear about events in Czechoslovakia, South Africa, Germany, Yugoslavia, etc., I'll stop to think and wonder if these people I met are all right.

Parting is also a time of saying "Time to go home." To think of a person who must face going home to Croatia is mind-boggling. What is going through their minds? Maybe I'll see some of these people again, then maybe not. Perhaps, I'll be spending a lot of money on international postage.

Sunday, 9 August 1992, 11:30 a.m.
on the train to Bodø en route to Lofoten Islands

We just finished our provisions for lunch. Cheese and whole-grain bread, tomato and a carton of Fanta orange drink. We finished the chips around 9:30. I wrote most of the previous entry during the train ride to Trondheim. The ride to Trondheim (or this route) is nowhere near as dramatic as the Oslo-Bergen route, but that one is hard to beat.

The early part of the ride to Trondheim yesterday took us along the Mjøsa, the largest lake in Norway. We went through Hamar, one of the three towns in the triangle that will host the 1994 Olympics, Lillehammer and Gjøvik being the others. From the train you can see the multi-purpose Vikingship Olympiahall, so-called because it resembles an upside-down Vikingship. It will host Olympic ice hockey, speed skating and figure skating.

We went past many forests and streams. There were some nice views during the last couple of hours. I didn't take any pictures. Alice tried to sleep during some of the trip. I read through Friday's *Herald Tribune*, getting irritated at the latest George Bush comments and wrote in my journal. Alice is enjoying the book *Three In Norway by two of them*, which I lent her. I had read the book before we came to Norway. It's a humorous diary of three British men traveling in Norway in the late 1800s, written by two of them.

We ate some of our *matpakkes* with juice, chips, chocolate and apples. We arrived in Trondheim at about 6:20 p.m., eight hours and 20 minutes after leaving Oslo. We got a map and started to walk to the youth hostel. A German woman, who was also looking for the *vandrehjem*, joined us. It was quite arduous and exerting with all the luggage.

We eventually got there. It was a nice-looking hostel – 130 *kroner* per night per person as members, including breakfast (@$21.67).

We washed up (after "roughing it") and set out to find a place to eat. The walk, this time, wasn't difficult. Trondheim, like Oslo and Bergen, is by the water, so there are views of mountains and fjords. But it has its own special charm. Like Bergen, Trondheim has retained the historical look. It was discovered in the 10th century and was the first capital of Norway. The main attraction is the Nidaros Cathedral, which was started in 1150. The coronation of Norwegian kings takes place in Trondheim.

We really only got to see the center of town. We found a pizzeria where it was all you could eat for 49 *kroner* (@$8), a real bargain. After eating, we walked back to the youth hostel.

Later in the evening, we met an American young man and German young woman. They were traveling through Norway, Sweden and Finland.

We woke up this morning at 6:30, had a good breakfast and caught a cab to the train station. In the Narvessen (newsstand/store) at the train station, we couldn't pass up buying a postcard of Hell. There is a town near Trondheim named Hell. Looking at the map later, I realized we had passed "through it" on the train (to Bodø). We can still say "We've been through Hell," and when we return, that "We've been through Hell and back."

The early part of the trip took us along the Asenfjorden. The train seemed like it was side-by-side with the water, so it felt like we were riding on the water. We've been going through a lot of beautiful forest areas. Alice has been amazed at the number of birch and fir trees, and the greenery we're seeing. She has said she would like to live in Northern Norway. We're getting farther North, and my line on the map is going farther up. The air is beginning to get chillier, and we're beginning to see more snowcapped mountains. A few more people in the compartment have taken out cameras.

Alice has spent the ride reading *Discover* and writing postcards. I spent the early part reading Mary Morris' *Wall to Wall: From Beijing to Berlin by Rail,* perfect reading for a long train ride. I read almost as many pages as I had during the six weeks in school.

As we travel, the scenery has become more and more dynamic and dramatic. The mountains are massive and rugged. There are streams running down through the forests and mountains. In some areas, all the trees grow on an incline, making a mountain of trees. You don't know whether to look left or right because you're afraid you'll miss something beautiful on the other side. Some areas are just rocks. On the right, now, are valleys of trees. At Mo I Ranna, there was a bust of Ole Tobias Olsen, the Northern Country's "father." At Dunderland, the clouds rest on the mountains.

4:45 p.m.

I just finished *Wall to Wall.* It's a wonderful book. Soon, in about 30 minutes, we will reach the symbolic point of our journey – The Arctic Circle. We thought we were nearing the *Polarsirkelen* around 15:30 (3:30 p.m.), but the conductor said we would get there at 17:15 (5:15) at Semska. There will be signs on the left and right.

The scenery continues to be majestic and dramatic. Mountains of trees. Mountains of awesome, rough-hewn rock. Patches· of snow appear in the mountains. There are the waterfalls that appear like veins, breaking up the pattern of the mountain. A few minutes ago, there were three waterfalls, like crevices, running down the mountain and then merging to become one. The train is going slower, perhaps to enable us to enjoy the views. The scenery in Norway is so magnificent. (Have you read this before?) It's as if humans set up these sights as tourist attractions. The sites are too awesome to really contemplate that people made them. People certainly didn't. Which means nature did. The tribute to humanity is the construction of the railroads.

We've done it! We crossed the Arctic Circle at precisely 17:15. It was announced the Circle would be marked by stone pyramids. Of course, if you blinked you might miss the marker. We managed to snap a couple of quick shots. In the distance, was the strange-looking Arctic Circle Museum.

It was remarkable that after seeing all the trees, there weren't any; just plain, rough terrain with rocks; some snow on the mountains on the left, but no snow on the right. Suddenly, the trees appeared again. There weren't any houses; although a couple of minutes later, we could see roads with a bus and cars.

Monday, 10 August 1992, 11:39 a.m.

The stretch run of the trip to Bodø yesterday took us along the water, the Saltdal and Skjerstads fjords. Sharp-peaked and snow-capped jagged mountains sitting in the water beckoned us. The sun shined down on the water. How about that? We crossed the Arctic Circle, and the sun was hot. We had a "Norwegian" meal on the train – salmon, cucumbers and potatoes. The salmon was one of our tins of salmon patè and the potato was *lefse.* In lieu of a knife, Alice improvised by cutting the cucumber with scissors. We finished this big cucumber, a tin of paté and four *lefses.*

We arrived at Bodø, the second largest city in Northern Norway, with 37,500 people. (The largest is Tromsø, which is even farther North than Bodø and the site of the country's northern medical school. Eivind went to school there.)

Bodø is the capital of Nordland County and is the gateway to the north; boats or planes can take you to the Lofoten Islands and other spots. Bodø is a new city, despite being founded in 1816. On May 27, 1940, the Nazis bombed Bodø, destroying two-thirds of the city. Bodø was famous for the herring fishery from 1850-1860. Bodø is the third largest congress city in Norway. The average summer temperature is 11.2° C (50s °F) and in the winter -1.8° C (around 30° F). Winter darkness lasts from December 2 to January 10 (*from the Bodø brochure*).

We grabbed a quick bite at the train station cafeteria and walked about 23 minutes to the *vandrehjem*.

Tuesday, 11 August 1992, 10:22 p.m.

We had quite a day yesterday. At the Bodø hostel, we were served breakfast in a styrofoam box – I don't think I've seen styrofoam in six weeks – but the food was fine – two very good rolls, cheese, margarine, jam, a hard-boiled egg, cereal. We pulled ourselves and luggage together and walked to the train station to put the luggage in lockers. We could then be more mobile around Bodø. We went "around the corner," to buy our tickets for the afternoon boat to Stamsund – 158 kroner for students (@$26.33).

We then set out in search of a *vinmonopolet* (liquor store) to buy some liquor to bring as a gift for our Lofoten hosts. We walked along *Sjøgata*, aptly named, for it means Sea Street, and it goes along the water. We passed the pier where the fishing boats had come in, and the fishermen were selling their catches. We found the *vinmonopolet* and bought some Portuguese wine. We tried to figure out how to get to *Turisthytta*, a restaurant/hotel overlooking the town. The guidebook said it was two miles from the center of town. Our timing had to allow us to be back at the train station to pick up the luggage before walking to the boat.

We found the bus station and learned (speaking in Norwegian) we could catch a bus that would take us near the *Turisthytta*. We asked the bus driver in Norwegian how close he was going to Turisthytta, and if we could walk there from the stop. He said (in Norwegian), "Yes, in about 20 minutes."

As it turned out, the stop was across the street from the hostel. As we got off the bus, the driver said, "*Det er oppover.*" "It is uphill."

Naturally, it began to rain lightly. We walked and walked. Alice was timing it to figure how much time we would need to allow for getting back. We had caught a 12:10 bus. We kept walking and finally met a man and woman walking down. I walked toward them, and they said, in a British accent, "Turisthytta? It's closed to 4."

"Why?"

"We don't know. There's just a sign."

"How much longer is it?"

"About 10 minutes."

So we pushed ahead, reached the building, which was indeed closed, and saw a couple of nice views in the rain. After a few minutes, we started the downhill walk. We stopped at RIMI, a grocery chain store, on the way back, and got some more potato chips and a carton of apple juice for the trip. We got to the train station at about 1:50, picked up the luggage and walked to the boat.

Once on board, we broke out the provisions – cheese, tomatoes, *lefse*. This time, we had mustard from the packets we took from the Bodø train station cafeteria the day before. We got through the apple juice and broke into the potato chips, devouring more than half the economy-size bag. The rest was polished off a couple of hours later.

We met a woman from Florida, who was originally from North Jersey. She was a member of Sons of Norway. She and her husband were taking the Bergen to Kirkenes ride, known as *Hurtigruten,* to the far north, and were now in the fourth day of the cruise. We met a student from Harvard who was majoring in mechanical engineering and had worked in Germany for the summer. He was now traveling through Norway.

In the cafeteria, we met a German couple who had gotten on the boat in Trondheim and suggested we look into that for our return trip. We have to be in Trondheim for the train anyway. Alice went to the ticket office to get information. It would be two nights on the boat. We were considering sleeping in the lounge, but are now considering a cabin. If we take the night boat to Bodø, we'll arrive at 1 a.m. and have to be on the street until the 10 a.m. train to Trondheim. The boat will get into Trondheim at 6:30 a.m., two days later, in time for the 8:05 train to Oslo.

Wednesday, 12 August 1992, 9:16 a.m.

The boat ride on Monday was calm despite the overcast weather. The steamers travel at a speed of only 15 knots. The views were of jagged rock structures of different formations. Sometimes, they appeared to come one after the other or next to each other, and then they merged together. On some mountains, there was snow. The boat left at 3 p.m. for the four-hour ride. It was clear at 4 p.m., so we could see the Lofoten Wall, i.e., all the islands and their mountains in the distance, sooner than usual. At 6 o'clock, the view of the Wall is even better.

For a while, we did not see any signs of life, then suddenly, houses appear on the rocks in the distance. You marvel that people came and settled here; and built roads and communities. We were nearing Stamsund.

From the deck of the ship, we could see a man on the shore holding a paper with my name on it. Nils, our host, and his 1½-year-old daughter, Helene, were there to greet us. He and his wife, Guri, live around the corner from the dock, in a house perched on top of a rock overlooking the sea. They have one of the bigger houses

– with an outdoor pool. Most houses are small "box-like" homes, some situated on sides of the mountains. From their living room, the window on the left offers a clear view of the dock and pointed peak rock islands, some small, some larger, jutting out of the water in the distance. From another window, one can see a rough mountain with some green and boulders. Out the right window, one can see houses on the mountainside, and mountains and fjords in the distance.

Despite being above the Arctic Circle, Nils told us the winter temperatures are mild, rarely going below –1°C (0=32° F) because of the Gulf Stream. It's milder than Oslo, he said. It's in the 50°s, maybe 40°s (F) here now, but the weather has been erratic this summer. It was hot for three weeks in June and snowed on June 20! The wind is blowing hard right now, and it's a good thing we have our Norwegian sweaters. Stamsund is a fishing village with a population of 10,500 people. The Lofoten Islands include about 30-40 islands, stretching 125 miles into the Norwegian Sea. Between 10-12 are inhabited, and six are communities/*kommuner*. Nils and Guri moved here from Oslo five years ago. They love it and feel they have everything they need – except a store for swimming-pool equipment.

Guri grew up on one of the islands; Nils is from Oslo. Nils enjoys the fact everybody knows each other.

"I can go back to Oslo many times and not see any-one on the street I know," he said. "I come back here, and without meaning to, I see people I know."

Nils is an environmental engineer, who taught at ISS one summer, and is in charge of the roads in the area (those that are not state owned). He is also one of the four district coordinators of fire services. He says there are 20-30 fires a year.

Guri is a psychiatrist and researcher, who has met my father. She was conducting research for a book about elderly women on the Islands.

There was a curious picture on a wall in the kitchen of three men dressed in 19th century British outfits in

Norway. They were relatives of Guri's. I think they were from Ireland, and they had retraced the route taken by the characters in *Three in Norway!*

She offered to take us for a ride around the island. We stepped out the door and heard the "bah" of sheep somewhere in the nearby mountains. We drove past valleys, immense mountains, that were pointed and jagged, and 3.5 million years old. There were small houses on the side of the road. Red is a popular color because it is inexpensive paint. From the outside, they're much less fancy looking than other houses we had seen in Norway. Then again, some of them are small summer cottages.

Sheep grazed along the side of the road, sometimes lying down on the shoulder because the road is warmer. The "spots" on the side of mountains were sheep. There are also cows around. Most of the farm area is grass. The growing season is very short, but vegetables are tasty because of the large amount of light in the summer. We were surprised to learn about a relationship between the sun and taste.

We went through a tunnel built into the mountain, which seemed more like a hole because of the solid rock on the sides. We came out of the tunnel and around a curve, and there on the left was a beautiful view of the sun going down. It was 10:08 p.m. Down in the valley were a smattering of houses, some red with blue roofs. Retired people lived in most of the houses.

The green pasture was laid out almost like an American football field without the yard markers. I took a picture of the sunset. We drove further and came to a beach. We got out of the car and opened the fence to the beach. The shore was full of large rocks. It was just a few minutes after I had taken the other pictures. The sun was going farther down on the orange horizon. We watched, as it slowly, but surely, dipped lower, and then the last dot disappeared. In the car, we discussed the Norwegian political parties, whaling and the island.

252

Later, after midnight, it was still not completely dark outside.

It is amazing that no matter where you travel, how far north you go, the memory and scars of The War – World War II – are present. This isolated island, where we came to get away from it all, was occupied by the Germans. Around the island are holes in the mountains, which the Germans dug as part of their fortifications. I think Nils said the Nazis built some of the roads. The city of Narvik is diagonally northeast from Stamsund behind the fjords. Narvik imported iron from Sweden, a valuable commodity for both sides. The North was also a route to and from the Soviet Union.

Yesterday was a vacation, take-it-easy day. I spent from about 11-3:30 writing two long letters to my brother, Albie, and my relatives, the Sufians. I then set out to search for a post office, hoping it would be open to 4. Guri gave me directions, but I took the wrong left at the bottom of the hill from their house. I walked for 30 minutes and saw nothing but the mountains, rocks and sea. A *car* would drive by every few minutes. You could see the bottom of the sea. After 30 minutes, it was now after 4, so I headed back. I went into the restaurant at the hotel across the street from Guri and Nils to look at the restaurant prices. As luck would have it, I could buy stamps there! But, I had an hour's walk.

After dinner, Alice and I joined Nils for a walk with Helene. We walked along another side of the water, and he pointed out the red cottages, *rorbu,* that fishermen used to use for lodging. Now, families can rent them at inexpensive rates. Helene let us hold her hand but tried to wander away at times, walking too close to the edge of the wharf.

Thursday, 13 August 1992, 7:39 p.m.

Yesterday – Wednesday – was another leisurely day, but heck, we don't have any obligations, now. This is vacation! The weather was blustery and cold. Tuesday was rainy and damp. We finally got ourselves out the door, about one or two in the afternoon. We followed the correct directions toward the post office. Along the way, we passed Helene's school. We saw her playing contentedly in the sandbox.

Across the street from the post office, we bought sodas and chocolate, of course. Alice decided to write some postcards and spent the next 30-40 minutes in the lounge of the post office writing them. By this time, it was close to four, and we met Nils, who was picking up Helene. He gave us a ride back to the house.

Dinner was a little later than Tuesday, but we read and watched Helene climb up and down a chair in the living room. She is, of course, into everything, throwing books and toys around the house. But, she always has a broad smile for us. I am joking that she will like gravy when she gets older because she likes to pour her milk or water on her food.

Dinner was a traditional Norwegian meal – mutton and cabbage with the obligatory potatoes. We had bought dessert as our contribution.

Well, she finally did it! Alice got me on a bike today. A humorous adventure to say the least. I tried to get on Nils' bike, but didn't feel comfortable. Alice managed to ride the bike, and we went to the "multi-purpose store," which rented bikes and rooms, as well as selling souvenirs and religious artifacts. We asked for the simplest bike – which turned out to be a woman's/girl's bike with brakes on the handlebars and pedals.

We started to ride. Alice got out ahead, though she wanted me to set the pace. I was trying to keep my composure, pedal, stop, steer and avoid the cars hitting me. I haven't ridden a bike in over 20 years. Finally, we reached a school. Alice tried the bike out in the driveway. "You can't use this bike. It doesn't have brakes."

Great!

We managed to get back to the store. Alice complained about the bike. The woman called her husband to check the bikes, while Alice rode up to the youth hostel to see if they rented bikes.

Meanwhile, I was willing, at this point, to chalk this up to experience. The husband checked all the bikes, including one his wife brought down from their house above the store. Alice tried it out and felt it was much better. So, we tried again.

Alice kept exhorting me from ahead to "keep pedaling;" "first gear uphill, third gear downhill;" "slowly close the hand brake downhill;" "don't stop." Some of it was easier said than done. The ride took us past beautiful scenery, but it wasn't advisable for me to glance up. We did stop to take some pictures. We went quite a distance – for me – and I convinced Alice to go back sooner. When we got into Stamsund, we stopped for our daily dose of chocolate and soda. I made it back, and my rear still hurts.

The baby was quite pleasant before dinner, playing with books, throwing toys on the kitchen floor for the sake of it, while Mommy cooked dinner. Helene was completely naked and walked into the next room and climbed up on a chair, and started drawing with markers. It is 10:30 now, and she is still not asleep.

One advantage to staying with natives is you never know what you'll get for dinner. We ate tongues of cod, with cooked carrots and potatoes. The tongue was quite good – fried – and had a muscle taste. It is a custom that children get to cut the tongues out of the codfish. Guri remembers doing that as an eight-year-old.

"But we realized knives were dangerous. They were never around when there were fights," she said.

As we had done every night, we cleared the table, washed the dishes and swept the floor. We've been good about trying to contribute and be of help. We also bought food today to make up for some we used.

King Harald has been traveling around the country. Nils told us this evening King Harald and Queen Sonja will be coming to their *kommune* of Vestvågøy Saturday, but not to Stamsund. But Nils is one of 50 people invited to meet the King on the King's ship! He is quite excited.

This led us to a discussion about security and safety in Norway. The King travels with very small security forces. His father, the revered King Olav V, would take the *trikk* with the people to Frognerseteren to ski during the energy crisis in the 1970s. When a journalist asked him if he was concerned for his safety, King Olav replied, "The people are my security."

This sense of safety is shared by the people, particularly in small areas like the Lofotens. Nils and Guri do not lock the house doors, and today she left the car doors open with the keys in the ignition. In Rauland, too, Torbjørn and Debbie left the house doors unlocked. These feelings come from a sense that people know and trust each other. If the King can feel safe, then why shouldn't we? Even Oslo, though the atmosphere is changing, is still a relatively safe city.

The conversation then moved as usual to the Norwegian and American systems. Why does Norway have a sense of social responsibility for its people?

"In Norway, having a job is dignified," said Nils.

Employment is given a priority by the government, because unemployment is viewed as a "waste of human and economic resources." The government will bail out companies and industries or start new ones to ensure employment. Following World War II, the Norwegian government set up industries in every region and sub-region of the country, so that businesses were established in rural areas where the materials were to be found. People in those areas were employed in these businesses, and cities developed around some of these rural factories.

The result was that through the '80s, unemployment was around one percent. When it creeps to two percent, there is great alarm. Unemployment reached four percent in 1982-83. Reasons cited were international recessions; baby boomers looking for work and more women seeking paid work. On the other hand, more people are working. The percent of women between ages 16-67 working increased from 53% to 65% between 1972-79; among married women, from 46% to 61%. But, employment among men remained at 90%, meaning they did not suffer as a result of the increase of women in the labor force. Unemployment is currently (1992) at six percent; in 1990, it was 16% among youth 16-19 years old.[28]

The (overall) salary gap is not as great between jobs, say between a banker and bus driver.

There was more to the conversations, but, alas, no tape recorder. We talked a little bit about the same issues with Guri later, as each parent took a turn trying to get Helene to sleep

Saturday, 15 August 1992, 10:28 a.m.

Aboard the *Polarlys*, heading to Trondheim. We closed out our stay in Stamsund yesterday – Friday – with an energetic day and quite a send-off meal. We were blessed with a beautiful day.

In the morning, I jotted down notes about Vestvågøy and the Islands from the map Nils had lent us. The history of the Lofotens dates back to the Ice Age, 20,000 years ago, and the Islands' mountains are the oldest in the world. It is an area where there is 24-hour sun from the 28th of May to the 14th of July and darkness from the 5th of December to the 6th of January. This is the Land of the Midnight Sun in the summer and Land of the Daylight Moon in the winter.

The arrivals of the boats are significant for the people because it is also their means of transportation and their links to the mainland and other islands. In fact, the steamers are modern and refurbished old mail boats.

Stamsund has the largest trawler company in Norway, farms that research the breeding of cod, factories that

---

[28] Arne Selbyg, *Norway Today*, 1987, and 1995 correspondence with Mr. Selbyg. Used with permission 2005.

process raw fish, and a fishing college. All the fish in the Lofoten Islands waters are edible with salmon, trout and char most abundant. The villages of Steine and Ure are the oldest fishing hamlets.

Vestvågøy, which has the oldest mountains in the world, is 422 square kilometers and is the largest district in the Lofotens, with a population of 111,000 people. There are many dialects, traditions and lifestyles. There are 400 different types of plants and 180 different birds.

The community/trade/administrative/educational and cultural center is Leknes. Also, one of the largest community art schools for children in Northern Norway is located in Leknes.

The area is full of history, as it has been populated since 9000-6000 B.C. The village of Sværika has 22 Stone Age sites. There is a bridge dating to the Viking Age, with the piers still standing, the only Viking Era span in the country.

Red, blue, green and yellowish brown are the colors of the Lofoten Islands. Most of the houses are small and box-like, and some are built into the sides of the mountains. The houses are red or yellowish brown. The sea is clear blue-green. The sky is bright blue; some of the mountains give off a blue hue, and there is plenty of green landscape. There are many hiking trails and places to rent bikes. The Lofotens also has the town with the shortest name in the world – Å, pronounced *"aw."*

As for accommodations in Stamsund, there are a few rooming houses and a hotel. The youth hostel in Stamsund is inexpensive (approximately $11.50-$14 a night), but very basic, and you have to bring your own food, utensils and sleeping bags. The red *rorbu* or cottages are old lodgings for fishermen. A family can rent one inexpensively. Next to the *rorbu* are the triangular, wooden, drying racks for fish.

Speaking of food and fish, we started yesterday by first shopping for food for our trip on the boat that night.

Then, we took about a two-hour hike. First, we took a left uphill on a road that I think was called Halstadveien. From the main road, Johannsen's Vei, you could see sheep at the top of the mountain. We reached a dead end, but it gave us a panoramic view of the center of town, houses and the mountains and fjords in the distance. We walked back down to the main road and toward town. I found the road leading to the path through the mountain range. Along the way, there are red "T"s on trees or rocks outlining the trail. We walked through marshy, muddy areas following the "T" until there were no more "T"s. We walked down a steep hill and found yellow arrows leading back up the other way. We followed them and made the circle back to town.

Along the way, we kept following the sound of the bells on the sheep somewhere in the mountains. We can't pass up a day without Freia chocolate, so we stopped for it on the way back to the house.

We also went comparison herring shopping for the trip. Alice bought dry fish (*lutefisk*) for gifts.

We were sent off with a "real" Norwegian treat for dinner – reindeer meat in cream sauce, with mashed potatoes and Brussels sprouts. Nils and Guri had really treated us well. We were two strangers who stayed four nights. They talked to us and told us things to do. They offered us their sleeping bags for the boat, but we were already weighed down with enough baggage.

After dinner, we cleaned up as we had been doing every night, while Nils took a nap and Guri got Helene ready for bed. We read some and watched TV. We were taking a 9 p.m. boat. Guri brought Helene down to say good-bye, then went upstairs. Alice wrote a note to them, which we both signed. I left it on the kitchen table with a chocolate bar. We grabbed our luggage and slipped out the door.

It was an hour before the boat was scheduled to leave. We sat on our luggage, read and looked at the sea life. Alice walked down the dock a couple of times to see if the boat was in sight. It wasn't. She asked me if I wanted to break into the paprika potato chips (with 30 percent less fat!). I had the same thought.

A few minutes into our little feast, the horn of the boat sounded. It arrived about nine, instead of leaving at nine. The German couple that we had met on Monday's ride was standing on the deck.

We bought two student tickets with a cabin for two nights – @$241 total. Transportation (except on city transit) seems inexpensive, particularly for students. It allows this country, separated by mountains, terrain and water, to be connected. But, Norwegians value their leisure time. The costs of transportation and inexpensive alternative accommodations make holidays affordable.

We were given two small bent copper tubes or pipes. These were the keys to the room, located on the lower level near the whoosh-whoosh of the water and the hum-hum of the motor. The room had a bunk bed and sink. We barely got in with our luggage. After dropping our stuff off, we went on deck and found a vantage point to get a photo of the house – in between the movements of the crane lifting cars onto the boat. When the boat pushed off, we went to the back deck. The sun wasn't visible, but there was an orange glow on the horizon. We were able to see the Lofoten Wall for the entire trip to Bodø. We alternated between indoor looking and on-deck watching. We were mesmerized, almost in a trance by the vista.

The sky began to look like there might be a tremendous storm. We then realized it was the descending darkness, and it made a very interesting view. It was like a split screen, a shade or curtain coming down. But, there was still lit sky over the Lofotens. The curtain descended more, but never completely covered the horizon, forming an ellipse.

Why did we sit in the back, staring for three hours at the same view? Yes, for the view. Yes, to marvel at this mysterious phenomenon of light. Perhaps also to remember what we were leaving and to try to avoid thinking about where we were going. Our "trip" is finally coming toward its close. We were going from the northern parts of the world, the oldest mountains in the

world, above the Arctic Circle. More, we were going from
the isolation, serenity, relaxation and beauty of an island
back toward the rat race of America in a few days. We
were leaving the amazing hospitality of two Norwegian
strangers and their baby daughter, who hosted us for
nearly five days and gave us a taste of real Norwegian
foods. Judging by my past experiences, should I have
been surprised?

We went to bed around two a.m. when the boat
finally arrived at Bodø. Sleeping was an interesting
adjustment. I could tell when the boat was turning or
nearing a stop. I felt like my body was being sucked up
into a vacuum cleaner.

We woke up this morning at nine. Alice headed to the
deck while I dressed.   She returned shortly, excited.
"We're passing the Arctic Circle again!"

I quickly finished dressing and grabbed my camera.
We now had passed the Arctic Circle twice, once by land
and train, and once by sea and boat.

We ate our breakfast of bread and herring. What a
life! Alice has found the German couple and is outside
with them now.

Monday, 17 August 1992, noon

We're back in Oslo, glad in a way, but it's a strange
feeling also. We trudged in yesterday afternoon.

On the boat, we spent time reading, eating, gazing at
the scenery and breathing in the sea air. There are so
many mountains of different textures and so old. Rock
islands, along with the mountains, all on the water. Some
have trees, some don't. No signs of civilization, then a
solitary house. At one point, we passed the Seven Sisters
formation, seven mountain peaks side-by-side. Alice
marveled at the engineering that went into building the
boats and figuring out what would hold up on these
isolated waters.

We got off the boat when it docked at Brøyersund
and walked a little way with Kristen and Herman, the

German couple. We then separated. We walked back toward the boat – took pictures of the wrong boat – and bought ice cream. We got on the right boat. Kristen found us again on the boat. She had collected four-leaf clovers and gave us each one.

The boat docked in Trondheim at about 6:57 a.m., almost a half-hour late. The alarms on our watches worked, and we were able to get up. With the motor running in our head – still is – we didn't get much sleep anyway. The train station was back-to-back to the dock, so it was a walk around the corner.

We bought our reserved seats for the train and actually received a refund for our unused Bodø-Trondheim train tickets. There were many people traveling. All of a sudden, Kristen came running into the station outfitted in her motorbike gear. She was looking for a place to buy more film, but also to say good-bye to us. She and Alice exchanged addresses.

The Narvessen – newsstand and food store – opened, and I bought some apples, chocolate and Friday's *Herald Tribune,* even though it was two days old. I hadn't read any news in a week. The train was nice, with automatic sliding doors between the compartments – that didn't always work. It was a quiet ride back, taking breaks for salmon from the tin, chocolate and apples. We spent most of the time reading. Alice had bought a *Reader's Digest* before leaving Oslo. There were a number of interesting articles and jokes in it. I was also catching up on back issues of other magazines. Alice is in the midst of three different books.

The scenery was nice, but it was raining. During our time in Norway, we had been on the train and boat to Bergen, traveled to Bodø, spent four days in the Lofoten Islands, cruised from Stamsund to Trondheim amidst beautiful mountains and rock islands; so anything else now would be anticlimactic – no matter how many announcements the conductor made about where we were. When we came to Hunderfossen, they played a children's song about Hunderfossen. The Olympic bobsled and luge competitions will take place in Hunderfossen, so it wasn't long before we stopped at Lillehammer. This time, I didn't get off the train.

The Sentral train station in Oslo was quite crowded. As with each of our return trips to Oslo this summer, it was raining. In the Narvessen, I bought some cheese and *lefse* to help tide us over for a couple of days. Having lived on tins and tubes for the last couple of days, we decided we needed a meal.

We got off the *trikk* at Majorstua to search for a restaurant. Alice looked around and said, "It's good to be back in Oslo, but I'm looking for familiar faces. You can't look back, just ahead to good experiences (to come)."

The Krishna vegetarian restaurant, where we had gone with the ISS students before leaving for the Lofotens, was closed, so we tried the Chinese restaurant across the street. It was good, but in the middle of the meal, I began to feel very hot and dizzy. Once out in the air, I began to feel a little better. We took the *trikk* and bus to the *vandrehjem,* which is also student housing for the University. By now, it was pouring. We checked in and got directions to the building. We made the wrong left and wound up back at the reception area. Back in the rain again.

After dropping the luggage off, I called the Dalgards and Berit about any plans for the next two days. My parents were due to arrive/have arrived this morning.

I came back to the room. It was only around seven. We met our neighbors, who were from Italy. We keep meeting Italians and Germans, which is amusing. In Norwegian class, we had translated a satirical newspaper column about foreigners protesting Norway's renewal of whaling and whether this was a threat to tourism. The writer wrote: "There are 50 percent more Germans here this year than there were in 1945 (at the end of WWII). But now for the time (being), they are not armed with anything other than mobile homes, and as roadblocks, they are rather peaceful."

We were so exhausted; we dropped on the beds and fell asleep until around nine a.m. We had a leisurely breakfast – four slices of bread, two slices of cheese, two different types of jam, butter, onion-cheese spread, choice of coffee, tea, milk and juice.

My parents have arrived, but not at Odd's office. We are getting ready to go pick up the rest of our luggage at Blindern.

Tuesday, 18 August 1992, 11:33 p.m.

Returned from Dalgards and are doing last-minute packing. The last two days were filled with good-byes, reunions and returns. We went back to Blindern yesterday to pick up the rest of the luggage, which we were able to store there. It had only been 10 days but what a change and different feeling being on the campus. We walked into the plaza, and it was full of students. A new banner, advertising a student festival beginning 31 August, now hung from Fredrike, replacing the old one. I don't even remember what that old one said.

There were students streaming down the hall in Fredrike. The campus had been transformed. We were not of these students. We didn't belong with them. The "real" students had returned!

In the ISS office, the man who had worked in the language lab was at the desk. He took us to the basement to get our luggage. I went back up to the fifth floor to call for a taxi and to call my father. We agreed to meet at 4:15 at the (Ulleval) Hospital.

The cab was already waiting when I met Alice in the lobby. As we drove through the campus, there was graffiti on a building: "Pakis Go Home." We didn't remember it being there before. It was alarming, especially after our summer school experience.

On this day, the *sporveien* (transportation system) had converted the Route 13 *trikk* to a complete bus route because of construction. During the summer, we could take the *trikk* from Blindern to the Ulleval Stadion stop and transfer to a shuttle bus. The *vandrehjem* is located along the route. Because of the construction work being done around the Stadion, people returning to school and work were caught in a massive traffic jam! The new bus route also stopped near the Hospital. We took a 3:28 bus. We sat for 20 minutes at one light. We got off at the stop closest to the Hospital around 4:08. According to the schedule, the total time to Majorstua should take 19 minutes. We walked down to Sognsveien and found a back way onto the Hospital grounds and found the meeting place.

My father's cousin, Marion, who was accompanying them on the trip, was waiting in front of the store on the grounds of the hospital. We greeted each other, and shortly thereafter, my parents arrived. We went to the cafeteria, but it had closed at four. Alice and I suggested going to the vegetarian restaurant at Majorstua, and we caught the bus along Kirkeveien.

It was good to see my parents again and to have people to relate our experiences.

A familiar face came into the restaurant, one of the weekend receptionists from ISS. He sat with us for a while. After dinner, my parents, Marion, Alice and I walked toward Frogner Park, although it started to rain. We only got to show Marion some of the Vigeland statues, and Alice didn't get to take pictures as she had wanted. We took refuge from the rain in the outdoor (covered) café in the park.

On Tuesday, we met Mom and Marion and went to Holmenkollen and Frognerseteren. Alice bought the *rømmebrød* cookies (sour cream bread), and Mom bought a few postcards in the Holmenkollen gift shop.

The four of us, with me as the able guide, walked back to the *trikk* stop and went up to Frognerseteren, and the Restaurant, where we wanted to eat. Alice and I had one of the best meals we had in Norway, certainly the best in a restaurant. We had the deer burgers, which came in a cream sauce, with boiled potatoes and parsley, peas and whortleberries. Mom and Marion had poached trout with shrimp and muscles, boiled potatoes and cucumber salad.

Alice and I had arranged for a quick visit to Berit and needed to get back to Majorstua to buy some wine, as well as flowers for the Dalgards that night. In between, we happened to finally find UFF, a secondhand store where you can get sweaters inexpensively. Alice managed to buy two, one for herself and one for her mother. We rushed to catch the 13 bus to Berit, who lives across from the hostel.

Berit was delightful, as usual, serving us drinks and snacks and wanting to know about everything we did. Some of the experiences came gushing out. Alice read her essay from the exam. Berit was quite impressed with the essay after only six weeks of studying the language. I caught Berit up with my Lillehammer interview and class activities.

Berit then said she had wanted to give us a gift. She had thought it was courageous for us to make this trip together. "I don't know if you'll stay together or not, but here's this book by a friend of mine." *"Og de levde lykkelig...Om forelskelse og kjærlighet."* ("And they lived happily...about falling in love and affection.")

Inside Berit wrote: *"Det har vært så hyggelig å bli kjent med dere. Jeg ønsker dere alt godt videre i livet."* *("It has been so nice to become acquainted with you. I wish you both all the best in the future.")*

And then it always seems to come down to the Dalgards, probably our family's closest and dearest Norwegian friends. My last dinners the night before leaving Norway have always been with the Dalgards, dating to 1970. Their last dinner in Philadelphia in 1973 was spent with us. Sometimes, the trips begin with them also, perhaps being picked up at the airport.

It was a full house at Odd and Ragnhild's – Eivind (Angela was sick), Olav and Florence with the two children, my parents, Marion, Alice and me. It was hard to believe this was the first time in our seven-plus weeks in Norway that I had seen Florence. She was away the first few weeks when we had seen the Dalgards.

For the first time, we got to test our Norwegian. As my father said, "They needed to get feedback." He, like Eivind and the others, was impressed as I told them in Norwegian what happened in the interview in Lillehammer.

There's a warmth and always humor that emanates from get-togethers with the Dalgards. Florence asked Alice whether she had obtained the "Steiners passion for Norway," meaning to say "Kleiners."

I said, "Kleiners. I didn't know *stein* (stone in Norwegian) had passion."

Olav teased Florence, who is half French, half Danish, about her "passion" for Norway.

Alice again read her essay to positive reviews. I read my "fairy-tale" essay about the American who wanted to be a Norwegian (a satire about me), with a lot of inside humor. At one point, I have the character visit a psychiatrist. Florence joked, "(That's) Odd."

At the conclusion, Eivind said, "That's a fairy tale?"

I kidded, "Well, it borders on it."

Olav and Florence had to leave early to get the kids home. Florence so much wanted us to come back to the house with them.

"Can't you extend your stay?" she asked.

As we went back to the youth hostel on the bus, I suddenly realized something – it was 11:00, and it was dark. I suppose that was an indication we had been here a while. Summer was nearing its end.

I also reflected that I'd known the Dalgards – as well as most of the other Norwegian friends – for 22 years. I can only think of one friend in the U.S. that I have known for that long. Of course, some of this connection is due to my father's numerous return trips and some of these associates coming to the U.S.

I think back to when we first met the Dalgards in 1969-70. Eivind and Olav didn't know English, and my brother and I didn't know Norwegian. Somehow, we communicated. In 1972-73, the Dalgards spent a year in Philadelphia and lived in our neighborhood. My brother and I hung out with Eivind and Olav all the time. They knew some English then (and certainly learned more). We introduced them to baseball and Harvey's Pizza Den, which was across the street from their apartment.

Since then, I have seen them in snippets, frames. But, it is a friendship that has endured. In the U.S., a friendship is sometimes considered over if you haven't seen or talked to someone for a couple of months. There has been little regular letter writing from them, but when we are together, it can be like time has not passed.

Several years after they were in Philadelphia, Olav came through town with five boys from The Traveling School they were attending. Students chose topics to study, and the classroom was the world. They had been in Central America and decided to come through the U.S. and stop in Philadelphia. These six Norwegian boys showed up and stayed for a couple of days. Olav just had to go to Harvey's for pizza.

When I made my first return trip to Norway in 1986, it was the first time I saw Eivind in 13 years. Yet, the friendship immediately picked up again. In 1990, it had been several years since I had seen Olav in Philadelphia. The friendship was still there as well. We have gone from barely being able to communicate to talking sophisticatedly in English to talking Norwegian again! Angela and Florence are now just as important. Three friends and a cousin of mine have felt accepted.

All the Dalgards tried to call us several times during the summer, but we were hard to reach. But, they tried.

Eivind drove us to the airport the next morning. He said the school was a good experience for us because, as a tourist, we only see the "surface" of the country. When Alice thanked him for all he had done for us, he said, "You haven't seen my bad side."

We all have our good and bad sides. And, yes, as a tourist, you do see a "surface of the country." There are good and bad sides of all countries. No one, and no place, is perfect. I've never said living in Norway would be Utopia. This trip was different because of the ISS, and we weren't here strictly to visit. I have had the advantage of knowing people so that I haven't felt like the average tourist. But, I also saw some things about Norway that weren't perfect.

The racism toward immigrants is disturbing, but yet, there was a large anti-racism rally last year. Conservatives are trying to chip away at the welfare state benefits, like the health-care system. Health care has become less efficient. Yet, there's still a strong feeling of social responsibility for others. The anti-immigrant feeling is due in part to the government instituting programs to help the immigrants.

Berit says, "Norway is not as good a place to live in as it once was."

Prices are high, especially for food. Unemployment is up in a country that once had the lowest unemployment in Europe. However, the gap in salaries is not as high as in the U.S., and everyone is entitled to decent housing. We would never consider slums what they consider slums.

Women for the most part enjoy equal status. The prime minister, Gro Harlem Brundtland, and the Mayor of Oslo, Ann-Marit Sæbanes, are women. The right to vote was granted to women in 1913. Nine of the 19 ministers in the cabinet are women, including Brundtland. The leaders of the Labor, Conservative and the Center Parties, the three largest parties are women; and 59 of the 165 members of the Parliament are women (June 1991, *New York Times*). Their participation is taken for granted. That 36 percent figure has remained the same in 1992.[29] The result has been programs for childcare and more emphasis on children and family issues. Women are guaranteed paid maternity leave and their job when they return.

---

[29] Arne Selbyg, *Norway Today*, 1987, and 1995 correspondence with Mr. Selbyg in 1995. Used with permission 2005.

Most Norwegians grew up in the countryside or on the coast and moved to the cities. On farms, women were main contributors. Fishermen were often away for months at a time, so the wife, along with the sons and daughters, had to run the household. Therefore, their equal status was established and accepted.

Norwegians, as the "stereotype" goes, are "reserved," "cool" and "hard to get to know." There are probably some who are. Explain Ana in the Heathrow Airport, who within a few hours is inviting us to dinner; the man at Frognerseteren driving us around the area; and the hospitality of Guri and Nils in the Lofoten Islands. Norway also gave me the experience of the International Summer School. Amidst the racism of some elements of the Norwegian population was the ISS, bringing people together from different countries and backgrounds.

Each time I visit Norway, I seem strengthened in my feelings toward the country and its people.

Monday, 24 August 1992, 11:53 a.m.

Philadelphia. Home again, although since I'm house sitting for my parents, I won't get a real sense of home for a couple of weeks. The time away in one respect went by quickly, yet in another, it felt like we were away a long time. It takes a little while adjusting, remembering where things are and how to get there.

Once again, it was tough to leave Norway because I didn't know whether it would be a year or more before I'll see these friends again. Maybe that's what makes it so special to visit. Maybe it's better that way?

And now, some "welcome home" notes...

Read two days worth of *Herald Tribunes* on the plane and got sick reading the rhetoric coming out of the Republican convention. Later that night, I listened to Barbara Bush lecture about "family values." You'd think Democrats never hugged their kids!

We got through immigration and customs pretty quickly, then waited two hours for the limo. There were so many people at Newark Airport, but the atmosphere was still not the high pressure that JFK would have been in New York.

As soon as you arrive in the U.S., the atmosphere is immediately different. At the airport, I stepped outside to scout for the limo. All of a sudden – "chaos." Noise and pollution. Travelers with carts of luggage maneuvering around. Cabs, buses, vans, cars, one after the other, trying to gain position as they drive along the roadway. Such differences from the calm of Oslo's Fornebu Airport. At Fornebu, you walk outside and see a view of the fjord! Buses and taxis wait in line for their turn to move.

Alice ran into a man who had lived in the same co-op house she did in Buffalo, nine years ago. She called her parents, and we were invited to dinner, so we had the limo take us directly there.

The next day, I "sprung" Buddy, our dog, from the vet and stopped at my apartment. Alice and I had dinner together. One of the first calls I received was from Textile personnel about whether I wanted to stay on the medical plan at $152.89 for medical and $29.92 for dental care, per **month**. Only $182.81/month for an unemployed person! Great safety net, Prez George! Talked to Albie and D.X. at length Thursday night, then fell asleep to George's speech. The economy and unemployment somehow escape him.

Had lunch with Andy on Friday, and talked with him by phone. Stopped at my apartment again. On the way, I noticed that the car wash where I took my car had closed. Steve was also one of the first to call me.

Talked to my friend, Mark, on Friday and spent a pleasant Sunday with him at Beachcombers, the swim club. Played tennis. Several people at BSC welcomed me back and asked about the trip. My welcoming committee, I suppose. It was apparently one of the few nice weekends of the summer in Philadelphia.

Talked to my Aunt Bevy Sunday morning.

In Oslo, there is more concern for safety now than when we lived there years ago. People lock doors, and we were told to be careful of our things. In Rauland and Stamsund, the house doors were unlocked. In Stamsund,

271

car doors were left open with keys in the ignition. Nils said, "Why not?"

Back here – to locked doors, clubs on car steering wheels, feelings of worry walking on the street, feelings of mistrust. Is my waist bag safe? Fears of this magnitude are not even prevalent in Oslo.

Welcome back to my reality. I'm in the unemployment office now to reopen my claim. Certain things have changed here, too. I arrived around 11 a.m. to get a head start on my 11:30 reporting time. There was a line to the door for the reception desk. To my left, where once a line snaked, are now chairs for people. How courteous. Gone is the separate section for opening claims. The new innovation is numbered tickets.

Now, home to tickets in the unemployment office and waiting time that is endless. I suppose it's meant to improve efficiency, but it creates a line at the reception desk, which is where one gets the ticket. There's a feeling of being personally devalued by the whole process.

My number was 96. They were at 7 when I sat down at 11:10. It's 12:50 and the counter says 66, although it may be higher. They don't always change it. What hasn't changed is the number of people. There are still plenty of them. Gee, George, great recovery, 89 people in front of me. But, maybe that's a change too. There are more people here than in June. Maybe that's why the office went to numbers? Family values? Does that include making sure people have jobs so they can support a family? Family values? Mothers sit here with their children for hours. I guess that's quality time, George!

I came prepared for the wait: a newspaper; June *Focus*, which lists businesses in the Philadelphia area; August *Public Relations Newsletter*, and a pad for journal writing. On the reporting day for unemployment, you might as well scratch the day from looking for work.

Welcome home.

Finally, around 1:35, they reached 96. It only took me a few minutes to do what I had to do. I was out of there at 1:42, slipping through the line that was still reaching to the door. I exited into an uncertain future.

Chapter 6
Transition, America
1992-94

Summer 1994

It has been almost two years since I wrote those words about an uncertain future. Though my situation is better for me than two years ago, there are things – financial, in particular, that are still a struggle. The last two years have not been easy.

I am now a graduate student working toward a master's degree in educational media at Temple University, integrating technology into education and training, a field that is current, which should enable me to have choices for occupations when I graduate a year from now. One of the reasons I chose this program was the interest and caring the professors showed toward me, something that few people in America had shown for over six months. I signed up for a photography course in January 1993, and the day after the first meeting, the teacher offered me a part-time job, working in the computer lab.

I am also a graduate assistant in the College of Health, Physical Education, Recreation and Dance (HPERD), writing and editing their publications, a position that pays me a stipend and tuition. I am appreciated and respected for the work I do.

As people in HPERD or Ed Media will tell you, Norway is never far from my thoughts. Most of the positive things that have happened to me in the last two years have a Norwegian-Scandinavian connection. I have been able to draw even starker contrasts between the way people deal with people in Norway, and the way they do in the United States, because my evidence is personal.

My Olympic dream did not materialize. Though the Lillehammer Olympic Organizing Committee never sent me an official letter, I am indebted to them for twice letting me come to Lillehammer to meet with them. It was arranged with just a phone call, courteously and pleasantly. When I called Frode in October 1993, he told me he had forwarded the letters I wrote to him to the right people, and told me to fax an updated resumé and letter to the personnel consultant at the LOOC.

Meanwhile, back here, calling CBS would get different responses. I don't think I ever spoke directly with the people I was calling. I would get told my resumé was lost, or my name wasn't on a list, even though I had been writing to CBS since 1991. I never received an interview for the one Olympic researcher position, or an interview for any other position. Never was I asked to come to New York for a tour. I received letters that would say hiring had been completed, then letters saying they were still reviewing resumés. There was never any personal touch. By the time the local TV affiliate tried to get involved on my behalf, it was too late.

TNT didn't turn out any differently. I never received a letter from them after a note in April 1993 saying they would be reviewing resumés in September. They never responded to faxes.

Here I was with knowledge of the Norwegian language, history and culture, as well as the professional experience and interest in the Olympics, and I wasn't worth the time in the United States. There are people who will say, "CBS and TNT are such large operations." So was the LOOC, but they made the time for me, and not begrudgingly.

It's not just the networks. The American job market has become so inundated with job seekers that it is rare to even get a rejection letter. That's usually a form letter anyway. Sometimes, the letter comes so many months after you applied, you forgot you sent a resumé. Often companies tell you not even to call.

By contrast, in January 1993, I sent a letter in Norwegian and a resumé to a magazine Frode had given me, *Norway at your service*, an English-language magazine published by the Norwegian Trade Council in Oslo. During the next couple of months, I sent out 24 letters to editors of travel sections in newspapers around the United States, offering to do an article on either Lillehammer, the International Summer School or the Lofoten Islands.

In March 1993, I received a message on my answering machine from the editor of *Norway at your service*, not the editor I had written to, but the new editor, an American woman who had lived in Norway for a number of years. My letter had been forwarded to her. The message asked if I was interested in writing an article for the magazine. She said when I returned her call, she would call me back, so I wouldn't have to pay for the international call! They were asking me to write an article, and she had the courtesy and common decency to say they would pay for the call.

The article was to preview the world cycling championships, to be held in Norway for the first time, in August 1993. She had the option of giving the assignment to a Norwegian journalist, and then translating the article into English, or giving it to an English-speaking sportswriter who could read Norwegian.

"How well can you read Norwegian?" she asked.

"Good enough. There's always the dictionary and my tutor," I said.

All the information she sent was in Norwegian, and I soon was seeing a benefit of the Summer School. In addition, in our subsequent conversations, we developed a pleasant rapport. She said she'd pay me a fee for the article plus expenses. When the expenses exceeded the original figure, she didn't demand proof, even though I sent receipts.

The result was the cover story and two articles that covered five pages of the glossy August issue and an invitation to write for the magazine again. The magazine is distributed in 31 countries.

Meanwhile, I got one bite from the 24 newspapers and then a rejection. Not all the newspapers responded.

Among those that did, many letters seemed curt and short, or a form letter. Little encouragement was ever offered. *The New York Times* sent a letter back that included my resumé, asking for my resumé and clips. They called back. My excitement was short-lived. No one there knew who had sent me the letter asking me for my resumé and clips!

At the same time, I was taking the photography class at Temple, and my slide-show final project in May 1993 was on the American Swedish Historical Museum in Philadelphia, which welcomes all people of Scandinavian descent as well as other interested persons. Not only was the show successful in class, but also when I gave a video copy to the museum, the staff was so overwhelmed they used it at their booth for the Pennsylvania Convention Center opening.

I have been to activities at the museum. The staff greets me cordially. There is a special feeling hearing Swedish spoken, which is close enough to Norwegian, and by parents to their beautiful blond children. It's as if I've been transported for a few hours to Scandinavia. Besides, the gift shop used to sell Freia chocolate!

The possibility of being in Lillehammer in 1994 was diminishing, but I decided if I couldn't be in Lillehammer, I would bring it here. For my fall '93 semester classes, I produced a two-slide projector show and video, *Introducing Lillehammer to the World.* I was able to use all the magazines given to me by the LOOC, *Norway at your service*, back issues of *Sports Illustrated* and *Olympian* for the visuals. The productions were well-received and sparked interest among students for the Olympics. I began the show by speaking in Norwegian. I used David Foster's *Winter Games* as background music, my motivational song.

I was successful in selling a Lillehammer preview story to *Olympian*, the magazine of the United States Olympic Committee. I was able to work on all the Lillehammer projects at the same time. In that call to Frode in October 1993, we talked for quite a while, and he told me who I could interview at the LOOC. The article appeared in the January/February 1994 issue, just prior to the Olympics. I had two articles appear in major magazines and both dealt with Norway.

Watching the Olympics was a bittersweet experience. Tears came to my eyes during the opening ceremonies when the Sami entered on the reindeer sleds, and I remembered my experience at Geilo. It was wonderful to see the shots of Lillehammer and Norway: the children, the Norwegian crowds cheering for everybody, the Norwegians doing well and some of the features on Norwegian culture. I longed to be there and was annoyed with each mispronunciation of Lillehammer and other Norwegian words. I videotaped every night's activities. However, I think the enduring memory for journalists of the 1994 Olympics was the hospitality of the Norwegians, which was mentioned by many broadcasters, something I know quite a bit about.

My boss at HPERD thought I should be interviewed by the media during the Olympics and made some attempts, but nothing ever came of it (not because of him).

When I returned from Norway in 1992, I never realized how much my life had changed, and would change, in America, besides having to look for a job. I was not prepared for these changes, and I am still dealing with them.

Being unemployed removed the network of people I knew from work. The Jewish organization I belonged to disbanded. Andy got married while I was in Norway, moved to New Jersey and started graduate school, too. Seth and Gwynne moved in together in the next building, and they, too, began graduate school. Less free time, distance and life changes have resulted in seeing or talking to each other less. In January 1993, Alice and I broke up.

My friend, Mark, and I have become better friends. He has been there for me, inviting me to social activities. He has heard about and seen the pictures from all my

Norway trips, and is anxious to travel to Norway. Except he wants to do in one trip what it took me four journeys to do.

Distance has hurt regular communication with friends in Norway, but not the friendships. Despite marriage, I am as much friends with Angela and Florence as with Eivind and Olav.

What can I say about the Breviks who I have known for such a short time? I received a postcard from them, written by John Ivar's wife, who I had never met. For Christmas/Chanukah '93, they sent me a silk tie with the image of the rock carving of the Olympic torchbearer on the front and the rock carving images of the Olympic events on the underside. The images are based on 4,000-year-old rock carvings depicting skiing, which were found in Northern Norway. There was also a tiepin of the torch. Included with the gift was a Norwegian letter, with a note from Marit and Andreas, who had driven me to Lillehammer, and two articles from the *Aftenposten*. They were about the torch relay around the country and a book on etiquette the LOOC had published.

I have had some correspondence from Bea and Erica, and at Christmas '92, the Norwegian staff at the ISS sent a letter to the students.

There are other gestures from Norwegians. When I talk to Norwegians at the Norwegian Trade Council or the Bergen Line (the cruise line for the Bergen to Kirkenes trip) in New York, or people regarding the articles I have written, they are happy to hear of my affinity for their country and are very receptive and courteous. This gives me a real good feeling inside.

When I interviewed the woman in charge of protocol for the cycling championships, she mentioned grants awarded to journalists to write about Norway, and faxed me the information the next day.

After I "pitched" the story idea about the International Summer School to *Norway at your service*, the editor recommended another publication that might be interested. Within a week of faxing that magazine a query letter in Norwegian and a resumé, I received a package with a letter written in Norwegian. It complemented my Norwegian, and offered me the opportunity to write the article. A little more than a week after faxing a letter and resumé to the Norwegian Trade Council in New York, I received a call acknowledging receipt of my resumé and that they would be in touch at a later date.

These are gestures and elements of public relations that don't seem to exist very much anymore in the United States. Our society has changed greatly in the way we deal with, or don't deal with, people. We've become very impersonal. There are many good things about our country, but we can be better. There are also many good and caring people in America, too.

Since returning from Norway in 1992, I have seen more clearly how American society is based on fear. It grips all of us and is uncomfortable: Fear of crime. Fear of walking on the street at night. Fear of walking to your car alone. Fear of walking from your car to the door of your home. Fear of taking public transportation at night. Fear of guns. Fear of not having guns. Fear of not being able to step out of your house in certain neighborhoods because you might get shot by a stray bullet. Fear of nudging someone in a line or a crowd because he might harm you. Fear of drugs. Fear of AIDS.

Fear of losing your job and health insurance. Fear of making politics socially responsible to people. Fear that America could be inferior to any country in any category. Fear and distrust of people. Fear of helping a homeless person because they may be faking or use the money for the wrong purposes. Fear of showing compassion.

Our humanity has been taken from us.

The tragedy is this list could go on and on, and all of them would be true. Always, I find myself comparing these facts to my image of Norway and Norwegians, which continues to grow positively with each encounter.

These comparisons do impact on my view of Norway and the United States. Is this fascination with Norway really overblown and romantic? There must be some deeper reasons for my feelings for this other country, which I hadn't quite sorted out. It would take a *visit to Philadelphia* to bring some clarity.

Chapter 7
The Bridge
June 1994

December 1993 to June 1994

I was occupied with one of my usual December activities, writing Norwegian letters to our friends, when the phone rang.

"Michael? This is Eivind from Norway."

It was around 9 p.m., meaning it was around 3 a.m. in Oslo.

"I just mailed a letter to you today!" I exclaimed.

"I'm planning a visit to the United States around the time of the (soccer) World Cup in June," he said. "I'm coming with a friend. Could you see if you could get tickets for the games? It is so hard to get tickets here."

I said, "I'll see what I can do. I had been wondering if you would try to come for the World Cup, especially after Norway qualified."

"I'm coming partly for that and partly to see all of you and America after 20 years," he said. "Are you coming to Lillehammer? We have some tickets."

For a moment, I was very tempted, but told him I wasn't.

"You know, we now have a daughter, Andrea, six months old," he said.

"It's about time you told us," I said. "And Olav and Florence?"

"They have a daughter, too – Agnes, three months younger than Andrea. It should be interesting for them as they grow up. I had a letter written to you, but I lost it. I didn't want to write in English."

"You could have written in Norwegian," I said.

"I know. That's what Angela said."

We finally got off the phone. Over the next six months, we communicated through letters and faxes, almost as much or more than we had in the previous 21 years. In one letter, right before the Olympics, he mentioned how ridiculous it was that I wouldn't be at Lillehammer.

I had no luck tracking down tickets for the Norway soccer games, but kept writing to him about whether I should try to get tickets to a Phillies baseball game. Then he wrote that he and his friend had worked out a package deal with Delta Airlines that included tickets to Norway's games in New Jersey.

When I hadn't heard from him about his definitive plans by mid-June, I called him in Norway a few days before he was scheduled to leave. "Didn't you get my card?" he asked.

"No," I said.

He gave me his plans for arriving in New York

I asked how he felt Norway was going to do in the World Cup.

"I don't expect them to do well, so I'll be surprised if they do, and not disappointed if they don't do well. Besides, I'm coming to visit the United States after 21 years and to see you."

On looking forward to the trip, he said, "It's strange. I don't remember much about my life before the year in America, but remember things vividly from that year. Then I came home. I remember some things from high school. I talked to Olav about it, and he said the same thing."

"That's interesting," I said. "I have similar feelings about the year we spent in Norway, and that's why I'm writing this book."

We were on the phone 30 minutes.

He said he would call when he got to New York.

I eagerly awaited his next call with the definite arrival times in Philadelphia. His call came from a pay phone in New York the following Friday, June 24, the same day his postcard arrived. The picture on the card was the July

282

midnight sun over Vestvågøy, where I had stayed in the Lofoten Islands.

I was intrigued by his requests for activities in Philadelphia: swimming, downtown Philadelphia, a baseball match, the Ellwood School (which he attended with his brother and my brother) and the old neighborhood.

26 June 1994

He would arrive Sunday afternoon at the Mt. Airy train station, my local station. I even finished cleaning up the apartment. The sticker of Norway's flag that I had displayed on the TV during the Olympics, I taped again to the set for the World Cup and the Norwegians arrival. I bought a World Cup shirt and hat. The photos of Norway all over my living room got an extra dusting. I saved the sports sections that mentioned Norway and the World Cup. As the days passed, I kept smiling with anticipation.

Finally, Sunday arrived. I was at the train station about 20 minutes early. Mark, who lived around the corner, soon joined me. He looked forward to meeting Eivind, whom he had heard so much about, and also because Mark and I were discussing a trip to Norway next summer. Mark would spend the day with us.

The train arrived two minutes late, and I was relieved to see him appear quickly in the doorway. All the Norwegian I planned to say didn't come out, except maybe *"Velkommen."*

I introduced Mark.

We walked to the car. I drove around some of the scenic areas of the neighborhood and past our food co-op. I explained with a mixture of Norwegian and English about the co-op. Although this was Mt. Airy, which borders Germantown, Eivind remembered that I had gone to school in Germantown.

As I pulled into the parking lot of my apartment complex, my parents were arriving. We were all going to

Beachcombers, our swim club. After a quick stop in my apartment, we were on our way.

During the phone call to Norway a week before, he had said he remembered Beachcombers and the activities there. Perhaps, he remembered Beachcombers, as I remembered Frogner Park or Frognerseteren.

He wanted to relax and get some sun. It had been so hectic before he left Oslo, with a birthday party for the baby with 20 people the day before, that he had forgotten the baby pictures, and had no time to buy me a Norway World Cup shirt. "I was lucky I made the plane," he kidded.

My father asked him about his visit so far.

"The change is the proportion of things. I remember things as a child, when they looked bigger," he said.

I brightened.

"That's the way I felt when I first went back to Norway!" I said.

He read my articles from *Norway at your service* and *Olympian*.

"The Lillehammer story was so accurate," he said. "I didn't know Norway's name came from the god NOR."

Conversation was easy. At the snack bar, he had his third or fourth soft pretzel of the day; the first time on his trip to America he enjoyed our local delicacy in Philadelphia. Afterwards, Eivind, Mark and I played tennis. Eivind was the better of an unspectacular trio, although he hadn't played in a year, but we all had fun. For a few minutes, Eivind and I just hit the ball around.

After a swim, he asked what changes had occurred in America. My father explained that crime, unemployment, drugs, racism, anti-Semitism were worse. He added that there was so much difficulty trying to get a universal health-care bill passed. I mentioned that when I was working in 1992, the employer covered my health care. When I wasn't working, I was able to stay on the group plan by paying $152 a month.

"You weren't working and didn't have money and you had to pay?" he replied, picking up immediately on the irrationality of the situation.

The conversation ended as we prepared to go to dinner at the restaurant down the road. Earlier, he recommended that if Mark and I traveled to Norway, we should take the Oslo-Bergen trip on Flåmbanen, which I had taken with Alice. He said we should stop overnight at Flåm to do some hiking. As we got in the car, Mark said, "Maybe you can go with us."

"On the Flåm trip, I would like that very much," Eivind said.

We enjoyed a steak dinner, but most importantly, the time spent was long and leisurely, so typical of dinners with the Dalgards and Norwegians. We were there so long that the waitress came by to offer us complimentary loaves of bread to take home because the restaurant was preparing to close.

Back at my apartment, Eivind and I talked about how to arrange our schedule for the next day and about meeting his friend.

We watched my videos from class about the American Swedish Historical Museum and Lillehammer. He then wanted to see the tape of the Olympic opening ceremonies to see the American coverage. He was shocked to see how many times I had to fast forward through the commercials and the constant talk of the announcers.

We were up till 1 a.m.

27 June 1994

We had a busy morning before we even left the house. Eivind called his friend, Espen, and it was arranged we would meet him at one of the train stations in Center City.

I wore my Norway T-shirt.

I laid out a real Norwegian *frokost* (breakfast): *sild* (herring), *gravlaks* (lox or ground nova) and Jarlsberg *ost* (cheese). The unsliced brown bread from the restaurant the night before just made it complete since you never see already sliced bread in Norway.

"I love herring," he said.

Eivind asked about Andy and Seth. I said I hadn't heard from Andy much since he got married and moved to New Jersey, and I occasionally saw Seth on the train or around the apartment complex. We were all in school, which limited our free time.

"I am not good at keeping in touch with people," Eivind admitted. "I am not a letter writer or someone who gets on the phone. I have a number of friends in Tromsø whom I mean to keep in touch with, but don't."

He called Seth and left a message on the answering machine.

After breakfast, I showed him the draft of a letter I had written in Norwegian to a magazine in Norway about a story idea. He willingly looked over the letter.

"I have no problem understanding the letter, but there are 30 or 40 mistakes in it," he said with humor. "Would you like me to correct it?"

We agreed he shouldn't make it perfect because the editor would either assume I got a Norwegian to write it or that I was more fluent in the language than I really was.

"Prepositions are a big problem in language," he said, noting my weakness. "This is a good letter. I give you a B for it."

We had a lengthy conversation on a variety of topics, but we had to stop, or we would never get to the old neighborhood.

As we drove back into the time warp, to his – no, *our* – history and memories – Eivind looked out of the window of the car. He seemed genuinely happy.

"Should I be recognizing something soon?" he asked.

He noticed the predominantly black neighborhoods.

"Do blacks and whites keep separate?" he asked.

"My neighborhood is integrated," I said. "But blacks and whites for the most part keep separate. There are blacks who want to be separate."

"Nothing has changed in 21 years," said Eivind. "I remember it was all right to be friends with the blacks at school, but they never invited you home."

Later, he would recall the games on the school playground.

"When we were choosing teams, Olav and I would pick the black players because they were the better players," he said. "Some of the other kids would get so upset. 'You can't pick them! You have to pick the whites!' they would say."

This observation from someone, who until recently had lived in a homogeneous white society.

Then we were there, the old neighborhood, which was my old neighborhood, too.

"Are you recognizing anything, now?" I asked, as we crossed 12th Street, then 11th Street, my old block.

"Yes," he said, brightening.

First stop was 10th Street and his apartment building.

"Is that it?" he asked, as we neared an apartment building.

"No, although I remember we looked at apartments in there for you," I said. "Your apartment building is next."

I turned left into the driveway.

He needed film, and I had forgotten the rolls I had at home. I knew there was a drugstore up the street.

"Let's go to the store where we used to shop for food," he said.

"A supermarket?" I tried to remember.

"It was on a corner," Eivind insisted.

"Well, let's go to the drugstore and get the film," I said.

I drove toward the drugstore. He looked out the window, at the overgrown grass on some of the sidewalks, and down the side streets.

"Somewhere is the park where we walked to play tennis," he recalled.

I reached the CVS drugstore.

"I think the market was here," Eivind said.

"There once was a supermarket here," I said.

I had been heading here anyway!

I waited in the car while Eivind went in the store to buy the film and perhaps remember where the milk had been stacked.

Once back in the car, we continued on our tour through time and down memory lane. I drove around the corner because I knew there was a small park there, and I had this memory that the Dalgards walked there.

"I remember this, but I don't think this is where we played," he said.

"There is another playground a couple of blocks away," I said.

First, we returned to the apartment building. He wanted a picture from across the street, where he could get as much of the building as possible in the picture. Just as I had wanted to take pictures of Tidemands Gate.

"You may have to be a model, today," he said to me.

He took out his camera. It was the same as mine. Was this eerie or what?

He took pictures of me with the building as a backdrop. Shouldn't I have taken pictures of him in front of the building? Then, maybe not. Perhaps, he wanted a picture of a person who made that memory special.

I asked if he wanted to take a picture of what had been Harvey's Pizza Den, which is now a fast food seafood restaurant. "It's no longer there," Eivind said.

I then drove toward the playground.

"There was a field where we played soccer," he said, recalling more fond times.

"There's a high school, maybe that's where you played," I said.

We came upon the playground and then I turned onto the main street, and pulled alongside the curb.

"There are tennis courts back there," I said.

"This is the place," Eivind said, looking at his Frogner Park. "I remember the club houses."

"The high school is across the street; maybe that's where you played soccer," I said.

"No, I remember they didn't let us play there," Eivind remarked. "Let's go to your house."

So, I drove to the big brown house built in 1897, which my parents had sold a year-and-a-half before. Children played by the driveway. There was something obviously missing, although I had noticed it when I drove by on another day.

"They cut down first base," we said, referring to the big green tree in the yard by the house.

Remaining was the big cement roller that had sat under the tree since before we moved in because it couldn't be budged. Actually, a branch of the tree had been first base. The tree stump that had been second base was barely noticeable, too. The bushes by second base, where we lost many a baseball, were cleared, but my parents had that work done.

"I remember when we first started to play, and Olav and I threw the ball real wild and hard," Eivind said. "You looked at us and said, 'You don't have to throw it that hard.'"

He took a picture of the house. He tried to get pictures of the street signs at the corner but couldn't get a good shot. Then we drove around the corner to the school.

He recognized the neighborhood, remembered how to get around, just as I had in Oslo. We both looked at the school.

"My last year here was 1968-69, before we went to Norway," I said.

"That long ago?" Eivind asked.

There was a teacher watching young children in the playground. He asked her if his teacher still taught at the school. The night before at dinner, Eivind had said the teacher, Mrs. Williams – a Black woman – was the best he had ever had. His parents had invited her for dinner. The woman said Mrs. Williams had retired four years ago. This teacher would send her Eivind's regards.

Eivind looked at the playground with probably the same distant gaze I had when I looked at Majorstua's huge schoolyard. His memories may have differed somewhat, but, like me, he took a picture.

At dinner, he had also mentioned a girl, Randy, who had been in his and my brother's class. Ten years ago, she was in Norway and had looked up Eivind, but he wasn't home. My mother had mentioned that Randy's father had been our vet for a number of years before he died. One of the sons had taken over the practice, and it was still located at their house.

"Let's go to Randy's," Eivind said.

As we drove away from the corner of the school, he asked, "Wasn't there a girl down that block, Joan?"

"Yes, there was," I said, surprised. "I know the family no longer lives there."

We passed another house. "That's where Bobby lived," he said. "Weren't there twins who lived on this block?"

When we reached the small stretch where there were stores, he remembered them.

I parked in front of the vet's office. We went inside.

"I'm from Norway, and I lived here 21 years ago," he said to the receptionists. "There was a girl who lived here who I had contact with, Randy. Ten years ago, she visited me in Norway, but I wasn't home. Do you know if she's here or where she might be?"

"Randy's not here, but she's doing well in North or South Carolina," one of the receptionists responded. "We don't have her address, but we could get it for you, if you come back tomorrow."

"I'm leaving for San Francisco tomorrow," Eivind said. "Perhaps, you have a telephone number."

They gave him Randy's number in South Carolina.

"Perhaps, I'll have a doctor's conference in South Carolina," Eivind said, as we left.

"I've thought of looking up some of my classmates from Norway, but I don't remember many of their last names," I said.

Then, he saw the 7-Eleven across the street and remembered that, too, although now there is a 7-Eleven down the street from his parents' apartment in Oslo.

"I have to get a soda," he said.

So, we stopped.

Time was beginning to be important if we were going to meet Espen in town. We stopped along 11th Street and he took a picture. We took a brief walk.

"Michael, are you patriotic to Philadelphia?" he asked.

"I guess I am," I said. "There aren't many places in this country I can see myself going to. I'd like to spend some time in Norway."

"I think the movie *Philadelphia* is good for the city," he said.

"I just hope it doesn't bring negative publicity," I said.

"I don't think so," he said. "In Norway and Europe, not many people know about Philadelphia or have heard of it. Now, they'll know."

We went back to the car and drove to the subway.

"We took the subway to the baseball games, didn't we?" he said, while we waited on the platform. "I remembered my father didn't like that. I guess he didn't think children should take the train at night."

It was remarkable that not only did Eivind want to do the same things I wanted to do on my first trip back to Norway, but also he was expressing so many similar feelings.

On the train, he seemed to be deep in thought. I asked what memories were going through his head.

"The people I met when we lived here," he replied. "I've always found it easy to talk to Americans. It was a good year, one of the best I had."

I thought about it. Though, I had troubles at school in Norway, that year was one of the best I ever had. The people I met made it special. The year the Dalgards spent in Philadelphia must have also been one of the best I ever had. It was one of the few times I had people to hang around with, and we were still friends.

He recalled the soccer team he and Olav had played for while they were here, something I didn't remember. The two of them and a Colombian boy, who they befriended, were the best players. He had asked me about him on a couple of my visits, but I only knew him the year Eivind and Olav were in Philadelphia.

"He wrote to me once and I never wrote back, and I felt that wasn't nice," said Eivind.

He also remembered the gesture the coach made when Eivind and Olav left.

"The coach and team wanted to give us a gift before we left and asked what we would want," Eivind recalled. "I said, 'We don't need a gift; the team shirt is enough of a gift.' Olav was so mad at me. 'We could have had anything we wanted and you said the shirt was enough!' He was probably right because I don't think I ever wore the shirt."

Soon, we were at City Hall, got off the train and walked underground to Suburban Station to meet Espen's train. Our timing was perfect. The train's arrival was announced just as we walked down the steps to the platform. People disembarked, but Eivind couldn't find Espen. He got very nervous and raced down the platform, looking in the windows of the train, but didn't see him.

"We did say 'Suburban Station' didn't we?" asked Eivind. "How close are the other stations in town?"

I assured him we had told Espen Suburban Station, then asked, "What does he look like?"

"About your height, curly hair, earring in the ear, striped shirt like the guy at the top of the stairs," he replied, squinting his eyes. "I don't think that's him. Yes, it is!"

We raced up the stairs to meet Espen.

"*Så hyggelig å møte deg,*" I said.

"*Du snakke norsk?*" Espen asked. "You speak Norwegian?"

It is interesting to me that I get the same response when I greet Norwegians with that phrase. Literally, it just means "So nice to meet you." Culturally, it is a courteous, warm greeting. The stranger always seems flattered and asks if I know Norwegian, as if to say that if I know that courteous greeting, I must know Norwegian. It probably helped Espen and me to get off on the right foot.

We stepped outside, and I was beginning to point out City Hall and the statue of William Penn (Philadelphia's founder), on top, when the rainstorm hit. We ducked inside Basset's Turkey restaurant for lunch. Espen and I split a hoagie, so he could get a taste of Philadelphiacana. I mixed Norwegian and English, often in the same sentence, particularly when I was trying to explain baseball. I was amazed at how much Eivind remembered about the game, and he was a big help explaining the game to Espen, especially about the strike zone.

When the weather had finally cleared, I took them for a walk along Benjamin Franklin Parkway. Eivind had kept mentioning that he remembered a colored and painted street. I did not know what he was referring to.

"This was the street," he said about the Parkway, which was no longer painted.

As with most out-of-towners, he remembered the Art Museum for the scene in *Rocky* when Rocky ran up the steps. He told Espen about it. I was taking them in that direction. We walked past the fountains, the Academy of Natural Sciences and came to the Franklin Institute, passing the long row of international flags that line the Parkway. They commented how pretty Philadelphia's Center City looked.

I told them I always know where the Franklin Institute is because the Norwegian flag is at the corner. Eivind remembered the Franklin Institute and Planetarium, and told Espen about the famous science museum. I pointed out the Central Library and the Rodin Museum.

Finally, we reached the Art Museum steps. We looked back at the beautiful scene of the Parkway and Philadelphia. They took pictures. We walked up a few of the steps. They asked me to take a picture of them boxing on the Art Museum steps.

We walked up the rest of the steps and sat for a little while. Other people were climbing the steps and doing Rocky imitations. I walked Eivind and Espen around the back, and then along a small stretch of Kelly Drive where they could see the boathouses and the scullers on the Schuylkill River.

Time was getting short, so we started back. It was nice how quickly Espen and I became friends. Along the way, somehow our conversation got to Columbus and Leif Erickson. In Norwegian, I mentioned the story about when we came back from Norway, and the teacher in my brother's class asked, "Who discovered America?"

My brother eagerly raised his hand. "Leif Erickson."

The teacher looked startled and said it was wrong.

"A similar thing happened to me, when I was here," said Eivind. "The next day, the teacher said I was right."

This was in the same school.

I also mentioned having read in *Nytt fra Norge* a couple of years ago about a book, claiming that Columbus could have been part Norwegian, which drew laughs from Espen and Eivind.

We stopped for a breather and drinks at the vendor by the Norwegian flag at the Franklin Institute. Eivind couldn't pass up another soft pretzel, like me and Freia *sjokolade* and Maarud *potet gull*. We continued on, reached City Hall and took the subway back to the old neighborhood.

Espen needed film, and Eivind, a couple of other things. We headed back to the drugstore. We drove past Eivind's old apartment building again. The woman at the checkout counter noticed their accent and asked where they were from. She asked if they liked it here.

"I like it very much," said Eivind. "I lived here 21 years ago. Wasn't there a supermarket here?"

"Yes," she said. "I think that was 10 years ago."

She looked at me, and I said, "I live here, and I'm their host."

Eivind insisted the soccer field was nearby and could we try to find it. He mentioned it was near these things that collected water.

"Oh, the reservoirs!" I exclaimed, suddenly knowing where he was talking about.

We went by the field. Espen got to see the sights, as we drove by my old house and the school.

As we drove to the school, Eivind recalled, in English, "I remember the first day of school. All the kids laughed at us because we spoke Norwegian. In two weeks, it was fine."

I recalled in Norwegian, *"Mit først dag i Norge, guttene spurte 'Liker du spiller fotball med oss?'"* "My first day in Norway, the boys asked, 'Would you like to play soccer with us?'" (in English).

We both remembered the experiences fondly.

At my parents' apartment, they got to meet Buddy, the dog, as well as see the apartment and get a good meal. My mother made a feast, and the two Norwegians ate plenty. Eivind had mentioned the day before that he had lived on pizza from vendors on the New York streets.

Eivind recapped the visit to the old neighborhood and mentioned he didn't remember Oak Lane having so many churches. He said "our house" had lost personality with the tree torn down. Espen and Eivind mentioned how impressed they were with the Parkway.

Espen told us he had worked in the theatre for 11 years doing lighting. My mother recalled seeing Henrik Ibsen's *A Doll's House* in Norwegian at the National Theater in Oslo in 1991 with Eivind's parents. She had read the play several times in English so she would understand it. My parents enjoyed the performance. Espen lives near Eivind, and my parents were familiar with the neighborhood. Espen invited us to visit the next time we were in Oslo, and we had only known him for a few hours.

My mother and I had bought baby gifts for Andrea and Agnes, the "new" Dalgard babies.

We then showed Espen a diagram of a baseball field and tried to explain more about the game. Dinner was very nice, but we had to get to the game.

On the way to the stadium, Eivind told us that doctors in Norway earn between $30,000-$100,000 per year and that no one in Norway earns less than $20,000 a year. There is a flat 28% tax plus 8% that pays for health insurance. Books are not taxed.

They got to experience everything at the game, including a rain delay. Dad and I took a lot of time explaining the game. Eivind bought another pretzel. He asked how much they owed us for the tickets.

"It's on us," I said.

"I ought to come to Philadelphia more often," he said. "I don't have to pay for anything."

After the rain delay, Eivind and I sat next to each other. I was shocked when he remembered the names of the Phillies from his year.

"Luzinski, Bowa –," he began.

"He's the third-base coach, now," I said of Bowa.

"Schmidt, Carlton," he continued. "Did the Phillies ever win a championship?"

I pointed out the decals in right field.

"They won the Eastern Division in 1976, 1977 and 1978, but did not reach the finals. In 1980, they won the championship."

"With those players?" he asked.

"Yes," I replied.

"Good," he said. "I saw the start of something, and they eventually won. They were good in the 1970s and now in the 1990s."

The Phillies won 5-1, so it made the night special.

On the ride back to my parents' apartment, Dad extended an invitation for Eivind's parents, him, Angela, Olav, Florence, the kids to visit. "We have room."

I said, "It's not a matter of room. We want you to come."

At my parents' apartment, we switched to my car, and I drove to my apartment.

On Sunday, I thought I understood Eivind to say, "Over a couple of beers, I'll give you some tips about getting a job in Norway."

Now, as we reached my apartment, I said, "We never did talk about tips on getting a job in Norway."

He was confused.

I said, "Remember, you said, 'Over a couple of beers...'"

He replied, "Oh, I didn't mean a job. I don't know anything about your field. I said, 'I could help find you a girl.' I could find a nurse for you."

I said, "Hmm. A Norwegian nurse. Start looking."

From the back, Espen said, "You've never made that offer to me."

We again retired at 1 a.m.

28 June 1994

We were up early, so I could get them to a 7:30 train back to New Jersey for the soccer game against Ireland. Breakfast was simpler this morning, just cereal and tea.

Mark stopped by the station to say good-bye.

In Norwegian, I said to Eivind, *"Takk for reise."* "Thank you for traveling."

"Takk for besøktet." "Thank you for the visit," he corrected me.

Then I said, *"Du hadde å reise tilbake til Philadelphia som jeg hadde å reise tilbake til Norge."* "You had to travel back to Philadelphia as I had to travel back to Norway."

The train pulled in. They thanked us.

"Hopefully, next year in Norway. Mark, you are welcome," Eivind said.

"Some people just say that to be nice," Mark told me. "I felt he really meant it. The gesture made me want to visit Norway even more. It's always nice when you can visit another country and know a native because they can give you an experience other tourists don't get."

Then I took Mark to meet the limo that was taking him to Kennedy Airport for a trip to Israel. By 9 a.m., I had dropped off two – three, counting Espen – friends, which left me with a strange empty feeling. As I drove home, tears started to come to my eyes, as I thought about the quick visit by Eivind, and how my visits to Norway also seemed to go fast.

I began to feel that longing for Norway. I thought how the feelings on my first trip back resembled Eivind's feelings on this, his first, trip back to the U.S.

Something special had happened to both of us during our respective year away from our native lands, that we had kept within ourselves over all these years. We both reflected on people we had met, whom we had not seen or even written to since our years away, and who we didn't know if we'd ever see again. We remembered a portion of our childhood, relived it as adults. The constants throughout those years and my visits were the *memories* of people we had met, and our implicit relationship with each other. That is the positive result or power of cross-cultural exchange.

This visit bridged the Norwegian-American and American-Norwegian experiences. Some of our family's best friends have kidded us about the way we refer to Norway, as if it's a romanticized image or a silly obsession. Eivind's visit proved my 25-year fascination and emotional attachment to Norway was not a silly obsession or something artificial. It was real, so very real.

Nature of Friendship

*"A bad friend
is far away
though his cottage is close.
To a true friend
lies a trodden road
though his farm lies far away."*

-Hávamál *The Sayings of the Vikings*[30]

---

[30] Hávamál was a special metered poetry of the Vikings. The poem is excerpted from *Hávamál, The Sayings of the Vikings*. Some of the poetry dates 1,000 years.

Part 2
1994-Present

Dedicated to my wife, Lisa, who wanted to visit "the country I talked about," and my children, Matthew and Devra, may they be the third generation of Kleiners to fall in love with Norway.

Chapter 8
1994-1996

I would spend the next year finishing my master's degree studies at Temple and working as a graduate assistant in the College of Health, Physical Education, Recreation and Dance.

Through the wonders of e-mail and the Internet, I would also find ways to bring a little bit of Norway to me and to educate others. This would range from joining a Sunday night online chat session with Norwegians of American descent from around the United States, to answering questions about Norway on the Norweaves listserve and on "travel" and "language" boards, to being invited to "speak" about student travel to Norway in a special chat session. In the Sunday chat sessions, we actually got to "speak" – or type – Norwegian, and I described the book to positive anticipation. Through the Internet, I also hooked up with a Scandinavian travel agency outside Tacoma, Washington – Five Stars of Scandinavia – which coincidentally booked many of the flights for students attending the International Summer School. The owner knew my Norwegian teacher from the ISS, Audun, who taught at Pacific Lutheran University in Tacoma.

In some cases, my unique screen name of "MKLNORWAY" resulted in unsolicited inquiries about Norway. This expanded my contacts with Americans who have been to Norway and Norwegians living in the United States. This technology gave me an avenue to market this book. Many of these people expressed interest in the book, and some of my best marketing agents for the unpublished tome were the Norwegians on the Sunday night Norwegian chat sessions. They not only asked me about the progress, but also mentioned my project to newcomers to the sessions. The fun of the chats – conducted in both Norwegian and English – and the correspondence between sessions, or just answering questions, has reinforced the feelings for the country and its people that have dominated the pages of this book.

And the coincidences. In addition to the Tacoma travel agent knowing Audun, a woman on the chat sessions from Olympia, Washington, was attending PLU and knew Audun, too. She had also grown up in Asker, where the Dalgards had lived in 1969-70, and she remembered walking past their street every day on her way to school.

Unfortunately, as people switched e-mail clients, the chat and contacts faded.

Norweaves also put me in contact with Arne Selbyg, who wrote a book, which I have cited as a source of information. I was able to update some of the data through an e-mail correspondence with Mr. Selbyg.

I began to subscribe to *The Norseman*, a wonderful magazine published for Norwegians abroad and friends of Norway by the Norse Federation in Oslo. Part of the magazine – which featured articles about Norwegian history, culture, politics, contributions of Norwegians in other countries – was in English, and part in Norwegian. So, I had the opportunity, on occasion, to practice *norsk*. I would write two articles over the years for *The Norseman*, one on the ISS (the Federation had been an early sponsor of the School), the other the excerpt from the book about attending the speed-skating champion-ship and Holmenkollen in 1970.

In January 1995, Mark mentioned a meeting of a Jewish *havurah* group that held a *havdalah* ceremony, bidding farewell to the Sabbath on Saturday night. They met once a month. We were shocked to walk into this couple's home and find 30 people. The group held a service followed by a potluck dinner and discussion. On this particular night, the topic was the Religious Right. We found the atmosphere light, people down to earth, and we began attending the monthly meetings on a regular basis. In April, when discussion arose about a topic for the May meeting, I offered a suggestion. May would mark 50 years since the end of World War II. I had the collection of stories of rescue and accounts of War experiences of people I had personally met in Europe over a number of years. I was willing to make a presentation.

The next meeting was my first public reading from *Beyond the Cold*. At the same time, I was receiving an e-mail newsletter, *News of Norway*, which included brief excerpts from Norwegian newspapers in English. A number of items mentioned Norway's commemorations of its liberation. I added this to my program. The presentation was warmly received by the *havurah* group and gave me confidence the book could be successful.

I began dating a woman from the group, Lisa Roth, in February 1996. The previous October, we had been paired up to prepare and lead the service. She was receptive and more comfortable with my Secular, non-religious approach, and our program was well-received. We didn't "get together" until February, when another Lisa in the group, who worked where Lisa Roth did, hinted to me that Lisa Roth was interested in me. She also lived in Mt. Airy.

Our first date was warm and pleasant. I was a bit disappointed when she said she didn't have much interest in sports. However, she would later disclose she liked football, and we would watch the Eagles games on

Sundays at my parents' apartment, and she would wear one of my Eagles hats.

She had grown up in Glen Rock, New Jersey, then came to Philadelphia to attend the University of Pennsylvania. Lisa then received a law degree from Temple, but hated working in law and went to Bryn Mawr College, where she received a Master's in Social Work. She works at a large non-profit company, Philadelphia Health Management Corporation, which is involved in public health education. Her area is Research and Evaluation of the needs of clients and writing proposals to obtain clients. Many of the people in her department, including her boss, had my father as a teacher at Temple. In another coincidence, when my brother was in his 20s and was an emergency medical technician, he worked with someone at PHMC, in its early days.

We would find another ironic coincidence. In one of my last classes at Temple, we had to design either a training program or educational curriculum complete with lesson plans, complemented by multi-media. I chose Eastern European Jewish Immigration in the late 19th century through the early 20th century. In showing the contributions of Jewish immigrants to American life, I needed to show it for both men and women. When citing the labor movement, I chose Samuel Gompers and Rose Schneiderman, the latter a union organizer among women, who also served in Franklin Roosevelt's gubernatorial and Presidential administrations.

Lisa was showing me around her house, and we came to a fascinating picture. It was from a 1915 women's suffragette rally. The women were all dressed in aprons and holding signs, "If you think politics is dirty, then call in the cleaning woman. Don't deny us the vote that you give yourselves." Lisa said, "This is my grandmother, Jane Schneiderman."

"Is she any relation to Rose Schneiderman?" I asked.

Lisa was surprised. "You've heard of Rose Schneiderman? They were sisters."

I mentioned my project and would later show it to her and her family.

We were finding compatibility on many levels: Jewishness, politics and, to a degree, sports.

I received my Ed.M. in Educational Media in August 1995, and in October was named Director of Communications at Abington Friends School in suburban Philadelphia, a school that went from preschool to 12th grade. Not only were my professional qualifications important, but also my experiences with multiculturalism and Norway were impressive to the administrators because it indicated the depth and breadth of my background. In addition, having graduated from a Friends school – even if it was a rival – seemed to make this a good fit. I was primarily responsible for public relations and a monthly newsletter, which I improved upon in substance and pages.

This job would have its ups and downs, but it allowed me to become part of the educational process and would provide me a forum to spread the word about Norway in a remarkable number of ways that I couldn't have imagined. There would be other multicultural experiences at the school.

As I settled in the first week, I noticed on the soccer schedule that the team was to play the Cuban junior national team the next week as part of a goodwill tour of Friends schools. Coincidentally, Fidel Castro spoke at the United Nations the day before the Cuban team was to play AFS. The tie-in presented a perfect PR opportunity.

The game was secondary to the exchange. The AFS players presented gifts; AFS students read poetry of Jose Marti, a famous fighter for freedom in South America. In a high school Spanish class, students from both countries laughed as they tried to converse and learn about each other's countries – which were enemies – and cultures. The Cuban players knew little English, so the AFS students had a practical use for their Spanish. There was competition for the Spanish teacher's assistance.

Meanwhile, a girls' soccer team was being started, and the coach was a woman from Sweden. That was another interview. When we would meet around campus, I would try to talk Norwegian with her.

However, the first story the Head of School wanted me to pursue was the return of two Bosnian students, a brother and sister – an eighth grade boy and an 11th grade girl. They had been "rescued" from their war-torn country and placed at AFS the previous year. Janna had become close with an AFS classmate, Emily. When I left the Summer School, I thought how I would be able to put faces to war-torn areas because I had met people from those countries. These Bosnian children, with their horror stories, did the same for Emily and the school community – and now for me.

When the grim prospect arose that the Bosnian students would have to return to their country after the 1994-95 school year, Emily undertook a fund-raising campaign and raised the $4,500 needed to bring them back. I interviewed them and pitched the story to the press. It generated much publicity, and as a result, the two girls "adopted" me as a friend and would stop by my office to chat.

And there was the evening of November 21, 1995. It is amazing how you can spend all day in an office and not know the news of the world. The time was 4:30 p.m. when the phone rang, and a reporter from a local TV station informed me a peace accord had been reached in Bosnia-Hercegovina. She understood AFS had Bosnian students, and the station was interested in filming them watching the 6:30 news and interviewing them. That gave me two hours to pull this together. I called the home of the teacher who was hosting the students, and no one answered. Maybe, the teacher was still here, and I raced down to the school and found her in a computer class. I told her the news. She gasped, "Oh, my!" and put her hands over her face and heart. We announced the news to the other staff in the room. "And Channel 10 is coming to my house!" she said.

There was an alternate number to reach the students, so she called home. Meanwhile, I went back to the office. This news could not be celebrated without Emily. She wasn't home, but I left a message. When I got to the house, the teacher had also called the host family from the year before, and they were there. There was excitement, tears and overwhelming emotion. Janna and her brother wanted to call home, but I advised to wait until the TV station arrived, so they could film the call. When Emily arrived, she and Janna embraced. The emotional call was placed. The adults had tears in their eyes. The strong friendships that had been established with the community – a multicultural experience unfortunately brought together by war – were evident that night. As I watched, I couldn't help but think, "This is what happens when peace breaks out."

There would be the annual AFS Winterfest program in December where Christmas, Chanukah, Kwanzaa and the Chinese New Year were recognized. In February, there was a Chinese New Year Parade. Two Upper School students, who had emigrated from China when they were nine years old, explained the traditions to fellow high-schoolers as well as kindergarten students.

Later in the school year, a world-renowned Russian theatrical folk dance teacher would teach students of different ages dances related to their studies and their particular heritages in a 10-session course.

Then, in March 1996, Tom Sørensen traveled to Phila-delphia to work with Dad for a week. His son, Andreas, wanted to see America. The infant at Torbjørn's house on my first visit back to Norway was now 10 years old. Since his father would be busy working, what would Andreas do? Since I worked at a school, maybe Andreas could visit for a few days. The school was open to the idea, and he would spend time in one of the fourth-grade classes.

However, before his arrival, I visited the class and taught them welcoming phrases in Norwegian; showed slides of Lillehammer, the mountains, fjords, the Arctic Circle and Lofoten Islands; discussed the history, culture and sports of the country; and showed them the Lillehammer tie that the Breviks had sent me. I also taught them to say, "My name is..." in Norwegian.

When Andreas showed up for class at 8 a.m. the first morning – after arriving at 5 p.m. the day before – the class gathered for morning circle. Each student introduced himself or herself in Norwegian. "I didn't expect they would learn Norwegian and say it so well," Andreas said. "It meant a lot that they used their time to learn Norwegian just for my coming. That was nice and helped get things started well. Everybody at the school was welcoming, and the teacher made me feel part of the class."

I slipped out of the class and returned to my office. For the rest of the day, I was like an anxious parent wondering how things were going. There was one anxious call from an art teacher that he had a minor accident in class.

When my mother asked him a couple of days later if he wanted to take the day off, Andreas said he didn't want to miss school. He shared his own slides and Norwegian chocolate with the class. One student noticed she had the same spider picture book as Andreas, except Andreas' was in Norwegian. She brought in her book, so she could learn the Norwegian. Andreas presented the class with a parting gift – a toy moose with a ribbon that had the colors of the Norwegian flag.

At the same time, the high school students were organizing the annual school-wide International Day, scheduled for May 17. The date was not lost on me. I became involved with the organizing group – PRIDE – and proposed a parade in honor of Norwegian Independence Day. After all, 17 *mai* is celebrated with parades of schoolchildren. Workshops, an international luncheon featuring food donated by families representing their heritages and an international fashion show were planned. I contacted the Leif Erikson Society, and they brought a replica of a Viking ship. Members came dressed in Viking gear. The ship was placed in the middle of campus, and students were allowed to board the ship. Three women from the local chapter of Sons of Norway came dressed in *bunads* (traditional regional attire) – two Norwegians, one Swedish – participated in the fashion show and made dessert for the luncheon. I introduced the parade. In my research, I had found that Quakers had been among the first Norwegians who arrived in America in 1825.

The fourth-graders with whom Andreas visited led the parade of nations along with myself. I provided a Norwegian flag. The class pulled out the toy moose Andreas had given them and paraded, holding it aloft.

Indeed, this had been an eventful year and a remarkable first one at AFS. After four years, it was time to return to Norway. It was finally Mark's turn to travel there with me. But there was another reason to return as well: The International Summer School was celebrating its 50th anniversary. I wanted to be part of the celebration, but I would be more than just part of the fete.

Chapter 9
July-August 1996

Wednesday, 17 July 1996

We arrived in one piece and pushed ourselves to make the most of the first day. There were some delays with the flights, and we landed at Fornebu Airport 20 minutes late at 11:20 a.m. My excitement built during the descent and landing in Oslo. There were some great views of Rådhuset and Holmenkollen from the plane, and I shouted to Mark, "There's Rådhuset! There's Holmenkollen!"

Customs didn't take long, except the agent took my passport, then smiled and said, "There's something wrong with your passport."

"What?" I asked, getting nervous.

"It's not signed," he said.

After the passport had been checked in Philadelphia and London!

Waiting for the luggage took a while, but finally, we were outside with the view of the Oslofjord. We took a taxi to Thomas Heftyes Gate, the Dalgards' apartment. The driver turned left at the corner, when I was trying to indicate the building was on the left side of the street. My first frustrations with the language today.

I was soaking in the familiar surroundings; Mark was soaking in every sight. Since the Dalgards were going to be away, Ragnhild had left the key at the corner dress shop, and I walked down the street to the shop. I started to explain to the salesperson in Norwegian that I was a friend of the Dalgards, then got stuck trying to remember the phrase "left the key," and slipped into English.

"And your name is?" the woman asked.

"Michael," I replied.

She went to the back and gave me an envelope.

I returned with the keys, and Mark and I began our trek up the four flights of winding stairs to the apartment. After some fiddling with the top lock, we were inside. I showed Mark the library, then took the luggage to the room in the back, where I presumed we would stay.

Ragnhild had left a note for us, and one for Eivind, on the counter in the kitchen. Pictures of the grandchildren were in a basket on the same counter. Though the photos were not labeled, I could tell who Andrea was. There was definitely Angela and Eivind in her, but she was a spitting image of Angela, with the similar hairstyle.

We unpacked the gifts, hung up clothes and washed up. I showed Mark around the apartment and the view of Holmenkollen from the dining room window. There was an old rosewood, *rosemåling*, chest from 1841 and other old items in the dining room.

We checked the food supply in the refrigerator and tried, unsuccessfully, to find the freezer. I called the Summer School so they could e-mail home our arrival, but found JoAnn Kleber busy. I left a message on Berit's answering machine and reached John Ivar Brevik. He was anxious to see us and invited us to visit the family in Askim. He offered us different days, before they were to leave on vacation. I told him we would get back to him, once we knew the other details with Eivind. A return call to the ISS reached JoAnn's husband, who took the e-mail information.

We then hit the streets of the neighborhood. I showed Mark the Narvessen (a little more than a newsstand) with the numerous newspaper choices. We walked down Thomas Heftyes Gate toward Frognerveien. As I walked around, and for most of the day, I felt strange. This was a different country, with a different language. There has been much talk about Norway being a second home to me. Everything was so familiar and not foreign. I knew this neighborhood so well that the familiarity didn't make it seem foreign at all.

I remembered looking at the addresses of the boys from my class at Majorstua in 1969-70 (I still have the address book, having found it at the bottom of a desk drawer after thinking it had been long lost) and seeing two of them lived at Thomas Heftyes Gate 60 and 62. I looked now and waited anxiously just to see 60 and 62, knowing that they certainly didn't live there now. At Frognerveien, we stopped by Peppe's Pizza and checked the prices and menu (around $20 for a pizza). I asked Mark if he wanted to see the house I lived in before we went to the Park. He said if it was on the way.

"It's certainly on the way," I said.

We turned down Frognerveien. "I want to walk down Frognerveien at some point," I said. "I haven't done that since 1970."

"I thought you've done everything," Mark said.

Turning around, I said, "And up that way, I want to find where I skated."

We came to Tidemands Gate. I pointed out to Mark, "At this corner was a bakery where we bought bread." The bakery was no more.

Like an assured tour guide, I took us to the left across Frognerveien, up Tidemands Gate.

"There were embassies on this street," I said. "Turkey and Brazil. We used to smell the coffee every morning."

Soon that wouldn't be the only smells of history I would experience.

Now, we found the Belgium, Thai and Bulgarian Embassies.

Finally, we came to the brown house with the 20 on the iron gate. I somewhat confidently pushed the gate open. "We were on the first floor. And here was the yard," I told Mark.

I forged ahead to the back and the entrance. "We played in the back here too."

I opened up the door. The door of the apartment a few steps up still had the Magnusen nameplate. I walked up. "There was a Mrs. Vogt upstairs," I said, peering up the stairs. "Notice the winding steps (a habit in Norway)."

I had been past the house on my previous trips; a couple of times, I had opened the entrance door, but stopped short of going up the steps, or lacking the courage to knock on the door. Before leaving on this trip, I had told myself, maybe this time I would knock; maybe I would get inside.

Now, I stood at the top of the stairs; Mark, a few steps down. I took some breaths. "Should I ring the bell?"

I was nervous. "What should I do?" I asked.

"You've got nothing to lose," Mark said.

Taking a breath, I gave the bell a short ring. We thought we heard some movement, but weren't sure. An elderly woman's voice came through the door. I explained in Norwegian that I had lived here with my American family in 1969-70.

"So you would like to see?" she said in Norwegian. "Can you come to the front on the other side?"

We went to the front of the house and up the stairs to the porch. I tapped a couple of times on the living room doors. But a door on the side opened. A white-haired woman with a metal cane stood there. Again, I tried to explain in Norwegian who I was. "Do you speak English?" she asked.

So, in English, I explained again. "Are you Magnusen?" I asked.

"Yes," she replied. "We lived in the Netherlands for seven years and rented the apartment."

She asked, "Was your father a professor?"

"Yes," I said.

"Are you the two boys?" she asked.

"No, this is a friend," I said.

"Come in," she said.

And, suddenly, we were in the dining room. There was a long table with a white tablecloth, and the place was well-kept with very nice things around.

Mrs. Magnusen had trouble walking, and I wondered if I was imposing. She led us into the living room.

"Sit down." Mark and I each took a chair. She dropped herself onto the couch – the same blue one that had been there in 1969-70. I couldn't help but think that she let us in. An elderly woman, who could hardly walk, let in two foreigners. Unheard of in the United States.

I looked around the room. There were many more things in the room then when we lived here. Gone was the old television with one channel that sat in the corner where I was now sitting. It had a radio on top, and my father and I used to pin our ears to the radio to catch the baseball and football broadcasts on armed forces radio. A newer TV was in the other corner. There was a piano with family pictures.

The floor revealed only part of the hardwood floors, where my brother and I played hockey, sliding on our slippers and using plastic golf clubs as sticks. I looked toward the room on my left, with the table and phone, and the stairs that led to the basement, which served as one of the hockey goals.

"I played here," I said.

"There were two boys. Was there also a girl?" she asked.

"Yes," I said, impressed that she remembered.

"The new apartment building on the block wasn't here in 1969," she said. "They won't knock this building down until I'm gone. It's 104 years old."

"I remember your son," I said.

"That's his picture on the piano when he was younger, and his wife," she said. "They have two children, and my daughter has two children, 16 and 19 already. I wish it was 1969."

For a moment, I half agreed.

"How are your parents?" she asked.

"They're retired from work now, but find many things to keep them busy," I replied.

She asked about my job. She had a hard time hearing me. I tried to ask about Mrs. Vogt. Mrs. Magnusen had the most trouble with "Vogt." I tried Norwegian.

"You're asking about the people upstairs?" she said. "They've been here a year" – in essence answering my question. "They're crazy. I don't like them. They don't like curtains."

Finally, she mentioned her husband. "He should be home around 3 p.m. He runs a limo company from the airport."

"Can I see the rest of the apartment?" I asked.

"Sure, but we can't see the bedroom. It's not in order." She struggled to get up.

"May we help?" I asked.

We went out of the room and to the left down the hallway. On the right appeared the bathroom. There at the end of the hallway was the bedroom my brother and I shared. The room was smaller than I remembered. There seemed to be just one bed. "How did we squeeze in here?" I thought.

"This is a nice room," she said. "You two boys would've been in here."

"We shared this room," I said.

We walked down the other end of the hallway, past the wc (water closet, toilet) and what was my sister's room. "This was a small room, but serviceable," Mrs. Magnusen said.

Then, we went into the kitchen. She sat down. "There have been changes to the kitchen since 1969," she said.

"Was your father from San Francisco?" she asked.

"Philadelphia," I said.

She told us how in 1982 she had visited 20 states in the U.S. and loved New Orleans. She had met Eric Heiden in Wisconsin.

It was time to leave. I said, *"Tusen takk."* "Many thanks." We walked back through the dining room. "We had a Seder here," I recalled to myself.

She told us she suffered from gout and showed us her hands, which had endured much surgery. Then we were outside again, back in 1996.

"You went back in time," Mark said.

"You got an experience no one else who has come with me had," I said. "You saw the inside of where I lived."

I kept thinking, she let us in. I was glad I did it. I saw something of my past in Norway that I had not seen before. The irony was that the Magnusens still lived there. I completed, or closed the door on, a part of my experience.

We moved on, down two blocks and turned left onto Munthes Gate. I pointed out where Dad worked. We continued down the block and across Kirkeveien to the Frogner Park and the Vigeland statues once again, which show the cycles of life. I had just been back and forth between my own.

The Park now took on a strange feel and look. It was so familiar. Yet, the statues were still impressive, as I pointed out ones to Mark, and he to me. He was impressed. Since he had seen my pictures, he was surprised how small the statues were. The Park was full of people, both tourists and Norwegians. Yet, it didn't feel congested. I was wearing a T-shirt with a large Norwegian flag on it, which my aunt had sent me from Houston. A tourist asked where I had gotten it, thinking she would be able to buy one in Oslo.

At the entrance, there was now a statue of Vigeland, surrounded by flowers, and a visitors' center.

On a large lawn, people gathered to watch a performance. Families abounded. Children climbed on the statues. The circle below the bridge has statues of infants. In the middle, there is an upside-down baby, indicating birth. A (real) father explained to his child that the statue was like the baby inside his pregnant wife's tummy, tapping her stomach at the same time.

After a stop in the Visitor Center – where we had our first chocolate and got our first looks at the prices of sweaters and postcards – I suggested we walk toward Majorstua. We cut through the old, virtually destroyed Frogner Stadium, one of the stadiums for the 1952 Winter Olympics. I stepped on the track. I ran in a track meet here the first week of school in 1969; I think I also played soccer here. Again, touching a piece of my past, I had not touched before.

We went down to Majorstua. A high-school classmate, a novelist, had read the first 50 pages of the book. He suggested visiting the school not just to see it, but also to feel and remember the emotions of the memories, sort of like an exorcism. But, the gates were locked and chained. I could only look through them and not see enough of the playground. I felt locked out.

We continued down to Majorstua Station, then back to Thomas Heftyes Gate and the Dalgards' apartment. First, we stopped in the RIMI market to buy some food we could make for dinner, and also buy some food for our weekend trip to Bergen.

Back at the apartment, we now had to get acclimated to the stove, oven, switches and temperatures. This proved complicated. I finally found the freezer was built into the wall. Once we got heat from the oven, we figured we were on the right track. We were both in need of rest, so napped until the timer rang.

The frozen cod was now cooked, and then we finally found a burner that could heat the vegetables. The food was good, but there was a Maarud potato chip bag lying around, and we broke it open. Mark loved them, and neither of us could stop eating them. Like with the chocolate, my culinary recommendations proved accurate.

I called Berit again and learned that Odd and Ragnhild had forwarded their calls to their cottage, so no one could return our calls.

We rested again until there was a turn of a key in the door. Eivind was back from Germany. We asked him about the stove, and he told us the burner we had first used was broken.

It was around 10 or later, but he took us to Aker Brygge, a group of shops, cafés and restaurants by the harbor, much like the Inner Harbor in Baltimore. He ran into a friend, who joined us at a café for a little while.

Mark had a number of questions, particularly about the medical-care situation in Norway. Eivind said there are three options now: patients who come to the hospital and the state pays; patients can go to private-practice doctors, pay one-third, while the state pays two-thirds;

and a third development, more distressing, where care has become more privatized. People can pay far more expensive rates for immediate care. The wealthy are usually the ones who can afford this, and Eivind said this is creating a more distinct higher class, "who give extravagant parties." Eight percent of people's incomes go toward medical care. But poor people are not neglected in health care. He was surprised when we told him about Republican cuts in welfare, job training, medical coverage, feeling it was cruel.

It was chilly, but not completely dark. Eivind dropped us off at the apartment after midnight, and said he would meet us tomorrow.

Thursday, 18 July 1996

Having now mastered the teakettle, we were able to have breakfast. I took out the *frokost salat,* breakfast salad, I bought at RIMI. I thought it was *sild,* herring, in sour cream sauce, because it was stacked next to the other *sild* jars. I couldn't find any herring. I looked at the jar and it said, *"God smakk til sild!"* "Good taste with herring!" Without the herring, it didn't have much taste, so the bread and cheese and a little *rekkeost* (cheese flavored shrimp that comes out of a tube like toothpaste) had to do.

Eivind came by around 10:30. We gave him the gifts, the tile of the shaking hands Mark's friend had made, of which we ordered several to take with us as gifts. We felt it was an appropriate expression of peace and friendship across the oceans. I also gave him the gifts for the children, and the Norwegian words I had written. There were American and Norwegian flags and the words expressed our years of friendship and looking forward to it continuing in the future.

En gave som symbol
av vår vennskap
tvers over sjøene

317

og gjennom årene
Mange tider alle sammen i fremtiden
Vennlig hilsen
Michael and Mark

A gift as a symbol
of our friendship
across the seas
and through the years
Many times together in the future
Friendly greetings
Michael and Mark

Eivind was touched by the presents and the words.

"A Norwegian poet," he said.

Eivind had to be at work at 1 p.m. for a 26-hour shift, but wanted to give us whatever time he could. The plan was to take a ride up to Frognerseteren and Holmenkollen Ski Jump.

Mark had also given Eivind a tape of Irish harp music performed by another friend. In the car, Eivind played the tape and enjoyed it very much. He said it would be nice music to relax to after a long day at work.

He was as pleasant and hospitable as ever. As he drove toward Holmenkollen, we passed the neighborhood of Gaustad, and he mentioned that was where his family lived before moving to Asker, where my family had visited them in 1969-70. He said the area was where many of the wealthy people lived. "People who sit around counting their money," he said.

He was quite excited about our trip to Bergen the next day, particularly the leg to Balestrand. "I've been to Germany, the Grand Canyon, some beautiful places in the world," he said. "When I saw the fjords last summer, it brought tears to my eyes."

When we mentioned how early we had to get up to catch the train, he said something that would stay with us. "You can sleep for the first two to three hours. All it is is trees!"

"To Mark, it's all new," I said. "It's all going to be beautiful to him."

After a brief look around Frognerseteren and Holmenkollen, we took a quick peek into the Skiing Museum and stopped in at the Fridtjof Nansen Café, both located underneath the jump. I had never been to either place. We sat outside where we could capture some more views. Mark and I shared an open-faced sandwich with goat cheese.

On the way back into town, Eivind drove by his house. He dropped us off in front of the Oslo *Sentral Stasjon* (Central Railway Station) by Karl Johans Gate. We walked up Karl Johans, which was full of people, shoppers, stores and stands outside the stores. We stopped at a couple of stores, but needed to push ourselves to do the things we wanted to do. Besides, we were skeptical of the 299 Norwegian *kroner* sweaters being sold at one stand.

We took a ferry around Oslofjord. The tour guide spoke English, Norwegian and German. At different junctures, she went to each row of the boat and asked where everybody was from and if they could hear and understand. She spoke Norwegian slow enough that I was able to understand. When she described Aker Brygge, she said, people come to the cafés to shop or just to "sit and enjoy life." I told her when we left the boat that I was able to understand the Norwegian, and she was pleased.

We crossed from the harbor to Akershus *Festning* (Fortress), built in the 1300s. Within the fortress is the Resistance Museum, a tribute to Norwegian resistance during the Nazi occupation from 1940-45. Mark was quite moved by the museum. Following that, we made our way back in the direction of the Rådhus, along Rådhusgate. We came across the building where the offices of *The Norseman* and Nordmanns-Forbundet are located. I thought about stopping in, but it was after four in the summer, so the offices were probably closed.

We stopped in an inexpensive souvenir store where Mark spent $100. Once again, I felt confident and thrilled that I knew my way around Oslo. However, that didn't go for locating the Vegeta Restaurant, a vegetarian cafeteria near the Rådhus. Once we found it, we enjoyed a good meal. It was a buffet, all-you-can-eat for 98 *kroner*, approximately $16.

After dinner, we returned to Thomas Heftyes Gate, first stopping at RIMI for the bare essentials for the next day's trip – potato chips and cartons of iced tea. Mark had already figured out the priorities. We rested at the apartment, then woke up and decided to go up to Frognerseteren for *eple kake med krem*. Our one-day Oslo Card still entitled us to a couple more trips in order for it to pay off. However, we missed the train to Frognerseteren by three minutes. As a second choice, I suggested going up to Sognsvann, a lake near the Studenterbyen, off-campus housing for University students. There is also the Norwegian Sports College and an Olympic office or training center located by Sognsvann. We sat there for about a half hour, not bad for a second choice, before heading back. I had forgotten my Oslo Card in another shirt, but there is little checking on the trains. Technically, I had still paid for it, and if I was stopped, I would have paid again.

Back home, we packed and went to sleep, thinking of our trip the next day.

Friday, 19 July 1996

We were able to get ourselves up early, had breakfast, packed sandwiches and got ourselves out the door and caught an early bus to Oslo Sentral Stasjonen. We were traveling light, just backpacks, cameras and a small nylon "playmate cooler" for the food. I was about to find out how light. It was on the bus when we checked to see if we had everything.

Mark said he didn't take his wallet and didn't see a need for it, since the hotels, trains and boats were paid for. I said, "Credit card," and Mark hit his head as if he wanted a V8. But we couldn't go back now. He did have cash with him.

We got to the station in plenty of time. I told Mark, "Prepare yourself for the trip of your life." I bought a map so we could chart the trip.

As usual, this trip can be hard to describe in words; it needs the pictures. I started to collect quotes. Foremost, were Eivind's comments the day before about the first few hours just being trees. Certainly, there were plenty of trees, but lakes surrounded them and mountains, and it set up the rest of the trip. How can it get better? But it gets much better.

After Eivind's two-hour period, I was scripting the slide show for when we returned. "We can call this part, 'the boring scenes,'" I joked.

Then, Mark broke my cardinal rule that this is not a train ride you sleep on. He kept nodding off – and this was after the two- to three-hour time frame set by Eivind. I nudged him continuously, "You're not allowed to fall asleep."

By the time we got off at Myrdal, our first change, Mark was saying, "It's not fair that one country has so much beauty."

And there was still much more to come, the train to Flåm, boat around the fjords to Balestrand, the overnight stay in Balestrand, and the three-and-a-half hour boat ride around Sognfjord to Bergen the next day.

The Flåmbanen is four levels of track through the mountains, and riders are provided with a guided tour. A few minutes into the ride is Kjofossen, the largest waterfall in Norway. The train stops to allow people, most of whom are tourists, to get out and take pictures. There were Americans, Japanese, French. Along the way to Flåm, we saw smaller waterfalls, many looking like they were cutting paths down the mountainside. The Flåmbanen, which took 20 years to build, has 20 tunnels, 18 of which were constructed by hand, and no bridges. Brentfoss fall is 420 feet. The train passes by the old center of Flåm and a church that was completed in 1667. There are 375 inhabitants of Flåm, most of whom make their living from tourism and farming.

The Flåm train station is backed by a massive, imposing mountain. Ahead are restaurants and shops along the dock, from where you can take a number of ferries around the fjords. In 1992, I went to Gudbransdal; this time we were going to Balestrand. Or you could take a ferry all the way to Bergen. At the end of the dock were some grassy areas on the left, with a view across the water to a mountain and fjord. Here, with the mountain in the background, is where we took the first pictures of ourselves, proving we were on this trip.

We had a couple of hours to kill before our boat would leave. We finished off our sandwiches and the chips, sitting at a table outside a restaurant. Afterwards, we looked around the souvenir shop, where they had some good deals on sweaters, but I didn't want another cumbersome thing to carry, and Mark didn't have enough money. I bought us some booklets about Flåm and the fjords.

I changed some travelers' checks, took a quick look in another shop, then we walked along the dock and snapped our pictures.

Finally, it was time to board the blue and white boat. It was a bright, sunny, clear day, perfect for the ride and views. The disappointment and frustration was there wasn't a large deck at the front of the boat. There was only a deck in the back, so most of our pictures were of from where we had come, and not in the direction we were going. In order to get the forward shots, we had to lean over the railing amidst the other tourists. Besides, it was too windy and cold to stand for long on the deck. A number of our pictures were shot through the windows from inside. Many of the fjords converge or meet each other and give the impression of touching, when they're not. It seems like there's just a narrow way to navigate between them. That's why it's dramatic to get the shots in front of you.

Nevertheless, this didn't diminish the powerful impact of the views, the massiveness and majesty of the mountains and fjords, the blue water, the snow and the glaciers along the caps. It brought to mind Eivind's quote the day before: "I came to the fjords last year and tears came to my eyes." Mark, with a lump in his own throat, repeated numerous times, "Wow! This is incredible!"

As the boat drew near Balestrand, it was announced that we were looking at the largest glacier in Norway. After an hour-and-a-half of drama, we finally docked at the village of Balestrand, which was surrounded by the water and views of the fjords. It was 5 o'clock in the afternoon and still bright and sunny.

The Kvikne Hotel, originally built in 1877, was a short walk up a hill from the dock. It was the nicest hotel in Balestrand and must've been included in all the tourist packages. The lobby was full of Americans, British, Germans, Japanese, French. (There must've been Italians somewhere, too. We could've had World War II.) There were two elevators, more like rooms. You had to open the door. One elevator's capacity was six people; the other was eight. With everybody's luggage, the capacity was more like two to four. We squeezed in with a German couple. I saw the man looking at the cramped quarters, and I could tell what he was about to say. *Kleine lift,"* he said. "Small elevator." I started calling the elevator "The Kleiner Elevator."

The room was quite nice. There was a blow dryer in the bathroom, a TV with cable, and a terrace with stupendous views no matter which way we looked. There was a booklet with things to do in Balestrand, room service, etc. I turned on the TV and found Sky television, England's CNN, and our first chance at English-language news. This was the first time we had heard about the explosion of TWA Flight 800 over New York, which had occurred two days before and a day after we left. I remembered that our British Air flight from Philadelphia had been delayed because they couldn't find a passenger whose luggage was onboard, so they were removing the suitcase. I had turned to Mark and said, "I hate to sound paranoid, but that sounds weird and a bit scary." And the seat on the other side of me was empty. We were stunned by the news and a little bit leery, but there was nothing we could do.

We took a nap before waking to tackle our dinner adventure. First stop was the buffet in the hotel restaurant. Once crossing the reception area, we found ourselves in what must've been the old part of the hotel. Beautiful lounges and sitting rooms with gorgeous furniture – mainly wood – with paintings on the wall, led to the spacious dining room. Then we got quite a shock. The all-you-can-eat buffet was 240 *kroner*, nearly $40, and the salmon, served a la carte, was 198 *kroner*, nearly $31. With Mark's financial situation, not to mention my own wallet, we couldn't swallow this.

The receptionists directed us to another hotel, which we, of course, got lost finding. Once we found it, the salmon was now knocked down to 135 *kroner* with vegetables ($21), but we had seen signs for another restaurant and decided to check it out. It was small "grill," but the salmon was now 98 *kroner* ($15.55) with vegetables. Our walk had knocked the price down 100 *kroner*. Mark got a salad for around 78 *kroner*. We'll never know if the salmon at the hotel would've been better, but this sufficed for dinner.

We walked back to the hotel and decided we wanted to go out again when it was close to midnight to see how light it was. At 11:30, we went outside. Dark was descending, but it was not pitch black. I snapped a few pictures, and you could still see the clouds. We returned to the room and went to sleep. We had an 8 a.m. boat to catch in the morning, and a long day behind us.

Saturday, 20 July 1996

Breakfast wasn't a problem because the smorgasbord at the hotel was included in our package. The dining room looked out on the sea, and it gave you a dizzying effect. The buffet offered hot and cold cereal, hard-boiled eggs, scrambled eggs, different kinds of herring, fried potatoes, sausages, cheeses, meats, breads, jams, fruit. We ate relatively quickly, as we had to catch the boat.

As opposed to yesterday, today was overcast, but the clouds just engulfing the tops of the mountains and fjords provided an interesting sight. We walked around outside, snapped a few more pictures and then our boat came in. While we waited in line to board, the hotel van driver decided to back up to unload people's luggage. Except he was backing up right into the line. People started to rap on the van and tell him to slow down and stop. He didn't hear anybody, and why he wasn't looking or couldn't wait until people boarded, I don't know. I felt something brush my backpack and thought it was a person in line. I turned and the van had hit the backpack – but fortunately not my body!

We got on safely. We had the same problem with this boat as the one the day before. There was only the back deck. This time, they didn't allow anyone out on deck, so all our pictures were from inside through the windows. In 1992, when I took the boat from Flåm to Gudvangen, the boat was open. I think these boats we were taking these two days were a combination tourist boat and transportation between different villages because they made a number of stops. In some ways, these stops added something to the trip, because at a number of docks, there was nothing around. A couple of houses – if even a couple – dotted the mountains.

Despite the overcast day and the restrictions on the boat, the views were still dramatic, and we both clicked away. By the time we reached Bergen, I had taken 87 pictures, and Mark, 82 – after only two days.

As you enter Bergen, houses dot the mountain and hillside. Bergen is known as the City Between Seven Mountains. Being on the Western side of Norway, it is closer to the rest of Europe and was one of the principle players in The Hanseatic League of the 15th and 16th century. It has maintained that old-time look. As we disembarked and started to walk from the dock, the row of old-looking buildings at the *bryggen*, the wharf, stared at us from across the water.

"I feel like I'm in a fairy tale," Mark said, when he saw them.

Walking from the dock also took us right into the bustling, crowded *Fisketorget,* the Fish Market. Several tables sell fresh fish from the boats – shrimp, salmon, *gravlaks* (like our lox), whole crabs. While originally a fish market, other stands selling sweaters, T-shirts, souvenirs and skins have now claimed their piece of the turf. At one table was a sign, "We speak English and love American dollars." There were also similar signs for Norwegian, French, German, Italian, Spanish, Hebrew and Japanese.

We bought a half roll with *gravlaks* and weaved our way through the crowd. Our goal was to get to the Tourist Information Office to find a bigger and better map, so we would be able to find the *pension*. It was naturally crowded, but we were successful in our mission. It was a sunny day, unusual for Bergen, so we decided to walk.

We walked around the town, along the cobblestone streets, by the oldest church in Bergen, Mariakirken, and in the area where Morris Gardner had lived. It was not just disappointing I wouldn't be seeing the Gardners on this trip; it was strange, because I learned shortly before we left for Norway that Morris had died. As I walked the streets, I kept thinking of potato chips, the food that we had shared happily in 1969-70. I thought of this when I visited him in 1990, for the first time in 20 years; he had six different varieties of potato chips lined up on his kitchen counter.

Torgalmenningen, which becomes Torggatan, is the main street by the harbor, and most of it is just for pedestrians. A large old church, Johanneskirken – Bergen seems filled with old, large churches – was at the end of Torggatan. There were steep steps along the left and right sides leading up to the front of the church. According to the map, the *pension* was down the street from the church, but it also showed a side way of going without climbing the steps. Intimidated and tired, we cut through the other streets until we got to the Park *Pension* on Harald Hårfarges Gate. Harald was a Norwegian king in the 13th century, and there was a bust of him on the side of the building.

The hotel, from the 1890s, was quaint with wood chairs and tables in the dining room and all kinds of old objects on the walls. In the hallway on our floor were an old spinning wheel, old desk and old phone.

Now, that we were in Bergen, we may have hit the wall of fatigue and jet lag. We were really exhausted, so napped before heading back out.

We discovered that the street by the hotel, Strømgaten, was a direct and easier route to town and a five-minute walk to the train station, which was good to know since we would be catching an early morning train to Oslo on Monday. We stopped in Lille Lungegård, a park, sat on a bench by a huge fountain and started to finally write postcards. Satisfied we had written enough for now, and sufficiently starved, we walked to a restaurant we had passed on the earlier walk around the cobblestone streets. It was near where Morris Gardner had lived, *To røm og en kjokk.* Two rooms and a kitchen. And it was about that small. I enjoyed my meal, and Mark got by on another large salad.

Afterwards, we stopped at the tourist office again and asked about bus schedules and sites. We were interested in going to the Aquarium the next day. The woman told us the Aquarium was a 25-minute walk from the hotel, and by the time we walked to the bus stop and caught the bus, we could be there.

We walked back to the hotel, wrote some more postcards and watched some of the Olympics.

Sunday, 21 July 1996

While the breakfast at the *pension* was not as extravagant as at the Kvikne Hotel, it was sufficient, and the atmosphere with the old wooden furniture made it intriguing. Cold cereal, hard-boiled eggs, cheeses, meats, a couple of choices of herrings, bread, Wasa, jams, coffee, tea and juice were the offerings.

Afterwards, the Norwegian navigator and his companion 10 feet behind started on the journey to the Aquarium. We weren't doing badly until the map got confusing. The street names were changing from Sydnes*plassen* to Sydnes*veien* to Sydnes*gaten*. We reached this major street, and we should've been able to turn left at the next street. The name of the next street we came to was the name of the street after the street we were looking for on the map. I figured if we turned left on this street, we could find a street where we could turn left and follow to Klostergate. A left-hand street never came.

Utterly confused, we stood on a corner looking at the map, when a gentleman walked up to us and said, without waiting for a response, "Aquarium? Straight on!" And he walked away.

Shortly after, we found it. A slight left and right turn were required after straight on. We had left with plenty of time for the penguin and seal feeding time. We made it just in time. Besides the fish on exhibit inside, there was an interesting model of how Norway uses water for electricity – 99 percent of the electricity is through water. I managed to translate enough of the Norwegian – without a dictionary – to get the context. There was also a description of how water is pumped in and out of the aquarium.

Before heading on, we stopped for a drink and a package of *lefse* in the museum cafeteria. We were really feeling the fatigue, as I almost fell asleep at the table. We pushed ourselves to the Natural History Museum at the University of Bergen, at the top of the steep steps by the church at the end of Torggaten. Naturally, we took a scenic route by the harbor area, which took us down into town, where we would then have to backtrack up to Torggaten and up the steep steps. But, this was due, in part, to the fact I had developed a bad case of chapped lips and needed to find someplace to buy chapstick, and that was only going to be in the area of town. I found chapstick at a large *narvessen* in the middle of Torbelga-tan. We also bought some energy food – chocolate – and stamps for the postcards.

As we progressed along Torggaten, we saw a man walking his pet black pig! Ragnhild Dalgard would tell us later that pet pigs were becoming popular. We also passed a bar/restaurant with a sign advertising that night's Olympic soccer game between Norway and Brazil – a women's game.

By the time we reached the top of the steps to the church, we were feeling exhausted. Finding the museum was another bit of an adventure. Once we found it, we could only manage part of the first floor, which dealt with volcanoes and how the continents formed over time. I had little energy to translate the Norwegian. We walked back to the hotel and took a nap.

The Køne Restaurant was the site for dinner that night. It had special prices. I had Wiener Schnitzel, and Mark, the salmon.

Throughout the weekend, we walked everywhere in Bergen – a city of hills that reminded us of Manayunk in Philadelphia and San Francisco – except when we took the funicular to Fløien after this dinner. At Fløien, there are panoramic views of the city. We were there around 8 p.m., and I got a nice shot looking right into the sun, and then other photos looking to the left of the sun. I spotted our hotel.

There was a plaque at Fløien designating Bergen as a Sri Chimnoy Peace City. Sri Chimnoy is an Asian musician, who we had never heard of. The designation, basically, meant a city dedicated to human understanding. We were also intrigued because Philadelphia was among the other peace cities.

In addition, a large, laughing stone statue of a troll dominated the playground area next to the snack bar and souvenir shop. We photographed each other with the troll's arm wrapped around our shoulders.

Down below, we walked the easier route up Strømgaten, which gets hilly as you get closer to the hotel. Now, we looked back up to where we had been and could see the shop, restaurant and the funicular.

I cheered on Norway against Brazil before retiring, amidst panic since I suddenly could not find my travel journal anywhere in the hotel room. Not in my backpack, under beds, under piles on the coffee table or hidden in the couch. Lisa had given it to me before I left. Not only did it have pages for writing, but maps, including time zones, temperature and clothing size conversion tables, pages to record travelers' checks, expenses, photos and addresses, world currencies, languages and climates, international flight times and distances, addresses for American and Canadian embassies and high commissions, and also amusing quotes from famous travelers. Bruce Chatwin's was now seeming prophetic and true: "To lose a passport was the least of one's worries; to lose a notebook was a catastrophe."

Monday, 22 July 1996

We woke up at 5:30 a.m. for our 7:30 train. I made another search for the journal. I suggested to the people at the reception desk that perhaps it got stuck in the sheets and when the cleaning woman came in, the journal got wrapped in the sheets when she stripped the bed. They doubted it, since the sheets weren't changed since we stayed two nights. They would keep an eye out for it and send the journal to me if they found it.

We ate breakfast amidst my distress, made some sandwiches and walked down Strømgaten to the train station. Finding potato chips was the order of business, but the shop at the station didn't have Maarud, so we had to buy them on the train.

Most of the day was the return trip. We were taking the train straight through, about a seven-hour ride. We hadn't seen the scenery between Myrdal and Bergen on Friday. I still nudged Mark to stay awake to see the views. Past Myrdal, he slept. I snapped a few pictures, then used the time on the train to work on my speech for the 50th anniversary party of the ISS. A few days before we left, I had received an e-mail asking me to be the alumni speaker at the festivities. Now, I had some time to commit thoughts to paper.

When we got back to the Dalgard apartment, we found Eivind waiting for us. We watched some TV, including the Olympics, and tried to decide what to do for the evening before Eivind met a friend.

I wanted to try to arrange days and times to see people. Thursday seemed to be the magical day when everybody was leaving on holiday. So we had to cram visits in the next couple of days.

I reached Berit, who invited the three of us for an impromptu dinner of pizza and beer and the best view of Oslo from her terrace. She suggested we bring an extra frozen pizza.

This call was followed by one to John Ivar in Askim. My suggestion was to go to Askim for lunch on Tuesday, and leave for Oslo around three or four because Odd Steffen and Ragnhild would be returning to Oslo that evening. But Askim was an hour-and-a-half away. "The problem is my wife, Margareta, works until after four," said John Ivar. "I am not good in the kitchen, but we'll work something out. Maybe we'll buy lunch."

Eivind, Mark and I decided to go up to Frognerseteren and get the *eple kake med krem* out of the way. Frognerseteren is not far from Berit's home. We had to go inside the restaurant to get the dessert specialty of the house. The weather was nice outside, so we wanted to sit outside and admire the panoramic views of Oslo.

Eivind and I found a table. Eivind began to speak in Norwegian, asking me if I had a chance to use the language. We began to have one of my few Norwegian conversations, when this repartee was suddenly interrupted by a crash. We looked up. Mark was standing at the bottom of the stairs, still looking ahead; the tray, I believe, was still in his hands. But the *eple kake med krem* – after all the buildup – was splattered on the ground, the plate and teacup broken. I went over to see if he was all right.

"I'm fine. It's the apple cake that's a mess," he said.

He had tripped on the last step. Eivind and I shared our piece of cake with Mark. Eivind attempted some negotiation with the waitress who was cleaning up the mess.

Back in English conversation, we talked about the American political system, safety in America and the media.

As he drove to Berit, Eivind became curious about the address. It turned out he had a friend who lived in the same complex as Berit, and that was the friend he was meeting tonight! Berit knew the friend. Eivind said hello, then excused himself to meet the friend.

It takes only a few moments before there's laughter with Berit. We gave her the tile and the Norwegian words I had written. She was overcome and tried to find a place in the kitchen to hang the tile. Eivind's reaction to my words was "Norwegian poet." Now, Berit said, *"Norske dikt."*

"Norwegian poem."

We ate salad, bread, little strombolis, and ice cream and *jordbær* (strawberries). She was impressed by what I told her of Abington Friends. She still teaches kindergarten teachers in a college and evaluates teaching. "I'd like to visit," she said.

She was also interested in Mark's job, which was working in the fair housing division of the Federal department of Housing and Urban Development.

Before we left, we got her e-mail address. "I don't use it too much," she advised.

Berit gave us each a hug.

"I'll be thinking of you around eight Friday night during your speech," she told me.

Tuesday, 23 July 1996

John Ivar picked us up around 10:30 for the ride in the countryside to Askim. He had shaved off his beard, and I didn't quite recognize him at first. He showed off his sense of humor along the way. Who said Norwegians don't have a sense of humor?

I asked about Marit, who had driven me to Lillehammer in 1992.

"This summer she is in the mountains with a friend milking cows," he said.

"Is this part of her veterinary studies?" I asked.

"I suppose it could be, but it's for money," he said humorously.

He joked that the size of Askim was two intersections. After about an hour or so, we reached their beautiful house. We met his son, Erland, who at first was shy. John Ivar realized that Odd and Ragnhild would have to pass by Askim on the way home, so they could pick us up. But we had trouble reaching them on the mobile phone.

In the meantime, the options were lunch or a walk into Askim.

"I am not good in the kitchen, but I make this pizza very well," he said.

Not very hungry yet, we opted for the walk to town.

About six months before, the *Senter for Socialt Netverker og Helse at Ullevål Sykehus*, Center for Social Networks and Health at Ullevål Hospital, which my father had helped create, and where he met John Ivar, was closed. Since then, John Ivar had been unemployed. He had refused to file for compensation. He was due to start a job with the military in August. John Ivar said unemployment was around six percent in Norway. He also said everybody in Norway gets four weeks vacation to start. "It's a right, not a privilege," he said.

The town was a little bigger than two blocks, and there was a shopping mall. We priced sweaters, but weren't satisfied with the choice and the fact they weren't made in Norway. We also couldn't find this SELSUN product my mother had asked me to buy. We tried some other stores, without success. The area was suburban looking; we walked along some quiet streets, past houses and some developments. John Ivar showed us Erland's school and the local athletic fields.

His wife, Margareta, was a child psychologist at the local hospital, and we stopped there so we could at least meet her. Mark admired the windows in her office, and they seemed surprised. "In Norway, all offices must have a window," she said.

By the time the three of us returned to the house, it was around two, so John Ivar, Mark, Erland and I were famished. John Ivar's pizza was a group effort and included everything you can imagine. Pepperoni, pineapple, onions, mushrooms (not on Erland's part), meatballs and ham went on this rectangular pie.

While it cooked, I showed them the Lillehammer videotape I had done for class at Temple. Erland began warming up to us, telling jokes, helping with my Norwegian, explaining the articles in the local newspaper. He was 12 and quite bright, loving to name the European capitals. But he couldn't name the capital of Pennsylvania.

We enjoyed the weighty pizza on the outside porch. We finally reached Odd and Ragnhild. The cat – a mean, black cat – was missing, delaying their departure. She always seemed to disappear when they were leaving someplace. They would call when they found the feline, or she found them, to let us know when they would be leaving for Askim.

Since they were going to pick us up, we had flexibility to spend more time with the Breviks. Margareta came home early. She brought out her photo album of their trip to the United States and Philadelphia, where they visited my parents in 1992, the summer I was at the ISS in Oslo.

When Odd and Ragnhild arrived, we all had ice cream and strawberries. Ragnhild told how the cat had bitten Eivind last year and how embarrassing it was for him to go to his own hospital's emergency room for treatment. Speaking of Eivind, we had to get on the road, because he was waiting for us at his house to say good-bye. He was leaving for the mountains the next day. For the trip back, the cat resided in a traveling cage.

When we got out of the car, Ragnhild took out a frozen pizza. "More pizza," I said.

Imagine – there was no pizza in Norway in 1969-70, and now in 24 hours, we had bought a pizza to take to Berit's, had pizza with John Ivar and here was another pizza.

We sat around a table outside and had dessert and tea. Eivind talked about how distressing it was to feel that Norway was becoming more like America. He meant in the sense that the news coverage is emphasizing the murders, with less substantive stories. People are becoming less educated about politics, he said.

Back at the Dalgards, we were up late discussing the European Union, difficult situations in Norway, biological treatment vs. community-based treatment of the mentally ill. Books by Odd's father were on the shelves, and we looked at some of them. His father was a political prisoner during World War II. There was a picture of him in one of the books as a member of a *fotball* team. One of his teammates was the future chancellor of Germany, Willy Brandt.

Wednesday, 24 July 1996

At 7 a.m., Odd had to take the car in for repairs of a previous problem. He had offered to take us to the Munch Museum, so we had the morning to relax while we waited for him to return.

Ragnhild pointed out the errors of our ways, starting with the cheese we bought at RIMI.

"You used this cheese?" she asked. "For real cheese, you have to go to a cheese store. This cheese!" she said, waving her hand in disdain.

Suddenly, bread appeared in drawers, real cheese, real goat's cheese. We had not known where to look. We learned which drawers were broken.

It was interesting going to the Munch Museum with Odd. He presented the psychiatric and psychological aspects or analysis of Munch's life, who was a very depressed person. Odd also talked about history. Taking off on our conversation the night before, I asked, "Should Munch have been treated biologically or community-based?"

At the same time, he pointed out, to me in particular, that Munch and playwright Henrik Ibsen were virtually ostracized from Norway and gained fame after leaving Norway. "You'll have to reform your view of Norway," he said.

After the Munch Museum, Odd drove to Blindern, so I could pick up a schedule of Friday's party activities. I met JoAnn Kleber who was happy to see me.

Next stop was the Vikingship Museum, but Odd opted to wait outside while Mark and I engaged tourist congestion. Mark once again was thoroughly fascinated by the ships, the history and the artifacts that were found.

We returned home, where Ragnhild was really going all out. To hold us over till dinner, she had made *vafler* – thin, light waffles – that like many Norwegian baked goods, are good with sugar on top. She spent the day preparing the dinner and doing the laundry.

As promised, dinner was reindeer meat in cream sauce made with goat's cheese, *ripps* (berries, similar to cranberries), mushrooms and onions. She threw in salmon for an appetizer. Boiled new potatoes, broccoli and carrots were the vegetables.

Food and company were delightful. The black cat had been the subject of some joking since Tuesday. Even Odd didn't want to say much about the cat.

"You're going to miss the cat," Ragnhild insisted.

"I don't think so," Odd replied.

They also tried to clear up what they thought was my rosy picture of Norway, as well as talking about their views of America and Americans. At one point, Odd said, "Generally, I think Norwegians are good people."

They were planning a trip to Australia and hoped to make it to America and Philadelphia.

"You'll make dinner for us in your place," said Ragnhild.

"I'll be glad to," I said.

We retired to the terrace for tea and coffee. I had always noticed they had a dead-eye view of Holmenkollen from the terrace. Now, Ragnhild pointed out they also had a view of The Monolith in The Park. "We have a view of the two biggest attractions in Oslo," she said.

Mark and Odd remained on the terrace talking, while I worked on the speech, and Ragnhild did something else. I asked Ragnhild for some assistance for the Norwegian part. She got a laugh from my Norwegian humor.

Before we went to sleep, Odd showed me how to use his computer, so I would be able to type the speech. It was strange seeing the Norwegian in the menu items.

Thursday, 25 July 1996

The earlier phone calls didn't seem promising. Torbjørn was leaving for Portugal Tuesday, the 24th, but he said Debbie was coming down from Rauland Tuesday night because Ingrid and Anja were returning from the United States. I was hoping Debbie, who went to the Summer School in 1973, would consider staying until the ISS party Friday night.

"I haven't seen the girls for four weeks," she told me Tuesday night. "They're going to be tired, and I may just want to get them back to Rauland Thursday. Maybe we can get together for breakfast or something. Go to the Park; let the girls run around. Let's talk Wednesday night."

337

On Wednesday night, she called me from Torbjørn's Oslo house.

"Right now, the girls are watching a video they got in London, but they're tired. Maybe we should just have breakfast tomorrow. But there's not much in the house. If you can bring some more bread or cheese, that would be great. It won't be anything fancy."

"That doesn't matter as long as we have a chance to get together," I said.

She gave me the instructions on how to get to the house, and we agreed to meet at 10 a.m.

It was amazing we got there. We made great connections and caught an earlier train. When we got off at Skådalen, we found the only road going downhill and kept following it around. I finally agreed with Mark – we were lost. We trespassed through a lawn and asked someone how to get to where we wanted to go. She told us to take a right down this road and cross the tracks. We walked on and suddenly found ourselves at the train stop *before* Skådalen. We had walked for about a half-hour since getting off the train, and the two trains following that one had already passed. Another one would be by in a few minutes. And we didn't have to pay an extra fare.

This time, when we got off the train, we crossed the tracks and at least the house numbers made sense. We eventually found the house with the Citroën in front, and climbed up a hill through trees and found the door. It was still around 10.

We walked into a day that never seemed to end and that we hoped wouldn't.

Ingrid, now eight years old, was in a chair, and Debbie sat in another, holding four-year-old Anja in her arms. I was struck by how much Ingrid changed since I saw her in 1992, the big jump from four to eight years old. When I saw Anja last, she was seven months old, so naturally, she had changed dramatically.

Ingrid would later say to me, "You see the big differences. I see the little ones."

She claimed not to remember me. Debbie said to her, "Remember, he gave you the maroon shirt that had Philadelphia..."

"Philadelphia College of Textiles and Science," I said.

I had brought a bunch of the shirts for Christmas gifts in 1990 when Ingrid was two. She wore it as a nightshirt. When I visited when she was four, she wore it for me.

We gave Debbie the handshake tile, and I gave the girls the gifts I bought for them, and then we sat down for breakfast. The girls were busy opening all the gifts they received in the United States, although Debbie had hoped they would wait until they got home.

Ingrid's English was impeccable for an eight-year-old. Anja's English was quite good, too. Ingrid is quite a craftsperson. She is making jewelry, earrings and rings. Debbie was wearing some. Ingrid brought her work out to show us. She sold almost her entire stock at a fair in Rauland, with pieces selling for as much as 70 NoK (almost $11).

Debbie told us she was struggling financially in her job, and paying for day care. However, she couldn't see herself working in the States, where she believed it would be far worse for a single mother with two children.

Up until now, Anja had said little and was trying to figure out what she wanted to eat. Soon, though, Anja was acting just as Ingrid did with me, when she was four. Suddenly, this figure appeared next to me, requesting my lap as a seat. Then, she took me by the hand to the couch to look at a book. There were two books with pictures from *The Lion King*. Objects or figures had to be found in the pictures on each page. One book was harder than the other. Anja had chosen the harder book. With her head on my shoulder, we both struggled to find the pictures. Meanwhile, Mark was engaged with talking to Ingrid and Debbie. Then Ingrid joined Anja and me and took the difficult book.

"If Anja doesn't find the things on one page, she thinks they're on the next page," explained Ingrid about why Anja kept turning the pages.

Debbie was getting anxious about getting them ready for the trip. She also had to send an overnight letter for Torbjørn, and the post office closed at one p.m. Our simple breakfast had already gone past 12. Mark made sandwiches because he and I were planning to go to Bygdøy to the museums. Debbie was trying to figure out if there was a place she could drop us off. Was the train station the best with her in a rush?

"You can find things in the book later," she told Ingrid.

"But, it's more fun doing it here with Michael," Ingrid replied.

"That's a nice thing to say," said Debbie.

Soon, Ingrid and Anja were all over me, laughing like a Vigeland statue. Ingrid had discovered a game. She took my Philadelphia Eagles cap off my head with her mouth. Naturally, Anja had to copy her older sister. We were laughing, and Mark snapped a picture. Ingrid then started playing the "scissors, paper, stone" finger game with me, with no limit.

Debbie wanted to get everybody out. I wanted to take pictures before this special morning ended. After the pictures outside among the trees, the seating arrangement for the car had to be resolved. Would Mark or I sit in the front? Ingrid had a solution.

"You two will have to do scissors, paper, stone," she suggested.

The girls decided. They were each holding my hand. We sat in the back. Anja had to sit strapped on a cushion in the back seat between Ingrid and me.

We checked our watches, and it was around 12:47 or 48. We should have time to make the post office.

"It's such a nice, hot day," Debbie said. "Maybe, I should take them to a beach at Bygdøy, cool off before we head back." She asked the girls how they felt about the idea.

As Anja got out of the car at the post office, she tripped and in catching her, my finger grazed her eye. Crying ensued, but within moments of apologies, Anja put her arms around me, and the four of us were off to a RIMI down the hill from the post office, while Debbie took care of the letter. The stop at RIMI was meant for them to buy stuff for the ride home.

As Debbie drove to Bygdøy, the route took us to Kirkeveien and into our neighborhood. Suddenly, Debbie asked, "Maybe you guys would like to join us at the beach? Do you have bathing suits?"

"Back at the apartment," I said. "What's your feeling Mark?"

In his typical decisive manner on this trip, Mark replied, "We can."

Debbie stopped by the apartment, and we went upstairs to get our suits. "You didn't expect this, did you?" I said to Mark.

In our American mindset, we thought, "Will there be a place to change? Probably."

So we didn't change, just put stuff in a backpack.

When we hit Bygdøy, we made a right turn away from the tourist traffic. Cars were parked alongside the road. We walked through the forest paths cutting through, trying to find a place along the rocks close enough to the water. It meant walking or jumping down rocks and up rocks. You couldn't help notice the facility and confidence of Ingrid and Anja. We finally found a spot where there were maybe 10 people. Most of the women were sunbathing topless.

Ingrid and Anja undressed and got into their suits. Debbie slipped into hers underneath her dress. There didn't seem to be a "private area" where Mark and I could change so we never did. I rolled up my pants, and we walked to the edge of the water. We took our sneakers off and started to wade in. It was cool, but pleasant. Across the bay or fjord not that far away was Oslo, and here we were in this quiet, serene place with the natives. Kayaks, sail boats and boats occasionally passed in front of us. Mark and I made our way to a rock where we could sit, admire the views, talk to Debbie, and watch

Ingrid and Anja. Ingrid immediately made friends with a girl, and they collected starfish.

Debbie said we looked so relaxed and took a picture of us sitting on the rocks with the fjord and Oslo in the back. She told us when she worked in Oslo, she would come down here after work and kayak, swim or just sit.

In going back to move our stuff closer to the shore, I slipped and got my foot stuck between three rocks, opening up a gash. I soaked it in the water. It was the only casualty of the day, but couldn't dampen the spirits.

We watched Ingrid and Anja, which we enjoyed, allowing Debbie time to swim. This simple breakfast had now reached 2:30. The five of us sat on the rocks, with Mark and I eating the sandwiches that we were going to eat on our museum trips, and Debbie and the girls eating the fruit they had bought for their trip back to Rauland. The girls were hungry, so we shared our sandwiches.

Around 3:30, two women and a man came walking along the rocks. One of the women looked like Berit. She looked up and gave a startled look.

"What are you doing here?" Berit asked.

Earlier, Debbie had said she hadn't seen Berit in a long time. Debbie also knew Berit's friend. Imagine that, all of us finding the same rocks.

When we left, Berit shouted to me, "I'll be thinking about you tomorrow night at eight during your speech."

Mark suggested to me that maybe we could convince Debbie and the girls to have dinner with us. Debbie was concerned about the expense, but on the other hand thought it would be great to find someplace where we could sit by the water, and the girls would be fed before the trip. Then, when we saw the line of cars leaving Bygdøy back into Oslo, staying on Bygdøy seemed like a good idea. I mentioned there was a cafeteria at the end of Bygdøy by the Kon-Tiki, Fram and Norwegian Maritime History Museums. First, we checked The Laternen, but it was far too expensive, then went to the end of Bygdøy. There was a small kiosk by the Fram, but I went to check the outdoor cafeteria I had mentioned in the car. The prices were much more reasonable, and Ingrid would be able to get her cheeseburger. There were tables right by the water, and naturally, it was still bright and sunny. Mark and I treated.

While we ate, Debbie mentioned we could take a train to a town an hour away from Rauland if we wanted to come on the weekend. Ingrid and Anja invited us.

Mark had always heard from me that Holmenkollen could be seen from anywhere in Oslo. Sitting at the table, he teased me, "I don't see it now."

"It's there, but the buildings are blocking our view," I said.

After eating, we stopped at the ice cream kiosk. I had been dying for a (vanilla) *soft is* (soft ice cream, custard) with the chocolate powder crumbs on top. With our ice creams, we walked toward the dock where the boats from Oslo harbor stop to drop people off at Bygdøy and vice-versa.

"We should be seeing Holmenkollen soon," I said. We all waited for it to come into view, and it finally did.

Debbie, Mark and I sat down while the girls ran around. If this is how they were on jet lag, how were they when normal? Then Anja came up to me and asked, "Michael, could you push Ingrid and me?"

They were trying to climb a statue of an anchor and wanted me to push them up. Then I caught them sliding down. We all gathered together again, and Debbie read a letter from Ingrid's teacher in Salt Lake City. The family had spent a year in Salt Lake City a few years ago.

We loaded back into the car. Debbie figured she should do some food shopping, and RIMI was down the street from us. The girls could stay with us while she shopped.

Debbie caught Anja in the rear-view mirror, starting to doze off. "Please stay awake longer," she said. "Then you can go up to Michael and Mark's and draw."

I, too, was hoping Anja could hang in there because I could see what was coming. When we got out of the car, she said, "Carry me."

Up four flights of winding stairs I walked, with her in one arm, the keys in the other hand. She had already been grazed by my finger and Mark's watch. "What a bundle you are carrying," Mark said.

We made it, and they admired the apartment. They were suddenly revitalized.

I found some paper.

"Farger?" asked Anja.

"You want colors," I said.

I hadn't been able to find bread in the apartment, but somehow found a colored pen. Anja drew a picture of Mark and me, and Ingrid a picture of me. They gave them to us.

"You made a picture last time, and I still have it," I told Ingrid.

Then they wanted to play hide and seek, but I knew the secret rooms, and they had difficulty finding me. The second time, I heard them shout, "You have to come out," indicating Debbie had arrived, and they couldn't buzz her in.

Debbie thanked us, and we thanked them for the day.

"Could we have your address?" Ingrid asked.

"You can use that e-mail address," Debbie told us. "I'll send you the address for the Rauland Web page."

They were walking out the door. Anja was *walking* down the steps. "After this day, you're just walking away," I said.

She came back and gave me a hug.

Breakfast ended at 8:30 p.m.

Friday, 26 July 1996

In the morning, I made some cuts and put the final touches on my speech for the ISS party that night. I was getting some butterflies, mainly because I didn't have a chance to practice it.

The itinerary for the day had us going to Bygdøy to see the *Fram* and *Kon-Tiki/Ra*; a quick glimpse of the

Rådhus artwork; check out The Nobel Institute, and be at Blindern by about 5 p.m. for dinner (yum!).

We caught the bus into town. I, of course, knew where I was going. Mark was his usual 10 feet behind. After getting off at the Nationalteatret stop, we walked down to the harbor, where the next ferry to Bygdøy was preparing to board. The boat service is treated like other public transportation, so it was the same fare, and free with our three-day Oslo Card. The boat takes only about 15 minutes and makes stops at The Lanternen Restaurant, near the Vikingship and Folkmuseum, and then by *Fram* and *Kon-Tiki/Ra* Museums. Here we were back at where we spent last evening with Debbie, Ingrid and Anja. The incredible day was still fresh in our minds, and we wouldn't stop talking about it for days.

We whisked through the ticket line at the *Fram* because of our Oslo Card. Once inside, we followed our usual habit of going in the opposite direction of the traffic. If you want to board the ship, you have to turn right after the ticket office to climb the stairs that take you to the entrance of the polar ship. We went in that direction, but didn't immediately go up the steps, and started viewing the exhibit downstairs, and since we were now going the wrong way, we read from the third expedition to the first. Of course, we once again were hitting tourist congestion. We boarded the ship, but went in all the right directions, which was fortunate, considering how narrow the paths were.

We then moved across the plaza to the Kon-Tiki/Ra Museum for more tourist congestion. Greeting us at the Ra exhibit was a relief Thor Heyerdahl had found in recent years in Peru that depicted reed-like ships. There was also an interactive kiosk about Kon-Tiki. The CD in the store was 475 or 498 NoK ($74-$77). There is also an exhibit of Heyerdahl's Tigris Exhibition in the 1980s. If he keeps going on expeditions, the museum is going to run out of space! Mark was once again thrilled with the two museums.

We caught the ferry back just before it left. The harbor is located in front of the Rådhus, City Hall, the red brick building with the two towers. The right tower has a clock. Oslo has many statues, besides those in Frogner Park. Right by the harbor are statues and a fountain. In front of the Rådhus, completed in 1950, are individual statues showing various workers and laborers. Inside, however, are murals on the wall and ceiling depicting the history of Norway, mostly life in World War II. I found our way to the main hall, the area where the ISS had the reception with the Mayor in 1992. On the walls and ceilings are more magnificent paintings. The rest of the building was roped off, except for guided tours.

"I see why you wanted to show me this," Mark said.

From there, we walked to *Det Norske Nobeliske Institut*, The Norwegian Nobel Institute, with the nice gardens and statue of Alfred Nobel in front. We managed to get in the big iron doors. There were bells for the library, Director, Research Director and a couple of others. A woman came out.

"What do you want?" she asked.

"To see the library," I said.

"It's closed," she said. "How did you get in?" She hustled us out the door.

Odd had mentioned it was difficult to get in. He had also said he believed there was a book about all the Peace Prize winners. I checked some bookstores on Saturday, but they had not heard of one. This was in an effort to assist the AFS headmaster, who was interested in setting up a tribute to the Peace Prize winners at AFS. He wanted to honor the approaching 50th anniversary of the American Friends Service Committee receiving the Nobel Peace Prize.

We returned to the apartment and grabbed a quick nap before heading off to Blindern for the party and my big night.

Upon reaching Blindern, we saw signs about the cultural evening on the steps outside the *studenterhjem*, and on the bulletin boards inside. Other "signs" of the evening were all over. In the lounge, exhibits about Ireland were being put up in one corner; Spain in another; India; Turkey; Pakistan; Hungary; Germany; Austria, too. On one side of a table was material from Azerbaijan; on the other, Netherlands. Ukraine, Latvia, Estonia were also represented.

The Palestinian display was a bit disturbing. There were three maps from 1947, 1948 and 1967, and the text was in Norwegian. There was part of a map, which is Israel, that seemed to be designated Palestine. The rest was designated as the area partitioned by the United Nations for a Jewish state. Israel also had a display.

At the check-in table, a woman was selling ISS 50th Summer Session T-shirts and sweatshirts, and a 50th anniversary commemorative book. There were also schedules for the evening, and there I was on the program. I bought a T-shirt, while Mark tried to make me buy four. The woman at the table insisted I should wear the shirt for my speech.

There were some old directories, and I looked for 1973, Debbie's year, but couldn't find it.

"I have a friend who came in 1973 and stayed," I said.

"Didn't everyone?" said another woman behind the desk, an alum from the 1940s or 1950s.

JoAnn Kleber was outside in a meeting. She introduced me to a 1949 alum. Astri, the housemother during my summer, was again the housemother. She remembered me. I asked JoAnn if she could introduce me to Cecilie Finkelstein so I could put a face to the e-mail.

JoAnn found her. Cecilie introduced herself, but as the lead organizer, kept having to excuse herself.

Mark and I decided to get dinner. The girl at the desk at the dining room said we had to buy the tickets at the reception. We went there and Zivojin, the Yugoslavian night watchman, walked in.

"I remember you," he said. "Wasn't it two years ago?"

"1992," I said.

"Four years?" he said, reflecting as I that the time had passed so quickly.

Once into the dining hall, I ran into Audun, my teacher. He began, naturally, to talk in Norwegian. We talked briefly, and then he said Mark and I better get something to eat. It was pleasant seeing familiar faces and being recognized among this sea of unknowns.

The food was rice, salad and something like a beef burrito, which turned out to be too spicy for my taste. Then again the food was not one of my favorite memories. The butterflies were beginning to churn.

Cecilie found us and apologized for leaving us and asked if there was anything I needed.

"I'm just concerned whether it's too long, and that I haven't practiced it," I said. "It's a very personal account."

"Don't worry," she said. "Whatever it will be, will be fine."

She excused herself again. "South Africa is in trouble."

As Mark and I sat there, I looked around at the familiar dining room. "There's a table over there that says, 'Only Norwegian is spoken at this table,'" I said.

"So how do you feel sitting here?" Mark asked.

"It's strange," I said. "I look around and don't see familiar faces among the students. But I see the different nationalities, and it could just as well be my year."

I spotted Kaare, who had worked in the office in 1992, and was now excursions manager, and he saw me. We said brief hellos, and he said we'd talk later.

Mark quickly got the feel for the atmosphere. "I've never been in a room with so many different people," he marveled. "It should be a requirement for college students to attend some type of international program."

We moved back to the lounge where there was plenty of activity. Cecilie and a woman wearing a United Nations T-shirt with the world's flags were working at a table. "That's a perfect shirt," Mark said.

"It's my favorite shirt," she said. "I thought it was appropriate for tonight."

"Are you nervous?" Cecilie asked me.

"Yes," I said.

"It'll be fine," she said. "It's like I have all these details to worry about, and then everything will turn out fine. Where are you from in America?"

"Philadelphia," we said.

"I'm from New York," she said. "My brother used to own a furniture store in Philadelphia."

She was looking in a book. "I'm trying to find a good quote for tonight, and then people can write their own thoughts," Cecilie said.

I showed her the Mark Twain quote I was using in my speech, which is my motto for ISS: "Travel is fatal to prejudice, bigotry and narrow-mindedness."

"That's great!" Cecilie said.

"I saw that in a travel journal," said the woman in the U.N. shirt.

"That's where I got it before I left for the Summer School in 1992," I said.

Cecilie went off to get some paper. The other woman was making up paper for people to write their ideas of a perfect world. One student drew the ISS logo. We had to fill them out, too.

Mark asked if there had been any Israeli and Palestinian discussions. "It was attempted, but the man who tried to organize it didn't realize what he was getting into," the woman said. "It never happened. But Palestinians and Israelis were purposely made roommates. It seems to be working, but you don't see them hanging around with each other all the time."

I also mentioned the Viking poem about friendship that I had cut from my speech as a possible quote for Cecilie's board. She tried to convince me to put it back in the speech.

I found Kaare again and asked him about his studies. He said he would either study history or law, and it seemed more likely to be history now. His studies had been slowed when he was operated on for a brain tumor. A week before, he had an epileptic seizure. He was continuing, and said he had to, as if everything was normal.

Soon, it was time to move to the gymnasium, which was decorated with flags. Einar Vannebo, the Director of the ISS, walked up to me.

"I am Michael Kleiner," I said.

"So, you're Michael Kleiner," he said. "I've heard about you. Thank you so much for speaking tonight."

The program opened with songs by the ISS choir after just a few days of practice, and a men's choir. Dr. Kjetil Flaten, former Director of ISS, spoke on "The Summer School Experience." One thing, he mentioned, was that in the early days of the school, the American students would come on a boat, and the choir was formed en route, so by the time they reached Norway, the choir was quite good.

Following Dr. Flaten, one student played a violin piece, and another a piano piece.

Then, it was my turn. At the last minute, I had written on Einar's introduction for me, that AFS would be celebrating its 300th anniversary in 1996-97. In closing his intro, he said, "Perhaps this 50th will inspire him on the 300th."

There were 500 students from 90 countries, plus faculty, staff, administrators and alumni in attendance. I opened with my Norwegian paragraph – which Ragnhild had helped me with – about what an honor it was to speak, and hoping this meant I passed the Norwegian oral exam. Then, I just continued. I caught Mark wiping tears from his eyes – he had not heard the whole speech. I could see others nodding. I paraphrased the Viking Hávamál poem, which Cecilie encouraged me to put back in, at the close, and I saw Cecilie smile. The audience applauded. I took a breath and walked to my seat.

Einar told the audience, "Maybe in Michael's experiences you saw your own." When he returned to his seat next to me, he said the speech was very nice and had come from myself. He asked for a copy for the files. Cecilie walked over and said, "It was wonderful. So heartwarming and straight from the heart. Thank you."

Now, it was time for the International Fashion Show. When I had spoken about Norwegian Independence Day at Abington Friends' International Day, I followed the fashion show. Now, I preceded it. Students were dressed in colorful national outfits of their countries; some students wore clothes of a country other than their own. Poland, Norway, African countries, Latvia, Scotland, Palestine, Netherlands, to name just a few, were featured. One of the emcees was Canadian and paraded around with a Canadian flag and ice skates.

Activities continued back at the *studenterhjem*. Audun thanked me for the nice words I said about him in my speech. I told him it's a good recommendation. We agreed we had a good class, and he asked if I had been in touch with any of them. Now, he knows there are nice words in my book about him. He concurred and asked about the progress of the book. This entire conversation was in Norwegian.

The dining room had tables of food samplings from different countries or more displays. The only food we got to was the shrimp creole at Scotland. The United States offered popcorn in honor of Native Americans. There were tables for Poland, Guatemala, Venezuela and more. The room was quite congested. Einar stopped me again to talk about the speech and asked about my remaining schedule in Norway.

Outside in the courtyard were dance and song performances of different countries: South Africa, Germany, Palestine, Bosnia-Hercegovina, Ghana, Croatia, Bangladesh and Zimbabwe. Students from three Baltic countries joined together to perform three folk dances. U.S.A., Canada and Belgium did line dancing together; Canada and Germany sang a song, and various countries did a martial arts display.

At one point, I said to Mark, "I want to sit on the front steps symbolically. We never sat on the steps until the last day in 1992."

Although there was plenty of entertainment remaining, we had to leave because it was getting late. I found

351

JoAnn sitting on the bench outside the building. She said the speech was good, thanked me and also expressed interest in a copy. She asked about the progress of the book. Mr. Kleber and Zivojin joined us, and I recalled how the three of us were always searching for a *Herald Tribune*.

Cecilie was sitting with Astri, her mother and aunt on a bench in the courtyard.

"Thank you for asking me to talk," I said.

"No, thank you," she said.

"Where in New York do you live?" I asked.

"Brooklyn," she said.

"My mother grew up in Brooklyn," I replied.

"I'm half Jewish. My father is Jewish; my mother, Norwegian," she said.

"We said Cecilie sounded Norwegian, Finkelstein Jewish," I replied.

"You got it right!" she answered.

She asked if we could get a picture of the three of us. Her mother took one picture with Cecilie's camera, one with mine.

Mark and I then continued down the hill toward the train – as I had done four years before. This return and speech were important for me in a couple of ways. Much of that 1992 summer experience was paired with Alice. Certainly, the two of us had some good times at the school, but there was tension and anxiety. In my retrospectives and writings since, I was able to pull out my own individual experiences that made ISS a worthwhile experience for me and allowed me to stand independent of Alice. The letters I've exchanged with friends reinforce that. I returned to this campus as Michael with my own story.

REFLECTIONS ON THE 50TH ANNIVERSARY OF THE INTERNATIONAL SUMMER SCHOOL, UNIVERSITY OF OSLO

Presented at the 50th Anniversary Celebration

By Michael Kleiner

July 26, 1996

God kveld. Det er veldig hyggelig å være her og i Norge igjen. Det er en stor ære for meg å snakke i dag kveld fordi Norge og menneskene her betyr mye for meg. ISS har også spilt en role i denne sammenheng. Jeg håper at jeg nå har bestått muntlig eksamen!

For those of you who don't know Norwegian, here are the subtitles:

Good evening. It is very nice to be here and in Norway again. It is a great honor for me to speak tonight because Norway and the people here mean a great deal to me. The ISS has played a role in this context. I hope that now I have passed the oral exam!

My experience with the International Summer School in 1992 was a bit different in the context of Norway. This was not my first trip to Norway, but the fifth over the course of more than 20 years. During that time, I developed a deep-rooted affection for this country and its people.

I had been here as an 11-year-old child in 1969, when my family spent a year in Oslo. I attended a Norwegian school – Majorstua. The reason we were here was a young man came to Norway with the Allied liberation forces in 1945 and fell in love with the country. A few years later, he returned to study at the University of Oslo, but left because he was in love with a young woman in the United States. That young man was my father; the young woman, my mother. He vowed he would bring his family here. In 1969, he fulfilled that promise.

In the succeeding years, a connection to Norway continued through visits by my father's Norwegian colleagues to the United States and his visits here.

When I returned to Norway for the first time in 1986, and in subsequent visits, I was always welcomed warmly by our Norwegian friends, and enjoyed wonderful times that the average tourist doesn't experience. This week was no different. Meeting Norwegians outside of our family's circle of friends added to my feelings for the country.

A year ago, my father was honored by his Norwegian colleagues for his 25 years of work with them. Some of that work deals with cross-cultural research. Now, a year later, I am asked to speak about my experiences at the International Summer School in a country that has meant so much to me.

I need to give this background to put in context who I was when I came to the ISS in 1992. For these prior experiences with Norway contributed greatly to my interest in other cultures – primarily Norway – respect for people who were different, and peace. ISS also allowed me to continue the pursuit of a goal. I was studying Norwegian at home with private tutors for professional reasons, and I had the desire to learn the language of my friends. ISS provided the opportunity to study the language intensively, a setting to use it, a chance to see my old friends, and hopefully make new ones from around the world.

My time at ISS contributed and helped mold my overall relationship with Norway, adding some more wonderful memories.

As we arrived, the news headlines told of gloom and hope: war in the former Yugoslavia, possible peace in the Middle East. Prior to leaving, I found a quote from Mark Twain, which became my motto for the ISS: "Travel is fatal to prejudice, bigotry and narrow-mindedness."

For the next six weeks, the ISS experiment to reduce prejudice, bigotry and narrow-mindedness was undertaken.

This campus, too, already held a special place in my memory. In 1969-70, I took Norwegian lessons with a University student. I traveled here from Majorstua on the trikk by myself. Back then, that one stop to a child from another country seemed long. In the winter darkness, scary. I believe we met in the *Matematikk Bygningen*. Now, on the first day of class in 1992, I walked across the same plaza with a lump in my throat. In this class were an

Iranian and an Iraqi sitting next to each other; students from Portugal, Canada, Estonia, Latvia, Italy and Germany. Later in the week, I was moved to an intermediate level class where there were four Americans, two Czechs, two Spaniards, two Japanese, one Dutch, one Austrian, one Belgian, one Canadian, one Afghan, one German and one Estonian.

I remember how intimidating that first day in the intermediate class was, with everyone speaking Norwegian. I was in a small group with women from Slovakia and Japan. I struggled with the Norwegian; they struggled with their English. At the farewell party, we were taking pictures together and signing directories.

As the course continued, I grew to respect the teacher, Audun Toven. He encouraged us to speak Norwegian; he taught us to sing "Happy Birthday" in Norwegian in honor of a classmate's *fødselsdagen*. The material we translated dealt with Norwegian history or contemporary issues like immigration and cultural identity in Norway and the Norwegian welfare system. We learned about Norway as we learned Norwegian. We laughed in class. He was patient and interested in the students, and was available outside of class for assistance.

The meals – although the food was often forgettable – provided even a brief opportunity to spend time with people from other countries. Perhaps, it would be only a one-time thing, but just having that one meal with people from, say, Mauritanius, Benin, Vietnam or Mozambique could have an effect. In some cases, those meetings led to more get-togethers.

Students also served as "educators" themselves, with organized evening discussions. Four South African students talked about apartheid; an Israeli and Palestinian discussion had a Peruvian moderator and Egyptian interpreter. Or there were casual discussions about life in each other's countries.

And the talent show showcased a multicultural evening of music, singing, dancing, poetry and storytelling.

The front steps and other activities provided chances for talking, laughing, playing and singing together.

The weekend excursions were a great time to relax and get to know students away from campus. A highlight of the weekend to Noresund was a hike to the top of Høygevarde. For me, the lasting impact was that people from America, Slovakia, Nepal, Benin, Norway, Slovenia, Canada, Italy, France, Germany, Philippines and Palestine walked up and down the mountain together. If someone tired, others would wait until the person could resume walking.

During the last week, there was a bonding with the students in class, teachers, administrators and staff that made up our community. Some of us knew about each other's goals and reasons for learning Norwegian, so in a way, our lives became intertwined.

So, when I faced the choices for the essay question on the written Norwegian exam, there was only one option: "my candidate for the 1992 Nobel Peace Prize," and only one answer – the International Summer School.

The strength and power of the ISS are seen in the good-byes at the end of the summer. At the farewell party, the cameras were clicking and the pens writing. As the campus emptied out, there were teary good-byes. I became friends with a German couple – and found the German students very friendly – important to me as a Jew; and became friends with a Russian man – important to me as an American. A Bulgarian man gave my friend a tape of Bulgarian folk music. Friendships were developed with classmates from Slovakia, Canada and Spain. There were hugs all around, including from the house-parents.

The strength of the ISS is that through meeting people from countries in turmoil, it put a face to those troubled areas. I was left with the feeling when I heard about events in Slovakia or South Africa or Germany or "Yugoslavia," I would wonder if these people I met were all right.

The strength of the ISS has been seen in the follow-up. In the last four years, the letters haven't been flying back and forth, but I have had correspondence with friends in Russia, England, Germany, Bulgaria and Slovakia. The letters are filled with warmth, humor, caring and hopes for a better world.

As I try to figure out a "secret" to ISS success, I, of course, can only speak from my year. For the most part, we talked and listened to each other without regard for what country or culture we came from. The classroom provided a common ground, where the struggles together to learn Norwegian superceded our national and ethnic backgrounds. Other students may have found a common ground in music. There was desire to meet people. The dining room was always full of noise from conversations.

Another unique aspect of ISS is that the student body crosses so many age groups and offers an additional forum for intergenerational mingling.

There is ancient Viking poetry known as Hávamál, which is 1,000 years old. The following poem is called *The Nature Of Friendship:*

> *A bad friend*
> *Is far away*
> *Though his cottage is close*
> *To a true friend*
> *Lies a trodden road*
> *Though his farm lies far away.*

The Summer School provides the first steps. Even if our correspondences are in letters, perhaps we're bringing the farms closer together. *Gratularer med dagen. Takk skal dere har.* Congratulations on the occasion. Thank you.

Saturday, 27 July 1996, 9:57 p.m.

It's been a week since I wrote in the journal, but the last six to seven days have been full of events and seeing people. And, last Sunday in Bergen, I couldn't find the journal and didn't locate it until we unpacked back in Oslo. Then, I didn't write anything until now, as we prepare for our last day in Oslo. As usual, the time suddenly went by so fast. We were busy, and I had a speech to write.

We got some of the main chores done today – shopping. First, we made our prerequisite chocolate purchases for the trip home, made easier when I noticed a Freia chocolate store on Karl Johans Gate.

After having done enough store-hopping to price sweaters from Oslo to Flåm to Bergen and back to Oslo, we wound up back at The Oslo Sweater Shop because we could get 10% off with The Oslo Card plus the tax. However, we found out we could only get the discount if we paid in cash. So, Mark and I scrounged up a combination of travelers' checks, American dollars and *kroner*. We'll be like The Bobbsey twins since we each bought the same traditional sweater – black and white with metal clips halfway down and the red and green flowery design next to the clips. I also bought a scarf for Lisa.

While we were at the store, the salesman suddenly said, "Did you hear what happened in Atlanta?"

"No," we said.

"A bomb went off at the Olympics and someone was killed," he said.

He didn't have much more information, and it was unclear if the bomb had exploded at an event or someplace else. The news was dramatic and left us with a weird feeling. Since we had left the United States, there had been a plane crash that might have been tied to terrorism – and had our families nervous about our travels home – and a bomb exploding at the Olympics. Getting more news was difficult. Back at the apartment, I tried unsuccessfully to find Armed Forces radio or Voice of America on the radio to get an English broadcast. I got through some of the Norwegian in the newspaper and a little bit of the TV, but was not able to piece everything together until I got a *Herald Tribune* and a British newspaper on Monday.

Well, back to Saturday. Our day started slowly as we started to pack. We thought about the night before at ISS, and continued to talk about our special Thursday with Debbie, Ingrid and Anja.

We headed to Bygdøy, once again; the fourth straight day we went to the peninsula. Today's museum stop was the Folkmuseum, the open-air museum of buildings, farmhouses, stables, lofts dating from 1200s-1900s. All the buildings are made of wood, and they are laid out amidst trees, forest, small green pastures, where you might find cows, horses, chickens or rabbits. At each building, there is a host or hostess dressed in regional *bunads*, who can answer your questions.

The centerpiece is the stave church from Gol, dating to circa 1200. It is quite tall, though small inside. It was made without nails and has very pretty carved art on the door and doorposts. There are dragon heads protruding from the roof, a symbol to scare away the evil spirits. The churches mix the clash of Norwegian architecture and the arrival of Christianity in the country.

What is fascinating to me about the Folkmuseums here and in Lillehammer is that, though the buildings span different centuries and are from different regions, they look very much alike. There may be a series of buildings near each other that are from different centuries. You can walk in the houses and see the furniture – such as the small beds. A guide said the beds are not necessarily as small as they seem, and that visitors from other European countries have commented that the old beds in their countries were also small.

At different buildings, there are various demonstrations, such as pottery making and traditional food. We found the food. Women were making *lefse*, a thin pancake of rolled dough, often served as a dessert. For five *kroner*, we could enjoy it hot off the griddle with butter. We also got the recipe for two *kroner*. For added entertainment, I embarrassed myself with my pronunciation of *pølse*, which means hot dog or sausage. I had seen Norwegians eating *pølser* in what I thought was *lefse*. Actually, it was *lumpe*, a thinly rolled-out potato cake that looks similar. The way I was saying *pølse* sounded like *poser*, which are bags or pouches, which obviously left the women quite confused.

There is also a replica of an Old Town, probably Oslo from the 1800s.

Mark and I had been overcome by the tourist invasion at the other museums and always had the habit of going in the opposite direction to the flow of the exhibits. The Folkmusuem is spread out, so we were able to be away from the "disease" and plan our own route, so it didn't matter which way we went.

At the start, we passed a building called Bethlehem 1876. The description called it a "chapel/meetinghouse." It was closed so we couldn't go in. Looking through the windows, I could see benches similar to Quaker meetinghouses, but saw a podium for a minister, a piano and artwork. Quakers don't have ministers, and activities like music and art were scorned upon at one time. But, there was a Quaker presence in Norway, and this could have been a meetinghouse of a sect that had ministers and accepted music and art, or by 1876, music and art were deemed permissible.

After finishing at the Folkmuseum and doing the sweater shopping, we went back to the apartment. Mark called Debbie in Rauland. Ingrid answered and wanted to go back with us. Debbie asked how the speech and the evening at ISS went. I called Olav because the Dalgards thought he might be back Sunday. But a person answered the phone and said he wouldn't be back until August 4. I also tried to reach Camilla Sørensen, Tom and Inger's daughter, but was told, she, too, was away (although I found out later that wasn't true).

The cash outlay at The Oslo Sweater Shop left us short on money, but we treated ourselves to dinner at Café Elise near the Dalgards. It was the restaurant Dad, Steve and I treated the Dalgards to on our last night in June 1990. We still managed to keep each order under 100 NoK, as we each got the rigatoni with salmon and bacon, and paid with VISA.

We then took a walk to the Park. I had said I wanted to walk up Nobels Gate to find the place where I skated as a child. I had not done it on any of the other trips. Mark said to save it for another trip. I wanted to do this because I think this was one of the last childhood spots I had not visited in Norway.

I also talked about walking down Frognerveien, which I didn't do. But Eivind had driven on Frognerveien, and we had seen it enough times when we were on the number 12 tram.

I remembered the "rink" wasn't a very long walk. I tried to estimate it in children's shoes. It couldn't be too far because we would reach the end of the park. The Vigeland Museum appeared on the left across the street. Directly across on our side was an entrance to the park. We turned and...

There was a big round flowerbed with benches around it. It caught me by surprise, not that I was expecting ice in the summer.

"This conceivably could've been it," I said.

I walked back to see if there were any other round surfaces, but could not find any. Mark suggested the pond, but it wasn't round enough.

"The benches are around it," I said. "People could sit down and put their skates on. They've either replaced the rink with the flowers and don't use it anymore, or maybe they ice this over in the winter."

At the time, the latter didn't make much sense, and I was left with mixed emotions. If they replaced the rink with flowers, at least it was replaced with something pretty; if the flowerbed is permanent, where do the leisure skaters skate?

I took a couple of pictures anyway. As we walked around it, I went into a brief skating motion. We walked through the park, past picnickers (it was around 8-8:30 p.m.), geese and walkers, and finally came to the bridge of statues.

"Are you satisfied now?" Mark asked as we came to the gates of the park. "Have you visited the final scene of your childhood in Norway?"

"I guess I am," I said softly.

We walked back to Thomas Heftyes Gate, stopping at the 7-Eleven for another bag of potato chips. As we walked up the hill, we counted the times left that we would have to walk up the hill and climb the steps, looking forward to the next visit when there would be an elevator that Odd insisted was being built. We watched some TV and retired early.

Sunday, 28 July 1996

Despite going to bed early, the body clock woke me around five a.m., but I tried to get back to sleep. After some packing and a leisurely breakfast, we finally got ourselves out the door. As I said, we were short of funds so I wanted to find a MINIBANK (an ATM) so I could use my VISA PIN to get some cash. Then, we wanted to walk to The International Children's Art Museum, about 30 minutes.

We found a MINIBANK on Kirkeveien, near Majorstua. I intended to withdraw 100 NoK. The machine offered an English version of the instructions, but that didn't seem to matter to me. In the States, you type in 10000 and the decimal is put in automatically. When I reached 1000, I realized this wasn't the case and hit *KLAR for* CLEAR, instead of *FEIL* for MISTAKE, and wound up with 1,000 NoK or approximately $158 which I didn't need for less than a day. It was good to still have a padding.

Next, we found an *apotek*, a pharmacy, which was closed, as I continued my search for SELSUN, a shampoo, for my mother.

We continued on to the museum. The International Children's Art Museum is one of those off-the-beaten-track places, which is a treasure. It's on a residential street in a blue and white building that could pass for any other house on the street. The museum opened in 1986, founded by movie producer Rafael Goldin. He and his wife traveled to different parts of the world, collecting the art and encouraging participation in competitions. The museum has been honored by such organizations as The LEGO Group and UNESCO. Artwork by children ages 2-18 from 150 countries is exhibited.

The purposes of the museum are to collect art, literature, films and videos by children from all over the world and preserve it for the future, and to collect books of art and literature about children's art. It is seen as a place where children, adults, artists, teachers, researchers and politicians can gain value and perspectives. The brochure notes: "Children and adults will meet each other on the children's own terms. The Museum wants to remove the gap between generations, integrate the culture of children and adults. The Museum arranges collective creative activities, drawing and painting, music, dancing and singing and concerts where the young ones and the established artists can perform together. Discussions, conferences both for adults and children, will alternate with playing and artistic activity." Traveling exhibitions can be arranged.

You enter by walking downstairs. The attempt to meet the children on their own terms begins immediately. There are benches and cubbies like in kindergarten. You have to take your shoes off here, and walk around the museum in your socks. On the walls are copies of press releases, newspaper clippings, announcements and posters.

The museum starts as soon as you enter the reception area. Admission is 30 NoK. There are postcards of the artwork and some posters. On the floor are mats of different animals. Every area of wall space is practically filled, and almost every area of floor space is filled with sculpture or masks.

Pictures are grouped thematically, but a common thread was the family: *My Family; What Is A Family?; My Father; Symphony of the Family; Home Activities*. Then, there are themes like Ecology and Peace. The museum is about four stories, but we could handle only two. There was so much to see; it was overwhelming, touching and moving. As you ascend the steps, there is artwork on the walls on each side of you, so you must stop at each step to look to the left and the right.

Some children wrote poems about the theme of their work, or descriptions of the painting. You read the material, look at the painting, then are amazed when you see the age of the child. Much of the work we saw was by Norwegian children, but there were a number of pieces from Sri Lanka, Asian countries and the Netherlands. There was just one we saw from the United States. There were some group efforts on some magnificent wall-length paintings by Sri Lankan children, showing events of life. On the second floor were a piano and a room with a number of drums and instruments. This is one of the "inspiring rooms." According to the brochure, children and adults can participate in drawing, painting, dancing, playing, making music, singing and dramatizing, weaving, embroidering, making books, animation films and videos. The artwork gives you an insight into the difficult lives some children endure around the world, even in Norway.

From the museum, it was a short walk to Blindern and the University. I wanted to drop off copies of my speech. As I entered the *studenterhjem*, two male students were sitting on the steps. I was wearing the ISS 50th Summer Session T-shirt I had bought on Friday.

They said, "Hi. Weren't you the guy who gave the speech the other night?"

"Yes, I was," I said.

"It was good," they said. "Very good."

"Thank you."

I dropped the envelope at the reception and came back outside. Mark was sitting on a bench. We tried to decide what to do next.

"Now, that we have money, we could take the train to Majorstua and go home, or head into town and look for a troll for your niece," I said.

We headed into town. Upon exiting at Nationalteatret, we immediately stopped at the Narvessen for our "lunch"– chocolate and a drink. We walked along Karl Johans Gate. We had not taken any pictures along the main street, which is mainly for pedestrian traffic.

The *gate* was not as mobbed as on weekdays, though there were still plenty of people. While some people were selling wares on the streets, most stores were closed, and except for a group of Andes musicians – who weren't even playing – the multicultural musicians were gone.

Suddenly, we passed an open apotek that had lines like a take-out place. I asked about the SELSUN, and the salesman said, "Liquid or cream?"

After all this, I'm faced with another question. I went with the liquid, and so at the 11th hour, I had gotten the SELSUN for my mother.

We eventually wound up back at The Oslo Sweater Shop, where Mark bought the troll. We then headed back to the apartment, watched some of the Olympics and read some of the paper. I gave another call to Olav, but once again was told he would be back 4 August; left a message for Eivind; and there was no answer at the Sørensens.

For dinner, we warmed up the leftover reindeer meat Ragnhild had made Wednesday. We still didn't trust the burners, and actually had not used them since the first night, when Eivind told us the one we had been using wasn't working. Eventually, we heard the sauce bubbling. And we ate.

This was the first of my trips where the last meal wasn't with the Dalgards, but we were eating Ragnhild's meal, so maybe in spirit, they were there.

Ragnhild left us a checklist of things to do before we left the apartment, and we started to check them off. We took a walk down the hill to the taxi stand at the corner to inquire about the availability of taxis in the morning. Then, it was to the 7-Eleven for one last bag of *potet gull*. Upon returning to the apartment, we watched some more of the Olympics; I reached the Sørensens, but not Camilla; left a good-bye message for Eivind; left a note for Odd and Ragnhild, and went to bed about 9:30.

The Road Home
Monday, 29 July 1996

I am aboard the British Air flight to London Gatwick, the first leg of my second leg of the vacation, which will take me to Nice/Vallauris to visit my Uncle Irwin, who is battling cancer, and his wife, Mireille. He has lived in France for around 40 or so years. Norway has finally disappeared under the white cloud cover, I've finished the Saturday-Sunday *Herald Tribune* and the breakfast.

We had to get up at 4:30 a.m. to get to the airport. Mark and I are going separate ways in a manner of speaking. He is also heading to London – Heathrow – and should be in the air now. Then, he's on to home. He got the 8 a.m. flight; I got the 7:15. Yes, in order to get the British Air Visit Europe package, I had to fly to London before flying to Nice. We naturally came to Fornebu together.

Our last shots of Norway were of Oslo's five a.m. light. We dragged our luggage down the four flights from the Dalgard apartment, down the hill to the taxi stand. We had checked with a driver the night before, who said there should be cabs at the stand, and if not, a cab was certain to drive by, or we could call from the pay phone. There were no cabs, but after a few minutes, Mark waved a cab down. In contrast to the normal day when different buses, cabs, cars, trucks are on the streets making noise, at this hour, the streets were empty and quiet. We got to Fornebu in about 10 minutes, waited in line to check in, navigated our way through the airport, passport control, and found the Tax Free Refund booth, only to find it wasn't open until 6:30. We walked away, but soon headed back to find ourselves in a line behind a tour group from Houston. A woman heard us talking about my earlier flight and let me in front. I got $16 back for the sweater and scarf, $3 for some of my Norwegian coins, and exchanged 200 NoK for French francs.

Mark walked to the gate with me, and sat with me until I boarded. He said he had a wonderful time and enjoyed meeting the people the best, and said most of my pre-trip talk was justified. He thanked me for being his tour guide. Except for a few minor things, the trip worked out well for us. We got along and had few disagreements.

There is much to catch up on with my journal writing, and now I have the time on the plane.

We were in a holding pattern before finally landing at Gatwick, where it was raining, after two weeks of sun in Norway. I followed all the "Flight Connections" signs, walked through the security check, up the escalator to a large hall. Apparently transferring in North Terminal wasn't going to be simpler than changing terminals at Heathrow. The flight to Nice had disappeared from the screen, without even a "Wait in the Lounge."

I went in search of a phone that might have a telephone book so I could look up Bea Shapiro – a classmate from the Summer School – and the hotel I would be staying at on my return to London. No luck. I rechecked the screen, and Nice was still lost in space. I went to Flight Information where everybody in line seemed to be asking about the Nice flight. The woman said it would be posted shortly, and to just keep watching the screen. It hadn't been on the board for five minutes.

The crowd gathered around the screens was looking for the Nice flight. I then heard Norwegian being spoken.

I was wearing my Norway T-shirt. Two sisters, their husbands and father were traveling to Nice. We started talking. The gate was finally announced as 81, which of course, was downstairs, through a hall, downstairs again, where there was a waiting area for the bus that would take us to the plane. There was a wait, then people started checking in before an announcement had been made. We were transported a further distance than at Heathrow to the plane. We got off the bus at 10 a.m., which was the scheduled time of departure of the plane.

We finally got in the air 10:50 London time; 11:50 Oslo and Nice time, 50 minutes late. In between writing, I ate lunch and read *The Daily Telegraph* and watched the plane fly over the Alps.

Finally, we landed in Nice.

After two weeks in Norway, there were some difficult culture shocks and changes moving from Norway to England to France to England and then home to the U.S.

Mark and I had talked often about the prevalence of languages – English and others – in Norway, from airports to museums to restaurant menus. Mark commented how great it felt to be in a country where he didn't understand anyone.

To England, where just in the airport, there was only one language. Even though it was English, the British terminology is different than American terminology.

The landings in Oslo and Nice are quite unique and dramatic. In Oslo, the plane lands in between the fjord; in Nice, you are surrounded by the Mediterranean Sea. Passport control, customs and baggage claim were the extent of English that I saw in the Nice airport.

I saw the Norwegians I met in Gatwick at the baggage claim. *"Sammen til slutten,"* I said. "Together to the end." They laughed and asked me to take a picture of them.

Teres, a friend of Mireille, who was visiting, accompanied Irwin. She didn't speak English and had been working on "How are you?" in anticipation of my visit. I had not had any opportunity to look at a French phrase book, although I had brought one with me. Though we found some way to communicate, it was difficult for her not being able to talk in anything but French, and for me not being able to understand her French or speak French. To find a Norwegian who doesn't speak some English is very unusual. Mireille's English was better than in 1992 when she and Irwin visited Philadelphia, and we could talk. Most of the conversations were in French. As opposed to Mark, hearing conversations, that I couldn't understand, was uncomfortable. Irwin said it took him three years of working and living in France before he became comfortable speaking and understanding French.

The menu at the restaurant we ate at tonight was entirely in French. People in stores seem to speak only French, or that's the only language they wanted to speak. Even if you look confused or like a tourist, they speak French.

Mireille began to play a game. Whenever I said a French word I might remember, she would count. "Five. He knows five words."

In addition, I had Norwegian and English words rolling around in my head, and my instinct was to speak Norwegian.

In Norway, Mark and I seemed to manage without lunch most of the time. In France, lunch is a big meal, and the meals concluded with *fromage* – cheese.

In the car on the way back from the airport, Irwin asked if I was hungry. I had a small breakfast on each flight, so I wasn't terribly hungry.

"Would you like an omelet? A grilled steak?" Irwin asked.

I opted for the omelet – "with some French cheese."

It was a beautiful, sunny, hot day. So, when we got to Irwin's house, I took a dip in the pool. July 29 and this was the first time I was in a pool. The water was pleasant.

We ate lunch outside. Lunch was not simply an omelet. There was tossed salad, potato salad, green beans, head cheese (you don't want to know). Fruit? Pluck a peach from the tree. Wine was served, but I opted for a soda.

When Mireille came home, she was charming and bubbly. She requested the French tradition, a kiss on each cheek from me.

I was exhausted, so I went to take a nap. There was a choice of rooms, and I chose the one with the computer and without a window. The room was too dark, and the hallway was not lit often. This was a bit different than almost 24 hours of light in Norway. I conked out right away and woke up two hours later at 6:30.

A friend of theirs had recommended a restaurant for dinner, but it closed early. We went to a seafood restaurant about a block from the port of Cannes.

"We went here with your parents, and they liked it," Irwin said.

"It passed my dad's approval?" I asked.

"It must've. He paid for it!" laughed Irwin.

Traffic was virtually bumper-to-bumper and that was the pattern during my two-and-a-half days.

When in France, do like the French. We ate outside. Irwin suggested I get the fish soup, a specialty of the house. It came with a special paprika garlic sauce, shredded cheese and toast crackers on the side. The soup came in a really big bowl, but the sauce was too spicy for me, and Teres had to finish it for me. I had large grilled shrimp over a salad.

For dessert, Mireille had chantilly; I believe it was some kind of ice cream (*glace*) with whipped cream. I had some kind of vanilla lemon ice cream in a small crust.

Mireille asked if I had a girlfriend, and I said yes. I asked if she remembered baseball from their visit four years before, when we went to a game.

"Every time she sees baseball in a movie, she says 'Phillies!'" said Irwin.

When we reached the house, the others retired. They went to bed, and I went to my room and continued to write in my journal, trying to catch up.

Tuesday, 30 July 1996

Later in the morning, we went to the Museé de Automobile, a museum depicting the history of automobiles, primarily sports cars and luxury cars. There was a whole row of Rolls Royces from different years. There was an early 1920s Renault and Citroën. I had to take pictures of these cars because Irwin had a Citroën for 17 years, and now had a Renault.

Irwin told me that when he had the Citroën, the Citroën owners would come to the museum to exchange parts. There was a mechanic's garage from the 1930s with the cars, tools, pumps from that time. The proprietor died, and the family gave "the garage" to the museum.

The people who designed The Maeght Foundation Museum in St. Paul Vence also designed this museum. Outside, there were some odd sculpture; a pond with geese, and an old, maybe military, car that children could ride.

We went back to the house for lunch. Irwin said Mireille was cheating today. In honor of my being here, she was coming home for lunch. She then had a client to see nearby. Irwin had joked about the hours she put in on the job, and predicted she would return to the office after seeing the client, rather than come home early. She said it would depend. If she were done by 4:30, she would come home. I put my hand out to Irwin as if to collect the money from a bet. I don't remember what was then exchanged, but it caused Irwin to put his hand out to me to collect the money back.

Lunch was grilled lamb chops on the barbecue. Knowing the French penchant for eating meat rare, I made sure to put in a request for medium well, much to their "disdain." In addition, there was eggplant, tossed salad, potato salad. Then there was the dessert. I broke out one of the large chocolate bars with hazelnuts, which I had bought in Oslo. On top of that were Häagen-Dazs chocolate-chocolate chip ice cream and vanilla ice cream bars with chocolate nut covering. Mireille was a real French chocoholic.

After lunch, Irwin took a nap; I did some more writing; Mireille went to visit the client; Teres washed dishes and the laundry, and did some sun-bathing.

When Irwin woke up, the three of us went to Antibes, a fortified town from ancient Greek times, when it was known as the acropolis of Antipolis. In subsequent years, it became a Roman "castrum," and medieval bishopric. The Grimaldi family occupied the castle until 1608, and gave the castle its name. In 1928, Antibes obtained the castle for a Museum of Art History and Archaeology. In 1946, curator Dordela Souchére offered Pablo Picasso space within the castle for a studio. Now the castle houses the Picasso Museum. Much of Picasso's works in the museum are from 1946 on, and show various techniques and media such as industrial paints, fibrocement, plywood, "illustrating the hard times in these post-war years (for materials) and his extraordinary propensity for experimenting with new materials."

The museum also houses work by other artists such as Matisse, Leget, Miro, Braque and some others I had never heard of.

You enter by going up stone steps, past canon aimed directly at the Mediterranean. A courtyard has a view of the bay and sculpture, which was not by Picasso. All the captions were in French.

There were narrow roads around the castle and homes within the castle grounds.

Irwin videotaped the museum visit, but had trouble with the camera at first. So, when he asked me to say something, I walked over to the camera and said, "You finally got it working!" But he cut that part of the tape.

On the way back, we stopped in Golfe-Juan. We were dying of thirst. Teres went to a bakery, while Irwin and I got a couple of iced teas, and then bought some food for dinner.

The Norwegian salmon caught my eye, and we bought lox, which the man sliced from the fish.

Mirielle was home when we arrived. "Four thirty?" I asked, and she nodded.

I took a quick swim and returned to my journal writing. Lox and salad were served for dinner. A humorous scene developed. Mireille and Teres took the salmon and began to delicately cut it with a fork and knife. But Irwin and me – the Jewish Americans – tore off a piece of the baguette, opened it, put on some cream cheese, and stuffed in the lox and salad. The two women stopped and looked at us, wondering what the heck we were doing.

I wanted to call the hotel in London where I would be staying Wednesday night to get the address and distance from the airport. I asked how much a cab from Heathrow would cost, and the man said £30. Irwin said £30 was a lot of money, and added to the hotel rate made my brief stay expensive. I might be able to get a room closer to the airport for around the same £89. Irwin suggested I go to hotel information at the airport when I arrive at Heathrow.

The trip wouldn't be complete without playing the tile game, Rummy-o. We always remember the game in Philadelphia. My parents and I had just taught them the game, and Irwin won a round before I had gone down yet. I was left with 142 points. Games between my parents and them are becoming legendary – with different versions naturally.

Mireille has become the real shark. I followed her and Irwin, so anything I saw to do, I either forgot, or it wasn't available when my turn came. She takes so long with her turn, "You can fall asleep," said Irwin. At one point, I asked Irwin, "So, what's new?" to pass the time. Mireille won twice, Irwin and Teres once each, results my parents were disappointed to hear when we called.

Wednesday, 31 July 1996

I was sent off with a steak lunch with fried potatoes, pasta, etc. and my trusty Coke. Teres always drank wine. With my soda, I wasn't very French.

About an hour before we were to leave for the airport, I was sitting by the pool writing, when Irwin came out and said, "Your father just called, and the Scheiners will pick you up at the airport."

Since I knew some Scheiners, this confused me.

"In Philadelphia?" I asked.

"No, in London," replied Irwin.

"Why would the Scheiners be picking me up in London?" I said. "They live in New York."

"Well, your father said he just sent an e-mail," said Irwin.

We checked the computer, and Dad's mail hadn't arrived yet. Suddenly, I figured out it must be the Finers in London. They needed the flight information, and said I could stay with them.

We called them and left the info on the answering machine.

Now, we had the problem of my hotel room in London. Irwin called the hotel to cancel the reservation. "He missed his plane," Irwin told them.

The hotel said they needed 24 hours notice to refund the money, so I lost the money.

At Heathrow, again – the London airports seem to have endless walking – down stairs, up stairs. There was no customs because I was traveling from one European Community (EC) country to another. I was able to take the Blue exit. Among the crowd was a man with a sign, "MR. CLEINER." Close enough, except I didn't recognize him.

"Mr. Kleiner?" he asked.

"Yes, and you are?" I asked back.

"The cab driver," he replied.

Not knowing who was paying for this, I rushed to exchange more money. About 25-30 minutes later, I was at the Finers. They had paid for the transportation in advance.

Again, the time passages were striking. I first met Anne Sussman in 1968 when she visited us in Philadelphia when she was 18 or 19 years old. I had seen her in 1969-70 when we stayed in London en route to Norway and on the return trip. She was dating Michael Finer at the time. I last saw them when I visited London in 1988. Now, Anne was 46 or 47. Her own children, Paul and Jonathan, were now 20 and 18. Paul was currently in Nice as part of a month-long rail journey through Europe. Paul is at Leeds University studying History. Jonathan was in Spain and would be attending a local college to study Hotel Management and Leisure.

Anne was still working at a college, maybe a sports college. It sounded like her job had something to do with business or admissions because we compared American and British standards for athletes. Michael had always been heavily into computers, and now runs his own business, which involves some travel and a lot of hours.

He is also still involved in cricket as a watcher and player. He insisted he had bought his last glove. I don't remember which son's room I used, but it had cricket posters and record books, much as an American boy's room has baseball paraphernalia. When I visited in 1988, I went with Michael to one of his cricket matches, and I interviewed some of the players. Michael remembered that.

The plan was to have dinner, then go to Anne's parents, Jack and Cissy. Jack had suffered a couple of heart attacks in the last year. Michael called them and said, "Put the strudel and apple cake on. We're coming over!" and then hung up.

Salmon was part of dinner.

I attempted to find the telephone number of Bea from the Summer School, but they were an "x-directory." That meant they didn't want their name given out.

After dinner, we left for Jack and Cissy's in Michael's "baby SAAB." The little white house was the same. Jack and Cissy were surprised and happy to see me. These were the first people I met when I first came to Europe, 27 years ago. Cissy put tea on. The strudel, cake and "biscuits" came out. While Jack was thin and conscious of his trembling hands, his humor was still there. Cissy sat in her usual chair, talked continuously and humorously in her Cockney accent, and managed to keep track of every conversation.

One of the first things she said to me was, "Your American fans are behaving miserably! Take that back with you!"

I never realized what a sports fan she was. They were bemoaning the performance of the Brits in the Olympics, the lack of youthful Olympians and proper facilities to train in England.

"We sent the darn old age home over there!" said Cissy.

Prime Minister John Major had said he would build facilities. "Probably just another campaign promise!" said Jack. "A week later, he'll forget about it!"

The conversation shifted. Anne gives Cissy mystery novels. Suddenly, Cissy said, "There's something wrong with that book you gave me. It's impossible for that woman to have committed the murder." She reads the end first.

It was a nice visit, even if it was short. Back at the Finers, we watched a little bit of the Olympic wrap-up, completing my trifecta of watching the Olympics in Norwegian, French and English.

Thursday, 1 August 1996

Anne drove me to the airport the next morning, and we talked about the political conditions in America and England, and found that the approaches of the Conservatives in England and Republicans in the United States, and the Labour Party in England and the Democrats in America were quite similar.

I was wearing my ISS 50th Summer Session T-shirt. As I sat down in my seat on the plane, the man next to me asked, "Were you in Oslo? I just came from Oslo. I met some students in Oslo who were from the Summer School."

He had been an exchange student in Stavanger in 1982, and had been in Norway now for a conference on

Arctic mining. He had been up North. Norway never seems to leave me. He lives in Anchorage, but his parents live outside Philadelphia. He had the *Dagbladet* and *Aftenposten* and offered them to me. The papers were highlighting Norway's *gull* in the 800 meters.

My parents were at the airport. I spent a good part of the evening at their apartment, telling them about the trip, showing off my sweater and the scarf for Lisa.

When I reached my apartment, there was a notice under my door that said an apartment on the second floor – under me – had been burglarized a few days before. The next morning, I dropped the rent check off at the office. The secretary said another neighbor witnessed the burglary and waited until Monday – after the weekend – to report it to management!

Welcome back to America.

Chapter 10
August-September 1997
Honeymoon

Sunday, 24 August 1997, early morning

The circumstances of this trip to Norway are far different than all the others. Foremost, it will be my honeymoon, and I will be showing off Norway and its people to my *wife*. And, the people who have been so hospitable and wonderful to friends, a cousin, and me will now shower that hospitality, and if possible, be even more special to Lisa.

I'm jotting down these notes in the middle of what seems like the longest night of my life, the last hours before my wedding. I'm trying to divert my thoughts away from my nerves.

I always envisioned that I might spend my honeymoon in Norway. When Lisa and I started discussing honeymoon spots, Norway was certainly on the short list, but I didn't want to force it on her if she preferred to go somewhere else. It's an expensive trip, and I wanted to respect her wishes. As we named spots, nothing seemed to grab us. And then she said, "What about Norway?"

Lisa reasoned that neither of us were "sit out in the sun all day" people. Why go someplace for the sake of going there because all newlyweds go there? "But, you've been to Norway so many times, I'm worried you'll be bored," she said.

"It's a big country," I said. "We'll go someplace I haven't been, and if you don't want to go to some of the usual museums, we'll go to others I haven't been."

So, we decided on Norway, and I made the arrangements through Five Stars of Scandinavia in Washington State, my pals who I had discovered through the Internet.

Tuesday, 26 August 1997

We are now here in Norway, resting at Odd and Ragnhild Dalgard's apartment. We are married! We survived the day you never forget, the events of which you can never remember. We made it through the ceremony, reception, responding at every twist and turn to guests showering attention. We were exhausted – still are, on top of the transatlantic flight, even though we left last night. We hardly had a chance to eat anything or even drink anything. We put together the ceremony ourselves. Everybody said it was the most beautiful ceremony they had ever seen. Trust me to find a way to get Norway into the ceremony. I had noticed the Norwegian word for getting married is *gift,* the same spelling as the English word gift. I discovered the origin of the English word came from the Old Norse. I wrote this as part of my vows, saying we are a gift in marriage to each other. Tom Sørensen represented Norway at the wedding. My Uncle Irwin died in France a month before the wedding, but Mireille came. Lisa's cousin and his wife came from Israel, so we had guests from four countries and about eight states.

On the way home, we dropped off rolls of film that my Uncle Dave took in to the slot at the photo store, so we would be able to pick them up the next day and take pictures with us to Norway. We ate leftover roast beef and some wedding cake at home and watched some old rerun on TV, which I believe had a wedding theme.

Our trip was relatively pain-free, except for the exhaustion. Uncle Dave had a flight to Houston leaving a few minutes before our shuttle from Philadelphia to Newark, also on Continental. He drove us to the airport after a half-hour with Aunt Beverly, Cousin Aviva, Tom and my parents at my parents' apartment. We got to the airport early enough for an earlier flight to Newark, but our luggage couldn't get on, so neither could we. So, we spent around an hour with Dave, as our respective gates were close to each other. Naturally, the shuttle left late, but this did not prevent us from making the connection, which required taking a bus from the plane to the terminal; going up an escalator; walking to an escalator to the monorail; taking the monorail to B terminal; taking a down escalator, and walking and walking 'until we got to the gate.

I embarrassed Lisa twice. As we boarded the SAS plane, I told the attendant, "We are on our honeymoon." When drinks were being served, I told the stewardess.

"Why are you telling everybody?" Lisa asked.

"Oh, congratulations!" replied the stewardess and placed two complimentary airline bottles of champagne on our tables.

"Well, we got free champagne out of it," I said.

Shortly into the flight, the pilot announced that they would be able to pick up time, and the plane would arrive in Oslo around 8:15 a.m., 45 minutes early! We left late, but would land 40 minutes early. We tried to sleep part of the time. As good as the movie was – *Everybody Says I Love You* (rather apropos) – we were too tired, and as usual, it was hard to hear. Dinner was very good with seconds of warm rolls. As I think about this trip, I realize that any subsequent trips to Norway will most likely be made with Lisa. I will no longer need to search for a traveling companion. So, I hope she enjoys the trip.

I also leave on this trip with a more secure feeling in my job situation. We had a successful 300th anniversary year at Abington Friends, and the people raved about the publicity I obtained. My boss gave the staff watches with the 300th anniversary logo on the face, and orchestrated a surprise shower party for me. It was nice having my department colleagues at the wedding.

During the year, I spoke to the kindergarten classes about my reindeer sled ride in Norway in 1970 with the Sami people, as well as serving *lefse*, which Lisa and I made. I was a big hit.

Tom's son, Andreas, made his second one-week visit to AFS, renewing ties he created the year before. He brought a book his class in Norway had put together with a little bio of each student with their picture. It was hoped pen pals could be developed between the two classes. When he returned to Norway, he brought with him similar books the AFS fifth-graders put together. And, some students are corresponding. Once again, I was able to bring a bit of Norge to the school.

What will also be interesting is that the *Storting* (Parliament) elections in Norway are in a few weeks. It will be exciting and interesting to listen to the discussions with our friends. I read my *Norway News*, which I receive on e-mail, for the first time in months a couple of days ago, The most recent poll showed the incumbent Labor Party with 27%, and the extreme right-wing anti-immigration Progress Party second at 22%, which is frightening. Liv Gardner wrote me a letter saying she would be busy with electioneering when we are in Bergen.

Well, we landed at Fornebu early. Passing through customs was a breeze, and our luggage was some of the first to reach the conveyor belt. But, since Odd Steffen Dalgard was expecting to pick us up at nine, we waited outside for him.

As he drove back to Thomas Heftyes Gate, he asked about the wedding, informed us Olav had broken his arm bicycling, and that the plans for the evening were to have dinner with Odd and Ragnhild, then go to Eivind and Angela's house to see Angela, the children and Olav. Eivind was working one of his 24-hour shifts, and it was difficult for Angela to come to Odd and Ragnhild with the children. This sounded like a good arrangement. I had not met Eivind and Angela's children, Andrea and Stian, or Olav's youngest, Agnes. Odd told us Ragnhild would be home around 4:30.

Their apartment building had one important addition. After years of talk, there is finally an elevator. You have to walk around to the back and have a key for the back door. It's a small elevator, but saves the effort of carrying luggage – and, for them, groceries – up the four flights of winding stairs, and it brings them right to the back door of their apartment. They didn't have an extra key, so we still got plenty of exercise during the week.

We had the usual guest room. Ragnhild had left two roses in a vase on a table. How did she know Lisa loved roses? Normally, I would push us to stay awake and take a walk, get into some activity, so we don't lose the day. We were wiped out, so we took a rest.

Then came the traditional Michael Kleiner First Day Tour. Down Thomas Heftyes Gate to Frognerveien, look at the menu outside Peppe's Pizza, get amazed or disgusted at pizza with pineapple, and recoil at the prices – at least $20. Turn right onto Frognerveien, walk two blocks to Tidemands Gate; point out the corner where there once was the bakery where our family bought bread in 1969-70; turn left, cross Frognerveien to walk up Tidemands Gate; comment how in 1969-70 the Turkish and Brazilian Embassies were on this street, and we used to smell coffee every morning; now we find the Thai and Bulgarian Embassies, to name a few; and then we come to the house my family lived in during that year. Lisa took a couple of pictures. This time, I didn't venture in.

We continued the tour walking two blocks to Munthes Gate, turned left and I showed Lisa where Dad worked; continued down the street until we reached Kirkeveien, directly across from Vigeland's Park. Refreshment was already needed, so we stopped in at the visitors' center for a Coke. We sat on a bench drinking and recapping the wedding.

Lisa was immediately impressed by the view entering the Park. We walked around, down to the pond with the statues of infants; back up to the bridge; and admired and wondered about the various statues. There were a few tour groups, but nothing overwhelming. Equally impressive were the different flower arrangements on the lawns. When we reached the steps at the base of the Monolith, we sat down and looked back toward the entrance for a while. The statues of old people were on our sides. I pointed out the detail of the wrinkled lines. Behind us, two young men leaned against the Monolith and sketched the statues. Two young blond children were with their mother and began to run around. Holmenkollen Ski Jump made its majestic stand and impression in the mountains on the right side. Funny, I always remembered it being on the left side from this vantage point! Looking back out at the park in front of us, I said you could sit here for hours. Look at all the benches that we could see just from where we were sitting! It was nice to sit here and relax from the hectic pace of the last few days and months.

We got up and walked around the statues. I pointed out the trails, talked of the people using the Park, and that the "art imitates life."

We headed back to the Dalgards. At Bygdøy Allé, I asked Lisa if she wanted to see RIMI, the local market chain, because she likes supermarkets. Lisa said yes.

As soon as we entered, the *potet gull* stared at us. I knew there was another reason I wanted to come in here. In the course of walking around, we ran into Ragnhild. The introductions, hugs, kisses and congratulations happened in the middle of RIMI! Ragnhild was standing by the cauliflower and asked if I liked it or would I eat anything? Noticing the broccoli on the other side, I said, "I prefer broccoli." So, she bought both.

At the checkout, we grabbed a sour cream and onion potato chip (*rømme og løk*) bag sitting along the side and bought it. The three of us walked back to the apartment toward the shortcut away from the steep hill. Along the way, we passed a fruit store where Ragnhild looked at a couple of things, rejected them and exchanged a few words with the salesperson. Next door was a fish store – "the best," said Ragnhild – and a cheese shop. Last year, Ragnhild teased Mark and me about buying packaged cheese at RIMI and not at a cheese shop. This must've been the cheese shop! We reached the building and rode the elevator up to the apartment.

Dinner was reindeer, with the little berries – I think they're cloudberries – often served with reindeer, new potatoes and broccoli. Lisa loved it. Odd and Ragnhild learned about Lisa's job, and there was much humor exchanged during and after the meal. When I said, *"Takk for maten."* ("Thank you for the meal," which is always extended after a meal), they replied that it is a custom for the person on the right of the hostess to say *"Takk for maten,"* and also make a speech about the hostess. Most of the speeches include jokes. Sometimes a person is told in advance and has to prepare jokes. This makes Odd nervous. One time, Ragnhild had too much to drink and kept repeating herself, and Odd was too far away to stop her. After all these years visiting Norway, sharing so many meals with friends and saying, *"Takk for maten,"* I was never aware of this cultural custom.

Ragnhild said dessert would be later at Angela's, where we would also receive our wedding present. We retired to the terrace for tea, where we could see a view of both Holmenkollen and the Monolith. It has been an unusually hot summer for Oslo, and the forecast was for more hot weather this week with some rain. Odd said people are saying the hot weather might be a result of the greenhouse effect.

"Nonsense," Ragnhild said. "They had this kind of weather 100 years ago."

"Were you around then?" asked Odd.

The black cat, Fantastik, who is only nice to Ragnhild, was actually letting Lisa pet her, when suddenly without warning, Fantastik hissed, showing her whole mouth and teeth, and lashed out with her paw. Then again, this is a cat that attacks Odd when he tries to get into bed. Well, she won't get nominated for any Nobel Peace Prizes.

As we left the apartment, I asked Ragnhild when the election was and she said September 15. She is a member of the board of the apartment building and will be busy politicking before and during Election Day. Ragnhild was worried about the election, but suddenly stopped on the steps, and smiled.

"Reuters interviewed me last week about the election and that was exciting," she said.

"I saw a poll about the election, and it wasn't very good," I said.

"It is bad," concurred Ragnhild, shaking her head and sighing. "We are too rich in Norway now. I don't like Norwegians anymore."

The line struck me hard and stayed with me for quite some time in the car. Throughout my years, I had met many good Norwegians, notably the people in this car with me now and their families. Certainly none of the people I know fit the racist, Norway-for-Norwegians-only platform of the Progress Party. That gave me comfort. I'll always have these people.

Eivind and Angela live in East Oslo, part of the old section of the city. "You will see there are many people of color living here now," Ragnhild said.

At dinner, she mentioned that the year they lived in Philadelphia, Eivind was named most popular student. "In Norway at the time, there wasn't a race problem, so Eivind treated everybody the same, and that's why he won the award," she said. I remembered Eivind telling me about White students being upset when he chose Black students for his teams in games on the playground, and that one of his best friends was a boy from Colombia. With an influx of immigrants, primarily from Asia and Africa in the last 20 years, Norway has had to face a race problem.

We entered the house – the door was unlocked – and a four-year-old girl with blonde braids met us.

"Hva heter du?" I asked. "What is your name?"

"Andrea," she replied clearly.

"Jeg heter Michael," I said.

Angela appeared and was soon hugging and congratulating me and greeting Lisa. Stian, 14 months old, was with her. Momentarily, Andrea carried a gift and presented it to Lisa.

"Takk for gaven," I said. "Thank you for the gift."

"Vær så god," she replied. "You're welcome."

We were in the kitchen and dining room now. Proud *bestemor* Ragnhild held Andrea, then Stian, in her arms.

"Michael er de pen?" Ragnhild asked. "Michael, aren't they beautiful?"

"De er ditt bestebarna!" I said. "They are your grandchildren."

The weather was nice, so we set up for dessert outside. Andrea kept saying, *"Åpen packet,"* referring to the present. "Open the present." Stian kept showing me a toy car. Olav arrived and joined us on the porch.

There was so much activity and laughter. For me, I felt at "home" again in Norway among the Dalgards. For Lisa, still tired as was I, it might have been a bit overwhelming. But, everybody was being nice to her. It was Olav's turn to ask if this was her first trip to Norway, what she did, where we met.

"Michael has told me about Norway," she said.

"Probably exaggerated," Olav said.

Cake, tea and coffee were served, but there was great interest in the package. For one, it was a joint present, and Odd, Ragnhild and Olav had not seen it. Of course, the children were excited.

"Har du kjøpt gaven?" I asked Andrea. "Have you bought the gift?"

"Ja," she replied. "Yes." Andrea is also learning German from Angela, and her only words in English seem to be, "See you."

Stian stood on a chair next to me, and then put his arms out to me, indicating I should pick him up. This was actually a ploy to get closer to the package, as he kept poking at it.

Finally, I opened the present. It was a lovely pewter bowl that was a 17th century Norwegian pattern.

Everybody wanted to know about the wedding and out came the pictures. They said they got a real feel for the wedding. Ragnhild commented that Eivind had said, "If I had the money, I would've come." My mother had cut a CD of her singing as a wedding present for us, and it included young and current pictures of us, and a big photo of me in Norway. They were quite taken with it and wanted to play the CD, but Angela said the speakers on their player were broken.

Florence called during the evening. Andrea got on the phone. *"Kan du kommer over nå?"* she asked Florence. "Can you come over now?" Florence wanted to invite us over to their house during our visit. (Eivind would later tell us that he called and talked to Andrea while we were at the house, and she told him, "There are two people here speaking English, and Grandma and Grandfather are also speaking English.")

It was time for the children to go to bed, and us too, so we prepared to leave. Angela said Eivind would be in touch about seeing us Thursday evening. Andrea's room was near the door. "Michael, do you remember this?" Angela asked.

There was a mobile hanging from the ceiling above Andrea's bed. It was a gift I brought last year (I think the mobile was for Stian).

"Det var gave fra meg," I said to Andrea. "That was a gift from me."

"Takk," she said. "See you."

"Those are nice first two words in English to know," I said to Angela.

We exited and walked back to the car. Odd was driving Olav, who now lived on Bygdøy, home. Our conversation shifted to the elections, and I asked Olav if he was also active in the campaign.

"Me?" he asked. "No. I'm a cynic. I'm of the belief that it doesn't really matter who is in power. I will probably vote for Labor."

There's a difference. An American cynic would probably not vote.

"The problem," Olav started to say.

"Is the Progress Party," I said.

"They are right-wing extremists," Olav said. "One of the reasons I voted 'yes' to join the European Union was so many of the 'no' people were these right-wingers. I think 100% of the 'no' voters were selfish."

Ragnhild gave him a look, and pointed to her and Odd, who both voted 'no.'

"Alright, 2% weren't," Olav said.

In the car, he asked me, "How would you have voted?"

"I don't know," I replied. "I know the issue was debated a long time, and the issues were complex. I think the concerns Norway had are proving true because the Union can't agree on anything. Countries who are already members are having second thoughts."

I asked about the structures of the electoral process in Norway. "Do you have to register in your party, declare what party you are a member of and vote just for them?"

"I receive a paper in the mail that tells me when and where to vote," Olav said. "We don't have to declare a party."

We explained Americans have to register as a Democrat, Republican or Independent, and in many states, including Pennsylvania, can only vote for candidates of our party in the spring primary election. In Norway, electors vote for a party, and then select local candidates from a list.

"You can mix up the list," said Olav. "That's when it gets confusing."

Ragnhild would be working inside the polls on Election Day.

When we got back to the Dalgards, it was only around 9:30, but Lisa and I were exhausted, so we went to sleep. During the night, I had some trouble sleeping, thinking about the overwhelming first day, but also about this election. The phrase, "a vote for the soul of Norway," kept coming to mind. I also felt I had an investment in this election because I have such an emotional attachment to the country. How would this election impact on my emotions for Norway?

Wednesday, 27 August 1997

I fell asleep, eventually. We woke up around 10, showered, ate breakfast – food was left out for us – and tried to decide what to do today.

It also meant the start of phone calls to arrange seeing people. I always bring this long list, including people I haven't seen in 27 years. By the time I'm finished with the regulars, the time is up. That's why two weeks is never enough for me, particularly with travel within the country in between. I could spend the whole time in Oslo looking up people.

I began alphabetically, and a good start was Berit Bae. I tried her work number and found it had been changed. I got a pen and called back to get the new number.

I rang the number, and Berit answered. "Berit," I said.

"Mi-i-chael," she said, drawing out the letters in syllables. Her voice could be heard through the phone, and Lisa laughed that Berit recognized me just at the sound of my voice.

"How are you? Congratulations!" she said, and I could see the everlasting smile on her face in my mind.

The idea, of course, was to see the stupendous view from her terrace. But, Berit was having a lot of work done on her apartment, so it wasn't in much shape for company, beyond looking at the view. She had talked to Torbjørn, who had suggested we come for wine and cheese this evening at his house at Skådalen, just outside the center of the city. We confirmed Torbjørn's work number with Berit.

I reached him, and Torbjørn further told me that Debbie was coming down from Rauland tonight with the girls because she was going to Paris tomorrow. This would be our only chance to see them. The arrangement would work out great because we would "kill three birds with one stone."

A family friend of Lisa's had a son who worked in Bekkestua, a suburb of Oslo. We gave him a call at work and home, but there was no answer.

So, we set out on our day, which was leisurely and spontaneous. We needed to get the Oslo Card, and we could purchase it at the Trafikkanten at Jernebanestasjonen, the central train station. The bus took about 15 minutes into town because of the traffic. We exchanged travelers' checks, purchased two three-day Oslo Cards, and began walking up Karl Johans Gate, the main street in Sentrum, the Center City, much of which is limited to pedestrians. As opposed to the height of summer, there were few stands set up outside the stores and few street musicians. Most of the musicians weren't even playing.

We stopped in Porsgrunn, which has different ceramic, pewter, wood and *rosemåling* items, as well as sweaters. We began to consider possible wedding gifts for our friend who had fixed us up.

We continued our stroll, looked in some windows, then cut through Lille Grensen, a small side street with stores and outdoor stalls, also limited to pedestrian traffic. The store Backe caught our eye because it advertised Orrefors Swedish glasses, which we had requested on our wedding registry. The store also featured glass from the other Scandinavian countries. Husfliden was another destination, since it is one of my favorite stores. We didn't make any purchases. After all this walking, Lisa asked if I wanted to get a drink.

We found a kiosk on Karl Johans by the park that separates the two sides of the street, bought a drink and a *Herald Tribune*. We found a bench by the spurting fountains. As we continued our walk, Lisa asked what the rose meant on this sign. I looked and the sign said, "Arbeiderpartiet."

"It's the symbol for the Labor Party," I explained.

There was a table with people distributing literature and talking to passersby. Then we noticed that up the whole block were tables one after the other with representatives from different political parties providing literature for the election. Every party was there: Christian Democrats, Progress Party, Red Electoral Alliance, Socialist Left, Liberals, Center, Conservatives and the

Green Party. The Center Party had a model of a wooden *hytta* (cottage), and one of their statements was if they were elected, they would follow the actions of the following candidates of different parties. We skipped past the Progress Party.

What was interesting was there were inquisitors at each table gathering information, asking questions and probably challenging party positions. The Green Party, though stressing the environment, had a broad agenda and platform. Because of America's two-party system, these rows of tables are a sight we wouldn't see in the United States. It would be rare to see a Democratic and Republican table next to each other.

We then proceeded to the seat of Oslo city government, but an international venue of great importance – the Rådhus, City Hall. The building with the tall twin towers looks out on the harbor. There was a guided tour of Rådhus at 2 p.m.

The reception area is quite significant. The room is wide and large. It is the host for many state and municipal functions, most notably, the presentation of the Nobel Peace Prize. Of course, for me, I remembered the Mayor of Oslo having a reception for the Summer School here in 1992. Covering the walls on the second floor are wall-length murals. On the bottom floor in the reception room are two smaller, but no less dramatic murals.

The guide told us it was decided in 1931 to construct a new City Hall. The war delayed construction, and the Rådhus wasn't dedicated until 1950. World War II and the occupation gave the artist subject matter.

The first wall on the second floor depicts a general history of Norway through the centuries. On the left wall of the first floor was the story of the occupation during World War II. The opposite wall told the story of the patron saint of Oslo. The other second floor wall depicted the life of Norway, primarily that of the fishermen. A room just off the reception area had two more murals on opposite walls. One showed the history of the labor movement in Norway; the other, the history of business and industry in the country. A large window provided a wonderful view, though the day was overcast, of Oslo Harbor.

The guide said all the materials used to build Rådhus came from Norway – the marble in the floors, the stone, etc. She explained the two towers represented the link between the two branches of city government. We were then free to roam certain areas of the second floor.

Two tapestries, completed in 1936, covered each wall of a room. One showed the downfall of King Harald Hårgrade (the Ruthless) at the Battle of Stamford Bridge in 1066; the other, the founding of Oslo. This room also serves as the room for civil wedding ceremonies.

At the beginning of the hallway was another monument – a working water fountain – a rare scene in Oslo, which I had not noticed on previous trips. It had not been this humid before.

The hallway was filled with gifts from various heads of states, countries and cities. There was a huge Kiddush cup with grapes sculpted on it from former Israeli Prime Minister David Ben Gurion. The design was similar to the cups Lisa's cousin had brought from Israel for the wedding. The end of the hall led us to another conference room with tapestries showing the development of the Norwegian constitution and freedom.

I suggested we catch the ferryboat to the Vikingship Museum, so we could experience the ride and see the museum. So, we crossed the street outside the Rådhus – another primarily pedestrian road – to the dock, where a ferry was just coming into shore. These boats are treated like the rest of the public transportation system and cost the same fare. With the Oslo Card, it was free. After disembarking, it was a few minutes walk uphill – uphills and downhills, Lisa would be learning, are a fact of life in Norway, even in Oslo. Therefore, this required an ice cream break at the kiosk outside the museum.

Lisa was fascinated by the Viking history, such as the shallowness of the boats enabling the Vikings to beach them easily, and escape quickly after attacking. She was impressed that a replica of one of the ships was built and sailed to the Chicago World's Fair in 1896.

By the time we got outside to catch the bus back to the Dalgards, the sky was cloudy, and it looked like rain. After getting off the bus – a three-minute ride – we walked back to find a florist. There are many of them. We bought flowers for Berit, then went to RIMI and bought cake to bring to Torbjørn's.

By dinnertime, it was pouring. Dinner was *pølser* (long hot dogs), mashed potatoes, orange slices with onions and cream of cauliflower soup. Ragnhild was going to get me to eat cauliflower one way or the other.

The rain was really heavy by the time we reached Berit's apartment. She greeted us in her usual jovial manner.

"So nice to meet you Lisa," she said.

"*Så hyggelig å møte deg,*" Lisa said for the first time.

"Oh, Michael has been teaching you," Berit said.

We walked into the living room. "I'm sorry the rain has taken away the great view," she said.

Lisa was still impressed by the depth of the view.

"I think we should have some champagne," said Berit. "I can't have much because I will be driving."

She also had a gift for us. It was Lisa's turn to open the present. It was a pack of candles and a black iron candlestick in a Norwegian pattern.

"I made sure it was small and light enough for you to carry," Berit said.

Of course, she wanted to know how we met, so we gave her the versions, as well as the planning for the wedding.

"I've been on my own for so long that I'm used to being independent and deciding what I want to do," Lisa said.

"Women tend to be independent, and men tend to take care of the person or be taken care of," Berit said.

Soon it was time to leave for Torbjørn's. We ran in the rain to the car, a 1981 Mazda. Lisa also has a Mazda, a

1994, so she and Berit compared cars during the ride. Skådalen wasn't much easier to find with a car in the rain than when Mark and I tried last year by train and foot in the light.

Are, Torbjørn's oldest son from his first marriage, was at the house. He must be about 21 now, and had just finished building an extension to the house, which was completely made of wood. Are had chosen conscientious-objector status rather than serve in the Norwegian military. He was in the process of a 14-month stint as a teacher's assistant in a school that was involved in forestry. I asked if he was interested in pursuing teaching, and he said no. College studies were on hold right now, but journalism interested him. He was also studying German.

It was Are's turn to ask how Lisa and I met, while Torbjørn prepared wine, crackers and cheese. Lisa deferred to me this time.

Then, Debbie and the girls arrived, earlier than expected. Ingrid was as social as ever, switching between English and Norwegian with ease. She remembered me this time, but couldn't quite remember when she had seen me last. Anja, who a year ago I had carried up the four flights of stairs at the Dalgards, said little more than hello. That day last year in her child's years was probably quite distant. Anja had changed her hairstyle. She climbed with facility all over the house, including the stairs and railings.

We got an update on Ingrid's jewelry, her sales and a look at her latest work. Later in the evening, Ingrid and Anja performed a musical routine for us. Ingrid hid in the next room and sang *Singing in the Rain*, while Anja, standing in the living room, moved her lips to the words. "Usually at home, Anja is very dramatic," said Debbie. "She throws out her arms and acts. She must be shy tonight."

Together, they performed *Get Me to the Church On Time* from *My Fair Lady* in honor of us, and Ingrid played *Twinkle Twinkle Little Star* on the flute.

The family had also bought us a special gift, two wooden cups made by the *rosemåling* artist of Rauland, with Lisa painted on one and Michael on the other. Custom made! Every gift we had received from Norwegians was a Norwegian craft.

We took out the wedding pictures and my mother's CD. They couldn't get over the shots of my beaming parents. As with the Dalgards, they, too, felt the excitement. "Torbjørn, we should have gone," said Berit. "I wish we were there. We must play the CD."

We never did, but Are was interested in the Yiddish titles because of his German studies.

At one point, Lisa snapped a shot of Ingrid on my lap, as we translated some Norwegian. Since she was four, Ingrid has helped me with my Norwegian.

Just before we left, Audun, now in high school, came home.

Berit drove us to Majorstua. In the car, she commented to Lisa how hard it must be for her to be meeting all these members of Michael's Norwegian family. Before we got out of the car, I told Berit there was a kindergarten class in America for her to see.

Back at the apartment, we joined Ragnhild and Odd in the study where they were watching TV. For some reason, Odd took out a small box.

"I don't know why I'm showing you this," he began. "My father was a prisoner in a concentration camp in Germany."

Odd took out a piece of fabric with a number on it. "This was his number," Odd said. "Prisoners exchanged different materials and made things. A Yugoslavian made this box."

In another small, but significant way, World War II had made an appearance on the trip.

Thursday, 28 August 1997

The calls for the morning were to Lisa's family friend, Richard, and John Ivar Brevik. I left a message in

Norwegian on the Brevik's answering machine. I spoke in Norwegian to the woman who answered at Richard's office and left a message. Afterwards, she said I spoke Norwegian well.

Lisa wanted to do something not too taxing. Although it was not a clear day, we decided to go to Holmenkollen and Frognerseteren. Little did she know that this could be strenuous. Several decisions were involved. The goal of reaching Frognerseteren was to get the famous *eple kake med krem* (apple cake with whipped cream) at the Frognerseteren Restaurant. The Oslo Guide said there was a surprise at the Holmenkollen Restaurant for holders of the Oslo Card. We figured it would involve eating there. But, we wanted to get the *eple kake med krem* at the Frognerseteren Restaurant.

We decided to first find out what the surprise was, so Holmenkollen was the first stop. From Holmenkollen Station, we started the uphill climb on the ramp from the tracks and the Restaurant appeared shortly. Then, we walked uphill to the Restaurant, which has a beautiful light wood interior. Inside, our climbing wasn't done since the restaurant was up another flight.

"We have the Oslo Card," I said to the hostess.

"You have the Oslo Card. You get a free coffee if you eat lunch here," she said.

It was too early for lunch, and free coffee wasn't a surprise enough, especially since we're both tea drinkers. So we left and continued the uphill climb toward Holmenkollen Ski Jump. I went around the side, so we could look up at the jump from the left side. Occasional stops were necessary. We then walked around to the other side and up toward the base of the jump.

Never far from a tourist sight is a kiosk, souvenir store, cafeteria or restaurant where one can buy a drink, chocolate, ice cream or something more. Maybe, it's because there's usually been a walk involved to get there. Liquid refreshment was definitely necessary. Since Lisa wanted to see the outside of the beautiful Holmenkollen Park Hotel and that was downhill, we decided to continue back to the train for the ride to Frognerseteren, rather than challenge more hills. After getting another burst of energy, we began our descent.

The train took us through five more stops and a winding ascent with increasing panoramic views from the left side of the train. Usually, public transportation stops are not directly by the sight one is heading toward. There is always some walking involved. Being at the top, our walk took us downhill on a pebble and stone path. It took only a few minutes before the beautiful wooden building with the artistic dragon heads protruding from the roof appeared. We each had a slice of *eple kake med krem*. Lisa also got a smoked salmon and egg *smørbrød,* and I opted for a shrimp *smørbrød* (open-faced sandwich).

Our next decision was whether to take the train to the Munch Museum or the Resistance Museum. We opted for the latter.

As we walked back to the train, Lisa mentioned Berit. "Besides being very nice, she is very perceptive," said Lisa. "Saying women are more independent. And she's never been married?"

"No," I responded. "And she recognized that you might be overwhelmed by meeting all of these people."

"I was feeling it, but not recognizing why," Lisa said.

Getting to the Resistance Museum required walking through the grounds of Akershus Fortress, which is perched on top of a hill overlooking the harbor on one side, and the Rådhus on the other. More uphills, then walking through the museum, which was hot. This wasn't going to be a taxing day. Lisa found the Resistance Museum quite interesting. Afterward, we headed back to the apartment and more steps.

Ragnhild said she had never been to the Resistance Museum. "I never go to war tributes or museums anywhere because history is always written by men, and men love to write about war. They never talk about women's contributions. I'm sure the Resistance Museum doesn't talk about women. Did you ever think about that?"

I guess it had crossed my mind on occasion. In thinking about the Resistance Museum, which I have been to several times, I don't think it speaks of women in particular, but in the underground newspaper section, periodicals to rally women to the resistance are included.

Dinner had been around 5 p.m., but was slightly earlier today because Ragnhild was going to the Oslo Konserthus with Olav to hear the Oslo Philharmonic Orchestra perform Mahler's 2nd Symphony. We had seen it advertised in the Norwegian paper on the plane. She was an avid concert enthusiast, and had been talking about this concert for a few days. Dinner was more reindeer stew. On learning about our day's activities, Odd told us that sometimes they take the train to Frognerseteren and walk back down to the apartment, about a two-hour walk. We were quite amazed.

We heard from both Richard and John Ivar. We slotted Richard in for the Wednesday evening we would be returning from Bergen; and the Breviks for Thursday. Inger Sandanger had called us at Torbjørn's last night, and we arranged to see the Sandanger/Sørensens on Friday. Our calendar was filling up fast.

Tonight, there was a debate – they called it a dual (without weapons) – between Prime Minister Thorbjørn Jagland of the Labor Party and the leader of the Christian Democrats, Kjell Bondevik. Apparently, each party leader gets a one-on-one shot with the incumbent. We watched the clips with Odd, and he translated for us. He said they didn't talk about the issues, which is not much different from American politics. Jagland had previously stated that if Labor didn't receive 36.9% of the vote, as in the previous election, the government would resign, a big gamble. Bondevik asked Jagland if Labor would join in a coalition with the Christian Democrats if they won. Earlier, Odd had said that part of the problem is there is no clear alternative to Labor, so the opposition is fractured. Most parties have at one time or another supported Labor policies. He and Ragnhild are Labor supporters.

Eivind arrived and we had tea on the terrace. Out came the wedding pictures, Mom's CD, the conversation about the wedding, how we met and Lisa's job. "If I had the money, I would've come," Eivind said.

I told him our calendar was filling up. He was not working next Thursday, but was working the following Saturday, and asked if we could switch our Thursday plans to Saturday. I said I would try.

Ragnhild came home in a cloud, enthralled with the concert. "I have been close to God tonight," she beamed. She played a CD of the music for us.

A little later, we played Mom's CD. On the sound system, it was beautiful. Ragnhild was overwhelmed for the second time this evening.

"*Så flott!*" she said. "So sharp and fine. It's like having Fran in the room."

One of the features of the CD is there is an encore performance of the entire CD. So we listened again. Lisa and I began singing and translating the words we knew.

"The next time Fran comes to Norway, I'd like to have her sing at the hospital," Ragnhild said. "I arrange arts programs at the hospital."

"A second treat for you tonight," I said.

"You should call them and tell your parents we listened," said Ragnhild.

So I called. Mom answered, and I said, "The organizer of arts programs at Ullevål Hospital would like to schedule a concert by a Fran Kleiner."

Mom didn't recognize me at first. Then we told them what we had been doing; Dad talked to his daughter-in-law, and Odd talked to Dad about when he was coming to Norway in October. Odd and Ragnhild were trying to plan a stop in Philadelphia in October as part of their around-the-world trip.

Friday, 29 August 1997

We tried to get an earlier start than our first couple of days. The sun was shining so it seemed like a good day for the open-air Folkmuseum. Before we left, I called John Ivar and was able to change next Thursday's plans to Saturday.

While we waited for the bus, I commented to Lisa how great it was to be able to take the bus one way and be in Sentrum in five minutes, and the other way be at the Folkmuseum and Bygdøy in five minutes.

As we entered the Folkmuseum, two schoolchildren with a video camera approached us.

"Are you from Norway?" they asked nervously in English.

"No, America," we replied.

"Do you have five minutes to answer some questions about your feelings about Norway?"

Obviously, they couldn't have found a better subject. I was already wearing a Norway T-shirt.

I probably shocked them when I answered the first couple of questions in Norwegian. Lisa poked me.

"Speak English to them," she said. "They probably want to practice their English."

The boys asked if this was our first trip to Norway; why we were here; did we find it expensive? Did we find it was hot? What do we like about Norway? Did we know the name of the King? They were 13 and doing a project for school on foreigners' views of Norway.

My moment of notoriety in Norwegian video education completed, Lisa and I proceeded into the museum. We covered quite a bit of ground, although we didn't stop every place. In the Old Town section, which replicates Oslo in the late 19th century and early 20th century, we saw a picture of a tiger on a *bensin* (gas station) sign. We read that the tiger image with Esso gasoline (later Exxon) originated in Norway in the 1920s, and eventually led to Esso's "Put a tiger in your tank" advertising campaign in 1964.

While walking along the paths with buildings from seven different centuries, we came across pigs, chickens and horses. We couldn't find the *lefse* demonstration again because it wasn't being offered today. I wanted to tell the women I had successfully tried their recipe, which Mark and I had bought from them last year.

From the Folkmuseum, we headed to the Oslo Bymuseum, located in Vigeland Park, which has exhibitions on the history of the city. But, first things first. We set out on a mission in search of salted potato chips – Maarud brand only – and chocolate. In the 7-Eleven at Thomas Heftyes Gate and Bygdøy Allé, we could only find lightly salted chips, and we bemoaned what had happened to this country! Undeterred, we set our sights on RIMI, but found the same predicament. Finally, we broke down and bought *lett saltet* – and a Freia hazelnut chocolate bar.

Immediately, we started eating the chips, as we walked toward the museum. Figuring we could take the chips with us on our trip to Bergen, we stopped on the chips, and then turned our attention to the chocolate. We didn't want it to melt in the heat. The humidity forced us to sit on a bench in the park before continuing.

The respite didn't last long because the City Museum was hot. That's the problem in Oslo. The buildings aren't air-conditioned and don't have drinking fountains (although there are plenty of sculpture fountains in the park and city), so there's no relief. The captions at the museum were in Norwegian only, as was the case when I was here in 1992. This is the only museum where I've encountered this. I did the best I could. The Berlitz book I had, only had English-Norwegian, so was useless. We were given an English pamphlet, which had general descriptions. After a while, it wasn't worth the trouble translating, so we just enjoyed looking at the exhibits and rushed through before we passed out. We sat at a table outside in the garden for a breather before heading back to the Dalgards.

As if a gift from heaven, people were handing out free Diet Cokes at Thomas Heftyes Gate and Bygdøy Allé. I didn't care that it was Diet; it was some relief. When Odd got home – he walked from work – he also had one. Ragnhild got her bottle, running for the bus in the morning.

Dinner – fish soup – was early because Ragnhild and Odd were going to a film premiere, which they had been nervously talking about all week. A son of friends had made a film in which he wanted to show the uselessness of violence, but he used a lot of violence in the movie. He considered himself a pacifist. There was an article about him in the newspaper. The parents were coming down from Trondheim and were quite anxious.

Eivind called and said they wouldn't be able to get together this evening. I told him I had been able to change next Thursday's plans to Saturday, so we were available to spend Thursday with him and the family. I said that Olav and Florence had also wanted to invite us over, and perhaps we could all do something together.

There were still some names on my list I wanted to call. I wanted to at least tell Per and Kare Hohle I was married, but I hadn't seen them since 1986, nor had my father because they had not been well and did not want visitors. I was nervous because I was afraid I would get bad news. I checked the Oslo phone book and there was still a listing.

I picked up the receiver and nervously dialed. Per answered. I knew I would have to speak Norwegian.

"This is Michael Kleiner," I said.

In 1969, Per recognized Dad's voice as soon as my father uttered, "Per," although they had not seen or spoken for 21 years. This would not be the same kind of conversation. Per couldn't seem to hear me, let alone understand, and kept saying, "What are you trying to say?" I spoke louder, although all I was trying to do was identify myself. I said, "Bob's son." He just didn't hear. Ragnhild came by to see if she could help. I asked to speak to Kare. Suddenly, he heard.

"Kare? *Hun er død. Åtte måned siden,*" he said. "She is dead. Eight months ago." He gave a date.

403

I said in Norwegian – I hope – I am sorry, and hung up. "I'll write when I get back," I said, sadly, hoping that he would be able to remember and recognize me in writing. Per had been my father's first friend in Norway, and the Hohles were among the first Norwegians our family met when we came to Norway in 1969-70. Per had become a well-known mountain climber and author of books about nature and outdoor life. How warmly Per and Kare treated us each time we visited, although they didn't speak much English. I will always treasure the visit on my first return to Norway in 1986 in their log cabin of a house; the laughter; their interest in me; wanting to hear me *snakker Norsk;* Per excitedly showing us slides of his recent trip to the Matterhorn; and Per giving me two books which he signed, one about Fridtjof Nansen and another about the Norwegian outdoors. Kare made the best *hveteboller.* Now, Per couldn't even recognize my voice, so I could share with him the latest development in my life, and Kare was dead. It is a fact of life that as I grow older and start losing family or family friends in the United States, the same will happen with my Norwegian family. Kare would now be added to Erik Rinde, who I never saw after 1970, and Morris Gardner, who had died last year. Life also must go on, and I had no choice but to move on to my next calls.

Lisa and I went to Aker Brygge, where we bought ice cream and strolled around town, then returned to the apartment to retire early, so we could be up in the morning to start on our three-day journey to Bergen.

Saturday, 30 August 1997

Ragnhild's alarm clock woke us at 5:50 a.m. We were able to eat some breakfast and call a cab, which got us to Sentral Stasjonen in plenty of time for the 7:30 meeting time. Five Stars had arranged this three-day Panorama Cruise to Bergen run by Tumlare Corporation. They had heard only good things about the trip. We would verify those sentiments.

Not only were we thrilled with magnificent scenery of waterfalls, mountains and fjords, but were also given such a wealth of information related to Norwegian history and legends that it made the trip fuller. I hope I can remember it all. We went by train, bus and boat.

At the train station, Lisa went to change money at an ATM (terrible rate) and bought some *lefse* and chocolate for the ride – the essentials. We had already packed the chips we bought on Friday.

Eventually, a blonde woman holding a "Panorama Cruise" sign came by the "Big Clock" meeting place. I alerted her that we were part of the group, and to my surprise, she said, "Mr. and Mrs. Kleiner?"

Her name was Carin, and the other guide was Tina. Carin informed us the entire group had a reserved car on the train; our luggage would be tagged, and after we reached Åndalsnes, the luggage would be transported the rest of the way for us.

Sitting across from us on the train were Jim and Mary from Jacksonville, Florida, and to their right, Harry and his wife, Linda, from Texas. Jim and Harry had just attended the annual aeronautics and aerospace medical conference in Oslo. Mary had her trusty Fodor's Norway guide. She would read aloud about an area we were passing.

"Wait until we take the bus on the hairpin curves in the mountains," I said, which didn't relax anyone. "And then there will be cows in the road, and the back of the bus will be hanging over the side."

"You've been on this trip before?" they asked.

"No, but I've been on other trips in Norway," I said.

Later, I was trying to read the train magazine. "Are you trying to understand it, or do you know Norwegian?" Jim and Mary asked.

"I understand Norwegian," I said.

Thus, began my Norway story, and my life as a guide. Whenever they needed a word pronounced, they asked me. If they had a question, they asked me. There was no touring information on this train, so I "became" the guide.

We were on the Trondheim train, but would be getting off at Dombås, where we would transfer to a train for Åndalsnes. Carin and Tina handed out itineraries, a map and a list of the group. There were 24 people, plus the guides, a woman from the tour office and her mother. The tourists were from the United States, England, Australia, France, Spain, Peru, Brazil and Italy.

The weather was constantly changing. First, it was overcast, then rainy, then sunny. At one point, Lisa thought it was snowing!

The scenery got more exciting as we proceeded. The train stopped at Hamar, and the Vikingship Arena from the 1994 Winter Olympics could be seen from the train. I pointed it out, which brought on questions from Jim and Mary about why the Olympics were held in Lillehammer. Eventually, the train stopped at Lillehammer.

"Don't you want to get a picture of Lillehammer?" Mary asked.

So, I took one. "They really spruced up the station for the Olympics," I said.

Another stop along the way that was nostalgic for me was Vinstra, the station for the Wadahl resort. In 1970, the Royal Norwegian Council sponsored a weeklong ski vacation at Wadahl for people and families from around the world who were spending time in Norway. I had never been able to locate it on any previous trips, even on a map.

All our meals on this tour were covered in the price of the package, and the box lunch served on the train was quite substantial. It took a little more than four hours to reach Dombås, and the weather was a little chilly. Though, the train was a little late, the connecting train was there waiting for us.

The scenery kept getting better and better, proving my oft used adage that you never know whether to look left or right in Norway, and never know what to photograph because you never know what's around the next corner. For a while, the scenery was on the left side; then as if to give equal time, the scenery appeared on the right side. And, of course, at times, they were on both sides.

By now, I had also gained a reputation as the shutterbug of the group. In a nice way, people, particularly Jim and Mary, alerted me to shots and moved out of their seats, so I could get a better vantage point. They warned me of oncoming tunnels, telephone wires, trees and when the view was clear. Waterfall on the left! Rapids on the left! Rapids on the right! Cows! Sheep! Horses! Goats!

At one point, we saw a flock of sheep, a man and a dog. The man sent the dog toward the sheep, and he shepherded the flock farther away from the train tracks. Tina "warned" us to look out for elk because one had been spotted. When she translated this for a couple, they stood up as if they had to move out of the way.

Around two hours later, the train reached Åndalsnes, where it was rainy and chilly. We were given time to stretch our legs, go to the bathroom and get some refreshments.

The thrills were just beginning. The group was split up – the English- and French-speaking people going on one bus; Spanish- and Italian-speaking people on another bus. This was to avoid everybody having to listen to four languages.

Tina was our guide. She introduced everybody. "Mr. and Mrs. Kleiner," she said.

I was still trying to get used to the sound of that.

The train experience was nothing compared to what lay before us. We entered Trollstigen, The Road of the Trolls. It is a two-way, one lane on each side, narrow road of hairpin curves. While the map seemed to indicate we were going down, the bus was going up and up around bend after bend. Legend had it that this was an area of "trolls." Tina explained that there were good and bad trolls. Children are told not to go out at night because the trolls will get them. Trolls took the shape of women or men and always had a tail. They could become part of stone or wood. The bus slowed down – from an already slow speed – because on the face of a mountain, we were supposed to see an image of a troll. Along the route, there were plenty of wooden images of trolls by campgrounds or souvenir stores.

The buses kept a significant distance from each other on these roads. Driving here demanded courtesy. If another vehicle came from the opposite direction, somebody had to back up, usually the car. Sometimes a bus came from the opposite direction. There were no guardrails on the road, just views looking down and down.

On the train, I had warned the people about the hairpin curves, and I had also said we would meet cows in the road. Sure enough, the cows were waiting, lying on the road, walking along the side, looking about without a care in the world. They didn't block the whole road, but the bus driver had to maneuver between them as the cows stared at us. The cows have the right of way. Later, we got stuck behind a woman bike rider at a small bridge. She, like the cows, was oblivious to the buses behind her and was biking real slow. "Sometimes the bike riders are slower than the cows," joked Tina.

The waterfalls were striking and magnificent, notably Stigfossen. As we climbed, we first saw the fall from its bottom. Then we stopped at a bridge "for a shower." We went outside, and the water sprayed us. Lisa and I asked Tina to take a picture of us by the waterfall.

Another stop was by Trollstigen Fjellstua, where we were given time to walk to a lookout point at the top of the waterfall. It was rainy, but warm. We reached there in the nick of time because suddenly fog descended, and we could hardly see in front of us. We found our way back to the *fjellstua* (a store and cafeteria in the mountain) and got a drink before resuming our journey.

Along the way, the bus was filled with the music of Edvard Grieg and flutist/recordist Egil Storbekken. I didn't know if this was to relax us on these roads, add a cultural touch to the trip or both.

Yet another stop was the bridge of Gudbransjuvnet. Legend said that parents of different farms had arranged a marriage between their children. The girl was in love with another boy, who came to the wedding and stole the girl. They jumped over this waterfall to escape. This bridge is where the gap had been.

People were commenting about the berry, apple and pear trees and low-ground crops. Tina explained that because of the Gulf Stream, the weather was humid here so it was a prime area for strawberries. The orange berries we were seeing were either cloudberries or rowanberries.

Finally, we could not go any further because there was only water and a fjord ahead. As we pulled into the dock, Tina pointed out the shape of a snake on the mountain. Olav Trygvasson, who brought Christianity to Norway, had to battle Vikings and snakes in Norway. The imprint was supposed to be a snake he threw against the mountain, 1,000 years ago!

It was amazing that the small boat could carry passengers, two buses, trucks and cars. This was a 10-minute ride, but we were still not at Geiranger yet, our final destination of the day. We docked at Eidsdal, and the group boarded the buses again for the ride on Eagle Road, "where we might see eagles." The buses stopped at a point overlooking Geiranger. On the left, a couple of cruise ships were docked in the water, with the beginning of Geirangerfjord on the right.

The view of Geirangerfjord was just like the picture postcards, except today the weather wasn't sunny. The clouds hanging over the mountains and fjords created an interesting perspective.

We could also see the zigzag roads on the left that would take us into the tiny village of Geiranger. The bus had to navigate more hilly roads to the Union Hotel, situated at a junction of a waterfall. The guides informed us our luggage would be delivered to our rooms; dinner was at 7:30; luggage should be left outside our door at 9 the next morning; we would leave the hotel at 9:30 to walk down to the harbor to catch our boat, which would leave at 10 a.m.

The hotel was quite nice with Norwegian style crafts around the lobby and beautiful views of the fjord from the dining room. The hotel, dating to 1891, had been in the Mjelve family for three generations.

Tables were reserved for us. The buffet was tremendous, and the food was excellent. A table of cold fish – salmon, smoked salmon, shrimp and herring, in different kinds of sauces. A table of different salads and breads. A table with meats – lamb and chicken mostly. A hot line with salmon, lamb, roast beef, potatoes (including boiled, of course) and vegetables.

Lisa and I sat with Seth and Edith, a couple in their 60s or 70s from New York, who had just completed an elder hostel biking in Denmark, where it had been extremely hot. He was a retired history teacher in Brooklyn, and she had taught kindergarten. Barbara and Jean joined us. They were born, raised and still lived in Oxford, England. They both worked at a museum, and were on this vacation without their husbands. Somehow, the conversation turned to the Inspector Morse mystery series, which takes place in Oxford. Jean's husband makes replicas of historical objects and made a replica of a dagger used in an episode. They had met the actor who plays Inspector Morse and the author of the stories.

Seth and Edith said they didn't watch much TV because they went folk dancing. This was getting scary for Lisa and me, because their interests were matching our parents. Seth knew several languages, but Edith knew Yiddish. But then the conversation turned to gloomy things like war, Ireland and Bosnia. When Barbara and Jean went to get dessert, Barbara said, "Find a happy topic for when we return."

So Lisa and I announced we had just gotten married and were on our honeymoon. Barbara and Jean offered a toast to us. We felt honored to be toasted in Norway by people we didn't know.

For tea and coffee, we retired to one of the sitting rooms for some more pleasant conversation. It really felt eerie when Seth mentioned that a brother or sister went on theater trips to London. Lisa's parents had gone on a theater trip to London in January!

As we headed back to the room, the sound of water could be heard from outside.

"Is it raining?" I asked.

"No, it's the sound of the waterfall," Lisa said.

We walked out front for a look, but it was dark and cold.

"You'll have to get a picture in the morning," Lisa said.

Sunday, 31 August 1997

The breakfast buffet was fantastic, too, with different kinds of sauces for herring; mackerel in tomato sauce; smoked salmon; cheeses; meats; breads; Wasa, other crackers; soft, hard-boiled and scrambled eggs; potatoes; cereals; etc.

But, when Lisa returned to the table after a trip to the buffet, she had shocking news.

"Did you hear what happened?" she asked. "Princess Diana was in a car in Paris being chased by photographers and it crashed. She, Dodi and the driver were killed!"

"How did you find out?" I asked.

"The Florida people told me," Lisa said. "They saw it on TV." (The room TVs had CNN International.)

I thought of Barbara and Jean, the British people we had just met. We didn't have time to turn on the news, and hoped we could catch up with English-language news when we reached that night's hotel. But, the world's weeklong magnificent obsession was beginning.

Our trip was not coming to a halt. We all walked downhill around a few curves into the village of Geiranger and the boat. Rowanberries lined the road, and we had a better view of the waterfall the further down we walked. The *MSS Starcruise* was strictly our group's boat, which was nice because we could spread out on the seats, leave our bags around and get to know the other members of the group more personally.

A Spanish man, using hand signals, offered to take a picture of Lisa and me from the deck of the boat with the fjord in the background. The sky was overcast, but again, the clouds engulfing the mountains and fjord, some below the peaks, made for interesting sights. It was as if the clouds were in suspended animation. I was disappointed not to see the sun glowing and reflecting on the fjords, like in the postcards, but Lisa and everybody else still enjoyed the views.

The weather was constantly changing. At times, it got very windy on the deck, so I had a turtleneck shirt over my Philadelphia Eagles football shirt. (It was Opening Day back home!) I had used around four rolls of film since yesterday. Geirangerfjorden is the most dramatic and narrowest fjord in the country. One of the first sights leaving Geiranger is the Seven Sisters Waterfall, side-by-side, beginning so far up the precipice, and then flowing down. Steam breathed out from some of the falls. The preponderance of waterfalls is due to the melting of glaciers high atop the mountains over thousands of years. We had seen plenty of glaciers and snow on the caps and slopes of mountains. Right after we came out of Geirangerfjorden, a rainbow appeared on the horizon. It was so windy on deck, with chairs blowing around, our hair and hoods flailing in our faces, that extreme patience was required in order to keep the camera still enough to snap pictures of the rainbow. My perseverance paid off.

The sun finally came out in the afternoon, which made the massive fjords even more remarkable. Lisa could see how different they looked with the sun splashing on them, and was already talking about returning to Norway to see the other scenic vistas of the country.

The lunch spread was spectacular with excellent food: lamb, chicken, tossed salad, potato salad, cole slaw, smoked salmon (*gravlaks?*), cold peel-your-own shrimp (including the eyes), a prawns and vegetable mold, half hard-boiled eggs with shrimp and caviar atop, cold cuts, cheeses and some kind of chocolate pudding for dessert. Unlimited free coffee and tea were served throughout the cruise. Soft drinks were extra.

Lisa and I sat with a French woman, who kept going back for more food, and talked to herself, praising the food with every bite. I began to think maybe she was a reviewer. Lisa spoke French to her and said the woman thought one of the cold cuts was elk.

During the cruises, Tina and Carin spoke three languages: English, French and Spanish. Whenever Tina spoke French, Lisa translated for me, even though Tina would be providing an English version. It was odd not hearing Norwegian. But, after Tina learned I could speak Norwegian, whenever she checked to see how things were with us, she would speak Norwegian to me. I would reply in Norwegian. As out of practice speaking as I was, on this entire trip so far, Norwegians understood me. I understood when she spoke *på norsk,* and it was good to be able to practice.

In the middle of the afternoon, the boat stopped, so we could take turns at some deep-sea fishing. On each side of the back of the boat were large cranks with the lines. From the back of the boat, people just adjusted the line. Jim wasn't having much luck getting a bite. His wife was sure she would catch something because she was a native Floridian, who fished with her father when she was young. She, too, didn't nab anything. Lisa remembered fishing with her father and getting seasick.

Jim helped me as I gave it a try and talked to him about the Jacksonville Jaguars football team, whose hat he was wearing. Lisa tried, too. The right side of the boat never caught anything, but others caught four mackerels, mostly by those who were at the middle of the back of the boat. Norwegians' facility with some of the outdoor life was seen when one of the fish was still flopping around in the bucket. Carin went over, and without thinking and in one motion, snapped the fish's neck. We were told the fish might be part of lunch tomorrow, although the chef muttered, "24 people, 4 fish!"

The boat ride was smooth, as they cruised at a real slow rate, and we were more inland. Rough seas lay ahead, so we had to dock at Leikanger to transfer to a bus. Our destination for the evening was Selje, the westernmost town in Norway, near the West Cape. The waters are very rough around West Cape, and passenger ships are forbidden there. The *Starcruise* would proceed without us, while we took the bus.

We were told the roughness of the West Cape dated to the Viking period, when they would beach at Leikanger and carry their boats through these mountains. It is amazing how often, even in the remotest areas of the country, World War II comes up. The road we were now traveling on was built by the occupying Germans. Round, layered, stone fortresses barely sticking out of the ground had been German fortifications, from where they could look out at the sea. However, Leikanger was also the dock from where Norwegian resistance fighters were ferried to the Shetland Islands in Scotland for training. This transport became known as the Shetland Ponies.

This road was also narrow, not as dramatic as Trollstigen, but cars did pass the bus. Besides the German fortifications, most of the landscape was rocks and boulders on steep mountainsides, and sheep grazing alongside the road. On the right were some spectacular views of the sea. At one juncture, the *Starcruise* in the distance was pointed out to us.

Finally, the bus reached the end of the road, which had a beautiful view of the West Cape. We were allowed to get off the bus and walk around – or buy food and souvenirs. It was interesting to watch the bus turn around on the narrow road. With the sun beating down on the Sea of Stad (it was around four or five o'clock) and a series of layers of mountains and fjords in the distance, the view was just incredible, spectacular and dramatic. It was only 500 meters above sea level, but Norway is already at a high elevation, being so far north, that you still feel high up.

Lisa and I took a walk to catch some more views, and found ourselves in the company of sheep. Lisa was able to get close enough so that I was able to snap a picture of her with the woolly friends. We walked back to the bus, and Lisa decided to walk further down toward the sea while I checked out the choice of ice cream.

Back on the bus, toward Leikanger, we went. We came to a large stone cross atop a hill at Dragseidet overlooking the fjord. This was erected in honor of this year's 1,000th anniversary of Olav Trygvason Christianizing the four counties in the area. King Harald had come here for the ceremony attended by 10,000 people. Leikanger's population is only 1,000 people. This became another stop.

Then it was on to Selje, another tiny village on the water, with some of Norway's oldest sites. Its claims to fame are the production of uniform shirts, fishing, fish breeding, farming, boat building, manufacture and service industries, and that it has a beach. These tiny villages make you realize that while we may take a bus or train to work, these people may take a boat. What are the industries in these villages? Do all the people who work in these villages also live in them?

We were told this hotel wouldn't be as nice as the one in Geiranger, but in some respects, this was better, and in some respects, the Union was better. There was a lovely view from our room and the dining room. Dinner was cream of asparagus soup, salmon with some kind of fish on top, in a creamy sauce, mussels, boiled potatoes, ice cream pie with chocolate sauce and berries. It was okay, but not up to the previous meals.

Seth, Edith and Jane from Australia joined us. The conversation went in interesting directions. Edith asked if Lisa and I had been to the Resistance Museum in Oslo. Lisa told them how interesting it was. Seth and Edith had been to the museum in Copenhagen and had been disappointed to learn that the Danes didn't do much in the way of resistance and didn't suffer the famines and other adversity that Norway did.

"You hear a lot about the Danes rescuing the Jews and don't always hear about the Norwegians," I said.

"With Denmark, it was more of a 'I won't bother you, you don't bother me' thing," Seth and Edith said.

"I can remember being a child in Scotland and the Germans bombing the Clyde shipyards," said Jane. "I could see the flames from 60 miles away."

I told how my father was with the Allied liberation forces in Norway.

The conversation then shifted to socialized medicine and Jane moving to Australia in 1961 with her pediatrician husband and two young children and the terrible conditions there. As with the night before, we took our tea and coffee to a sitting room. We had a small table, but made room for more chairs so Barbara and Jean could join us. The conversations continued from things like Jane surviving going to school in London by working as a babysitter for a Jewish family when she was 19. The couple recorded weddings on the weekend at the Dorchester Hotel and brought home the leftover food for Jane.

She then mentioned yogurt as a cure for chicken pox, to which Lisa said that research shows the more social people are, the more they build up their immune systems to colds because they are around people. To which I piped in, "Social networks." I explained Dad's research and interest in social networks, that the social settings people are in can help and hinder recovery from mental illness. They all responded, "That's so true," and began giving their own examples.

The hour was now after 10, but we still had a view from the sitting room window, although it was not pitch-black. It had been another long and full day, so we all retired. The TV did not have an English-language station, so I understood what I could of the Norwegian broadcast about Princess Diana and translated for Lisa. A 100-nation conference on the banning of land mines was opening in

Oslo on Monday, and Princess Diana had been scheduled to appear. The tragedy was the only story on Norwegian television, and was all over the Norwegian newspapers.

Monday, 1 September 1997

Wow! Labor Day! Breakfast was a substantial *smorgasbord/koldbord*. At breakfast, Barbara said how sad and shocked she was about Princess Diana's death, but couldn't get much news because it was in Norwegian.

"Michael was translating some of it from the TV last night," Lisa said.

"We should've been in there with you," she said.

Later, on the boat, she said she was stunned by the sorrow and interest on the part of non-British people. A woman at the hotel had said, "You've suffered a great loss." Barbara said this event will become in people's consciousness like the assassination of President John F. Kennedy for Americans. People will remember where they were when they heard of Princess Diana's death. She recalled as a teenager where she was when JFK was killed.

"I can't say the same feeling existed when Reagan was shot," she said.

This tragedy also left me with a weird feeling. Mark and I arrived in Oslo last year the day of the TWA Flight 800 crash, and around a week later, were shopping in The Oslo Sweater Shop when the salesman told us a bomb had exploded at the Atlanta Olympics. Now, a year later, I am in Norway again at the time of another tragedy that grips the world. Vacation is a time to escape, although I try to buy an *International Herald Tribune* every day. These horrible tragedies happening on successive trips to Norway show how hard it is to escape entirely from the world.

Back to brighter things. The weather again started out suspect. The deck was very windy, and it rained. The sun made its appearance in the afternoon.

The gaps between fjords were much wider, providing a comparison to the day before. We were not as far inland, so we sometimes saw the edge of the horizons like at sea. Other times, there were rock islands, or islands with birds. The scenery had become so overwhelming that we were actually on overload. I began to preserve my photos.

For large portions of the trip, the ride was rocky. It was stuffy inside and windy on deck, so we weren't sure where to go. Lunch again was a fabulous *smorgasbord,* and everybody had to snap pictures of it before we gorged ourselves. Included on the table were the fish people caught yesterday.

Once again, we were inundated with information.

Many of the houses in the mountains are painted red or red and white. Red is cheaper paint (I had heard this before), and the white is more expensive. The combinations allow people to give the impression that they can afford a little luxury – without showing off, so we were told. Another legend is that ox blood protected the wood. Lisa's explanation was so the houses could be seen.

Both days, we passed a number of fishing villages and "farms." In 1948, there were 85,000 fishermen in Norway; in 1989, 28,000. Only 2% of Norwegians earn their living solely from fishing, although fish is still Norway's largest export. The "farms" were enclosures in the water, either rectangular or circular, with nets probably in the water below. We also saw the wood triangular racks where the caught fish are hung to dry. Some villages were known for herring or salmon or trout or mackerel.

A few minutes from Selje, the boat pulled alongside an island that had an old monastery. There was a lengthy explanation about the history of the island. The Irish princess, Sunniva, landed here in the 11th or 12th century, escaping from a Viking who wanted to marry her. (So, why flee to Norway if you're escaping from a Viking?) There is a cave where she and her companion died as martyrs. Her body was dug up and found to be still as beautiful as she was before. She became a

Norwegian saint. Ruins of a church and the Albanus Benedictine monastery date to 1103.

We passed alongside a massive mountain 800 meters high. The mountain is gradually falling down, and one day will collapse, cause great flooding and destroy the towns in the area. No date was given.

On any trip around the fjords in Norway, one sees a solitary house or just a few homes in these isolated mountains where there are no roads. "You may wonder why people would live here," announced one of the guides, as I began to wonder, and as I always have on my trips to this country. "There was a population explosion in Norway in the 17th century and people had to find places to live." This gave me the impression that perhaps some of these houses were not inhabited anymore, but I never got to ask the question.

To further discuss the point, the *Starcruise* pulled up alongside a mountainside that had three farms, one toward the top, one toward the middle and one toward the bottom.

"Now, suppose the farmer at the top wants to visit the Jones' at the bottom?" I said to Lisa. "How do they get there? How do you get from the shore to the lower farm?"

As if on cue, one of the guides announced, "You might see a zigzag path on the right side through the trees. The people have to carry their groceries up along the path."

You start to wonder. Where do they buy the groceries? How many grocery bags do they have? How about furniture? Maybe they make their own furniture? That must be one heck of a walk to the upper farm! The tour group actually researched this mountain to tell us about the path.

By the time we reached Brekke, the *Starcruise* had taken us through rocky waters. Lisa was feeling queasy. Some of the people in the group, like us, were on a three-day trip; the others, on a five-day tour. At Brekke, we were splitting up. We disembarked and tried to regain our balance. The boat, though, kept rocking in the dock.

A bus waited to take us the final stretch into Bergen. It had brought another tour group, which was joining the *Starcruise*. Our luggage was the last piece off the boat. Meanwhile, Seth and Edith were taking pictures of us with Barbara, Jean and Jane. As the bus pulled away, the tour guides, Tina and Carin, and the people from our group remaining on the boat waved at us, and we waved at them.

Aboard the bus, we were exchanging addresses, which was not easy because of the winding roads. On top of the boat ride, the bus jaunt wasn't that comfortable or easy on the stomach. A paper went around the bus, so people could write down their hotel in Bergen. As a final show of courtesy, the bus was going to drop everybody off at their respective hotels.

There was a new tour guide, an older gentleman, who had a sense of humor. Everybody was real tired at this point. There were a great number of tunnels, which bothered the guide because at this rate, pretty soon there wouldn't be anymore landscape to see. Brekke also turned out to have been the site of underground resistance in World War II. He said there was a Resistance Museum in the town. Once again, the war wields its head, but the guides are always proud to talk of the resistance and point out important sites.

The man said Norwegians' average salary, after taxes, was around $2,000 a month. One of the fascinating facts was that the people or farmers own the mountains. This creates interesting debates when the state wants to build roads or tunnels. How deep can they dig before it's not farmers' land?

We crossed Europe's only floating bridge to enter Bergen. Naturally, it was raining – it does so 219 days of the year. Our hotel was the first stop. Another couple from a non-English-speaking country was also staying at the Bryggen Orion. Everybody said good-bye and wished us luck. "We'll probably see you walking around town," I said.

The Bryggen Orion was one of the Rainbow Hotel chains. It's relatively inexpensive, far less than the fancy ones. The price includes a large smorgasbord breakfast and the Bergen or Oslo Card. There wasn't much aesthetic about the outside. There was construction being done outside the Orion. The hotel and room – a nice size – were neat and clean. The hotel was located by the wharf, and we had a view from our window.

The room TV had British Sky TV – England's CNN – and Euronews in English, but no CNN. The only story on British Sky, naturally, was Princess Diana; on Norwegian TV, it was Princess Diana and the Norwegian election; and Euronews emphasized business with a Princess Diana twist. The *International Herald Tribune* devoted lots of space to Princess Diana's death. This just shows that the world doesn't revolve – or not always – around the United States as many Americans seem to believe. The same coverage might have happened if a famous American had died tragically. I don't remember obsessive coverage in Europe last year about the TWA crash or the bombing in Atlanta. While they were leading headline stories, particularly the Olympic bombing, it wasn't the only story on the news as is the case with Princess Diana.

Lisa was bothered by hay fever, and the Clarendin we bought in Oslo wasn't working, so we went to an *apothek* and picked up some different medicine. Nearby was a post office, where I exchanged travelers' checks and bought postcard stamps. We walked around the old cobblestone streets and along the *bryggen,* wharf. Along the way, we ran into Seth and Edith.

The Bryggen had several souvenir and sweater shops. It was interesting that these beautiful expensive sweaters were displayed outside the stores, without fear of them being stolen. We went into one, and Lisa bought a traditional black, white, green and red cardigan with the clips, similar to mine, except I have a pullover. We also bought a beautiful *rosemåling* tray, as a wedding gift for our friends.

We continued our walk down by the harbor and *fisketorget*, which was deserted now, being late afternoon. During the day, the *Fisketorget*, Fish Market, is full of activity. We walked up the main pedestrian walkway, Torgmeldingen, and met Jane. We took a break at Ole Bulls Plass by a fountain, and spotted Mary and Jim, and Harry and Linda in the distance.

Our walk took us back to the old area, and I found the restaurant *To rom og en kjøkk*, Two rooms and a kitchen, where Mark and I had eaten last year. Lisa and I enjoyed a good meal, then walked back to the hotel and relaxed. I talked to Liv Glasser and arranged for us to meet her tomorrow evening.

Tuesday, 2 September 1997

We woke up to clouds and eventually rain. The hotel provided an impressive spread for breakfast, including batter to make waffles, which neither of us tried. Outside the hotel, a statue was being put on the building. Lisa thought it might be Orion, except the statue was a woman.

Our first walk took us up and down the old alleys behind *bryggen*. We looked at the old buildings, which were now stores. There were jewelry stores with special stones found in particular areas of Norway. We went into a lace store, which had very specially designed tablecloths, runners and other items from Hardanger, an area particularly known for this style. We bought a runner.

On we went to the Fisketorget, where there are not only several tables selling salmon, shrimp, crabs, but also tables of souvenirs, including two *kroner* and one *krone* postcards, probably the cheapest in the country. Lisa was taken with the charm, architecture and stores of Bergen.

After wading through the fish market, we decided to take the funicular to Fløien because the weather had cleared some. As with the day, we went to Frognerseteren and Holmenkollen in Oslo, it wasn't a clear day, but we still got an impressive view of Bergen below, the city between seven mountains. A stop for chocolate at the kiosk was the first order of business. Then, we decided to take a walk on one of the trails offered. There were different distances and levels of difficulty. We chose the flat number 2, which ended at a large pond. Upon walking around the other side, we sat on a bench. A flock of ducks noticed and walked right up to us. Lisa had bought a kilo of plums at Fisketorget (I had one) and began to feed the ducks some plum pieces, much to their delight, as they battled for the bits.

We walked back to Fløien where families were taking pictures with the smiling stone troll. Hungry, we went into the restaurant, just in time, because rain started pouring down. While we ate and waited for the rain to abate, we debated going to the Grieg House or the Aquarium. I had not been to Grieg's Home. The catch was the guidebook said the bus ride from the terminal was 10 minutes, then a 20-minute walk to the home.

The rain subsided so we headed back down to town. We grabbed four two-*kroner* postcards at the Fisketorget and decided to try the Grieg House. I knew where the terminal was, but we took a wrong turn that got me confused. We were able to get back on track, but then the rain really came down. There were three buses we could take. We got on the first one that came, which was crowded, so we had to stand part of the way. I was under the open window of the roof, so the rain dripped right on me.

This was not a 10-minute ride. We noticed another unusual thing. The bus stops on the street weren't labeled. How were we going to know where to get off? When the crowds thinned out, we moved to the front end and asked the driver to let us know when we reached the stop. Fortunately, he didn't say it was three miles back.

Your destination never seems close to the transportation stop in Norway. We walked back to this highway and began walking up. There was a sidewalk on only one side and which side changed. Crossed the highway and continued uphill. I thought I remembered from pictures that the house was yellow; Lisa said it was on a hill. One time we walked up a steep driveway, which turned out to be a private residence. We saw a sign for Troldhaugen parking, which was a good omen. The parking lot turned out to be awhile coming. Then, from the parking lot, there was yet another walk through interesting woods with leaning trees. We knew we had to be on the right track when there were Japanese tourists coming from the opposite direction.

There is a Grieg Museum, his house, his composing room in the woods, his gravesite and a concert hall in another direction in the woods. All are separate buildings. Admission isn't included with the Bergen Card. The Bergen Card is not as good a value as the Oslo Card because you only get discounts at the museums in Bergen, not free admission.

We opted to visit just the home, but first walked around the back where there was a pretty flower garden and beautiful views of Bergenfjord. We walked down some rock steps to get better vistas.

Women in bunads greet you at the entrance. Though the home is two stories, they showed us only three rooms downstairs. The room that used to serve as the kitchen now has a number of pictures of Grieg, cases with some of his music and a trunk. The dining and living rooms were as they were when the composer lived here, with some beautiful furniture and several gifts given to him on his 60th birthday.

Grieg was born in Bergen on June 15, 1843, and gave his first concert here when he was 19. He spent 22 summers at Troldhaugen, which he had built for him and his wife, Nina. He was a contemporary, knew and worked with Norwegian composer Ole Bull (who also has a home in Bergen) and playwright Bjørn Bjørnsen. You can understand why he liked this site with the views and privacy since it takes so long to get here.

It seems like every museum has a café – maybe it has to do with the distance to bus and train stops. We had a cup of tea to replenish ourselves before heading back to town.

In the evening, we met Liv at the empty Fisketorget, and walked to the Holbergstua Restaurant on Torgmeldingen.

"Have you heard of Holberg?" she asked. "He was a Norwegian writer, but he spent a lot of time in Denmark so the Danes claim him, too."

Near the market is a statue of Ludwig Holberg.

The restaurant was on the second floor and had some beautiful wood furniture. We sat by a window overlooking the street.

"Usually, after our (political) party meetings, we come here for beers," Liv said.

"We saw all the party tables outside and on Karl Johans Gate in Oslo," I said. "We thought we might see you at the table."

"I'm responsible for getting people to work at the table," she said.

She was an alternate to the Town Council and said the local party's goal was to get two representatives from the county elected to the Storting. Liv was also concerned about the showing of the Progress Party, but "There are polls every day so you don't know what to believe."

Liv now works at the European Documentation Center, disseminating information, which makes her feel awkward because she had worked so hard against Norway joining the European Union.

The death of Morris the year before shocked her, Rachel and Rebekka. Rachel was working in Oslo; Rebekka, in London. She showed us a picture of them. Liv also told us the story of an American friend she had as a child in Norway, who she had not been in touch with for 30 years. The woman is now an American tour guide who brings groups to Norway. She looked up Liv, and now they see each other a few times a year.

Liv treated us to dinner. Back outside, Liv asked, "Do you want to walk back together, or do you have plans?"

"We can all walk," Lisa and I said.

"Have you been down these small alleys?" Liv asked.

She took us down this tiny alley we wouldn't have found on our own. We walked down these cobblestone steps into a basement bar, a wine cellar. It was small and made of wood. Liv talked to the woman bartender and ordered some wine for us, which we paid for. We found a table that had a lit candle in a wine bottle on it. Later, the bartender placed another candle on the bottle.

"The woman said they think the cellar dates to the 13th century, but it has had the same name since the 15th century," said Liv. "You can't get in here on the weekend."

We wouldn't have known about it without her. We sat there for a while, listening to Grieg music, *The Song of Bergen,* and talking some more. The three of us walked back in the same direction and parted at her bus stop. She was happy to see us. Lisa and I only had a little more to go to the hotel.

"What did you tell me about Liv?" Lisa asked.

"That she was quiet, quieter than the others," I said.

"She's just shier," Lisa said. "She's very nice."

"Shier, but very gracious," I said.

Wednesday, 3 September 1997

This was our departure day, so naturally the sun was out. But, it made for a pretty train ride across the country to Oslo. We were booked on the 10:20. Since I had been on this trip before, I was able to save photographs. Lisa finished reading her book, and I managed to write two days worth in my journal.

At Myrdal – which is the station connection to and from Flåm – a tour group got on our car, and we recognized some of the people as from our group. Carin, the tour guide, noticed us. She said once she got the group settled, she would come back and talk with us. We had hardly spoken with her during the trip because she was on the Spanish and Italian bus. She learned it was our honeymoon, about my connection to Norway and

426

that my father had been with the liberation forces. ("Thank him for that.")

"Have you been to the Munch Museum?" she asked, the umpteenth person to do so. "His paintings of women are very interesting. He was both fascinated by women and feared them."

The hotel in Oslo, the Gyldenløve, was another in the Rainbow chain. The room was very small with a bed and a cot. Each hotel has been different. The card key was put into a slot by the door, which activated the electricity. The shower floor was level to the floor, which I've seen before, meaning you have to sweep the water into the drain with the broom provided. The TV had CNN, which was also heavily emphasizing Princess Diana and the upcoming funeral on Saturday.

We arrived around 6:30 and called Richard, the son of friends of Lisa's parents. She really didn't know him as a child. While we waited for him to pick us up, we grabbed some dinner at the tavern next door.

We met Richard's wife, daughter and dog. A teenage son never came down. Their home was located on a farm with beautiful grounds and apple trees. The house was 250 years old. Richard worked for an oil company, and the family had lived in Norway for nine years. The children went to the Oslo International School, formerly The British, and The American School, with the children of diplomats and NATO service people, but no Norwegians. Neither Richard nor his wife knew Norwegian. The daughter, 12, would not want to go to school in America, but she had spent most of her life here. There were many things they liked about Norway: feeling safe about the children being able to take the bus to the mall; the outdoors; walking and skiing. They didn't seem anxious to leave Norway.

He asked me about the difficulty of going to the Norwegian school when I lived here. I replied, "It was difficult, but I wouldn't exchange it because that would've taken away the cultural experience of mixing with Norwegians."

427

Thursday, 4 September 1997

The morning began with a visit from the janitor. Last night, Lisa dropped the ball of one of her earrings down the sink drain. She called the desk, and the person said the janitor would be in at 8 a.m. At 8 a.m., he knocked on our door, and within minutes, had opened the trap and found the ball.

The arrangement for today was to see Eivind. We didn't know whether it was for a full day or the evening. We gave him a call and got the babysitter, so we left a message.

Finally, we took everybody's recommendation and went to the Munch Museum. The hotel was well-located, about six blocks from Majorstua Station. We walked up to Kirkeveien and caught the No. 20 bus to the Museum.

Lisa liked the paintings. Years ago on a visit to Oslo, her parents had bought her a poster of Munch's painting of women on a jetty. It hangs in the bedroom. We found some renditions of it, except the women were facing in the opposite direction as in the poster. The women on the jetty are in profile and don't have distinct features. We tried to take some of Carin's comments into consideration. The deaths of Munch's mother and sister when he was young had a profound effect on him, perhaps effecting his later relations with women. There are several paintings of his sister and mother on their deathbeds. I noticed that none of the people in Munch's paintings smile.

We caught the bus back to Majorstua and had lunch – and dessert – at a Møllerhausen Bakery.

Back at the hotel, the TV was on when we entered the room. "There is a message for you," said the screen. By punching in the room number with the remote control, we got the message. Eivind had called, asking us for dinner at his house for six, and leaving his parents' number. I called. He had been sick yesterday, but was feeling better now. I asked how to get to his house. He told me to take the 20 bus – our buddy today – to the last

428

stop; make a 180° turn with our nose and walk until we came to a flower shop. That street is Normanns Gate.

We were exhausted so fell asleep for a while. When we woke up, I turned on CNN, which had found another news story in the world. Three suicide bombers had set off three explosions on Ben Yehuda Street in Jerusalem. They were showing live footage of people running around and close-ups of bloody, wounded people. The commentary was not referring to any of the footage. It was an interview with a Palestinian. The same scenes kept being shown. "How much different is this than the *paparazzi* photographing after Princess Diana's accident?" I posed. "They're both getting a story. Do we need to see these pictures when the commentators are not even talking about them, just as do we need to see the pictures of the car accident?"

Suddenly, CNN was interrupted – that's a change – by a flash that I had a letter at the desk. It flashed twice so we figured I better go get it. It made us a little nervous. Perhaps, it was a telegram.

Instead, there was a letter from Einar Vannebo, Director of the International Summer School, which was ironic. I had been meaning to call him, but had lost the number. I had just found it in the phone book, and suggested to Lisa I call and see if we could just stop by and say hello.

Einar wrote that he had not received my e-mail until September 1 when we were already in Vestlandet (West Coast). He would be away from the 4th-11th and would unfortunately not be able to see us. He suggested I stop by the office to see who was there, and to stay in touch. It was a nice note, making me still feel connected to the ISS.

Then I called Inger Sandanger, Tom Sørensen's wife, to arrange Friday's plans. The line was busy, but as soon as I hung up, the phone rang and it was Inger. There was a lot of mental telepathy going on today. She suggested we meet her at the shops at Ullevål Hospital at 2:30 tomorrow. She also asked if there was any place we wanted to go that she could take us. Lisa was interested in going to the Hadeland Glassworks. Inger said it wasn't out of the way.

There was still more itinerary planning to do. Next was a call to John Ivar. Erlend answered and put Margareta on the phone. "Congratulations!" she said. "We are looking forward to seeing you. We are hoping for sunshine. Let me put John Ivar on who is more of an expert in English."

"What expert?" John Ivar said.

He debated whether to drive to Oslo on Saturday and pick us up, or drive us back. I had a train schedule and said we could take a train that arrived in Askim at 11:11. The train took just under an hour.

"As for food," John Ivar began, "is there anything you don't like or don't eat?"

About the only thing that appalled Lisa on the trip were pimentos.

"Pimentos," I echoed Lisa's request.

"What are they?" John Ivar asked. "If I don't know, then we probably don't have it," he said.

"Red, sort of like red peppers," I said.

"I think I know," he said.

Scheduling done, we could now set out for the evening's activities at Eivind and Angela's. After we got off the bus, we made the 180° turn with our nose, as per Eivind's instructions, and crossed the street. There was some initial confusion, but we asked a man for directions. We came across the flower shop, where we purchased flowers for our hosts. Lisa had noticed there are a number of florists in Oslo. She really enjoyed seeing the number of homes and apartments that had flower gardens. It seems like every apartment terrace has flowers. What a difference a new person's perspective brings to your own observations. I hadn't noticed this before. We continued our walk up Normanns Gate and knocked on the door, which, again, was unlocked. Andrea, again, met us at the door.

"Husker du oss?" I asked. "Do you remember us?"

"Ja," she replied.

Andrea returned to a table where she was painting. *"Du er en maler,"* I said. "You are an artist."

Lisa and I continued with the greetings. Andrea came over and handed us the painting and said something.

"She said this is a gift for your wedding," Eivind said.

We thanked Andrea, and I asked if she could sign her name.

"Jeg vet ikke bokstaver," she said. "I don't know letters." Her pronunciation is so sharp. I put the painting on a high shelf to dry.

We moved into the living room. Eivind offered us some wine. Stian kept grabbing at the glasses.

I noticed they had Moomintroll books, which my siblings and I loved when we read them in English the year we lived in Norway. They are the adventures of a family, that in the simple drawings look like hippos, written by Finnish writer Tove Jannson. These versions were in Norwegian, and I tried translating for Lisa.

"I started thinking the stories were boring," said Angela. "They're really quite good, and Andrea likes them a lot."

Stian found this huge book that was bigger than him. He was struggling with it, and I helped him along. He enjoyed standing on the pictures. Then his attention turned to a box of toys, mostly cars and trucks, but it also included a toy cellular phone. All over Norway, at bus stops and on trains, we saw people with tiny cellular phones. Now, here was a toy one!

That did not command Stian's main attention. As he had done a week earlier, he liked to show us the car or truck. He was particularly intrigued with me. At one point, he ran toward Angela in the kitchen, tripped and fell to the floor. From the prone position, he looked toward Lisa and me, then toward his mother, seemingly trying to determine the severity of the fall by our reactions in order to figure out his reaction. "Should I cry or not?" Then, he got up, ran and hugged Angela around the legs, then ran into my arms, evidently saying, "I'm all right."

But, then he got into a habit of hitting Lisa, and eventually me with the toy car or truck. I tried to tell him to stop. Angela tried Norwegian and German. The problem was we were also laughing. Stian would stop, cuddle up to us, then after measuring the effect, would resume hitting. Then, there were Norwegian and German demands of "don't hit," then Stian would cuddle and hit. He was trying to see what he could get away with. Dinner brought an end to it.

As we finished dinner, Eivind said he knew how I liked *Jeopardy!* and the international competition was on TV. So, we retired to the living room. The tournament had been on in America a few months before. A Norwegian was in the finals and won the first night of the championship round. It was interesting to see the game show with subtitles. We could read the answer before the contestant said it.

Tea was put on, and apple cake heated. Meanwhile, the children were put to bed before we could get a family picture. As a doctor, Eivind was interested in Lisa's job in public health evaluation and research. He was under the impression that everybody in America had health coverage, but the rich could afford a better quality of care. Lisa explained that anyone could *get* care, that if someone came to the hospital, they couldn't be denied care. We had to explain the concept of health insurance in the United States; that many people don't have insurance because they don't have a job, or work for themselves, or are poor and can't afford it. We explained the insurance companies' recent campaigns against President Clinton's medical plan and how the issue became clouded in language.

From there, the conversation shifted to AIDS and HIV in the two countries; gay activism on the part of AIDS; and the complexities of welfare mothers in the U.S. being able to get and maintain a job because they have to find day care for the children. In curbing the spread of HIV among drug addicts, Lisa said her agency wasn't allowed to distribute clean needles.

"I work at a drug rehabilitation center one day a week," Eivind said. "There are not many good things I can say about Norway over the past 10 years, but we've seen a reduction in HIV since we were allowed to distribute clean needles."

Switching to sports, Eivind said Norway could qualify for its second straight appearance in the soccer World Cup if it beat Azerbaijan Saturday. Soccer has become very popular in the nation. The Norwegians' appearance in the 1994 World Cup in the United States prompted Eivind's visit, and he hoped now to go to France in 1998. He also said I should look for the name of Espen Knutsen, a Norwegian ice hockey player who had just signed with Anaheim of the NHL.

Eivind called Olav. I arranged that Lisa and I would squeeze in a croissant visit with them Saturday morning before we left for Askim. Due to our popularity, we would have to take a later train.

Eivind drove us back to the hotel, first stopping at his parents, so Lisa and I could pick up our other suitcase. We were able to say good-bye to Ragnhild and have a brief conversation. She had packed the suitcase for us. We looked forward to their visit to Philadelphia in October, and invited her and Odd for dinner at our house.

At the hotel, Eivind got out of the car to say good-bye. "So, I won't see you before you leave," he said, sorry at the thought. "It was nice to see you and meet you, Lisa. Next year, here, or we'll visit you."

We parted. "They're really nice," Lisa said of Eivind and Angela. "I really like them."

Friday, 5 September 1997

We had the morning to get in a visit to a museum before meeting Inger. Lisa had wanted to go to the Museum of Applied Art (*Kunstindustri*), and it was a site I had never seen. Yesterday, I noticed a museum brochure in the hotel lobby, which said an exhibit, "1,000

Years of Silver in Norway," opened today. There had been a feature on last night's TV news.

Our walk along Akersgate from the Storting train stop took us through the business district, primarily newspaper offices. At a newsstand, I count around 10 daily Norwegian newspapers, which are distributed around the country, plus papers from Sweden, Finland, Denmark, France, England, Germany, plus *The International Herald Tribune, USA Today* and occasionally, *The New York Times*. Many Norwegians read more than one newspaper. Some papers are business-oriented publications, and some represent or lean toward a political viewpoint.

We reached the museum right before opening time – 11 a.m. A crowd had already gathered, mostly a school group. It was quite an impressive looking building. The silver exhibit took up three rooms. The descriptions were in Norwegian, the only museum besides the Bymuseum that I had encountered this. I did the best I could to understand and translate, but we would've been there all day if I spent time at each stop. Then, I noticed a computer in the corner that had Norwegian and English versions of the descriptions. The program also enabled the user to zoom in on different details of the artifact and read a description.

The exhibit was fascinating, and Lisa enjoyed it. The silver ranged from drinking horns, jewelry, crowns, miniature palaces, belts, bowls and plates. Mixed in with the centuries-old artifacts were pieces from 1997. It was interesting to see pins from the 14th century that looked similar to those that are worn on bunads today, showing that the traditions have been passed down.

After finishing the silver exhibit, we went to another floor for a quick look around. We visited the gift shop, where Lisa bought a pin of dragons for her sister. We then walked to Karl Johans Gate and dined on karbonade at the café by the fountains in a square off Karl Johans.

The campaign tables were still in operation, and I wanted to get a shot of the Arbeiderpartiet table. I picked up some literature, which I'll have to translate some time. Then, Lisa heard some music. "Look a parade!" she said.

Uniformed men on horses heading toward the palace were followed by a uniformed band and antsy drivers in motor vehicles. We figured this was probably a parade for the changing of the guard at the palace.

If we were to meet Inger, we had to get back to the hotel. We hopped the train for the one stop to Majorstua Station, made a quick purchase of flowers at a *blomster,* which had become our gift of choice for hosts, then walked the five to six blocks to the hotel. By now, it was about two, and we had to get back to Majorstua to catch our good old No. 20 bus along Kirkeveien to Ullevål Hospital. The TV in the room was on, meaning another message for us. Inger wanted to know if we could meet here at 1:30. A call to her office found that she had left. The man on the phone said he would go to the meeting place and give Inger the message.

We scurried up Bogstadveien – the street where the hotel is – to Kirkeveien, but just missed the 2:11 bus. There was another bus at 2:18, and the ride was about eight minutes. And, for a change, the destination was across the street from the stop. Ullevål is a huge complex. We walked through the iron gates. As we neared the shops, I spotted a woman wearing a Temple University T-shirt.

"Look, someone is wearing a Temple T-shirt," I began.

Suddenly, the woman was running toward us. She was Inger, and it had not occurred to me that the Temple shirt would be the identifying marker. She rushed us into the car. Inger was anxious to beat the traffic out of town, so was somewhat aggressive. Hadeland closed at 4, so she was also trying to get there in time.

Interestingly, this one road took us through Nittedal, where they live, to Hadeland. I was surprised how big Nittedal was. Inger said 17,000 people lived here. Rolling hills and lush green passed us, and there was also a horse farm used for training horses for riding.

Hadeland was situated by a pretty river and mountains. You could see the outline of a downhill ski course in the mountain. Hadeland is a glass factory from the middle of the 18th century, and most of the outside of the buildings reflected the period. The factories, which during the day give demonstrations, such as allowing you to blow glass, were closed. One of the gift shops was open, and there was some beautifully amazing and interesting stuff. On the other hand, with the glass we had already received as wedding gifts – and other gifts sitting unopened at home – we were afraid to buy anything. After a while, we didn't want to look at more glass. We looked in the windows of the other buildings, which included an art gallery and a store with stone objects.

The cafeteria was open so we got some tea – we're drowning in tea on this trip – and sat outside on a deck. A playground area was on the property right by us. From our table, we had a view of the road, lake and mountain. It was a beautiful, bright, sunny day, a little cool. Like our other friends, Inger commented how hot the summer has been. It was so unusual to be sitting outside comfortably this late in the year, and nice to take advantage of every opportunity to enjoy the good weather, she said. From the other side, "It was pretty and relaxing to sit and talk with her," said Lisa.

Naturally, the Princess Diana tragedy came up in the conversation. Inger said she thought about how fast she herself had driven to Hadeland; how she felt she should slow down. Going home, Inger said, we didn't have to be in a rush.

She called Tom, who was preparing the dinner. He had a reputation of being quite a gourmet chef.

"Tom needs to know if he can put bacon in one of the dishes he's preparing," Inger asked us, upon returning from the phone.

"Sure," we said.

Inger went back to the phone. When she returned to us, we asked if dinner was a surprise or could we know what was being served.

"For starters, there is a mixture of different fishes wrapped with bacon," she said. "That's why he needed to know if you could eat bacon. Then, there's mutton chops."

"Andreas is excited about you coming," Inger continued. "He broke his arm roller blading."

She was also hopeful one of her daughters would be able to stop by with a friend who had just returned from America. As we sat there, Inger got more hungry and thought of the dinner menu. "I didn't have lunch," she explained. The time was after five, so we got back on the road.

Lisa wanted to bring goat cheese and *multebær,* cloudberries, back home with us. In the morning, we were able to procure the requisite G35 Gudbransdal goat cheese at a store on Bogstadveien. The *multebær* was in the form of jams and in glass jars, which was too risky to transport. I had suggested asking Inger if she knew a good place to buy the *multe.*

"We can probably get some at the gas station," Inger said.

Isn't it nice to know the natives? *Multe* at the gas station! It kind of reminded me of the time Ragnhild Dalgard told me the best *hveteboller* were at the 7-Eleven. Actually, there was a vegetable and fruit stand by a gas station. They were offering a special by the case, and that was 10 kilos, which was far too much for us. We had to wait until the salesman took care of the other customers so he could weigh out the *multe,* especially for us. Inger thought 1½ kilos would be sufficient. Lisa and I planned on saving some for us, and splitting the rest with our parents. The price was almost $30.

On the way back to the house, I asked Inger about Guri, Nils and their daughter, Helene, who I had stayed with in the Lofoten Islands in 1992. Guri was now an advisor to the Minister of Health and commuting back to the Lofotens on the weekend. Her position could be in jeopardy because of the election.

"We're having an election here," Inger said. "Have you heard about it?"

We said we had and mentioned talking to others and seeing the booths on Karl Johans Gate.

"It's complicated," Inger began. "Things are pretty good. The economy is good; unemployment is very low, so there are arguments to stay the course. On the other hand, after all these years with the same (Labor), it might be good to see what someone else does, but the Center or center-type parties don't offer a strong alternative."

I mentioned the poll I had seen before we left Philadelphia, showing the Progress Party second.

"I think that will change, the numbers will go down," she said. "The Progress Party complains about everything, but doesn't offer their own program or budget or how to pay for things."

Inger drove up a hill. "That's Andreas' school," Inger pointed out. Then she made some other turns, up hills, until we finally got to the house, a three-story dark wood structure. Andreas greeted us at the door. He yelled to Tom, "They're here! They're here!"

Inside, we also met Øystein (who until we got home to the United States didn't realize he was Inger's son from a first marriage), who was in 10th grade. Then, the boys disappeared to play computer games and watch TV.

We followed Inger and Tom upstairs, where there were two bedrooms, a long kitchen, a dining room, a living room, bathroom, and a hallway with a computer and printer. Almost every area of wall space was filled with artwork, a number of paintings by Tom. There was an outdoor patio and grill.

I was curious about this evening. By strange sets of circumstances, Tom and Inger had never had a chance to host me when I was in Norway. I had seen Tom on a number of his visits to Philadelphia, and Inger on one of those visits. Of course, we had just seen Tom at the wedding. This was their first opportunity to host me/us.

Often, quiet and shy when visiting us, Tom was much more open, animated and excited, and made every effort to extend hospitality.

First, there were offers of wine. Inger found containers to pack the *multe* and wrapped and wrapped the containers with tape. Tom was busy preparing the meal. A *Larousse Gastromique* cookbook was open on the counter showing a recipe for braised mutton/lamb chops.

"This is a combination of a French and Norwegian recipe," Tom said. "The Norwegian part is that the chops are from the Lofoten Islands."

He took out a pan to make the bacon for the appetizer. We could smell the grilling chops in the oven. Rolls went into the oven. Tom took out the baking dish with the chops, which was the size of a long cookie sheet. There must have been 20 or more chops on the dish. First, Tom placed chopped pieces of garlic over the chops, and then sliced potatoes. The dish went back in the oven.

The appetizer had different kinds of fish with the bacon mixed in. The main course was outstanding. We didn't know what the gravy was, but everything tasted so good. Andreas and Øystein made a couple of guest appearances. Dessert was warm *multe* with ice cream. Inger added sugar to the *multe*.

During dinner, Tom talked about the number of cottages they had, and how they were selling one of them. He was very interested in history, particularly history of an area or region. He took out a report Andreas had done for school about a local area. "The parents were up late scanning the pictures," Tom said. He was just as interested in the history as Andreas. Tom had studied many regions of Norway, and his next project was Nordmarka, a forest near Frognerseteren in Oslo.

Switching back to the election, Inger asked Tom about the Progress Party's budget proposal. Tom said it answered a couple of questions. What that was, we didn't know. Later, when we had retired to the living room, Tom and Inger said voter turnout had been going down in recent elections. They disagreed if it had ever dipped below 70 percent!

Lisa and I showed the wedding pictures and again explained the Jewish traditions. They wanted to hear Mom's CD, and we struggled with two CD players before being able to hear enough of Mom's music.

Before we left, Tom and Inger wanted to have a conversation among them, Andreas and me. At the wedding, the AFS headmaster approached Tom about the possibility of Andreas spending a semester or year at AFS. There had been some letters exchanged between the AFS class and Andreas' class in Nittedal. Andreas was excited, but nervous about the prospect. He was quiet and didn't have many questions. Tom and Inger were worried about their own homesickness for Andreas and suggested they could visit during the time. Tom also suggested Andreas would have to do work in Spanish, English, American History and be up to speed on mathematics. I told them the best I could about the program in sixth grade. One issue was Norwegian schools had just changed to beginning school at six years old instead of seven, and Andreas had been skipped to seventh grade. It was agreed he should be with the sixth grade at AFS, the students he had met in his two previous visits. Inger reminded him this would not be a visit this time; he would have to do the schoolwork. I said this exchange didn't have to happen this year.

After a family picture, Inger drove us back to Oslo, though it was close to 11. It had been a wonderfully pleasant evening. "It was a very nice evening because it was relaxing, and they had a beautiful house," said Lisa. "The food was great. It was good to have warm *multe* with the ice cream. I already knew Tom and Andreas, so it was more relaxing because I was seeing people I already knew. It was easy talking to Tom and Inger and the conversation was pleasant."

Saturday, 6 September 1997

The challenge today was how much visiting could we squeeze in? When I come to Norway, I'm a popular guest, and now with a wife, even more so.

In the morning, we were going to visit Olav and Florence for a couple of hours before taking the train to Askim to visit the Breviks. Olav said he would drive us to the station. Getting to Bygdøy wasn't all that complicated. We walked to Kirkeveien and took the No. 20 bus in the opposite direction, about seven minutes to Olav Kyrres Plass, waited 10 minutes for the No. 30 bus for about a five-minute ride to Fredricksborgveien. We found the little shopping area, where on our first night, Odd had dropped off Olav.

Now, came the fun part. I remembered Olav going to a gate directly across from the parking lot. Lisa remembered him going to a house on a hill. Both satisfied the house across the street. Except I could've sworn Olav said his address was 31, and this house was 19. I climbed up the driveway and came to the door. But, the names were different, so I didn't knock, and walked down the driveway. We continued walking down the street of which only one side had a sidewalk. Eventually, we came to 31, but it was clearly not the house, and a bus stop was out front. Olav had clearly said to get off at the stop after the Vikingshipmuseet. We walked back in the direction we had come. At one point, we rang the doorbell of a house. The man knew of no one named Dalgard. Then, he asked, "Have they moved in recently?"

"Yes," I said.

"Oh, I think some English-speaking people moved in next door," and he gave us directions. We walked down his hill past some old American cars, and found ourselves next door, at a two-family house. We tried the right side, but the name outside the door was not Dalgard. We didn't even try the other side because we were convinced this was not the place and we weren't looking for "English-speaking people."

441

That left us with the original house across from the shops. We walked up the hill again. A young boy and young girl came to the door. I asked in Norwegian if their parents were there. Olav appeared in the doorway. Soon, we were inside saying hellos, congratulations, being introduced to the children. Siri, Florence's daughter from a previous marriage, was 14 now. Joachim was seven; Agnes, four, born a few months apart from Eivind and Angela's Andrea. They were still establishing themselves in their new home, which included replacing the nameplate on the house. Someone had opened a croissant store across the street, and they had become friendly with the owner. Olav went out to get some croissants and brought back some chocolate ones.

They were quite excited. Princess Diana's funeral procession was on TV. "Do you mind if we watch?" asked Florence. "We are so taken with this and upset at her death. Or do you think we're crazy to be so involved?"

The TV was moved closer to the table. For most of the time, we just saw the procession of the hearse. I was a little curious, but by now was overwhelmed by the media coverage, and response from people, even Olav and Florence. Siri and Joachim were glued to the set as well, and said little.

Olav suggested women were more affected by Princess Diana's death than men, which we agreed was partly true. In discussing the *paparazzi,* I commented, "I have a dilemma with their behavior at the accident. As reprehensible as they are for following her, and as reprehensible as the actions of taking pictures at the accident scene, the accident becomes a news story (as we've seen). The photographers are then doing their job. The problem is the *paparazzi* chasing the car may have contributed to causing the accident.

"It reminds me of the story they told in journalism school. A reporter is sent to cover a dance and comes back, and the editor asks for the story. The reporter replies, 'There wasn't a dance. The building had a fire.'"

"I think I understand what you're saying," said Florence.

"How different has the so-called mainstream respectable press been than the tabloids since her death?" I continued. "Pages in the papers every day, interviews with the doctor on the scene, the only story on the news, beginning to end coverage of the funeral. We were watching CNN the other day, and they were showing live footage after the explosions in Israel, with close-ups of bloody faces, people running around, and the reporter wasn't even describing what we were watching. He was doing an interview with a Palestinian. Do we need to see all of this? How much different is it than the *paparazzi* taking pictures at the accident?"

We soon learned there was another reason Olav and Florence were engrossed. "We're really Anglophiles," said Florence. "Like Michael has a passion for Norway, we have a passion for England."

Lisa was taken aback. "You're French," she said to Florence.

It caught me by surprise, too, since Olav had teased me that I had an exaggerated view of Norway, and they loved England and hadn't lived or visited there.

"We will live there eventually," said Florence. "We just like so many things about England."

"My mother's family is English," said Lisa. "So, I'm an Anglophile, too. I went on a garden tour there a couple of years ago."

"The forests, the parks," Florence exuded.

"Norway has forests," I said.

"England's are different," she said.

"Jane Austen," Olav said. "We like Jane Austen."

As time was getting short, out came the wedding pictures, the explanations, the "how we met" story and Mom's CD.

"Do you like sports?" Olav asked Lisa. "Michael knew every statistic over the last 20 years."

"I like football," said Lisa.

Speaking of forests, Olav was taking Joachim to bike in the forest – I guess Olav was cleared after his broken arm – and the two of them got ready. He would drive us to the train station on the way. Agnes won her request to join them. Before leaving, I took a family picture.

Joachim, who had been mostly quiet at the house, was now full of curiosity, asking Olav questions and offering commentary.

"He says he thinks all American children have square eyes because they watch so much TV," explained Olav. "I think Norwegian children are catching up because they watch a lot of TV. I think all Norwegians have a car. There are so many cars around."

Then, Joachim asked, "Does America have a king?" When told "No," he replied, "Why?"

I said, "Long story."

Olav repeated my answer in Norwegian, then seemed to be offering an explanation of American History, and may have still been explaining when we reached the station. We left them, and thought with amusement about Joachim's questions.

The train was a local train to outlining areas. The ride was just under an hour. As we pulled into Askim, I could see John Ivar from the window. As we got off, I noticed Margareta and Erlend were with him. *"Hele familien,"* I said. "The entire family."

I introduced Lisa. Congratulations and welcomes followed.

"We figured you took the later train because you were watching the funeral," said John Ivar. "We've been watching all morning and haven't even had breakfast."

It was after 1 p.m. They wanted to show us their Askim, a small town of around 7,000 people. "We're going to show you the big sights, the supermarkets," said John Ivar with a laugh.

"We could go to RIMI, but I like this store," Margareta said in the car. "It's bigger."

The store was called, fittingly, MEGA, though not as large as an American supermarket. Almost immediately, we came across the potato chips. They chose one, Kim's salted, and one paprika. I may have to change my loyalties. Then, they picked up the soft drinks. They wanted to make us something *Norwegian,* but we had already had reindeer. Eventually, we had all split up in different directions. "It's impossible to keep up," said John Ivar, when we all found each other again. I noticed he bought three newspapers.

We needed all hands to carry the bundles to the car. Then, they wanted to show us the center of town, which was just a few blocks long. They had thought about taking us to their cabin where they had a boat, but the weather had changed. John Ivar found a parking spot by a small restaurant, where you could get an American hamburger! Nearby was a Chinese restaurant. "See, we're international," he said.

We walked into the small mall, where Mark and I had went with John Ivar last year. Askim had been a center for making rubber for car tires. Viking Askim employed a few thousand people from many countries, and had operated out of the building that is now the mall. After walking around, we came out at the front where there was a bakery with seating outside. They recommended a couple of chocolaty treats, and we got tea again. We sat outside and talked. They reminded Erlend I could speak Norwegian, and I reminded him how he helped me read the Norwegian paper a year ago. Like Andreas, he had been skipped a grade and was in eighth. He wanted to show us where he played "chess."

We walked a couple of blocks, and then turned left down a pedestrian-only street. There was a large sporting goods store on one side. Then, we came to a "chess board" painted on the street. Huge black and white plastic pieces were in a box.

As we walked back to the car, Margareta said, "So, here, in Askim, we have everything we need."

It was decided any other sightseeing would be saved until later – although the hospital where Margaerta used to work and Erlend's favorite pizza place were pointed out on the ride back to the house. In the car, the subject of gardens came up. Lisa had made a rose garden in her yard. She had seen my pictures of the Breviks' garden amidst the rocks, right off the patio. "Maybe you should come and work in our garden," said Margareta. "We are so busy and don't have time…"

"So they don't bother," chimed in Erlend. He may be quiet, but every now and then Erlend comes up with a smart, funny line, and he always has a smile on his face.

Soon, we were at the beautiful three-story house, white with blue trim. The kitchen, living room, dining room and patio were on the middle floor. The bedrooms were on the third floor. There was a lot of light-colored wood often seen in Norwegian homes. A map of Lillehammer was on the wall of the living room by the TV. Piles of books were stacked under stairs.

Erlend went upstairs. "He has a special room and is very proud of it," said John Ivar. "He wants to show it to you, but he's getting it ready."

He called up to see if Erlend had things in order and was ready for the visitors. The size of the room would make a CEO jealous. A bunk bed was along the left wall next to a stereo system. On the immediate left, as we entered, I think there was a rock collection. Erlend was sitting at a desk that wrapped around him almost in a semicircle. He worked at a laptop, but a PC was close by. Behind the desk were at least two old computers. On the wall by the desk were *Far Side* cartoons in Norwegian. I recognized some of them from the English version. On the other side of the desk was a bed. The wall featured certificates from school including one for skiing and one for volleyball. He is also very proud to have attained a green belt in karate.

"I look at this room and am amazed," said John Ivar. "The things children have (access to) now. I never had any of this. I never had a room like this."

After showing us his environs, the proud proprietor disappeared to watch TV in the first-floor room. Maybe Olav was right about Norwegian children watching so much TV. To think in 1969-70, there was one station, and programming during the week began at 6 p.m.

John Ivar showed us *his* study, which was nowhere near the size of Erlend's, but had the computer Erlend coveted. John Ivar continued the tour of the house, taking us out on the patio deck. There was a table and chairs by the rocks and garden where Mark and I had eaten with the Breviks last year.

"This is nice for lunch or dinner," he said.

The deck continued almost entirely around the house. As we walked to the left, I tripped over a little step that was hard to see. "That is a defect in the building," John Ivar said. "They didn't make it level. You are not the first person to trip."

On the right side of the house was a small table with chairs. "This is our breakfast side," he said.

Margareta was still in the process of painting this side of the house – not right now. They had lived here 10 years and are the original owners. After all this touring, we finally settled down on the couch in the living room. They offered us some soda. Their mechanic arrived to deliver the Mazda and pick up the Volvo. "It's nice to know a mechanic," said John Ivar. "He doesn't charge much, delivers and keeps our old cars running."

"With me now working in Ski, we really need to maintain two cars," added Margareta.

Once again, out came our pictures and the CD. They also put in a request for a copy of Mom's CD. We repeated the "how did we meet," "Jewish traditions" and other explanations. Like some of the other Norwegians before, they asked if it was common for Americans to have large weddings. Like the others, they said Norwegian weddings were not extravagant, maybe a dinner with family. Many times a man and woman live with each other for a while and have a child, then decide to get married. A need for a grand celebration becomes less necessary. Sometimes, there is dancing and music. I find it hard to believe there isn't dancing and music, considering the traditional Norwegian dances and bunad outfits.

Unless that would be more likely in the countryside (see the "mock" country wedding fiasco in the 1992 section of the book).

"If we want to see more sights, we should go," announced John Ivar.

So, we got to ride in the Mazda through the countryside. The first stop was one of the three hydroelectric factories in the area. We drove over a narrow bridge, parked and walked back over the bridge. They explained this was the largest river in Norway. The building was a big stone structure but was quiet and inactive on the weekend. Falls fell along the side, and there were some rapids, contrasting the activity of the week, said John Ivar and Margareta. On the other side, the river's waters were calm. They said the water originated from melting glaciers in Røros in central Norway, and we were in Southeast Norway. Because of the preponderance of melting glaciers in the country, Norway utilizes the water to generate electricity. Close to 100% of Norway's electricity is hydroelectric, and this makes electricity extremely cheap. So, Norwegians leave lights on. Ragnhild corrected us when we turned off a light, and the bulb burned out.

Back in the car, we found ourselves on narrow roads, bringing up our experience on Trollstigen. They had a humorous story.

"When you drive on Trollstigen, you have to be careful and can't stop," said John Ivar. "You need a car with a large motor to handle the hills. So, people are told not to drive campers. This was a challenge our mechanic couldn't pass up. He borrowed our camper and couldn't make it. A policeman said, 'I've heard of people doing stupid things on Trollstigen, but a *Norwegian!*'"

We came to an area where there is a special stone, *potetsteiner*, potato stones, because they looked like potatoes. They are only found in Mexico, Askim and another unusual country I can't remember. The novelty brings tourists and other people to the site to collect the stones. Now, collecting is restricted, but John Ivar and

Margareta assured us that if we were interested, they had some at home. Following this geological experience, they decided we had exhausted Askim sightseeing for today and headed home for dinner.

While dinner was prepared, I looked at *Dagbladet* and tried to decipher the latest polling data. Labor had taken a jump close to the 36.9% Prime Minister Jagland had set as necessary to achieve in the election in order for Labor to stay in power. The poll also cited the Socialist Left's standing at around 8 percent, and the paper combined the two numbers seeing these parties as a potential coalition.

We were called to dinner, which was meat fondue. A fondue pot filled with boiling oil was in the middle of the table. We each received two skewers colored at the top. Little chunks of meat were on a dish. We skewered the chunks and placed them in the fondue pot where they cooked for a couple of minutes. There were three different sauces we could dip the done meat in. A salad and a choice of either paprika or plain salted potato chips were served. This was one of Erlend's favorite meals.

We enjoyed it, but just when we were full, John Ivar got up and chopped up more meat. And, we had to have more, he insisted. For dessert, Margareta had made "something you might not like." *Trollkrem* consisted of cooked lingenberries, egg whites and lots of sugar. Lisa had three servings. Erlend didn't like it and disappeared back to the TV.

Our conversation turned to politics. They had questions about the American system, while we asked about Norway. They had a slightly different outlook on their upcoming election. Margareta wasn't sure what she was going to do, although John Ivar countered she did. Either way, they didn't reveal their preferences to us. John Ivar said the immigration issue was complex.

"At what point do you say it's enough?" he said. "In Norway, there is a question of is it better for us to help these people in the country they are living, or bring them here and help them? Can we afford to have all these elderly people come here? Are we really helping them?"

Lisa had asked others if there were certain areas of the country that were considered Labor or Conservative. We had not gotten a clear answer. I asked who did these parties represent? They said the Center were generally farmers (and probably fishermen, I presume), and the Christian Democrats were missionaries or church people and people involved in charity organizations like The Red Cross. I gather from the name that Christian Democrats are people who believe in democratic principles and draw that from Christian teachings. The business community had generally found Labor to be favorable to them, so this had resulted in the weakening of the Conservative Party.

They had a sense from some people that the Democrats and Republicans in the United States were not much different. Although we said there were similarities, we disagreed that they were exactly the same. Lisa said Republicans are supported by the wealthy, benefit big business and don't believe the government should help people in need. The Democrats tended to be for the ordinary people, supported by unions, and believed that the government should help people.

Among the problems, we said, is that in America running for office costs so much money. Running becomes a matter of dollars and not beliefs. Lisa said that perhaps if people were voting for a party, a candidate would feel more beholden to a philosophy. We said campaigns deteriorate into name-calling, where candidates talk about how bad the other candidate is, and not about themselves.

They, too, were flabbergasted to hear we have to register in a particular party. "I don't know how you in America with your two parties can call it a real democracy," said Margareta.

Somehow, the topic moved to vacations. In Norway, everyone, by law, has a right to four weeks vacation to start. However, in some cases, in a person's first year on a job, they have a right to four weeks vacation, but it may not be paid.

Time was progressing, and we had to begin to think about how and when we were leaving. First, Margareta suggested that we call my parents. A little while later, the phone rang, and it was my father. I wondered how they found us. He had exchanged e-mails with Tom Sørensen, who said we had been at their house Friday night, and would be at the Breviks Saturday.

According to my train schedule, there was a 9:53 train from Askim that would get into Oslo around 11. John Ivar said there were more trains from Ski, about a half-hour closer to Oslo.

We said good-bye to Erlend. John Ivar raced to Ski. We got there about 9:30. I went into the ticket office. A local train station with an open ticket office that late on a Saturday night was a surprise. So was the fact the train pulled in while I was buying the tickets. There was a certain car we had to board so we had to race to it. We didn't need to because the train wasn't leaving until 9:34.

Lisa and I stood on the train saying good-byes. "Good luck," said Margareta. "Congratulations. Be nice to each other."

The train pulled away from another pleasant, warm, friendly experience with members of our Norwegian family.

There were many young people on the train, either heading back to Oslo, or heading into Oslo for a late night of activity. As for us, we had exhausted all our visits for this trip. We had one more day in Norway, all to ourselves.

Sunday, 7 September 1997

For the second straight trip, tradition would be broken, and the last evening would not be spent with the Dalgards. Odd's brother was having a birthday party. So, we were on our own.

We decided if it was a nice day, we would go to Frognerseteren, walk around, get *eple kake med krem,* sit, read and write, so we could relax. If the weather was bad, maybe we would squeeze in a museum.

Sunday was a bright and sunny day in the 70°s F. After breakfast and some packing, we set out toward Majorstuen station. Bogstadveien gave a perfect direct view of Holmenkollen, so I snapped a few photos. As we neared Majorstua, I noticed many people heading in the same direction. Suddenly, I remembered this is a Norwegian Sunday.

Whether summer, fall, winter or spring, if Sunday is a nice day, you will find most Norwegians outdoors. In Oslo, many are heading toward Frognerseteren. While Americans may enjoy taking a Sunday stroll, a Norwegian Sunday is a fascinating cultural phenomenon.

The Majorstua train platform was filled with people. Five train lines come through Majorstua. Two were of prime interest – the No. 1 going to Frognerseteren and the No. 3 to Sognsvann. Even on Sunday, they leave every 15 minutes.

I said to Lisa that we hadn't been to Sognsvann. Lisa asked where and what it was. Sognsvann is a lake with pretty surroundings.

"Could we walk around there?" she asked.

We decided to go to Sognsvann first, about 12 minutes on the train, spend a little time there, return to Majorstua, and take a No. 1 train to Frognerseteren.

As we got on the train, we noticed the picture on the side, indicating where to hook skis in the winter. Families were on the train, some with strollers or carriages. Fathers and sons. Mothers and daughters. Couples. Friends. People with dogs. People with bicycles. Older adults. All were heading someplace where they could be active outdoors.

Sognsvann is one stop past Berit's apartment, which is also the location of Studenterbyen, off-campus housing for the University of Oslo. People streamed out at Sognsvann – the last stop on the line. As we walked with the crowd, we passed a parking lot that was quickly filling up, and signs for the Norwegian Olympic Committee and Norwegian Athletics College. Maybe the people joining the crowd were coming from all these places. Of course, we passed a food kiosk.

When we reached the clearing that brought us to the lake, we came across an event we didn't expect. There was a tent city in front of the lake, which had something to do with a commitment to nature. This was the first day of a weeklong camping and nature experience. There was a finish line banner with a picture of a Kvikk Lunsj chocolate bar as if they were a sponsor of a race. There was a speaker – I believe a priest – on a stage right in front of the lake. Green landscape abounded, and with the bright sun, it accentuated the color.

Lisa and I followed the flow of the crowd toward a path on the right of Sognsvann. Again, it was a scene of generations. Young children with backpacks, racing ahead, laughing and enjoying themselves. Families. Bicyclists. Older adults walking with backpacks. Mothers with children; fathers with children; families with carriages and strollers. Friends enjoying themselves with a Sunday walk.

We became part of it all, walking on the path surrounded by trees, the lake or rocks. We reached an opening and saw people picnicking on top of a big rock. The path circled the lake, about a mile and a half. It came out at a horse farm and then right into the "city." Was there a Kvikk Lunsj bar awaiting us for completing the course?

There was lots of activity in different areas. Children were grilling hot dogs on sticks. The Boy Scouts were giving rides on a wooden ferris wheel. Children were shown how to make their own butter. An accordion player was providing the musical background for the activities. There were many canoes on Sognsvann.

We walked over toward the *mål* banner – the finish line – where indeed slices of Kvikk Lunsj bars were being distributed. It's like a Kit Kat bar, so the people at the table were putting the strips in a box, not fast enough for the hands grabbing at them. There was also free juice.

Several signs explained in Norwegian *Tryggv i Naturen* project. "Survival, safety or secure in the nature" is the translation. From what I gathered from translating the text, this was a collaborative effort of environmental and other nature groups with business – Freia Kvikk Lunsj was a major sponsor – and government to make people appreciate, enjoy and feel secure in nature and the environment. It was quite an interesting "accident" we happened upon.

We had another destination and appointment today – Frognerseteren and *eple kake med krem*. We walked back to the Sognsvann station and ran to catch the train before it left. This took us back to Majorstua, where we switched tracks and caught the train to Frognerseteren, about a 25-minute ride.

As with the trains to Sognsvann, the train was full of all kinds of people. Since it was a clearer, brighter day than the earlier time we had gone to Frognerseteren, the views out the window, as the train ascended the mountain tracks, were dramatic. We could see Oslo and the fjord on one side, and green land and trees on the other. Some people got off at earlier stops, including Holmenkollen. The rest filed out at the terminus, Frognerseteren, with the immediate view of blue sky, white clouds and the fjord below. We walked down the hill and turned right at the sign pointing toward Frognerseteren. Within a few minutes, we saw the dark brown wood Frognerseteren Restaurant with the dragon heads curling out from the roof. We noticed the weather vane on the roof had a sculpture of a rooster and the year 1909.

The last time we were at Frognerseteren, there was almost nobody here. But, this was Norwegian Sunday. Nearly every outside table was taken, as well as many inside. We went into the cafeteria. Last time, we had taken the last two pieces of apple cake from a case in the cafeteria line. This time, there were two trays just with *eple kake med krem* on a table in the middle of the room. And the line at the table was long.

I went outside and found a table. Every table had at least one *eple kake med krem*. I noticed a sign on the side of the restaurant that said Frognerseteren was 1,387 feet above sea level. We sat and ate our *eple kake med krem,* admired the views and enjoyed the sunshine and breeze. At one point, a group came out from a party inside. All of the people, including the younger children, were dressed in bunads. We took pictures of each other and the views. Lisa asked a woman to take a picture of us. This was the last photo on my last roll, our final picture in Norway.

We sat on a bench in front of the restaurant. Lisa read and I wrote in my journal, desperately trying to catch up. After an hour or so, we decided to head back by walking to Holmenkollen.

For dinner, we were on our own for the first time since Wednesday. The Oslo Card offered a discount at a restaurant about five or six blocks away in the other direction from the hotel, so we decided to try it. However, they were hosting a big party, so were closed to other customers. After some walking around, we opted for a place where we could sit in an open porch. The waitress was very helpful. There was a Sunday special for NoK 129 ($17) that included the main course, salad, vegetables and dessert. Lamb chops were the main course. There were three choices of potato. The waitress said the scalloped potatoes went well with the chops. I chose the boiled, however. The waitress offered to bring a big bowl of scalloped potatoes, so we could share them. The serving was quite substantial.

Dessert was supposed to be cake, but they were out of it. But, she could offer us an ice cream sundae with a scoop of three different flavors. She was trying to sell us on a particular flavor. Lisa decided to try the flavor. However, it turned out they didn't have a lot of the flavor left, so she gave Lisa an extra scoop of chocolate, which certainly didn't disappoint Lisa. Quite satisfied, we walked back to the hotel.

I was hoping to find a good movie in English on TV, and was successful. *A Few Good Men,* whose Norwegian title was translated as *A Matter of Honor,* was on. It was made longer by the number of commercials that have now invaded Norwegian television. There are not a lot of breaks. When there are, they are long. When the movie was finally over, we shut the lights out on another pleasant and wonderful trip to Norway.

Lisa had officially joined the Kleiners' Norwegian family. Now, we embarked on our journey into married life. Where and how would Norway fit?

Chapter 11
Passing It On

We would have the opportunity to host the Dalgards at our house, along with Mark and my parents, when Odd and Ragnhild came the following month. It was a small payback for all the special evenings and gracious hospitality spent at their apartment. As far as the Norwegian election, Labor fell just short of the percentage the Prime Minister had targeted. But, he kept his campaign promise and resigned the government. The Parliament discussed the problem and recommended the King pick the Christian Democrats to lead the nation. The Progress Party finished a disturbing second at the polls.

There would be a few more opportunities to bring Norway into Abington Friends and other special multicultural experiences.

I relate the following stories because I believe the cultural experience of Norway throughout the years, the International Summer School (ISS) and my Jewish background influenced me to become interested in other cultures and to respect them. Meeting people from all over the world at ISS – and the fact that happened in Norway – taught me how to relate to. people from different countries, and reinforced my own hopes for a better world. I wanted to share Norway with others, and the experience had now impacted my own work as well.

The Head of AFS had been building up toward having a program commemorating the 50th anniversary of the American Friends Service Committee and Friends Service Council in London receiving the Nobel Peace Prize. While Quaker schools and organizations around the world marked the day on December 10, 1997, none probably had the little extra touch of AFS. I suggested to the Head of School that I could read, in Norwegian, the excerpts from the 1947 presentation. A senior student read the English excerpts from the speech delivered by Gunnar Jahn, Chairman of the Nobel Committee in 1947. A student from England read excerpts from a lecture by a woman representing the Friends Council of London, and another student excerpts from a lecture by a representative from the AFSC. The Head of School then recited portions from the American's acceptance speech. Candles were lit in honor of peace.

A couple of weeks later the annual all-school Winterfest program took place. All the different holidays at that time of year are acknowledged. Sweatshirts were made up with "Peace" in different languages. A student said to me, apologetically, "We forgot to include the Norwegian. We'll remember next year."

This showed the impact that Norway and I had made over the years.

Andreas did come to AFS, intending to stay a semester and live with a host family. The experience of a few months 4,000 miles away from family was quite different than a week. The prolonged experience didn't work for him, and combined with homesickness, resulted in Andreas returning to Norway after two months.

There was another special exchange in the spring of 1998. In June of 1997, AFS was contacted for a possible student and faculty exchange with The Tianjin Fourth Middle School in Tianjin, China. A four-person delegation and a faculty member at Temple University, who was a native of Tianjin and the liaison, visited the school. I was the host for most of the day and had my picture taken with the English teacher from the Tianjin school. He sent that and other pictures to the school and made special mention in his letter: *"Please remember me to Michael...a picture for him."* Two of the interpreters for the day were a senior and a junior student, both of whom had been raised in China and immigrated to the United States when they were nine. The junior grew up in Tianjin. The Headmaster at the Tianjin school presented the senior with her diploma at the AFS commencement.

When the new year began, the remaining Chinese student began teaching students and faculty Mandarin phrases in anticipation of the exchange students' arrival. One delay after another occurred, and it seemed like the exchange was going to fall through. Finally, in April 1998, a call was received that four students and a teacher would be arriving within the week! They stayed two months for a wonderful warm exchange among students of all grades, faculty and staff. Following the school's annual Arbor Day Celebration, the Chinese students and teacher planted a tree on campus. They made 400 dumplings for students and faculty as part of their farewell, and the following day, AFS hosted a farewell party. Gifts were exchanged, and I was one of the people who received a gift from the Chinese teacher and students. It was a bookmark with a picture of a man playing a string instrument. It has been explained to me that this person might play at the King's house, and the image is symbolic of wonderful and happy times, and great respect. The salutation was in Chinese, but the words indicated they held me in great esteem, and hoped the friendship would be remembered and continue.

I, too, would be taking my leave of AFS. Ironically, my time had begun with the visit of the Cuban soccer team and was ending with the visit of the Chinese students. While there were these special things happening, there was another side. My first year of married life made me realize some important things about myself. Whereas, in the past, I might stay late to watch a sporting event, now at 5 p.m., I wanted to go home. While I might still enjoy attending extracurricular programs, I wanted to have more control of my time. At the newspaper, at Textile or AFS, I had to put in so much extra time. While I had the vacation time, heaven forbid if I took it. I was bothered that I received some flack for taking so much time for my honeymoon! John Ivar's statement, "Vacation is a right not a privilege in Norway," had special meaning for me. The opposite seems to be the case in America. Wherever I have worked, there was never a good time to take a vacation. I would return to learn that some "disaster" happened. Further, juggling so many different roles was no longer a pleasure. I wanted to see if I could combine PR with my technology degree. It was time to leave AFS.

Nevertheless, it was bittersweet. AFS, in other ways, was the best job I ever had. I proved I could do non-sports PR and was good at it. I put out monthly newsletters with substantive information and many pictures of which I was proud. My interest in adding Norway to their multicultural programs was welcomed, and I became an educator. After I announced my departure, I received numerous e-mails from faculty, praising my work, involvement in the school and wishing me luck.

Once again, I was going into an unknown.

During the summer of 1998, Lisa and I went to Cape May, New Jersey, visited my brother in Salt Lake City and traveled around Utah. There were no worries about what work was being left behind. I wrote about some of our funny experiences in Utah and worked on the second part of this book.

In 1999, I decided to start my own public relations and web site design business out of the house.

My first client was West Mt. Airy Neighbors, a community organization that was celebrating its 40th anniversary of maintaining diversity, integration and quality of life in West Mt. Airy. There was a similar organization in East Mt. Airy. The neighborhood is a national model. This led to working with Mt. Airy Learning Tree, an adult education program of "neighbors teaching neighbors." I also joined the Mt. Airy Business Association. I was aware of the special qualities of Mt. Airy, but was now working intimately with the organizations. Again, the goals of the community coalesced with some of the Norway experience and helped me appreciate the neighborhood even more.

MABA is a unique business association in that members include retail businesses; home-based businesses; community organizations; educational, cultural and religious institutions; political representatives; doctors. Members live and work in the area so we may evaluate the viability of a new business as it affects us as residents and business people. Members come from outside Mt. Airy as well. After serving as secretary of MABA for five years, I was Vice-President in 2005, and am President in 2006.

The biggest moment of 1999 was November 1, when Matthew and Devra – yes, twins – were born. I was able to go to every single appointment Lisa had with the doctor, and always wondered how I could have arranged that if I wasn't working for myself. I was happy to be part of the process.

Of course, in the early years, there wasn't much of Norway I could tell my children. But there were little symbolic things like watching them play with the wooden car I made in shop class at Majorstua, meeting Tom and Odd on their visits and receiving polar-bear toys. Of course, they didn't know from where Tom and Odd traveled. For the first three years, we had a sitter take care of them while I worked upstairs.

When I started to work with author Lois Young-Tulin, I found that working with authors, artists, musicians and small businesses might be my target market. The Temple University Small Business Development Center has provided invaluable free business consultation services, and the Creative Services Department developed my logo, brochure, business cards and stationery for material costs.

Business, though, has had its ups and downs, and I certainly could be making more money. Running your own business – when I am responsible for doing the work, gaining and retaining clients, billing and staying abreast of new trends – is challenging. But, I am available when the kids are sick, and the weekends are family time. Raising twins is a challenge in itself.

I hope to work with promoting Norwegian authors here. I even contacted Kjetil Flatin for suggestions. He had preceded me when I spoke at the anniversary of the

Summer School and was now publisher of *The Norseman*. He apologized for taking so long to reply, but he was thinking how he could help me. These instances of sincerity and willingness to find a way to assist are very touching.

Of the ISS students, I have had the most correspondence with Sultan, usually around Christmas time. A few years ago, he contacted me by phone from Moscow, interested in knowing if there was anything I could do to help him get a job in the United States. I looked into the rules, and there was nothing I could do.

We enrolled Matthew and Devra in the Summit Children's Program in 2002 after their third birthday. We have all loved it. They are excited about going; are taught about the value of friendships, "kind hearts;" and are in a warm, nurturing atmosphere. They are learning things we might've learned in first grade. There are the diversity and multicultural aspects that have become important to Lisa and me. A Chinese teacher taught students about the Chinese New Year and taught some Mandarin phrases. It also turned out she was from Tianjin and knew the teacher who had come to AFS.

I've reprised my Norway reindeer sled story that I presented to the AFS kindergarten classes. In March 2003, I presented the story to Matthew and Devra's class, complete with maps and video from the 1994 Olympics, which included the Sami, on sleds, leading the reindeer into the stadium during the Opening Ceremonies. Most captivating was probably the ski jumper going down the ramp with the Olympic torch. All those three- and four-year-old eyes were transfixed. The teacher said she had never seen the class so still and focused during circle time. It must've taken 45 minutes. I repeated the performance in December 2003 prior to Christmas, adding a little about Christmas in Norway and the Julenisse. Younger kids also attended. As part of their thank-yous, some students hugged me.

In November and December 2004, the class studied "Friends" and "Weather," respectively. I spoke – and showed slides and photographs – about the snow and fjords in Norway, dark days in the winter, light days in the summer, about my friends in Norway, taught them to count to 10 in Norwegian and how to say "my name is…"

Several months ago, I was sitting at the table with Matthew and Devra, wearing one of my Norway T-shirts. Matthew said, "I like your shirt." I said, "Remember when I talked about the reindeer sled ride? Norway is the place I had the ride. Some day we'll go there."

Devra, not wanting to be left out, said, "Me, too!"

"Yes, you, too. We'll all go," I said.

A promise, like my father before me.